A DIFFERENT DEMOCRA

A DIFFERENT DEMOCRACY

American Government in a
Thirty-One-Country Perspective

Steven L. Taylor
Matthew S. Shugart
Arend Lijphart
Bernard Grofman

Yale UNIVERSITY PRESS

New Haven & London

Yale University Press books may be purchased in quantity for educational, business,
or promotional use. For information, please e-mail sales.press@yale.edu (US office)
or sales@yaleup.co.uk (UK office).

Designed by James J. Johnson.
Set in Melior Roman, Copperplate Gothic, and Avenir Next types by Newgen North
America.
Printed in the United States of America.

Library of Congress Cataloging-in-Publication Data

Taylor, Steven L., 1948–
  A different democracy : American government in a 31-country perspective / Steven L.
Taylor, Matthew S. Shugart, Arend Lijphart, Bernard Grofman.
    pages   cm
  Includes bibliographical references and index.
  ISBN 978-0-300-19808-9 (paperback)
  1. Democracy—United States.   2. United States—Politics and government.
3. Comparative government.   I. Shugart, Matthew Soberg, 1960–   II. Lijphart,
Arend.   III. Grofman, Bernard.   IV. Title.
  JK1726.T38 2014
  320.473—dc23

                                                            2014014631

A catalogue record for this book is available from the British Library.

This paper meets the requirements of ANSI/NISO Z39.48–1992 (Permanence of
Paper).

10   9   8   7   6   5   4   3   2   1

To our many students who were not only our guinea pigs but also our teachers and who contributed to making this a better book

"Those who know only one country know no country."

—SEYMOUR MARTIN LIPSET

Contents

PREFACE

It is often said that the United States has an exceptional democracy. This can mean any number of things, but we are concerned with the question of whether the structure of American democratic institutions is similar or dissimilar to other democratic states. If it is different, in what ways is American democracy different—and do those differences matter? What explanations exist for these differences? These are the themes that animate this book.

Specifically, our book examines the choices made by the designers of American government at the Philadelphia Convention of 1787 and the institutional structures that evolved from those choices, and compares them to thirty other democracies. The basic topics for comparison are as follows: constitutions, federalism, elections, political parties, interest groups, legislative power, executive power, judicial power, and public policy.

Each chapter starts with a discussion of the feasible option set available on each type of institutional choice and the choices actually made by the US founders as a means of introducing the concepts, and then it discusses how specific choices made in the United States led to particular outcomes. We look at the discussions on these topics in *The Federalist Papers* and the debates in the Philadelphia Convention. This approach gives us a means of explaining the concepts in a comparative fashion (for instance, federal versus unitary government, unicameralism versus bicameralism, and so on) before moving into the comparisons of the American system with our other thirty democracies, which make up the second half of each chapter. Each chapter contains an explicit list of specific differences between the US and the other democracies as well as comparative data in tabular and graphical formats. All of the figures and tables contain comprehensive comparative data featuring all thirty-one cases (save in a handful of instances) or specific thematic subsets of the thirty-one cases (for instance, presidential systems or bicameral legislatures).

Our book can serve two important functions: as a textbook and as a scholarly contribution. First, as a textbook it can work in a variety of courses and course levels, depending on the aspects of the text a given instructor wishes to emphasize. On one hand, the text takes a fairly straightforward look at basic topics in government and mirrors the topics that might be used at the introductory level. On the other hand, the book demonstrates both rigorous comparisons and raises a number of theoretical issues linked to institutional design. It can therefore be used at multiple levels depending on the nature of the course and the focus of a given instructor:

1. The basic themes of the book, and the structure of the chapters, were chosen to correspond to the themes typically found in introductory American government textbooks. Our goal was to make it possible for the comparative-minded professor to use the book to augment a basic American government textbook. While some of the more-advanced themes might be downplayed in such a course, the book can very easily be used as a supplement for American government texts.
2. Our book can also be used as a book in undergraduate comparative politics courses. It can serve as an anchor text on a syllabus in such courses focused on democracy and institutional design, but also as a secondary text alongside more-general textbooks.
3. It can also be used at the graduate level, insofar as it provides a comprehensive comparative study of the thirty-one cases and makes a number of theoretical claims that can be delved into further at this level.

Our book also makes a scholarly contribution by means of its analysis of the variations of democracy between the United States and the rest of the world. There is a void in the literature in that few works explicitly treat the United States as one case among many. Rather, political science tends to be segmented into fields of American politics and comparative politics, with the latter often meaning, in practice, any country or countries other than the United States. We believe that this is detrimental to both the study of the United States and to comparative political inquiry. Our book seeks to stimulate placing the United States into a broader comparative perspective. At the moment the segregation of the United States from the rest of the world within political science—in faculty hiring, teaching from undergraduate to graduate levels, in many professional journals, conference programs, and university press catalogs—tends to give the impression that comparative institutional analysis is relevant only in foreign lands. There is a need to understand that the United States is not exceptional in the sense that we are just as bound by institutional constraints and pathways as is any other population. We think this can best be done by comparing US practices to those of other, relatively large, established democracies.

The origins of this book can be directly traced to two seminars taught jointly by Bernard Grofman and Arend Lijphart in the winter quarters of 1996 and 1999 to combined groups of graduate students at the University of California campuses in Irvine and San Diego. In four of the ten weeks the students from one campus attended the seminar at the other campus, alternating between campuses. The other six weeks the course was taught via teleconferencing, using the University of California network and facilities at each of the campuses. The seminars used draft versions of Lijphart's *Patterns of Democracy* as their template for how to situate the United States in comparative perspective. Grofman and Lijphart had met and become friends in 1977 and coedited three books, on electoral systems and reapportionment issues, in the 1980s.

In 2000 they agreed to turn their seminar on "The United States in Comparative Perspective" into a book. After Lijphart's retirement from teaching at UC San Diego, Grofman taught the seminar twice on his own as a required course for graduate students affiliated with UC Irvine's Center for the Study of Democracy (CSD), but progress on turning the seminar into a book was slow as a result of a multitude of competing commitments in the early 2000s, such as the completion of a fourth coedited book, on electoral and party systems in the Nordic countries. While both authors remained strongly committed to the project, it became clear to them that only with the collaboration of another scholar or scholars would the book ever get written. They invited Matthew S. Shugart in 2003 to join the project as a third coauthor. Progress picked up and draft chapters were written by Lijphart and Shugart in the mid-2000s. In the spring quarter of 2007, Shugart cotaught a course with his PhD candidate Royce Carroll at UC San Diego, building the course primarily around the draft chapters that then existed and drafting some new chapters. In addition, Shugart developed some of the themes that would later evolve into the theoretical framework of this book—especially the grounding of the comparative analysis in the writings of Madison—in his Policy-Making Processes, a course he taught for many years for the Masters of Pacific International Affairs program at UC San Diego.

Still, the now-three coauthors agreed that further energy needed to be injected, and in the late 2000s they invited Steven L. Taylor to become the book's fourth coauthor. Taylor and Shugart first became acquainted at UC Irvine when Taylor was an undergraduate and Shugart a PhD student, and Taylor took Shugart's Regime Change course in 1988. Taylor's subsequent work in his own PhD studies at the University of Texas at Austin and as a professor at Troy University focused on democratic institutional change in Colombia. After 2005, Shugart and Taylor began honing some of the ideas that they would later incorporate into revised drafts of this book on their respective Weblogs, Taylor's *PoliBlog* and Shugart's *Fruits & Votes*.[1] Also continuing the tradition of teaching courses based on the draft text, Taylor workshopped some of the early drafts of the text as part of his comparative government course, and later used an early manuscript of the book as part of an advanced undergraduate seminar, The US Constitution in Comparative Perspective.

The book in its present incarnation is far more comprehensive and cohesive than the course materials of long ago and far better suited to complement a standard American government textbook. However, although it has taken more than a decade to bring the proj-

---

1. http://fruitsandvotes.wordpress.com and http://poliblogger.com. In recent years Taylor has also been a regular contributor to Outside the Beltway (http://outsidethebeltway.com).

ect to fruition, one aspect of the project has never changed, namely the view that the United States can best be understood by seeing it in comparative perspective—as one democracy among many. The founder of CSD, Russell Dalton, opens his course in comparative politics by quoting Rudyard Kipling's aphorism: "What knows he of England who only England knows?" With the United States substituting for England, that quote defines the spirit of the original Grofman-Lijphart course and of this book.

We should like to acknowledge the financial support received from several sources. Grofman and Lijphart are grateful to the Intercampus Academic Program Initiative Fund, University of California Office of the President, for its support for travel costs and for the use of teleconferencing facilities that made their joint graduate seminars in 1996 and 1999 possible. Grofman would like to acknowledge the longtime support for his involvement in this project by the UC Irvine Center for the Study of Democracy and by the Jack W. Peltason (Bren Foundation) Chair. Shugart is likewise grateful to the CSD for providing funding to defray his research expenses related to this project. Taylor would like to thank the Troy University Faculty Development Committee for granting sabbatical time that was used to jumpstart this project.

In addition, we would like to acknowledge the invaluable contributions by several individuals. In particular, Grofman thanks Clover Behrend-Gethard for her secretarial assistance in the early days of the project. Shugart thanks the various senior colleagues and coteachers who nurtured him in his earliest years at UC San Diego's School of International Relations and Pacific Studies, especially Peter Cowhey, Peter Gourevitch, Mathew McCubbins, and Susan Shirk. All four of us also want to express our deep gratitude to our research assistants: Royce Carroll, Mark Gray, Stephen J. K. Lee, Jeff Daniel, and Mónica Pachón. Additionally, we owe a debt of gratitude to numerous experts who graciously answered our questions concerning a wide range of topics that helped enhance this book: David Fisk, Stephen Gardbaum, Mark P. Jones, Youngmi Kim, Joy Langston, Keith Poole, Kuniaki Nemoto, Peter M. Siavelis, Melody Ellis Valdini, and Gregory Weeks.

CHAPTER 1

INTRODUCTION

AMERICAN EXCEPTIONALISM

In what way can it be said (as it often is) that the United States of America has an exceptional democracy? That seemingly simple question is the basis for this book. We say "seemingly" because the very assertion of American exceptionalism creates a host of problems. The most obvious problem is simply determining what is meant by the term, as the word denotes both something that is unique, special, or different as well as an exemplar worthy of emulation. Further, the very assertion that the United States is exceptional has profound political and emotional implications that have the possibility of clouding sound political inquiry, as it can inspire a myriad of responses, ranging from deeply held patriotic views to serious resentments about American attitudes and power.[1] On that latter point, we hope that the empirical approach (one of comparative institutions) to be undertaken herein will quell such responses. We are simply seeking to answer the question, How distinctive is American democracy when compared to other countries around the word?

---

1. Indeed, the very usage of the term *American* can be seen as controversial to some, as citizens of other countries in the Western Hemisphere (i.e., the Americas) see the appropriation of the terms as solely being the domain of the United States to be problematic. On the other hand, the full name of the country is the United States of America, and the common referent to it is America. Regardless, while it may seem odd to some students, these discussions of semantics can have important political implications that have the potential to muddy analytical conversations.

The notion that the United States of America's democracy is somehow exceptional is not a new one. It dates back in many ways to the American Revolution (indeed, before)[2] and continues to resonate in contemporary politics. Whole books could be written on the subject,[3] and we do not propose a comprehensive discussion here. However, because any discussion of American democracy in a comparative context inevitably raises the issues of whether it is categorically different than other democracies, it strikes us as an issue worthy of addressing. Beyond that, it is our experience that students (and citizens in general) often use assumptions about American democracy to influence the way they view the concept of democracy itself, and so it is worthwhile to explore these issues before embarking on our analysis.

The very idea of "American exceptionalism" can take on a myriad of meanings, including culture, economics, military power, and historical development. This book is not oriented toward a comprehensive assessment or evaluation of these meanings, but is fundamentally focused on the question of institutional variation in a comparative sense. Still, it is worth considering two broad ways in which American exceptionalism emerges, which is relevant to our discussion. The first is an informal, general set of attitudes. The second is a more formal, academic approach. We sketch out both below and examine how they are relevant to our analysis.

Informal Attitudes to American Exceptionalism

It is certainly not unreasonable that Americans would have pride in their country and therefore think it exceptional. As a general principle, it is hardly unusual for citizens to see their home as special. Indeed, Americans need look no further than the attitudes of their fellow citizens within the fifty states to see this in operation. The

2. Think, e.g., of John Winthrop's likening of the Puritan colonies in North America as being "a City upon a Hill" (imagery from the Gospel of Matthew) in 1630, all the way to its later appropriation by President Ronald Reagan to apply to the United States in the 1980s.

3. Many have been written, and several are discussed in this chapter.

residents of the states have differing reasons for believing their state to be special, be it because of certain historical events, geographic features, or cultural contributions. It is therefore not difficult to see how such attitudes might exist in a broader, global fashion (in fact, the French see France as exceptional, as do the Germans, Germany and so forth). As such, it is to be expected that Americans would see themselves as unique or special.

Certainly the United States of America has a number of claims that it can make in this regard. First, it is one of the largest democracies in the world, both in terms of physical size (only Canada is bigger) and population (only India has more residents). Second, it is arguably the oldest continuous democracy in history (although that is a more complicated statement than it may initially seem to be). Third, it has the oldest democratic constitution, which has served as model to many other countries over time. In addition, there are a number of specific aspects of American democratic processes that are either unique or, at least, in the distinct minority compared to other democracies (such as the widespread use of primary elections to nominate candidates and the length of the ballot). Exactly what some of these observations mean will be explored in later chapters.

The pride that Americans have in their country and history, coupled with its power in international affairs leads to the idea that not only is American democracy special in and of itself, but that it serves as a model for the world. Basically, the assumption is that because of the exceptional (more in terms of excellence than uniqueness) nature of American democracy, it ought to serve as an example.[4] We can see this in two recent inaugural addresses. In 2005, President George W. Bush referenced the founding of the United States and went on to state "it is the policy of the United States to seek and support the growth of democratic movements and institutions in every nation and culture, with the ultimate goal of ending tyranny in our world." Likewise, four years later, President Barack Obama noted that the Founding Fathers' "ideals still light the world." These are

---

4. Another way of discussing this concept is to discuss American exceptionalism in terms of both uniqueness but also historical sequencing; i.e., being the first constitutional democracy meant that it was unique and therefore a model.

not new ideas. Thomas Paine wrote in *Common Sense* in 1776: "We have it in our power to begin the world over again."

Such a view also has the effect of leading Americans to assume that democratic governance in the rest of the world is pretty much the same as in the United States. After all, if the United States was first and best, surely younger democracies simply followed its lead, yes? And, there are some reasons to think this. For example, many Latin American constitutions adopted similar governmental structures to that of the United States (such as the widespread existence of presidentialism in the region). Of course, there are also a large number of differences (especially in the area of electoral systems) that exist. And, as we shall see, the exact manifestation of democratic governance globally differs from the US model.

Assumptions about US leadership on the issue of democratic development also skews American understanding of democratic governance, because if the United States is an exemplar to the world, then really what more does one need to know to understand democratic governance than the US model? These views are reinforced by the United States' relative isolation from other democracies. The continental nature of the United States leads its daily politics and press coverage to be rather different than, say, Europe's. While it is true that the United States is bordered to both the north and the south by democracies, the attention paid in the US press to either country is scant.[5] No doubt, too, the relative power of the United States vis-à-vis other states leads to the assumption that superiority in things like military might and economics must also mean superiority in other areas.

This all matters because it skews the way that students understand government. As Lipset once wrote "it is impossible to understand a country without seeing how it varies from others. Those who know only one country know no country" (1996: 17). A lack of understanding of the institutional variations within democracies, and

---

5. Indeed, whereas news from Canada tends to be almost nonexistent on a national level, news from Mexico is almost entirely negative, dealing either with the contentious issue of immigration or with the violence related to the drug trade.

the way those variations affect the functioning of government, leads to difficulty in understanding aspects of US democracy. For example, citizens often wonder (if not bemoan) why there are only two viable parties in US elections, or why the president and congress behave as they do, and so on. Such questions are all about institutional structure, and comparative inquiry in particular can shed substantial light on these subjects in ways that examining such processes in isolation cannot.

The Academy and American Exceptionalism

In a more formal sense, academics have found the question of American democracy to be an intriguing one. Most academic discussions along these lines focus primarily on issues like the conditions of the founding of the United States versus that of other countries (especially European ones) with a substantial emphasis on the nature of values and attitudes. Such studies are at least as old as Alexis de Tocqueville's classic work *Democracy in America*. Many academic studies have been devoted to the notion (for example, Lipset 1996 and 2003, Schuck and Wilson 2008, and Wilson 1998). The main emphasis in these works tends to be on the specific character of Americans (that is, on their beliefs and values) and how that translates into political attitudes and, ultimately, governance. These comparisons are also usually in the context of comparisons to western European states.[6]

Interestingly, one of the results of the academic study of US government has actually helped lead to the isolation of the case from comparative study, adding to the perception that the United States should be treated as a case apart. Such a statement may strike students as odd, but it is nonetheless true. Political science is divided into many subdisciplines, and two of the most prominent are American politics and comparative politics. The evolution of political science has, in large measure, classified those scholars who study the United States as Americanists, and those who study any other

6. For a concise yet fairly comprehensive summary of the standard discussion of American exceptionalism, see Brooks 2009: 21–33.

countries of the world as comparativists. This situation has created an isolation of the United States as a case in broader comparative theorizing and has also led to a literature on the United States that, by definition, treats the case as exceptional. While comparativists will sometimes use the United States as a case in their studies, the study of American politics rarely includes other cases. The typical student experience (especially the nonmajor) is to have a course on American politics that looks *only* at the United States, and perhaps a world politics course that looks at the rest of the world. Even a student majoring in political science can manage to take courses focused on either *only* the study of the United States or, conversely, courses that study other parts of the world to the exclusion of the United States. As such, the propensity to treat the politics of the United States as something set apart is not limited to casual observers or patriots. There is even a tendency in the literature on American political institutions to fail to examine the United States in a comparative perspective in any comprehensive fashion and to therefore treat it in isolation, if not as unique and special. We hope that this text will help remedy that general oversight. While it is true that all countries have unique features, the fact of the matter is that if each case is treated as sui generis, then the construction of systematic theories of politics is impossible.

The goal in this text is not to diminish Americans' pride in their democracy but rather to explain how it is (and is not) like other democracies in the world. Of course, if broader understanding should lead to a more critical eye regarding the institutions of governance in the United States, that should be seen as a positive, as the ability of citizens to be constantly self-critical of their government is key to the health of democracy.

Our Approach: Cross-National Institutional Comparison

What none of the manifestations of discussions about American exceptionalism, which we outlined earlier, accomplishes are systematic comparisons of the actual functional machinery of democratic governance in the United States to other established democracies. This book seeks to fill that gap. In so doing we will demonstrate that democracy in the United States does, in fact, function differently from other democracies on a number of dimensions. This investigation, too, is a means by which to enhance the general understanding of the way in which democracies operate and why institutions are consequential to the way in which democratic governance manifests.

POLITICAL SCIENCE, POLITICAL ENGINEERING, AND *THE FEDERALIST PAPERS*

The context of this study is that of *political science,* that is, the systematic study of human interaction, especially as it pertains to governing large populations of human beings. We are seeking to identify and explain specifically the way by which differing configurations of institutional structures within a state function together in democracies, and to compare a set of democracies to demonstrate how differing structures affect political behavior and outcomes. Our main focus in this process will be to see how those arrangements in the governmental structure of the United States of America differ (or are similar) to those in thirty other democracies.

In some ways the specific approach that we are taking, one that focuses on *institutions,* that is, sets of rules that dictate the creation of structures that define the parameters of options open to political actors, is also one that highlights the idea of *political engineering,* the application of the lessons of political science to specific settings. The implicit theoretical assumptions made herein are that the institutional choices made in our thirty-one democracies matter in terms of basic governance and public policy design and implementation. For example, policy outcomes are negotiated differently in a presidential system (like that of the United States) versus a parliamentary system, such as the one in India.

Clearly the constitution produced by the Philadelphia Convention of 1787 was a deliberate act of political engineering that reflected a specific set of assumptions about the political world. Those who came to be known collectively as the Founding Fathers (and especially that specific subset of the Founding Fathers, the framers of the Constitution) knew that the experiment in political engineering they were living under at the time, the Articles of Confederation, was failing and that a new set of institutions, with a different approach to governing power, needed to be put into place. The authors of *The Federalist Papers* were quite conscious of their own act of political engineering, as Alexander Hamilton wrote in *Federalist 1:* "It has been frequently remarked that it seems to have been reserved to the people of this country, by their conduct and example, to decide the important question, whether societies of men are really capable or not of establishing good government from reflection and choice, or whether they are forever destined to depend on their political constitutions on accident and force" (Madison, Hamilton, and Jay 1987: 87). Note, specifically, the notion that "reflection" (or applied reason) could be used to identify options for governing from which deliberate choices could be made. Further, note that implicit in this formulation is the notion that government could flow from the choices and preferences of the governed rather than simply from the desires of the strongest. In this statement we see an explicit endorsement of political engineering, and also a justification for what would become democratic governance in the United States.

In this book we develop a framework for comparing democracies and for highlighting the many ways in which the United States is organized and functions differently from thirty other democracies around the world.[7] The framework is derived, to a large degree, from that presented in *The Federalist Papers,* which we could call the original "statement of purpose" by which the framers of the US Constitution promoted its ratification. In those essays, James Madison, Alexander Hamilton, and John Jay[8] articulated a theory of how political systems work and advocated their design as best suitable to ensure good government. While this framework, updated with more contemporary ideas from political science and political economy, derives from the very design of the US Constitution, its application

7. The criteria for selection are discussed below.

8. Hamilton and Madison were the primary authors, and we draw largely on Madison in our discussion here. It is worth noting that these authors did not share a unified political theory, but rather we are engaged, primarily, in the political task of supporting ratification of the new Constitution.

to our full set of thirty-one democracies shows, ironically, just how unusual the US form of democracy is in many respects.

The basic ideas of *The Federalist,* drawing principally from the contributions of Madison, are that government institutions must channel and balance the ambition of political leaders. Madison considered government to be a delegation of authority from citizens to representatives, such that he explicitly defined a *republic* (what we would call a "representative democracy," as it has evolved over time) in *Federalist 10* as "the delegation of the government . . . to a small number of citizens elected by the rest" (Madison, Hamilton, and Jay 1987: 126). He further took for granted that these representatives would be self-interested. Therefore, it was necessary that "ambition must be made to counteract ambition" (*Federalist 51*) via proper institutional arrangement.

KEY CONCEPTS

Before embarking on our analysis, it is necessary to establish some basic concepts. While the fullness of these concepts will be explored in the chapters that follow, we need to provide the bases for our conversation.

Democracy

Following from the logic found in *The Federalist Papers,* we can understand the basics of democracy in its modern, representative form to be a chain of delegation.[9] Delegation theory gives us a set of analogies—derived originally from economics and management—that the ultimate holders of authority are principals, who delegate authority to agents in order to take advantage of specialized expertise of those agents. The chain of delegation is depicted in figure 1.1. The idea of democracy is that the citizenry governs itself, but, of course, only in the very smallest communities is that literally

9. Others have used the "chain of delegation" metaphor (Palmer 1995, Strøm 2000); Carroll and Shugart (2007) likewise draw on the logic of *The Federalist Papers* to highlight how authority is delegated in modern democracies.

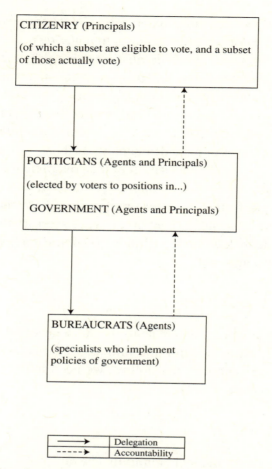

Fig. 1.1. Stylized chain of delegation in democracy
Key: Solid arrows indicate delegation relationships, with the direction of the arrows showing the flow of authority from principals to agents. Dashed arrows indicate accountability of agents to principals.

possible. Therefore, as shown by the first solid arrow from the top of figure 1.1, the citizenry delegates to politicians, who are the agents of citizens (or more accurately, of those citizens who are eligible to vote and who exercise their right to vote). As Madison wrote in *Federalist 39:* "It is essential to such a government that it be derived from the great body of the society, not from an inconsiderable portion or a favored class" (Madison, Hamilton, and Jay 1987: 255). Of course, at the time of the founding of the United States, there were still classes of persons (most notably women and slaves, but also the unpropertied in many states) who were not allowed to vote. As will be discussed in chapter 3 on constitutions, the definition of democracy has expanded considerably since the late 1700s. Still, we see here the basic notion of republican government (that is, government that derives from the consent of the governed, rather than from the powers of an aristocratic class or some other fount) being outlined. Further, we see the notion that the public delegates the basic power to govern to politicians, since it is impossible for the populace to directly govern itself. Madison continued by noting, "It is sufficient for such a government that the person administering it be appointed, either directly or indirectly, by the people; and that they hold their appointments by either of the tenures just specified" (Madison, Hamilton, and Jay 1987: 255)—in other words, the power to govern is delegated by the people to elected politicians.

Politicians are specialists in the techniques of winning elections and governing. However, politicians only rarely have the expertise of administering complex policy implementation, so they too delegate. In this second link in the chain of delegation, politicians are the principals, and bureaucrats are the agents. Thus, politicians are at once agents (of citizens) and principals (over bureaucrats). In modern democracies, what we call the bureaucracy is the set of organizations that are responsible for carrying out the public policies enacted into law by politicians. The bureaucracy is thus comprised of a panoply of "agencies" with specific functions, such as the Department of Defense, the Department of Health and Human Services, and the Environmental Protection Agency, to take three examples from contemporary American government. Bureaucratic agencies of this sort consist of individual bureaucrats (or sometimes "officials") who are hired for their expertise and specialized knowledge of actual policy. They function as agents because they only implement policies that are chosen by politicians; they must conform to the law in carrying out their professional responsibilities. Or at least that must be the case if democracy actually "works," because, as figure 1.1 reminds us, the citizens are the ultimate principals. Thus, if bureaucrats are not implementing the policies that politicians determine, democracy cannot be said to be working. Nor can it be said to be working if the orders that politicians give to their bureaucratic agents do not reflect the choices made by citizens at elections, where voters choose which set of politicians will exercise political power. While we can say, in very general terms, that democracy does not work if the decisions implemented by bureaucrats do not ultimately depend on the choices made by citizens, just how this process works varies in important ways across democracies. Of course, in reality, delegation is never perfect, insofar as politicians cannot be exact reflections of the desires of the citizens who sent them to government in the first place, nor can we ever be certain that bureaucratic decisions conform exactly to what politicians intended when they wrote a given law. More fundamentally, citizens themselves are divided in their preferences over policy, and any representative government necessarily must make compromises across these divisions, meaning that laws may actually reflect these divisions by leaving gaps that bureaucrats must fill in when they implement policy. For all these reasons, the institutional structures that delegate popular sovereignty into governance are likewise imperfect, and the degree to which politicians and bureaucrats can fulfill their roles as agents is flawed as well.

Government: Hierarchy versus Transactions

The term *government* has a dual usage in our discussion. In the broad sense, government is made up of the structures and leaders in charge of making authoritative decisions and carrying them out for a given country. The nature of who governs and why has to do with the regime type in place (that is, is it democratic, authoritarian, and so on). We are dealing solely with democratic regimes. The more narrow way that the term *government* can be applied is to the specific collection of individuals in a parliamentary system that are selected by a majority of the legislature to occupy the executive branch so long as they can maintain the confidence of that majority (that is, a prime minister and a cabinet). The specifics of such institutional arrangements and how they differ from those in the United States will be addressed in subsequent chapters (especially those on legislative and executive power).

BOX 1.1. STATES, REGIMES, AND GOVERNMENTS

Terminology in common use among political scientists, especially those of the profession engaged in the study of countries other than the United States, is often poorly understood in the United States. Here we seek to clarify three common foundational concepts: state, regime, and government.

STATE

The term *state* is used in a broad sense that is distinctive from its use in phrases like "the fifty states" of the United States. Or we could say that every country has a state, but not every country has states! The idea of states as political subdivisions in a federal country–the most common understanding of *state* in the United States –is completely separate from the idea of every country having a set of organizations and institutions that collectively constitute its state. In this latter sense, the state consists of the military, police, and the whole edifice of administrative organs that jointly exercise authority over a territorially defined sovereign entity. Thus we can speak of the "member states" of the United Nations, which means that each state has been recognized by the United Nations as having sovereignty–the right to make binding decisions–over some territory, as opposed to being subject to the authority of another state. So a new state is created only when a dependent territory becomes recognized as independent (for example, when the former dependent territory of Portuguese Guinea became the independent state of Guinea Bissau in 1974) or when an existing state breaks up into two or more new ones (for example, when the Soviet Union broke up into the Russian Federation, Ukraine, Kazakhstan, and so on, in 1991).

Each of these states then constitutes organizations–military, police, administrative–that carry out authoritative decisions within its territory. Thus the term *state* refers both to the recognized sovereign entities (which engage with other states in the sphere that political scientists call "international relations") as well as their internal organizational structures (which engage with citizens in the realm of domestic politics and policy).

Aside from cases of new sovereign entities being created through the independence of previously subordinate territories or the breakup of existing states, normally states persist even as their regimes and governments change–taking us to the definitions of these latter terms.

REGIME

A state has to be governed according to some set of rules and practices. It is the rules and practices that constitute the regime. Thus there is the basic dividing line between democratic regimes and authoritarian ones. As detailed in the main chapter, a democratic regime is one in which those who make decisions are ultimately accountable to citizens via elections (and, more specifically, elections that offer real choice and the freedom of parties and individuals to compete over differing visions of how the state should be governed). Authoritarian regimes are those in which power-holders are not accountable to citizens but rather to some narrow group, which might be a single political party (for example, the Communist Party in China), the military (for example, many regimes in Latin America before the transitions to democracy in the 1980s), or a royal family (for example, the House of Saud in Saudi Arabia).

As this is a book about democracies, we will not concern ourselves here with how authoritarian regimes are governed and how they differ from one another. We will, however, concern ourselves throughout with differences within the broad category of democratic regimes. For instance, we can speak of a presidential regime (for example, the United States) or a parliamentary regime (for example, the United Kingdom). Here the term *regime* signifies a set of rules and procedures that define how the executive power is constituted. We can also use terms like *presidential system* and *parliamentary system* to convey the same concept.

Many independent countries undergo changes in regime without a change in the state, per se. For example, in 1989, the military of Chile ceased governing the country directly and transferred power to an elected president and legislature. In that way, it changed from an authoritarian regime (or a military regime, more specifically) to a democratic regime (and specifically, a presidential regime). The state of Chile did not change, however, as the same military institution and all other administrative agencies remained fundamentally intact. We can now go a step further and also note that while the democratic, presidential regime of Chile has not changed since 1989, its government has changed several times.

GOVERNMENT

The term *government* as detailed in the text of the chapter, is used in two different (but closely related) senses. In general, the government refers to the individuals and political parties that occupy the top decision-making positions at a given time. If the regime is democratic, these office-holders may shift with periodic elections (or even between them, under some circumstances). In the United States, we often define governmental periods by the name of the president: "the Obama administration," where the word *administration* could just as easily be replaced with *government*. The practice in parliamentary systems is similar, in that a given cabinet that governed the country for a period of time is often referred to by the name of the prime minister who headed it (for example, "the Harper government" in Canada).

The identification of the office occupants of a specific period of time collectively as "the government" is much more straightforward in parliamentary regimes than in presidential ones, especially the United States. In many parliamentary regimes, the government (prime minister and cabinet) may resign between elections and be replaced by a new one, according to the basic institutional rules of the system. In such situations it is common to refer to a "change of government," because the personnel, and perhaps the political parties, are being replaced. However, it would be misleading to speak of a change of regime—or of the specific governments or administrations as "regimes" (for example, "the Harper regime")—because these changes of government occur according to the established rules of the game, and hence within the confines of a single continuous regime.

SUMMARY

Governments change regularly, especially in democratic regimes where there are institutional rules for such changes—in particular, elections. Regimes change less often, when the fundamental rules of the game are altered, such as when a democratic constitution comes into force and a previous authoritarian regime is replaced. (The reverse can also happen, of course.) States change less often still, only when an existing one breaks up or a dependent territory becomes independent or when the entire edifice has collapsed and a replacement is constructed.

Speaking in the broad usage of the term, the very structure of government is a *hierarchy*. In a hierarchy, one actor is subordinate to another. That is, agents *exercise authority,* but only at the behest of principals, who continue to hold *ultimate authority.* This is a hierarchy because authority flows in one direction, from the principals to the agents. It is also a hierarchy in another sense: *Accountability* runs in the opposite direction, in that agents are accountable to principals. In politics, accountability means that the agent's right to exercise authority can be revoked by the principal if the principal is not satisfied with the ways in which the agent is exercising the delegated authority. For instance, in democratic systems, politicians periodically face elections, and the voter-principals can vote their politician-agents out of their governmental posts. The chain of delegation depicted in figure 1.1 is clearly a hierarchy because voters hold ultimate authority, and, through elections, voters both delegate authority to politicians and hold them accountable. Similarly, the relation between politicians and bureaucrats is hierarchical because the authority that bureaucrats exercise is based in the laws and orders given by politicians in government; if politicians are dissatisfied with the actions of bureaucrats, the law can be changed or the agency can have its budget cut or its responsibilities transferred to some other agency.[10]

Few democratic political systems are purely hierarchical, however. In addition to the basic hierarchical framework of authority depicted in figure 1.1, there are also *transactional* relations within the political system. A transactional relationship exists whenever coequals must work together to accomplish their objectives. Working together means arriving at mutually agreed upon solutions, as opposed to the possibility that one simply overrules the other. Thus transactional relations are the opposite of hierarchies. In a true hierarchy, the principal prevails by revoking the right of the agent to exercise delegated authority. In a transactional relationship, on the other hand, two (or more) coequal actors must cooperate, or else refer their conflicts back to the principals to resolve (for example, in a democracy, the voters may ultimately decide to change the political complexion of their agents).

There are two basic forms that transactional relationships take in democracies, and we will discuss them at length in several of the following chapters. Briefly, they may take the form of transactions between *separate institutions* or among *political parties.* The tenets of constitutional design advocated by *The Federalist Papers* and embodied in the US political system entail the separate election of the Congress and president, whose distinct ambitions are made to counteract one another.[11] That is, Congress members and the president tend to have different preferences, in part because they are elected differently. Yet they serve for fixed terms. That is, there is no hierarchy between them, whereby one can dismiss the other when conflict over policy arises.[12] Instead, they exist in a transactional re-

10. Normally in modern democracies, however, politicians do not have the authority of outright firing bureaucrats, due the development of the professional "civil service."

11. Indeed, the earlier reference to "ambition countering ambition" from *Federalist 51* is precisely in reference to the notion that the institutions of government need to be constructed so as to require transaction to take place as part of the policy-making process.

12. While it is true that Congress has the power to impeach and remove a sitting president for "bribery, treason, or other high crimes and misdemean-

lationship with one another. They are coequals, and policy changes require the consent of both of them. In transactional relationships, individual actors may have *veto powers* within the governing process, and so the only way to avoid impasse is to compromise (that is, transact/negotiate). The term *veto* derives from the Latin *vetare* meaning "to forbid." In a political context, to veto is to stop an action from happening. The basic notion is well known to US citizens, as the president is granted the power to veto bills passed by Congress. However, beyond that formal veto power is the fact that multiple institutions in a given system may have the ability to stop policy from being formed. In other words, some political institutions behave as *veto gates,* in the sense that unless the gate is opened, action cannot flow through (that is, it is vetoed by being stopped). Depending on the institutional parameters and other factors, a given veto gate may require more than one actor to agree to unlock the gate (as one player alone lacks the needed key). A presidency granted veto power is a veto gate and it only takes one actor, the president him- or herself, to decide whether to open the gate or not. Legislatures, however, often contain multiple parties, or parties made up of various factions. Under those circumstances, a given legislative body, itself a veto gate, may have multiple actors, whom we can call *veto players* within it, who must agree (that is, create a legislative majority) so that the gate can be unlocked. The more veto gates in play, and the more veto players with keys, the more transactions that need to take place to put policy into practice. Institutional design therefore is relevant, for example, are there two chambers that act as one veto gate or two? Does the executive have veto power?

Making transactions between separate institutions are not, however, the fundamental way that politics works in most other democracies. More common is a system of transactions between political parties sharing power. As we will see, in most democracies two or more parties form *coalitions* or other working agreements over how governmental authority will be exercised and which policies will be enacted. Parties are coequals in the sense that all of the parties

---

ors," this process was one designed to deal with malfeasance, not policy disputes.

BOX 1.2. VETO GATES AND THE PLAYERS WHO HOLD THE KEYS

The concept of a veto gate is a metaphor for the steps in the process of making new laws. The idea is that for legislation to be created, it has to pass through multiple stages, which can be conceived of as gates that must be opened if the process is to continue. The number of gates that exist in a given country's government varies and depends on the institutional configuration of a given system. So, in simple terms:

Veto gates are stages in a legislative process wherein political power must be used to allow an idea to move from one stage of the legislative process to another. Depending on the institutional arrangements in a given country, there can be multiple veto gates. The more institutions present in the process, the more gates exist—for example, a bicameral legislature with coequal legislative powers or an elected president with a veto pen. There are three veto gates in the US legislative process (both chambers of Congress and the president) but only one in New Zealand (the unicameral Parliament).

Veto players are the political actors involved who have to act to open the gate. We can think of this as the holders of the gate's keys. If the veto player is a singular actor, such as a president who has the power to sign the bill (open the gate) or reject the bill (refuse to open the gate), then the process to turn (or not turn) the key is not especially complex, because individuals do not have to transact with themselves to make decisions—they are either willing to turn the key or not. If the gate is a legislative chamber that has one party with more than half the seats, then that party may likewise be a single veto player controlling the veto gate—provided that the party acts in such a cohesive manner that we can think of it as being one actor (even though it may be made up of dozens or even hundreds of individual legislators).

However, if a veto gate is controlled by multiple players, such as a legislative chamber populated with several parties, none of which has an absolute majority of the seats, then the gate requires multiple keys to open it. This means that the various players have to transact with one another to open the gate, and all the players may not be willing to do so or may require concessions in exchange for the turning of the key (that is, voting to pass a bill).

in a coalition must give their consent in order for the agreement to remain in place, although the bargaining power of parties may vary depending on their relative sizes and other factors. Each has its own electoral constituency, within a subset of the ultimate principal, the citizenry, and each thus has its own ambition: to advance policies that will lead its voting constituency to want to vote for the party again at the next election. Consistent with the ideas found in *The Federalist Papers,* though within a different institutional structure, the ambition of the various parties is checked by that of the others.

Articulating Citizens' Preferences: Political Parties and Interest Groups

So far we have spoken of different ways in which politicians exist within a set of hierarchical or transactional relations. Just as later in this book we will have to further disaggregate "politicians" and "government" in figure 1.1, so we will have to disaggregate the citizenry. We have already alluded to political parties and how they represent different constituencies within the electorate. As such, they reflect the *collective action* of sets of politicians, seeking to represent the preferences of groups of voters. Parties are thus a crucial link between citizens and the government. As we shall see, our democracies differ markedly from one another in the number of major parties and in how important a role they play in the process of government. The United States is not typical in having just two important political parties. Most democracies have *multiparty systems.* Moreover, parties play a lesser role in coordinating the actions among politicians in the United States than in most other democracies, partly for the reason mentioned earlier: In most democracies, transactions among political parties are the primary means by which democracy works, whereas in the United States transactions between institutions (presidency and Congress) play a more central role.

Parties are not the only means by which the preferences of (groups of) citizens are reflected in the political process. *Interest groups* are another. An interest group is a group of citizens organized around a common interest that they seek to have represented in the political process. Interest groups can be very narrow, reflecting only the preferences of a specific type of business, or they can be quite broad, containing a mass membership. Whether very narrow or quite broad, however, they are almost always narrower than political parties. Parties organize to contest elections and seek to control governmental authority, whether alone or in combination with other parties. Interest groups, by definition, are seeking to influence government, not elect members to it, on behalf of a specific purpose shared by their members. Interest groups are also important because their activities are not limited to attempts at influencing elected politicians, but also often focus their attention on the bureaucracy.

As we shall see, our democracies vary in the extent to which parties or interest groups are more important in the policy-making process. All democracies have both parties and interest groups, but it is probably true that a general maxim can be stated that where parties are more important, interest groups—or at least the narrowest of them—are less important. The reason is that, as noted, both are means of collectively organizing and representing citizen preferences, but parties tend to aggregate across a wide range of interests, while each interest group tends to be concerned only about the specific interests of its own members.

Institutions

A basic definition of *institutions* is as follows: "Rules that govern social interactions, constraining the behavior of and the options open to actors. Political institutions establish guidelines for deliberation, the aggregation of preferences into collective decisions, and the implementation of those decisions" (Carey 2000: 735). Institutions, therefore, provide the structures and processes by which the authority of principals are communicated to agents as well as through which the agents are made accountable to those principals. Further, institutions are the vehicles through which the preferences of the principals are made manifest via the actions of the agents. For example, citizens-as-voters (principals), make their preferences known via the electoral system (an institutional structure), to send politicians (agents) to serve in various aspects of government, such as the legislature and executive branch (other institutions).

This book is predominantly one that compares institutions. Specifically, we will be examining the following institutional variables: constitutions, division of power, electoral systems, political parties, interest groups, legislative power, executive power, and judicial power. The book also includes a look at specific policy variations across our cases. A main theoretical point that we would like to emphasize is how one set of institutional choices, such as choosing presidentialism over parliamentarianism, can limit and influence the institutional paths subsequently taken. And, indeed, note that the United States in particular, as the first country to start down the path of constitutional democracies, made choices that led to the fact that it is, in important ways, a different democracy than the others in the study.

THIRTY-ONE DEMOCRACIES

For the purposes of comparative study and the broadening of the understanding of democracy, we have selected thirty other democracies to compare to the United States, making this a comprehensive comparative study of thirty-one democratic countries. We would argue that to fully understand the degree to which the United States is or is not a different democracy, we need as broad a pool for comparison as is reasonable. We utilize two basic criteria for inclusion: democratic longevity and population size.

In regards to the issue of democratic longevity, our basic measure was continuous democracy since 1990 as measured by the NGO Freedom House.[13] However, we also have included a few exceptions that fall somewhat outside these parameters. Specifically, there were several cases that did not meet the Freedom House standards for the entire period (that is, those classified as "free"), but were deemed worthy of inclusion because of the general trajectory of democracy in the cases in question, and also for purposes of geographic and institutional variation within our pool of cases. Of the thirty-one cases included, twenty-four unambiguously meet the criteria laid down, but seven do not fully comply. Three of the cases in question do not meet the time-frame requirement: the Czech Republic did not exist until 1993, and Mexico and South Africa were still engaged in democratic transitions during the early part of the period being studied.

13. A complete explanation of Freedom House's methodology can be found here: http://www.freedomhouse.org/report/freedom-world-2012/methodology.

Four other cases were classified at times as only "partly free" by Freedom House since 1990, usually for reasons of violence, but were considered sufficiently democratic to warrant inclusion, and also for reasons of geographic and institutional diversity: Argentina, Brazil, Colombia, and India.

Because the United States is a large country (both in terms of geography, but more importantly in terms of population), it was thought that especially small countries should be excluded from the study. A lower population threshold of 5 million was selected, meaning that states such as Costa Rica, Iceland, and Norway were not included in the study. However, we made an exception for New Zealand (with a population of 4.3 million) because it presented a noteworthy case of political engineering and as a case with specific characteristics relevant to the United States (for example, English-speaking, once a strong two-party system, and so on).

Table 1.1 lists our thirty-one democracies, along with their populations, Human Development Index (HDI) score, and from which point they have continuously been democratic.

As the table indicates, we have countries from all regions of the world, although the majority of the states are European. Most of the states (twenty-six) are also classified by the United Nations Development Programme as having achieved very high human development, while three are classified as high human development (Brazil, Colombia, and Mexico), and two as having medium human development (India and South Africa).[14]

Interestingly, the plurality of the states under discussion, thirteen, are fairly young democracies, having made their most recent (if not first) transition to democracy during the third wave (which started in 1974), most of which democratized in the 1980s or later (nine of the thirteen). Although as we will see in chapter 3, many of these countries have vacillated between democratic and authoritarian regimes over time.

14. In the 2011 rankings, the very high development level was .793 and up, high development was .783–.698, and medium was .698–.522. In rankings before 2011, the system had different cutoffs linked to round numbers (e.g., medium ran from .500 to .799, and high ran from .800 to .899, and so on).

Table 1.1. Thirty-one democracies

	Population (2011)	HDI (2011)	Democratic since
India	1,205,073,612	0.547	Third wave
United States	**313,847,465**	**0.910**	**First wave**
Brazil	205,716,890	0.718	Third wave
Japan	127,368,088	0.901	Second wave
Mexico	114,975,406	0.770	Third wave
Germany	81,305,856	0.905	Second wave
France	65,630,692	0.884	Second wave
United Kingdom	63,047,162	0.863	First wave
Italy	61,261,254	0.874	Second wave
Korea	48,860,500	0.897	Third wave
South Africa	48,810,427	0.619	Third wave
Spain	47,042,984	0.878	Third wave
Colombia	45,239,079	0.710	Second wave
Argentina	42,192,494	0.797	Third wave
Poland	38,415,284	0.813	Third wave
Canada	34,300,083	0.908	First wave
Australia	22,015,576	0.929	First wave
Chile	17,067,369	0.805	Third wave
Netherlands	16,730,632	0.910	Second wave
Portugal	10,781,459	0.809	Third wave
Greece	10,767,827	0.861	Third wave
Belgium	10,438,353	0.886	Second wave
Czech Republic	10,177,300	0.865	Third wave
Hungary	9,958,453	0.816	Third wave
Sweden	9,103,788	0.904	First wave
Austria	8,219,743	0.885	Second wave
Switzerland	7,655,628	0.903	First wave
Israel	7,590,758	0.888	Second wave
Denmark	5,543,453	0.895	Second wave
Finland	5,262,930	0.882	First wave
New Zealand	4,327,944	0.908	First wave

Note: First Wave: 1828–1926; Second Wave: 1943–1962; Third Wave: 1974 onward.
Sources: Huntington 1991: 14–17 (and authors' classifications); United Nations; and CIA *World Factbook.*

STRUCTURE OF THE TEXT

We start our discussion with a look at the concept of political engineering, with the Philadelphia Convention of 1787 as the basis for that discussion. From there we look at constitutions and division of power (that is, unitary versus federal states). These topics form a foundation from which we can then discuss the structure of governance in our thirty-one democracies. From there we will look at electoral systems (or the rules for delegation) and then political parties and interest groups (the main agents who act on behalf of segments of the citizenry). From there we look at the three main types of government power/institutions: legislative, executive, and judicial. In the comparative conclusion, we will look at some specific examples of public policy variation across our cases.

Each chapter begins with a discussion of the institutional options that would be theoretically open to a political engineer approaching the given topic. This approach allows for an introduction to the relevant concepts germane to the chapter. From there, each chapter looks specifically at how the United States compares to its thirty democratic siblings. At a minimum, these comparisons should help answer, in an empirical fashion, how different a democracy the United States is in comparison to other such states and what that assertion actually means. One thing is for certain: Any claims to being exceptional (or oldest, or best, or any other superlative, or criticism for that matter) requires *comparison* inherently. We hope that this book provides a solid foundation for those comparisons at least in terms of institutional structures and their implications for governance.

CHAPTER 2

POLITICAL ENGINEERING AND THE US CONSTITUTION

Before embarking on a systematic comparison of key elements of the institutional configuration of the United States of America to the other thirty democracies in this study, let us consider the origins of that institutional configuration. Such a discussion will help us to consider not only the key ways in which the United States is a different democracy, but also underscores the theme of political engineering that is key to understanding the way in which institutional choices matter. Further, it is useful to consider the writing of the US Constitution of 1789[1] as an act of political engineering and compromise rather than as the mythologized political miracle that it is often considered to have been.

If political engineering is the application of the principles of political science to a specific set of problems, then the Philadelphia Constitutional Convention of 1787 is a perfect example of such an enterprise. Specifically, we can see that actors such as James Madison and Alexander Hamilton, to name two of the more prominent examples, were very much interested in taking their practical and theoretical knowledge of the political world and applying it to the problems facing the United States in its political operations. The challenge that faced the conventioneers of 1787 was the failure of an existing set of institutional structures and the need to design replacements. And, as is the case whenever political engineers meet to address such problems, the practical politics of the day intersected with the intellectual understandings of the political world to produce an outcome.

1. The US Constitution written in Philadelphia went into force in March 1789 and hence is referred to as the Constitution of 1789.

The main purpose of this chapter is to demonstrate the basic concept of political engineering in action as well as how specific institutional choices set the United States on the developmental path
that it has taken. Such a discussion will highlight the key institutional differences that exist between the United States and our other
thirty democracies and allow for the institution-by-institution comparisons in the subsequent chapters, and will establish the fact that
choices over institutions matter. A major focus here is the development of federalism and presidentialism. This chapter will be unlike
those that follow, insofar as it is looking solely at the United States,
although we would argue that what is discussed in this chapter does
have broad comparative applicability.

FUNDAMENTAL PROBLEMS AND
INSTITUTIONAL CHOICES

After the flooding experiences in the aftermath of Hurricane Katrina in 2005 and the failure of the levee system that was supposed
to protect New Orleans from the waters that surround it, civil engineers were called in to assess those failures and to propose and
construct solutions to prevent a repeat of that catastrophe. Those
engineers knew that a general problem existed and had to diagnose
the specific causes thereof and to put into place corrective measures
to ensure the proper functioning of the levees into the future.

So too did the political engineers who arrived in Philadelphia in
the summer of 1787 find themselves faced with a general problem,
that is, governing the thirteen states. The source of that problem was
within the structure of the country's first constitution, the Articles of
Confederation.[2] To put it as plainly as possible, the central govern-

2. It might be objected that the engineering analogy is not valid, as other
types of engineers might not have to compromise with those who favor alternative solutions, as is essential in politics. However, the differences should not
be exaggerated. To return to our Hurricane Katrina example, engineers designing improvements to flood-control systems had to contend with competing
objectives (e.g., aesthetic considerations, environmental consequences, and the
limitations of public budgets). All engineers face compromises of some sort
between their technical plans and practical implementation.

BOX 2.1. MADISON'S "VICES OF THE POLITICAL SYSTEM OF THE UNITED STATES" (APRIL 1787)

1. Failure of the States to Comply with Constitutional Requisitions
2. Encroachments by the States on the Federal Authority
3. Violations of the Law of Nations and Treaties
4. Trespasses of the States on the Rights of Each Other
5. Want in Concert in Matters Where Common Interest Requires It
6. Want of Guaranty to the States of Their Constitutions and Laws Against Internal Violence
7. Want of Sanction to the Laws, and of Coercion in the Government of the Confederacy
8. Want of Ratification by the People of the Articles of Confederacy
9. Multiplicity of Laws in the Several States
10. Mutability of the Laws of the States
11. Injustice of the Laws of the States

Source: Meyers 1981: 57–65

ment under the Articles lacked all capacity to govern. Box 2.1 contains a summary of the "Vices of the Political System of the United States," which detail a central government unable to collect taxes, enforce laws, conduct foreign policy, regulate commerce, or manage the interactions of the states themselves (among other problems). Indeed, the political engineers of 1787 faced the kinds of problems that political engineers have continued to face up to the present time: seeking, usually in the context of a political crisis, the appropriate institutional mix that would allow adequate governance in a manner that the stakeholders involved in the negotiation can accept.

The Philadelphia conventioneers arrived agreeing that there was a problem concerning the ability of the central government to govern and that the problem was grave enough to get them to travel from all over the thirteen states to come together so as to construct some sort of solution.[3] There was consensus about there being a problem,

3. Although it is worth noting that the Rhode Island delegation did not initially participate. As the smallest of the small states, it had the most to lose power-wise if the basic structure of the Articles was altered.

and there was general consensus on two other key issues regarding the design of the new constitution: the maintenance of a republican form of government and that the several states had to be preserved in their political and geographic characters.[4]

Maintaining republicanism meant, at a minimum, continuing to respect the notion of popular sovereignty as described by the Lincolnian formulation of government of, by, and for the people[5] rather than having the fount of government power being from some other source (like a hereditary aristocratic class). The real test of republican government, as noted in chapter 1, was Madison's statement in *Federalist 10* of the delegation of government power "to a small number of citizens elected by the rest." As such, any solution would have to include representative democracy (as it was understood at the time). The tougher problem was the continuation of the states while at the same time creating a functional central government. As we will see, fixing this problem is what led to the institutional innovation we know as federalism. And, of course, the different states, as represented by their delegations, had their own particular views about the nature and extent of the problems and the best way to fix them (indeed, those views often varied even *within* those delegations). The convention, therefore, is an excellent example of political engineering, as it contained both a set of institutional conundrums as well as very real practical political considerations.

Madison, Take One: Factional Balancing

One way to think about the proposition of political engineering is to consider how a specific thinker, as well as practitioner, engaged in the process. A singularly excellent example of this can be found

4. This is not to suggest agreement on other issues. However, in terms of the issues debated in Philadelphia, these two factors clearly guided the debate.

5. While made famous by Lincoln's Gettysburg Address, the origin of the formulation is likely Daniel Webster's, The Second Reply to Hayne, January 26–27, 1830: "It is, Sir, the people's Constitution, the people's government, made for the people, made by the people, and answerable to the people" (available online at http://www.dartmouth.edu/~dwebster/speeches/hayne -speech.html).

in the person and work of James Madison of Virginia. Madison was both a student of politics[6] as well as a politician,[7] who had seen firsthand the anemia of the Congress under the Articles. As already noted, he outlined in great detail the failings of the Articles (see box 2.1), and he also set about the process of devising an outline of how to remedy those failings, as we will see in a moment. Madison is a useful thinker to address here not only because of his historical significance to the events under discussion, but also because he was a pioneer in the realm of institutional design in representative democracies. In many ways he is the prototype of the political engineer of which we have been speaking. Further, his theories about the institutional parameters needed to make democratic governance feasible in large countries are central to the core themes of this book.

Madison is frequently called the Father of the Constitution, and not without merit. While it is true that the document that was eventually produced by the convention had many inputs from multiple sources and was a document ultimately produced by committee, much of the impetus for a new constitution, as well as its intellectual foundations, can be traced back to Madison. Madison was an early agitator for changing the Articles and was a sponsor of the first attempt at a national convention to address its ills, the aborted Annapolis Convention of 1786. He went on to actively think about the difficulties facing governance in the United States, especially as it pertained to the power of the central government in relationship to the states. As Madison argued in a letter to George Washington in April of 1787, "I would propose that . . . the national Government should be armed with positive and compleat authority in all cases which require uniformity; such as the regulation of trade, including the right of taxing both exports and imports, the fixing the terms and

6. For example, one of his endeavors leading up to the Constitutional Convention was a study of confederacies. See "Of Ancient and Modern Confederacies" as excerpted in Meyers 1981: 48–56. Also, see *Federalist 18; 19,* and *20,* in Madison, Hamilton, and Jay 1987.

7. Before the Philadelphia Convention, Madison had been elected to the Virginia Constitutional Convention, the Continental Congress (three one-year terms), and the Virginia House of Delegates. He also served, before his time in the Congress, on the Virginia governor's Council of State.

forms of naturalization, etc. etc." (Meyers 1981: 67). That letter also contained a sketch of a constitution that would eventually evolve into the Virginia Plan.

The Virginia Plan was a set of fifteen resolutions written by James Madison in advance of the Philadelphia Convention and that was proposed to the body on May 29, 1787 (four days into the process) by fellow Virginia delegate Edmund Randolph. A summary of the plan can be seen in box 2.2. The plan represents a direct example of applied political engineering, as it starts with a set of problems with an existing political structure and proposes a set of new institutions designed to fix those problems. Further, the proposed design is motivated by a coherent theory of political behavior, which is discussed below.

Also of specific interest is the fact that the design proposed in the plan was altered during the debate, as other engineers offered their

BOX 2.2. THE VIRGINIA PLAN

1. Common defense, security of liberty, and general welfare
2. Seats per state ("the rights of Suffrage") for the national legislature linked to the quota of contribution or number of free inhabitants
3. Bicameralism
4. First branch, elected by the people of the several states for a fixed term
5. Second branch, elected by the first from a list of nominees from the state legislatures
6. Each branch would have the right to originate legislation, also, the right to negate state legislation that was deemed to contravene the Constitution
7. National executive to be chosen by the national legislature for a fixed term
8. Council of Revision—made up of the executive and members of the judiciary to review acts of the central government
9. National judiciary chosen by the national legislature
10. Admission of new states
11. Republican government and existing state territories ought to be guaranteed
12. Continuation of Congress until a new constitution is adopted
13. Provision for amendment
14. States authorities ought to be bound by oath to support the new constitution
15. Ratification process

own suggested fixes to the existing structure and as the political give-and-take of a collective body worked its way through various conflicts. A note worth special attention is that, with the national legislature choosing both the executive and the judiciary, the Virginia Plan would have more resembled the fusion-of-powers system we see in parliamentary systems, rather than the separation-of-powers systems that emerged from the deliberations. As the chapter on executives will develop, separation versus fusion of powers is one of the fundamental differences among institutional designs, with separate elections and fixed terms for the president and legislature (as in the United States) contrasted with an executive that is selected by the legislature (and usually accountable to it, as in parliamentary democracies).

In addition, the Virginia Plan would have done away entirely with the coequality of representation of the states in the Congress, as had been the case under the Articles. Instead, the plan proposed a first chamber (also called the lower house) of the new bicameral national Congress in which each state had a number of representatives proportionate to its population. This first chamber then would select the members of the second chamber (upper house) from lists of candidates provided by the states. The whole national legislature would then choose the executive and judicial branches. In terms of the basic model of democratic delegation that we proposed in chapter 1, the voters of the nation, acting as principals, would delegate governing authority to the members of the first chamber, and they would be the primary agents of the people who would then delegate further authority to the other branches of government. Such an arrangement, it should be noted, fulfilled one of the main predicates of the convention, insofar as it maintained the republican character of the government. The plan also maintained the states as units within a greater union, but it significantly diminished the representation of the smaller states. This change proposed by Madison faced serious political obstacles from delegates of the smaller states in the convention because allocating legislative representation based on population would have created, in Madison's own words, an "extended republic" that was national in scope. We will return to that issue in a moment. First, let's consider how Madison saw this process as working from a theoretical basis.

Animating the plan was Madison's basic theory of republicanism, which was based on factional balancing rather than on separation of power and checks and balances. If we go back to the aforementioned essay on the "Vices of the Political System of the United States," we find that he builds his theory of republicanism on the issue of the motivations of office-seekers, as well as those of the general population. In regards to office-seekers (and thereby officeholders), he noted three motives for seeking such offices: ambition, personal interest, and the public good. He went on to lament that "unhappily the two first are proved by experience to be the most prevalent" (Meyers 1981: 62). He went on to note that "all civilized societies are divided into different interests and factions," which reflect similar motives that needed to be held in check. He noted that "the Society becomes broken into a greater variety of interests, of pursuits, of passions, which check one each other, whilst those who may feel a common sentiment have less opportunity of communication and concert" (Meyers 1981: 64).

The problem of conflicting ambitions (both among politicians but also in the broader population) is at the heart of what Samuels and Shugart call "the core hypothesis" of the political theory behind *The Federalist Papers* and really the foundation of Madisonian political theory. To summarize, it is that "the extent to which government ensures liberty or gives way to tyranny is directly related to the manner in which institutions of government structure the representation of societal interests and channel political ambition" (2010: 22). In other words, the only solution to maintaining proper republican government is appropriate factional balancing, which requires institutions designed to accomplish this task. Thus, it requires adequate political engineering: Good government is made (and often remade); it does not just happen. As Madison said, "The great desideratum in Government is such modification of the sovereignty as will render it sufficiently neutral between the different interests and faction" (Meyers 1981: 64).

This is all important in the broader discussion of republican government. Specifically, how to manage the problem of allowing the people to choose representatives when they are divided into numerous self-interested factions and therefore their choices reflect their factional interests, which Madison feared would run counter to the common interest. Indeed, he specifically feared the ability of a given faction to tyrannize the rest of society. How to prevent tyranny of a given faction over the interests of the whole? Madison's aforementioned study of confederacies led him to see that smaller states with fewer factions made it possible for one faction to dominate the others, leading to the lack of governability in those confederacies.[8] He believed that republican government would be most successful in an extended (that is, large) republic like the United States. This view was contra many theorists, specifically Montesquieu,[9] who predated him. He explicitly makes the argument in *Federalist 10* that a larger, "extended" republic has a better chance of ameliorating the problems of factions since the size leads to dilution and the difficulty of any given faction to dominate politics. As he wrote in *Federalist 10:*

> The smaller the society, the fewer probably will be the distinct parties and interests composing it; the fewer the distinct parties and interests, the more frequently will a majority be found of the same party; and the smaller the number of individuals composing a majority, and the smaller the compass within which they are placed, the more easily will they concert and execute their plans of oppression. Extend the sphere, and you take in a greater variety of parties and interests; you make it less probable that a majority of the whole will have a common motive to invade the rights of other citizens; or if such a common motive exists, it will be more difficult for all who feel it to discover their own strength, and to act in unison with each other.

Institutionally, therefore, Madison hypothesized that locating power in the national legislature, and specifically one in which the states were represented according to their population, was the best means for balancing the ambitions of various factions. For this reason, the Virginia Plan was very heavily focused on the legislature, and in particular on the first chamber (that is, in today's terms, the House of Representatives). It should be emphasized that, as Samuels and Shugart (2010: 29–30) point out, Madison did not conceive of the evolution of political parties and therefore did not foresee the

8. See, e.g., *Federalist 18, 19,* and *20,* in Madison, Hamilton, and Jay 1987.

9. Discussed by Hamilton in *Federalist 9,* in Madison, Hamilton, and Jay 1987.

ability of a given combination of "factions" (as he called groups with different interests) to form parties that would assume majority control of the chamber for an extended period of time.

Had the Virginia Plan prevailed in Philadelphia, the United States would have been set on a very different institutional path than the one it eventually found itself on (and that we discuss below). Not only would the relative power of the states in the institutions of the national government have been different (that is, tilted in the direction of population entirely) but the legislature, and in particular the first chamber, would have fully dominated the other two branches of government. In that realm it is possible that the executive of the United States would have evolved in such a way as to resemble more a prime minister than what we have come to see in the role of the president.[10] As such, the exact development of American democracy would have been different in important and fundamental ways for that reason alone.

The fatal flaw, from the standpoint of political viability, of the Virginia Plan was that it favored large states over small ones. This is a democratically defensible position, given that the power in a republic draws from the people. Moreover, as we shall see in the chapter on federalism, many other federal countries do not provide institutional guarantees to their smaller component units as does the US Constitution. However, the practical political considerations of the day, and the institutional constraints placed on the convention-eers, meant that a compromise was needed. In the next section we move back to the narrative to see the interaction of those practical political considerations with the theoretical propositions that were on the table.

Plan versus Plan and Compromise

The neat and tidy version of the story goes something like this: The large states pushed the Virginia Plan, which was countered by the small state–backed New Jersey Plan. A conflict arose because of the two opposing forces, until another small state, in what could be anachronistically called an "only Nixon can go to China moment,"

10. These different roles will be a core topic of ch. 8.

stepped in with the Connecticut Compromise, later dubbed the Great Compromise, to bring a solution to the impasse. The reality is bit more complex.

The fact of the matter is that the initial month of debate in the convention was mainly based around the Virginia Plan and was a point-by-point exercise, with some of the more complex or problematic issues being set aside for later discussion. It was clear from the beginning that the central government would need enhanced powers, as was the notion that a more-fleshed-out central government with legislative, executive, and judicial powers was needed. The idea of a bicameral legislature was also part of the prevailing consensus, and the notion that the first chamber would have seats allocated to the states based on population was fairly central to the discussion as well. As such, the early going of the convention (roughly a month) was focused in and around the fifteen points of Madison's proposal and was not a death match, as some texts often present it, between it and the New Jersey Plan. It is worth noting that other plans were offered as well, such as the Pinckney Plan[11] and the Hamilton Plan.[12]

11. On the same day that Randolph introduced the Virginia Plan, Charles Pinckney of South Carolina offered his own constitutional sketch, which had much in common with the Virginia Plan. The original Pinckney Plan can be viewed via Yale University's Avalon Project online at http://avalon.law.yale .edu/18th_century/pinckney.asp. The portions of note that it had in common with the Virginia Plan was a bicameral legislature and the legislature choosing the executive. It also contained what may have been the earliest references to what would become the Three-Fifths Compromise. The Pinckney Plan was not debated but was rather referred to the Committee of Detail, and Madison was not originally provided with a copy, so his original notes are incomplete (see Madison 1966: 33). If one looks at Elliot (1888: 145) one sees a well-developed draft constitution that would give one the impression that Pinckney practically foresaw the entire Constitution of 1789 on that fourth official day of the Philadelphia Convention. However, as fn36 in Madison (1966: 33) explains, the version provided by Pinckney in 1818 (when the journal of the convention was being prepared for publication) was from 1797 and was not the original proposal. A copy of the original was discovered in the papers of James Wilson and was later published in 1927.

12. The Hamilton Plan, also known as the British Plan, was proposed a few days after the New Jersey Plan. It infamously included a lifetime appointment

BOX 2.3. THE NEW JERSEY PLAN

1. The Articles have to be made adequate
2. Expansion of powers: taxation, commerce, trade
3. Requisitions made in proportion to the number of white and free citizens and three-fifths of other persons (excluding Indians not paying taxes)
4. An executive (made up of "persons") elected by the Congress
5. Judiciary, appointed by the executive (outlines powers and responsibilities thereof)
6. Supremacy clause
7. Admission of new states
8. Naturalization rules the same for each state
9. A citizen of one state who commits a crime in another state will be treated the same as would a citizen of the state in which the crime was committed

Indeed, the first introduction of the idea that would become the Great Compromise, that is, equal representation of the states in the Senate, was first proposed by Roger Sherman of Connecticut on June 11, 1787, *before* the New Jersey Plan was formally proposed and the idea was initially rejected (Elliot 1888: 169). The New Jersey Plan (see box 2.3) was not introduced until four days later, on June 15.

The basic purpose of the New Jersey Plan is made clear in the first resolution of the document, which states, "Resolved, that the Articles of Confederation ought to be so revised, corrected, and enlarged as to render the federal Constitution adequate to the exigencies of Government, and the preservation of the Union" (Frohnen 2002: 232). As such, the basic institutional design within the New Jersey Plan resembled that created by the Articles, but with augmentations. Interestingly, this included a fused power arrangement like that of the Virginia Plan, with the selection of the executive by the legislature. That executive (which, as proposed, would have been a committee) would have, in turn, been responsible for selecting the judiciary.

---

for the chief executive (called the governor in the proposal). Text available online at http://avalon.law.yale.edu/18th_century/hamtexta.asp.

Like the Virginia Plan, the New Jersey Plan represented a particular institutional vision for the country, and had it been adopted, would have set the democratic development of the *United* States on its own specific pathway. It should be underscored that the key institutional factor of that pathway would have been the enshrinement of minority privilege as a dominant feature of governance by maintaining equality of the states in the legislature.

As the classic narrative correctly notes, neither representation by population nor coequality was politically viable. And so the Connecticut Compromise reemerged in early July of 1787 and established a key institutional element of the US government: a bicameral legislature with symmetrical powers (that is, legislatively coequal) and yet incongruent in the sense that the basis of representation in each chamber was different. We will return to the specific meaning of such issues in chapter 7 on legislative power.

It is worth stopping for a moment to think about how a specific choice can be so significant in terms of political design. The Great Compromise was not a full-blown plan or even an alternative set of institutions; it was single choice concerning one institutional factor in a broader design: the representational basis of one chamber of the legislature. It was, as a political move, key, as it was what allowed the entire process to move forward. One could argue that without it the convention would have failed. It was also a key move in terms of political engineering, as it helped enshrine over-representation of smaller states into the US system of legislating. As we will see in the federalism chapter, the disparity in the representation between the largest and smallest of the states is quite dramatic and has increased markedly over time.

While the plan-versus-plan narrative emphasizes the fight over the structure of the legislature and the question of representation in the Senate, we emphasized earlier that presidentialism was one of the fundamental engineering decisions made at the convention. Yet it is striking that this choice emerged quite late in the process. In all of the formal plans presented, the chief executive (whether called president or governor, and whether singular or plural) was selected by the legislature. This was true again in both the Virginia and New Jersey Plans. Later in the process this shifted to the notion of the election of the chief executive to come from an electoral college, with the voters in that college being chosen by whatever process each state preferred.

The decision to have an executive chosen by a source other than the legislature created the fundamental basis for the separation-of-powers notion that is central to the design of the US government. It was also a move that caused Madison to have to alter and augment his theory of republican government. So it is interesting to note that two fundamental developments of the institutional design of the US government (coequal representation of the states in the Senate and the presidency, which laid the foundation of separation of powers and checks and balances) emerged from political compromise within the debate of the convention. As such, despite the well-crafted arguments provided in *The Federalist Papers,* these institutional innovations were not the result of grand theory but rather very much the result of the horse-trading associated with practical politics—or, we might say, with engineering meeting the practical constraints of the site.

Madison, Take Two: Separation of Powers

The exigencies of the convention led to the need for Madison to further adapt his theories in the context of the agreed-upon constitution. However, his basic theory of preventing tyranny and maintaining republicanism remained in place: the adequate balancing of ambition by the institutional design of the state. Instead of ambition being checked solely by a myriad of factions within an extended republic, it would also be checked within the structures of the government itself. So while the notion of factional balance remained part of his theories (again, see *Federalist 10*) he further developed his theory to encompass the separation of powers system that the constitution created.[13]

The way in which the institutional configuration of the government would help check ambition is outlined in *Federalist 51,* in

13. As Kernell (2003) notes, Madison never quite squared how one of these ideas furthers the other (because it doesn't).

which he argues that the following institutional features of the US Constitution would function to such an end: separation of powers, checks and balances, bicameralism, and federalism. It was in this essay that Madison famously wrote "that if men were angels, no government would be necessary" and that, therefore, the internal structures of government had to be constructed in such a way that would allow for governance to take place despite rival ambitions and interests, or what he called "the defect of better motives" (Madison, Hamilton, and Jay 1987: 320). He specifically notes the role of political engineering in numerous places in the essay (although he did not use those words). For example, he notes that the various "defects" facing governance can be addressed by appropriately "contriving the interior structure of the government" or, in other words, by appropriate institutional design (318).

He argues that ambitions of politicians can be curbed by the assignment of the three types of power (legislative, executive, and judicial) into separate "departments," with each being given "an equal power of self-defense" (320). In other words, we see here separation of powers and checks and balances. He notes in the essay the relative strength of the legislature vis-à-vis the executive and therefore notes the need for the executive to have the veto power, but he states that the power ought to be qualified and not absolute, hence the power of the legislature to override a veto. As such, we see a clear illustration of two branches being given power over each other, which could facilitate the need for the type of inter-institutional transactions noted in chapter 1. He further argued that because "in republican government the legislative authority necessarily predominates," it should be divided into two chambers, so as to limit its ability to dominate the government. Thereby Madison gave theoretical justification for the Great Compromise that the conventioneers reached to bridge the differences between small and large states.

The latter half of the essay moves from the design of central government to the role played by federalism in protecting liberty. He argues that not only will dividing the power delegated by the voters into separate branches of government lead to a security against tyranny by a dominant faction, but that in the "compound republic of America, the power surrendered by the people is first divided between two distinct governments, and then the portion allotted to each subdivided among distinct and separate departments" (321). In other words, power is diffused in the United States to the federal and state governments, and then within each government that power is further divided into legislative, executive, and judicial branches. Further, because of the size of the United States, the ability of factional majorities to dominate and tyrannize is diluted and curtailed.

Overall we see a situation in which it is clear that Madison is arguing that flaws in human nature lead to challenges for governing and that the most efficacious way to ameliorate those challenges is through proper institutional design.

A UNIQUE INSTITUTIONAL MIX

Ultimately the convention produced a set of institutions that are almost unique in key ways vis-à-vis the other democracies in our study. Specifically we have a mix that includes presidentialism, federalism, and a particular type of bicameralism, that is, one that provides equal power to the states in the second chamber and has the same basic legislative powers as the first chamber (known as symmetrical bicameralism). Of our thirty other democracies, the only countries with a similar institutional mix are Argentina, Brazil, and Mexico (and of these, Mexico's second chamber has no authority over the federal budget). Once we introduce three other variables—a strict two-party system, widespread usage of primary elections to nominate candidates, and single-seat districts with plurality elections—the United States has an institutional configuration that is unique in this study (and, really, globally).

Indeed, various choices made in Philadelphia helped lead to subsequent choices and behaviors. As noted earlier, the choice to have the executive chosen outside of the legislature created an important institutional dynamic in which the legislature and executive would have to transact with one another to create legislation (see box 1.2 on veto gates), and yet each would have no control over the existence or term of office of the other (unlike in parliamentary systems, where a no confidence vote can lead to a new executive or even a new election for the legislature). The creation of presidentialism meant that the parties in the legislature would not have the task of selecting the executive, but only of legislating. This dynamic helped create the structure of the US party system, which is uniquely dominated by only two parties, both of which are nonhierarchical in their organization and candidate-centric (as we will further discuss in chapter 6). Certainly, by definition, the process to elect the president is candidate-centric; additionally, legislative candidates, who are competing in single-seat districts, are also incentivized to run campaigns tailored to themselves and their parochial appeal, rather than having to make an argument for a party leadership that is national in scope and linked to the selection of a prime minister. These factors also help explain the near-universal use of primary elections, also candidate-centric, for the nomination process, instead of having candidate-selection processes that are heavily influenced by party leaders. At a minimum, since legislative parties do not have to form a government (see box 1.1), they tend to be more bottom-up, rather than top-down in structure. The rest of this section examines the key effect of the decisions made at the convention, as well as noting some choices not made.

Key Effects

There are a number of key effects that are a direct result of the pathways upon which the US system of government was set in 1789. Here we detail some specific issues that help us provide the foundation for discussing how US democracy is different from the others in our study. Each will be addressed in greater detail in the appropriate subsequent chapters.

1. *Created tension between the central government and the subunits.* By definition, federalism institutionalizes some amount of tension between the central government and the subunits. Certainly in the United States the ultimate example of this tension manifested in the Civil War. However, setting aside that rather dramatic piece of US history, it should be noted that because of the structure of federalism in the United States, it very much continues to shape public policy making as well as political struggles within the US system.

While the US Constitution delineates a basic division of policy authority to the federal government and to the states, the exact definition is somewhat ambiguous. Article I, Section 8 of the US Constitution details a set of specific powers, which address very much the kinds of problems that Madison wrote about in the "Vices" (see box 2.1). However, the final clause of the section contains the necessary and proper clause (also known as the implied-powers clause and the elastic clause), which notes that Congress shall have the power "To make all Laws which shall be necessary and proper for carrying into Execution the foregoing Powers, and all other Powers vested by this Constitution in the Government of the United States, or in any Department or Officer thereof."

The Tenth Amendment to the US Constitution attempts to clarify the relationship between the two levels of government by stating: "The powers not delegated to the United States by the Constitution, nor prohibited by it to the States, are reserved to the States respectively, or to the people." Of course, while there are powers enumerated, as noted earlier, in Article I, Section 8, the "necessary and proper" clause creates significant ambiguity, as does interpretation of the specific powers listed.

The issue of which powers belong to whom is basically as old as the republic (and is a struggle that continues to the present). A famous example would be the Supreme Court case, *McCulloch v. Maryland* (1819) which dealt with (1) whether the federal government had the right to establish a bank, and (2) whether states could tax federal entities. The Court ultimately ruled that (1) the federal government could establish a bank, even though the power was not an enumerated one (indeed, the Court relied, in part, on the necessary and proper clause for its argument), and (2) that the states could not tax the federal government, which partially helped establish the relationship between the two levels of government. The debate, however, was not settled, and we have seen over the decades a tension between the two levels, including questions of what particular words and clauses mean in Article I, Section 8, not the least of which is the meaning of congressional power to regulate interstate commerce.

2. Over-representation of small states in the Senate. A point related to central government/state tensions is the nature of bicameralism in the United States which gives a great deal of power to senators from smaller states, at least in proportion to their counterparts in larger states (in terms of population).

The practical institutional significance of the Great Compromise was the permanent enshrinement of minority privilege into the fabric of US governance. By this we mean that since individual senators represent widely disparate numbers of citizens, it is quite possible for a majority of senators to actually represent a minority of the population and for those senators to win the day legislatively. As we will see in our chapters on federalism and legislative power, the gap between large-population and small-population states has grown over time. The Great Compromise, which was an act of political necessity in the 1780s, has the effect in the current era of distorting the representational power of some citizens vis-à-vis others. The most glaring example of this is the comparison between California and Wyoming: The former has a population about seventy times that of the latter, yet each state has two senators.

3. Distortions in the process to elect the president. Since the method eventually agreed upon at the convention to elect the president was based on the relative representation of the states in the legislature, the distortions of relative power among the states present in the Senate are partially reflected in the distribution of the electoral vote. Each state has the same number of electoral votes as it has members in the House and Senate. There is, as a result, some over-representation of smaller states in the electoral college. Further, there are distortions based upon which states are competitive and therefore receive more campaign attention versus those that are considered locked into a highly likely outcome.

4. Presidentialization of party politics. As noted below, the conventioneers did not foresee the development of political parties. Nonetheless, the choice of presidentialism has had a long-term effect on the party system. In parliamentary systems, the primary electoral focus of parties is winning seats in the legislature. The hope of those parties is either to win an outright majority, and therefore put its leader in the position of prime minister, or else to join with other parties in a coalition. Because the path to executive office passes through the legislature in a parliamentary system, the entire political process in such democracies depends on the collective action of parties to a much greater extent than is the case in the United States or other presidential systems.

However, in presidential systems the emphasis invariably becomes the president or a given party's presidential candidate, more than the parties themselves. The very fact that a party can have a majority of seats in the legislature and yet not hold the executive—a common occurrence in the United States known as "divided government"— changes the dynamic fundamentally. Moreover, even when the president and the legislative majority come from the same party, the president has a different constituency from the legislators, due to the separation of powers. Unlike in parliamentary systems, the path to executive power in a presidential system does not run through the legislature, but rather through a distinct election process (and, in the modern United States, a nomination process in which legislators are not central actors). These features of separate powers mean that, as Samuels and Shugart (2010: 34–35) point out, parties themselves are separated into legislative and executive "branches." As President Jimmy Carter's chief of staff, Lloyd Cutler, aptly put it, parties and legislators in the United States are not set up to "form a government," as is the case under parliamentary democracy (Cutler 1980).

5. *A system of inter-institutional transactions.* Again, if we revisit the model of delegation of political power introduced in chapter 1, we can see that the basic institutional structure designed in Philadelphia created a system replete with the need for transactional politics. Building on the theme of the previous point, these transactions are not primarily between relatively cohesive political parties, as in many other systems, especially those that are parliamentary. In the United States, transactions are typically between institutions— which sometimes are under control of different parties but which have different interests when under unified partisan control. There is the need for the president to transact with the Congress, but also for the Congress to transact with itself, chamber-to-chamber, due to symmetrical bicameralism. This situation is made even more

complex due to the constituencies that delegate authority to each chamber and the president being differently constituted. While they all are ultimately elected by the same pool of eligible voters, representatives are elected in roughly equal districts, senators are elected from state-based districts, and presidents are elected via the mechanisms of the electoral college. This arrangement leads to separate institutions that must transact with one another, but they create a complex feedback loop in terms of accountability back to the voters.

We can contrast this with a parliamentary system where voters (principals) delegate power to political parties in the legislature (agents), who then delegate executive power to the prime minister. Thus the connection between voters and the executive is indirect, in that a voter can choose an executive candidate only by voting in legislative elections for the party whose leader the voter wants to see as prime minister. In a presidential system, the process of delegation to the executive is essentially direct (even given the US Electoral College), and does not run through the legislature and legislative elections. In fact, voters often are not really even delegating to legislative parties, per se, as their "agent" in the legislature may be an individual politician more than the party to which he or she belongs. This separate delegation process creates a very different governing and policy-making dynamic. One easy illustration of this fact is that in a pure parliamentary system, divided government (that is, the legislature controlled by one party and the executive controlled by another) is impossible.

Interestingly, Madison's Virginia Plan, as well as his basic theories of factional balancing as represented by the arguments in *Federalist 10,* fit the parliamentary model much more closely than they fit the presidential model that resulted from the Constitutional Convention. Of course, what the exact institutional evolution of a system based on the Virginia Plan would have been is, by necessity, speculative. Indeed, Madison's original plan did not include a no-confidence vote (that is, the ability of the legislative majority to remove the executive, which is another defining feature of parliamentary democracy), so it could have made the United States look more like modern-day Switzerland (where an executive is elected by the legislature but cannot be removed by it), rather than the parliamentary systems of Canada or Australia, for all we know.

Choices Not Made

It is important to note that not all of the institutional structures under discussion in this book were decided upon in Philadelphia. Part of this has to do with oversights and misunderstandings of the delegates. Indeed, it is important to understand that political choices frequently have unintended consequences and/or a given set of political engineers may simply not see or understand the implications of all of their choices. Also, in terms of the Philadelphia convention, they had the disadvantage of sequence: Theirs was one of the first such attempts at constitution-making, meaning that they had little in the way of practical experience with which they could compare their theories. Further, certain developments that now seem obvious in retrospect were utter unknowns to them.

The following were the choices not made.

1. Electoral system. While it was decided that the House of Representatives would be chosen by a popular vote, there was no debate about how its members would be elected, an approach that would be unthinkable if one were designing the institutions of a democratic regime in the twenty-first century (or even the late nineteenth, for that matter). Instead, the basic processes and the rules for suffrage were left to the states.[14]

2. Party system and interest groups. A key theoretical failing of Madison (and the founders in general) was the lack of foresight in regards to the formation and significance of political parties. While Madison

14. It is worth noting, however, that the mathematics and processes that would be used in subsequent eras for the design of electoral systems were being discovered, at least in part, by the political thinkers of this era of US history. Thomas Jefferson, as is noted in the appendix to ch. 5, developed a method for apportioning US congressional seats among the states, which was essentially the same as the D'Hondt method used to allocate legislative seats to parties in many proportional representation (PR) systems (to be discussed further in ch. 5). Likewise, Daniel Webster devised a system that was mathematically the same as the Sainte-Laguë method, another PR formula.

discusses the issue of factions in great detail in *Federalist 10*, he and the other founders failed to grasp the way in which parties and interest groups would emerge with the US political system. It is fair to state, however, that Madison's theory of faction is well in sync with the pluralistic interest-group system that would emerge in the United States. This topic reemerges in chapter 6. He was simply unable to foresee how different combinations of interest groups would form fairly stable constituent bases for political parties, allowing one of them to gain a majority and thus control a legislative chamber for a period of time.

3. The bureaucracy. The complicated bureaucratic structures that are a part of modern governance also were not something that the framers discussed or could possibly have foreseen. Indeed, while the Constitution clearly envisions an executive branch beyond the president and vice president, it does not spell out any details in that regard. Article II, Section 2 envisioned the president appointing "public ministers" and the like, but the notion of the massive federal bureaucracy that has emerged over the past two-plus centuries was unforeseeable, if anything because the Constitution was drafted prior to the Industrial Revolution and the general growth in significance of modern governments as a general principle.

4. Public policy. Certainly the framers of the Constitution understood that they were creating an instrument for the design and implementation of public policy. However, they were by no means in agreement over what that would mean, nor did they fully agree even on questions of the scope of government. They did know that they were expanding the powers of the central government in several key areas of policy, specifically commerce, foreign policy, taxation, and the regulation of slavery. They could not have conceived, by the way, of the scope of government in the modern era, so it is difficult, if not impossible, to project back and determine what the founders would or would not have supported in terms of contemporary policy debates (as we will see in chapter 10).

CONCLUSIONS

That the Philadelphia Convention was a quintessential case of political engineering should now be clear. To briefly recapitulate:

A problem of governance led to the consideration of fixes, which in turn attracted the generation of possible solutions based on a combination of practical political experience and applications of political theory. These possible solutions had to face contact with various political interests and forces before an acceptable solution was achieved. That solution, the Constitution of the United States of 1789, created a set of institutional parameters that set the development of the US government onto a specific set of pathways that have dictated the behavior of political actors in the country to this very day.

We can further see, in the political theories of James Madison, a central understanding of the concepts of political engineering. In regards to the United States itself, there are several key choices (and non-choices) that deserve restating, as they serve as key thematic issues throughout our discussion. First, the founders chose to maintain the states as politically significant subunits, thus creating federalism. As a means of connecting the subunits to the central government, they choose bicameralism and ensured state influence by creating equal representation of the states in the second chamber. This arrangement meant, at a minimum, that a dedicated alliance of senators from less populous states could control one veto gate in the process and force the first chamber to transact, if they so chose. The framers added another level of complexity when they decided—after making their choices on federalism and bicameralism—to have the executive be chosen from outside of the legislature. This choice created a specific arrangement between voters and legislators that would have been different if the legislators had been given the power to select the executive. Further, the lack of knowledge of electoral systems also influenced the development of the parties for the simple reason that the possibility of adopting an electoral system that might have promoted a greater number of parties or more hierarchically organized parties, or both, was never even considered. Thus we can already begin to see how the structure of institutional authority, starting with how many agents of the voters there will be, and of what sort, can have fundamental consequences for how a democracy develops and functions.

APPENDIX: THE PLANS OF PHILADELPHIA
AND POLITICAL ENGINEERING

As noted earlier in this chapter, the Philadelphia Convention of 1787 saw four detailed plans introduced for consideration. Each of these plans had their own institutional configurations, which would have resulted in different types of delegations of authority and, likewise, paths of accountability (to relate back to themes introduced in chapter 1) had they been adopted. Further, they serve as examples of attempts at applied political engineering. This appendix provides a basic overview of the four plans in terms of the institutional recipes (mostly in graphical form) that they proposed, as well as a map of the final product produced by the convention.

The four plans proposed at the Philadelphia convention are as follows, by sponsor and date of introduction in chronological order:

Edmund Randolph of Virginia	May 29, 1787	(aka, the Virginia Plan)
Charles Pinckney of South Carolina	May 29, 1787	(aka, the Pinckney Plan)
William Patterson of New Jersey	June 15, 1787	(aka, the New Jersey Plan)
Alexander Hamilton of New York	June 18, 1787	(aka, the Hamilton Plan, sometimes called the English Plan)

The plans in question did not receive equal treatment at the convention. For example, the Virginia Plan became a major focus for the convention, while the Pinckney Plan was tabled and never seriously considered. Further, both the New Jersey and Hamilton Plans died fairly quickly. As noted previously in the chapter, most discussions of Philadelphia tend to focus on a narrative that pits the Virginia Plan against the New Jersey Plan. Of course, the New Jersey Plan, with its basis in the Articles of Confederation, had no real political chance. Ultimately, a substantially amended version of the Virginia Plan came to be reflected in the final Constitution that went into effect in 1789.

Regardless of the general fates of these plans, they do provide an interesting opportunity for discussion insofar as their similarities help reveal the general level of consensus (as well as disagreement) over the shape of a new constitution, but also they allow for thought experiments as to what the shape of the US government could have been. They each are institutional recipes that produce different governmental outcomes that would have evolved differently over time.

If we examine the institutional recipes suggested by each plan, we can see both a strong set of commonalities and a number of important divergences that would have resulted, had they been implemented, in a significantly different institutional environment than the one that was eventually ratified. A basic comparison is found in table 2.1.

One clear area of agreement, the need for a national judicial branch, exists in all four plans and makes it to the final Constitution. Likewise, there is basic agreement over symmetrical bicameralism (with only the New Jersey Plan dissenting on that issue). Agreement over the legislature choosing the president, however, did not translate into that institutional feature being adopted (a key decision made that created the presidential model). Of course, the original conception of the electoral college was such that the framers assumed that the House would frequently choose the president (as Hamilton notes in *Federalist 66*).[15] The idea of a Council of Revision that would review all laws passed by Congress exists in two plans, but eventually was rejected.

15. Yet another example of a proposal that the legislature would select the executive: a January 14, 1787, letter from Henry Knox to George Washington, which sketched a new central government thusly: "Were it possible to effect a General Government of this kind, it might be constituted of an Assembly or lower House, chosen for one, two, or three years; a Senate, chosen for five, six, or seven years; and the Executive, under the title of Governor-General, chosen by the Assembly and Senate, for the term of seven years, but liable to an impeachment of the lower House, and triable by the Senate. A Judicial, to be appointed by the Governor-General during good behaviour, but impeachable by the lower House, and triable by the Senate." Letter available online at http://www.familytales.org/dbDisplay.php?id=ltr_hek4303&person=hek.

Table 2.1. Comparative Plans from the Philadelphia Convention

	Virginia Plan	*Pinckney Plan*	*New Jersey Plan*	*Hamilton Plan*
Symmetrical bicameralism	x	x		x
Executive chosen by legislature	x	x	x	x
National judiciary	x	x	x	x
Council of revision	x	x		

As discussed in the main body of the chapter (and as analyzed in great detail in Kernell 2003), the Virginia Plan reflected Madison's preconvention preferences for a new constitution and was founded on his theory of factional behavior. In terms of the framework introduced in chapter 1, the plan was especially noteworthy in the sense that it had a single clear path of delegation from the voters to the first chamber, which in turn further delegated authority to the other branches. This created a system that resembled more the fusion of powers seen in contemporary parliamentary systems than the separation-of-powers scheme that eventually was adopted (though lacking a provision for accountability of the executive back to the legislature, as in modern parliamentary democracies). The Virginia Plan also created weaker states than did the eventual Constitution. First, representation in the second chamber was, like in the first, to be allocated seats in proportion to the state's populations. That alone would have created a substantially different dynamic in the Congress. Second, the national legislature was to be given, in the sixth section of the Virginia Plan, the ability "to negative all laws passed by the several States, contravening in the opinion of the National Legislature the articles of Union." The lack of a reelection mechanism in the Virginia Plan did mean that

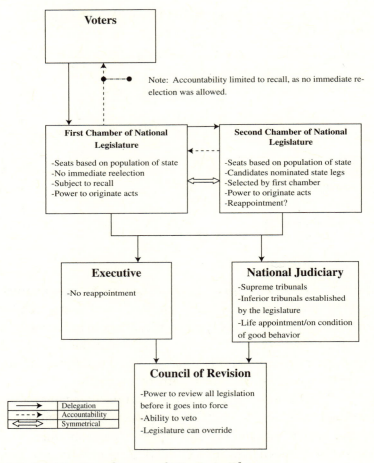

Fig. 2.1. Institutional map of Virginia Plan
Key: Solid arrows indicate delegation relationships, with the direction of the arrows showing the flow of authority from principal to agent. Dashed arrows indicate accountability relationships. The two-headed arrow indicates symmetry between chambers. The hollow one-headed arrows indicate one institution deriving from another.

an adequate feedback loop allowing voters to hold their agents accountable was lacking.

Like the Virginia Plan, the Pinckney Plan envisioned a flow of delegation from the voters to the first chamber (in this case called the House of Delegates). The House of Delegates would, in turn elect the senators, but instead of from the states themselves, they would be chosen from four districts. Under this plan, the two chambers of the Congress would choose the president. And, again like the Virginia Plan, the national legislature would have had veto power over state laws.

The New Jersey Plan was not much more than an attempt to enhance and retain the Articles of Confederation. It would have

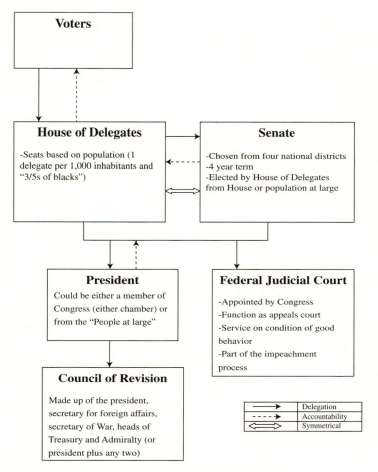

Fig. 2.2. Institutional map of Pinckney Plan
Key: Solid arrows indicate delegation relationships, with the direction of the arrows showing the flow of authority from principal to agent. Dashed arrows indicate accountability relationships. The two-headed arrow indicates symmetry between chambers.

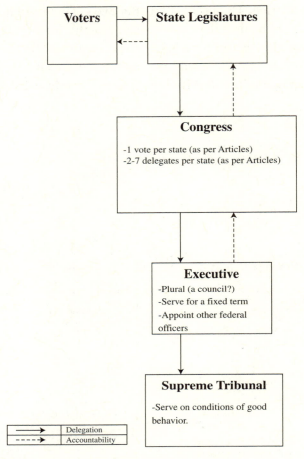

Fig. 2.3. Institutional map of New Jersey Plan
Key: Solid arrows indicate delegation relationships, with the direction of the arrows showing the flow of authority from principal to agent. Dashed arrows indicate accountability relationships.

maintained a system where the voters only had indirect influence over the national government, as it would have remained an agent of the state legislatures, not of the people themselves.

The Hamilton Plan would have created a system with the least amount of accountability, as the chief executive (the Governor) and the Senate would have been made up of lifetime appointees.

Of course, the eventual plan adopted contained a fairly limited accountability loop. Only members of the House were subject to direct accountability to the voters, as Senators were created as agents of state legislators. Further, the original mechanism of the Electoral College did not provide a direct feedback loop to voters, since voters

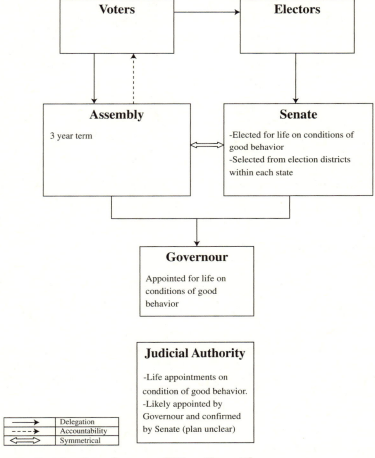

Fig. 2.4. Institutional map of Hamilton Plan
Key: Solid arrows indicate delegation relationships, with the direction of the arrows showing the flow of authority from principal to agent. Dashed arrows indicate accountability relationships. The two-headed arrow indicates symmetry between chambers.

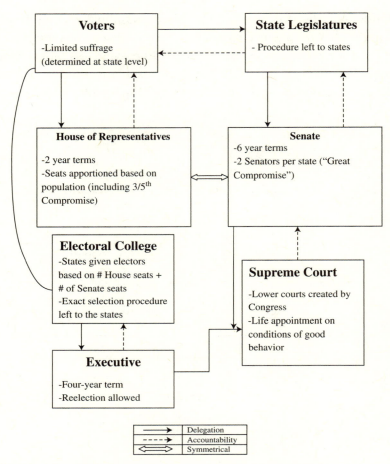

Fig. 2.5. Institutional map of Constitution in 1789
Key: Solid arrows indicate delegation relationships, with the direction of the arrows showing the flow of authority from principal to agent. Dashed arrows indicate accountability relationships. The two-headed arrow indicates symmetry between chambers.

did not choose the electors. Even once the shift takes place to electors being chosen by voters, the electors themselves have no constitutional obligation to follow the voters' instructions (and hence the occasional unfaithful elector who votes differently than the elector's state does).

CHAPTER 3

CONSTITUTIONS

The foundational act of political engineers is the creation of a constitution to govern a country. Or at least this has been increasingly the case since 1789, to the point that it is an almost universal process.[1] Indeed, for democratic polities in particular, constitutions form a container in which we can find the basics of most (if not all) of the other institutional variables discussed in this book, such as the design of legislative, executive, and judicial power or how policy-making authority is divided between central and local authorities.

This chapter will address the question of the basic options open to political engineers regarding constitutions, define the basic concepts associated with constitutions, and conclude with an explicit comparison of the US constitution to those in our other thirty democracies.

THE INSTITUTIONAL OPTIONS

When we consider the options open to the founders of the American republic, it should be noted that from a historical perspective, a written constitution was not a foregone conclusion. While it is

---

1. See Elkins, Ginsburg, and Melton 2009, esp. ch. 3. Specifically, the authors point out that while in 1800 almost no countries had formal constitutions in the modern sense of the term (which they meticulously operationalize), over the course of the nineteenth century the gap between countries in existence and countries with constitutions rapidly closed. Indeed, for new states formed after 1789, the adoption of a constitution was seen as an "obvious" action (41).

retrospectively obvious that the Philadelphia conventioneers should come together to write a constitution, historically speaking such an approach was almost novel at the time. What we think of as the norm in the early twenty-first century was a fairly new enterprise at the time. Indeed, the models available to the framers were limited. As Elkins, Ginsburg, and Melton note, "at least since Aristotle, the word 'constitution,' in its various translations, has been invoked to refer to the higher law of political jurisdictions. . . . Nevertheless, no universal model existed until the rise of the modern state at the turn of the 18th century" (2009: 41). As such, the number of models that could be consulted was limited, with the best pool of such examples being, in fact, the states themselves. It is therefore not surprising that *The Federalist Papers* make numerous references to those documents.

At least in theory, the United States could have followed the examples of other existing countries and could have functioned sans a formal, written constitution, as was the case in Great Britain. Under that option, a collection of documents and practices could have formed the US Constitution. Of course, there were several reasons this was not the case. First, as a relatively young entity, there were no distinct American traditions and practices to be followed in the way analogous to the British experience. Instead, the procedures needed to be spelled out. Further, the pathways toward a written constitution had already been set by the constituent states of the union (as early as 1776) as well as in the guise of the Articles of Confederation. As a result, the United States was a forerunner in a trend that would move from novelty to norm within fifty years.[2] Perhaps most important, the complex political relationships that exist in a federal and presidential system required a specific set of written parameters. Since such a system delegates specific powers to specific actors who control veto gates within the policy-making and policy-implementing apparatus, it is necessary to spell out the basic relationships. Imagine, for example, trying to determine the specific powers of the president and Congress without a written document.

A key need for a constitution for the United States can be found in the fact that the type of government that existed post-independence

2. Ibid., fig. 3.1.

was one that was vested in the basic notion of *popular sovereignty*. This means that it was a government that derived its authority to govern from the people, not from a king or aristocratic class that could assert power over a territory, or from a religious order that could claim a divine right to rule. Rather, when sovereign power comes from the populace, it becomes quite vital to define what that actually means in a practical sense. Along those lines we can consult *Federalist 51,* wherein Madison wrote, "In framing a government which is to be administered by men over men, the great difficulty lies in this: you must first enable the government to control the governed; and in the next place oblige it to control itself. A dependence on the people is, no doubt, the primary control on the government; but experience has taught mankind the necessity of auxiliary precautions." While not in the context of an argument for constitution writing, per se, the passage reflects the notion that for a government to properly function, it cannot rely solely on popular sovereignty, but that proper design of that government is needed, and by extension we can argue that having the basics of that design codified into a constitutional order is a desirable process.

Of course, it should be noted that having a constitution does not make a state democratic, nor does it mean that the government ordained by that constitution derives its power from the people. Indeed, in the constitutional era is it quite common for nondemocratic states to have constitutions. Many of the countries under study in this book have experienced authoritarian governments, including ones that installed their own constitutions. As such, some of the constitutional orders identified in table 3.2 count nondemocratic constitutions alongside democratic ones.

DEFINING THE CONCEPT

Constitutions are documents (with the notable exceptions in New Zealand and the United Kingdom, which famously have unwritten constitutions)[3] that establish a basic framework for governance. Constitutions are, by definition, the highest law in a polity and

3. These constitutions are unwritten at least in the sense of a unified document. This is further discussed below, along with the case of Israel.

therefore the source of all other laws. The creation of an efficacious constitutional order is understood to be part of the basic establishment of the rule of law in lieu of the arbitrary rule of aristocrats or some other source of authority answerable only to itself or some narrow segment of the society. In the democratic tradition constitutions translate the abstract notion of popular sovereignty to paper and serve as a foundation upon which to build government. This concept of constitutions has become directly linked to the development of modern democracy since the late seventeenth century (see, for example, Casper 1989, Dippel 1996, and especially Sartori 1962). Larry Diamond expressly links the notion of a fully democratic state to a constitutional order: "A constitutional state is a state of justice, a *Rechtsstaat* in the German, in which the state acts predictably, in accordance with laws, and the courts enforce restrictions on popularly elected government when they violate the laws, or the constitutional rule" (1999: 12). In other words, the notion of constitutional government is one of government limited to an agreed-upon set of structures and responsibilities as recorded in a fundamental document. The state then flows from that document (at least in terms of an ideal interpretation of the process and recognizing that the practical applications of parchment principals are often messier than their authors might like).

Constitution writers have to make fundamental choices about how to structure the relationship between citizens and their government, as well as to determine how the internal structure of the government will function. It is within constitutions that we expect to find the basic outlines of the rights and privileges of citizens and how the rights of citizenship can be used to influence the selection and behavior of politicians in government. As such, constitutions outline the basic parameters of the principal-agent relationship outlined in chapter 1 (and illustrated in figure 1.1). Further, constitutions detail the basic design of government and how the agents of the people will interact with one another as they attempt to make and implement public policy. A clear illustration of this idea can be found in a fundamental constitutional choice: between a parliamentary system, which fuses the legislative and executive powers, and a presidential system, which creates separation of powers. In a parliamentary system the legislature chooses the executive (prime minister and cabinet), and the relationship that is created is a hierarchical one in which the cabinet is ultimately answerable to the legislature, and thus the policy preferences of the cabinet and the legislature are typically aligned.[4] However, in a presidential system, wherein the legislature and executive are elected separately through differing methods and by different constituencies, the relationship becomes transactional. This means that the president must somehow secure the consent of the legislature, which may have different preferences, to achieve policy (more on this in chapter 8, "Executive Power").

Indeed, constitutions typically establish the basic parameters for practically all of the items under discussion in this text, that is, the division of power between the central government and localities, the locus and basic functioning of legislative, executive, and judicial power, and the parameters (if not the precise rules) for the electoral system. The functioning of all these institutions then directly shapes the development and behavior of political parties and interest groups and, ultimately, the production and implementation of public policy.

While constitutions are typically single, unified documents, this is not always the case. Some constitutions are considered "unwritten" because they lack such a single, unified document. The quintessential example of this is the British constitution, for while it does contain written materials, it is a collection of multiple sources and traditions rather than a singular document. The earliest constitutional document of the United Kingdom, the Magna Carta, dates from the year 1215. However, the Magna Carta is only a small part of the British constitution, and the British constitution is a so-called "unwritten" constitution, consisting of "an agglomeration of statutes, judicial interpretations, conventions, laws and customs of Parliament, common law principles, and selective jurisprudence, such that even scholars may disagree on what is and what is not a part of the constitution" (Maddex 2008: 470). The British constitution is

---

4. If they are seriously at odds, the provision for a no-confidence vote means that the legislative majority can change the composition of the executive, or an early election can be called.

therefore not included in many of the tables included in this chapter. Likewise, New Zealand's constitution consists of a number of documents, dating from the Treaty of Waitangi in 1840, but lacks a unified document. Israel's constitution is also often called "unwritten," because instead of a single constitutional document, it has a series of separate basic laws. Israel's 1948 declaration of independence has been called the "earliest quasi-constitutional document" (Maddex 2008: 226), and the oldest basic law is the 1958 basic law on the Israeli parliament.[5]

In addition to being the fount of many topics for discussion, constitution writing and reform is a fundamental example of the concept of political engineering as noted in chapter 1 (for a direct discussion of such, see Lijphart 2004). Indeed, one cannot find a clearer example of the principles of practical political experimentation and political engineering than the process of constitution building in the early United States (as we discussed in the previous chapter and outlined in its appendix). At the onset of the revolutionary period, the thirteen colonies that became the thirteen states originally organized themselves under the Articles of Confederation. However, the failure of that constitution to create an adequate governing structure for the United States led to the Philadelphia Convention of 1787, one of the most famous examples of political engineering of all time. Indeed, *The Federalist Papers* contain, primarily, arguments against one constitution (the Articles) and in favor of the one that would be ratified in 1789.

Constitutions tend to operate on a general level, providing a basic blueprint for governance without delving into the specifics of day-to-day public policy, although some do make explicit policy statements. The precise working out of this blueprint as well as the daily function of government is left to the legislative and executive powers of the state.

The comparative study of constitutions is complicated by the fact that over time constitutions come and go for a variety of reasons. Several factors ought to be considered. There are straightforward is-

5. Israel's basic laws can be viewed, in English, at the Knesset's Web site: http://www.knesset.gov.il/description/eng/eng_mimshal_yesod1.htm.

sues, such as the date of establishment of the current constitution governing a given country and therefore the age of a given constitution. Beyond that there are the questions of when the practice of using a written constitution was established in a given country (a practice, as noted earlier, that only started to become a global norm in the nineteenth century) and how many constitutions a given country has had.

Even the process of counting constitutions can be tricky, insofar as a given constitution might be used at different times in a given country's history. For example, a constitution might be abrogated by a military coup or war and be replaced by one or more constitutions before being restored at some later date. Let's consider a hypothetical case in which a country establishes a constitution in 1850, has a coup in 1860, which results in a new constitution, which in turn is replaced as the result of the country being occupied by a foreign power in 1870, only to finally restore the 1850 constitution after a successful war of liberation in 1880. How many constitutions did that country have? In terms of documents, the country had three (1850, 1860, 1870), but in terms of constitutional systems, four (1850, 1860, 1870, and 1850 again). Along these lines we adopt the counting process employed by Elkins, Ginsburg, and Melton: "A constitutional system encompasses the period in which a constitution is in force before it is replaced or suspended" (2010: 2).

In general the number of constitutional systems that a given country has experienced can be a measure of its long-term political stability as well as perhaps its vulnerability to outside political influence. Of course, not all constitutional orders are replaced as a result of violence or systemic failure but rather may be the result of political reform of a democratic nature. As we seek to understand political development in our democracies, it is useful to note when they adopted their first constitutional system as well as how many they have had. Table 3.1 contains this information for twenty-nine of our democracies (excluding New Zealand and the United Kingdom).

Several factors are worth noting. First, as described earlier, some constitutional orders are nondemocratic, imposed by authoritarian governments or occupying powers (such as France's 1940 constitution). Other times the result of loss in war can lead to the adoption

Table 3.1. Historical constitutionalism in twenty-nine democracies (1789–2006)

	Year of first constitution	Years of constitutionalism	Number of constitutional systems	Average durability	Most durable constitutional system in years
United States	**1789**	**218**	**1**	**218.00**	**218**
France	1791	216	15	14.40	49
Netherlands	1795	212	7	30.29	159
Switzerland	1798	209	7	29.86	125
Spain	1808	199	14	14.21	55
Sweden	1809	198	2	99.00	165
Mexico	1814	193	11	17.55	90
Argentina	1816	191	8	23.88	113
Chile	1818	189	8	23.63	92
Portugal	1822	185	6	30.83	95
Brazil	1824	183	8	22.88	67
Greece	1827	180	12	15.00	61
Colombia	1830	177	9	19.67	106
Belgium	1831	176	1	176.00	176
Italy	1848	159	2	79.50	82
Denmark	1849	158	4	39.50	54
Canada	1867	140	1	140.00	140
Japan	1889	118	2	59.00	61
Australia	1901	106	1	106.00	106
South Africa	1910	97	5	19.40	51
Hungary	1919	88	4	22.00	58
Poland	1919	88	9	9.78	24
Finland	1919	88	2	44.00	80
Austria	1920	87	3	29.00	62
Israel	1948	59	1	59.00	59
Korea	1948	59	1	59.00	59
Germany	1949	58	1	58.00	48
India	1949	58	1	58.00	58
Czech Rep.	1993	14	1	14.00	14

Source: Based on data from Elkins, Ginsburg, and Melton 2010.

of a democratic constitution (such as in Germany in 1949 and Japan in 1946), as can the exit (from various means) of an authoritarian regime (such as Brazil's new constitution in 1988 or Argentina's restoration of its constitution of 1853 in 1983).

Second, many replacements come about via a process of democratic reform, replacing one democratic constitution with another entirely without abrogating the democratic nature of the regime (for example, Colombia's replacement of its 1886 document with one in 1991, or France's move from the Fourth Republic constitution to that of the Fifth Republic in 1958).

Other new replacements are even less dramatic: Entirely new constitutions may be written and formally adopted that are substantively not very different from the preceding constitution. For instance, the 1999 Swiss constitution was largely an aesthetic exercise for the purpose of deleting outdated provisions and integrating accumulated amendments into more streamlined constitutional texts. A similar—hypothetical—rewriting of the US Constitution would entail such changes as (1) moving the two-term limit for presidents, specified in the Twenty-Second Amendment, to Article II dealing with the executive power; (2) deleting the no-longer-relevant provision in the Twenty-Second Amendment that the two-term limit does not apply to the president in office at the time the amendment was proposed; (3) removing the sections in Article I concerning how slaves and Indians would be counted (in Article I, Section 2); and (4) deleting both the Eighteenth Amendment and the Twenty-First Amendment (except Section 2) that respectively impose and repeal prohibition.

Third, many states have experienced a large number of constitutions in a short period of time, marking initial instability and then moving into a period of sustained constitutionalism (such as Colombia's eight constitutions from 1821 to 1886 and then entering into a period of 106 years without a replacement).

THE UNITED STATES CONSTITUTION IN COMPARATIVE PERSPECTIVE

All constitutions provide the basic rules for the organization and operation of governments. This is also the basic purpose of the US

Constitution. In addition, however, the US Constitution serves as a source of national pride—arguably more so than the constitution in any other democracy. Most knowledgeable Americans know that the US Constitution is the oldest constitution in the world, and they are proud of this special characteristic of their Constitution. They also know that it is a remarkably brief document, and they generally admire this feature. Because of their reverence for their Constitution, they tend to be very reluctant to change it; hence they also approve of the fact that the Constitution is very difficult to amend, and they generally know that in practice it has only rarely been amended. Finally, they also see the Constitution as the foundation for the establishment of democracy in the United States at a relatively early date, and they often call the United States "the world's oldest democracy." All of these judgments imply comparisons with other countries. This section of the chapter is devoted to an explicit and systematic comparison with thirty major democracies on these subjects.

1. An old and durable constitution. The proud claim that the United States is governed by the world's oldest written constitution is clearly justified. It was adopted in 1787 and became effective in 1789. In fact, the advent of the US Constitution was such that the Comparative Constitutions Project uses 1789 as the starting point for its study of worldwide constitution making.[6] If we look at the current constitutions of our other democracies (as listed in table 3.2), we can see that the US Constitution is the only one, from the twenty-nine democracies with written constitutions, that dates back to the eighteenth century and only one of four from democracies that were not established (or reestablished) in the twentieth century.

If we look back to table 3.1, we can further see that the United States has had a very long experience with constitutionalism, but one that shares eighteenth-century origins with France, the Netherlands, and Switzerland. It also has had a remarkably durable constitutional

6. The Comparative Constitutions Project is aimed at "understanding the origins, characteristics, and consequences of written constitutions for most independent states." It contains "nearly all national constitutions from 1789 onward" (Elkins, Ginsburg, and Melton 2009: ix). The project can be accessed online at http://www.comparativeconstitutionsproject.org/index.htm.

Table 3.2. Date of origin of current constitutions in twenty-nine democracies

United States	**1789**
Belgium	1831
Netherlands	1848
Canada	1867
Australia	1901
Mexico	1917
Austria	1945
Japan	1946
Italy	1947
Israel	1948
Korea	1948
Germany	1949
Hungary	1949
India	1949
Denmark	1953
France	1958
Sweden	1974
Greece	1975
Portugal	1976
Spain	1978
Chile	1980
Argentina	1983
Brazil	1988
Colombia	1991
Czech Republic	1993
South Africa	1996
Poland	1997
Finland	1999
Switzerland	1999

Source: Based on data from Elkins, Ginsburg, and Melton 2010.

system. Of the pre–twentieth-century constitutional systems, only two others share the distinction of still utilizing that same constitution (Belgium and Canada).

2. A short constitution. Determining the length of a given constitution is not as easy a task as it may appear at first glance. One problem, but only a minor one, is that in order to obtain comparable counts, English-language versions of all constitutions have to be used, and translations by different translators can obviously contain varying numbers of words. A more serious problem is that some constitutions affirm the validity of earlier constitutional texts without repeating them in the constitution itself. For instance, the 1958 constitution of the French Fifth Republic begins by solemnly proclaiming the attachment of the French people to the 1789 Declaration of the Rights of Man and of the Citizen, a separate document of more than eight hundred words. Another example can be found in the 1949 German constitution, which lists five articles of the previous constitution of 1919 and states that these articles "are an integral part" of the new constitution. The second problem is whether provisions that are clearly no longer relevant (such as in the example of the Eighteenth and Twenty-First Amendments to the US Constitution mentioned earlier) should be included in the count. Our decision was to be as inclusive as possible, but not to claim a degree of accuracy that is not warranted. Table 3.3 therefore shows the length of the constitutions of twenty-nine democracies (all of our democracies except the United Kingdom and New Zealand) in thousands of words.

The United States is near the top of the table, but not at the very top: both Japan and Denmark have shorter constitutions. Overall, the differences in the length of constitutions are not as great as the differences in their ages. Three constitutions in the middle of the table (those of Switzerland, Israel, and Spain) have constitutions that are roughly twice as long as the US Constitution, and only eleven constitutions are more than three times as long. The Indian constitution is an anomaly among democratic constitutions, with more than one hundred thousand words. The longer and more detailed constitutions are, the more often they need to be amended—a subject to which we shall return at the end of this chapter.

Table 3.3. Length of constitutions (in thousands of words) of twenty-nine democracies

Japan	5
Denmark	7
United States	**8**
Korea	9
Italy	10
Netherlands	10
France	11
Czech Republic	11
Hungary	13
Argentina	13
Finland	13
Australia	14
Belgium	14
Switzerland	18
Israel	19
Spain	19
Canada	21
Poland	21
Germany	26
Greece	29
Chile	30
Portugal	38
Sweden	42
Austria	43
Colombia	51
South Africa	51
Brazil	60
Mexico	78
India	118
Median	*19*

Source: Based on data available at ConstitutionMaking.org 2010; Political Database of the Americas at http://pdba.georgetown .edu/Constitutions/constudies.html; and Tschentscher 2010.

3. The world's oldest democracy? In his 1993 inaugural address, President Bill Clinton called the United States "the world's oldest democracy." He was not the first American, and will not be the last, to make this claim. How valid is it?

The best-known analysis of the paths that the countries of the world have taken toward (and away from) democracy is that of Samuel P. Huntington (1991). Huntington identifies a long first wave starting as early as 1828 and lasting until 1926, a short second wave from 1943 to 1962, and a third wave starting in 1974. Two reverse waves, in which democracy collapsed in many countries, occurred between the three waves of democratization.

It is worth noting that as time has progressed, the definition of democracy has deepened. Huntington's choice of 1828 as the beginning of the first wave, for example, illustrates this fact. Specifically he uses the following criteria: (1) 50 percent of males eligible to vote, and (2) a chief executive responsible either to parliamentary majorities or directly to the electorate (1991: 16). From a contemporary point of view, these are extremely inadequate measures of democracy. From a historical perspective, however, such a reliance on popular will was innovative, as was a chief executive who obtained power via some connection to that popular will (as opposed to, for example, being a monarch or military leader).

The United States is listed first among the democracies in table 3.4, because Huntington explicitly identifies the United States as the country where the first wave of democratization began in 1828. The other seven countries in the first group are listed alphabetically, as are the countries in the other groups with the same pattern of waves and reverse waves in the table. Of our thirty-one democracies, twenty-five can be called "old" democracies, in the sense that they all participated in the first wave of democratization, but only eight, including the United States, can claim to have been continuous democracies since the first wave. It is also worth noting how many of our democracies have experienced reversals: twenty of the thirty-one current democracies. Four countries—Argentina, the Czech Republic, Greece, and Hungary—have the checkered democratic history of having participated in all of the waves and reverse waves.

Table 3.4. Waves of democratization and reverse waves in thirty-one democracies

	First wave 1828–1926	First reverse wave 1922–1942	Second wave 1943–1962	Second reverse wave 1958–1975	Third wave 1974–
United States	X				
Australia	X				
Canada	X				
Finland	X				
New Zealand	X				
Sweden	X				
Switzerland	X				
United Kingdom	X				
Austria	X	X	X		
Belgium	X	X	X		
Colombia	X	X	X		
Denmark	X	X	X		
France	X	X	X		
Germany	X	X	X		
Italy	X	X	X		
Japan	X	X	X		
Netherlands	X	X	X		
Argentina	X	X	X	X	X
Czech Republic	X	X	X	X	X
Greece	X	X	X	X	X
Hungary	X	X	X	X	X
Poland	X	X			X
Portugal	X	X			X
Spain	X	X			X

(*continued*)

Table 3.4. (*continued*)

	First wave 1828–1926	First reverse wave 1922–1942	Second wave 1943–1962	Second reverse wave 1958–1975	Third wave 1974–
Chile	X		X	X	
Israel			X		
Brazil			X	X	X
India			X	X	X
Korea			X	X	X
Mexico					X
South Africa					X

Source: Adapted and expanded from Huntington 1991: 14–17.

Some of Huntington's judgments may be questioned. In particular, he argues that the German occupation of France, the Netherlands, Belgium, and Denmark during the Second World War constituted breaks with democracy in the first of his reverse waves, even though these breaks were externally imposed and lasted a relatively short time, after which democracy was immediately restored. Similarly, he includes India in his second reverse wave because of the so-called Emergency in India from 1975 to 1977, although this clearly undemocratic interlude was quickly ended by free elections after only about a year and a half.

A more serious objection to Huntington's analysis, and to his conclusion that the United States is the oldest of the world's democracies, is that he uses an extremely lenient definition of "universal" suffrage: the right to vote for at least 50 percent of adult males.[7] As a result, he ignores the exclusion of women and members of racial

7. Huntington (1991: 14) concedes that he includes both democratic and "semidemocratic" systems.

and ethnic minorities from the franchise in many countries. Truly universal suffrage, including the right of women and minorities to vote, is not a *sufficient* condition for democracy—for instance, the fact that all citizens of Iraq under Saddam Hussein had the right to vote obviously did not make Iraq a democracy—but is clearly a *necessary* condition.[8]

Table 3.5 lists our thirty-one democracies according to the year in which universal-suffrage democracy was established or reestablished. In just over half (sixteen) of our countries, especially the more recent democracies at the bottom of the table, such full democracy was instituted after a period of completely nondemocratic rule. An additional two cases established universal suffrage at the time of national independence. However, thirteen countries, generally toward the top of the table, already had extensive but not fully inclusive voting rights and adopted universal suffrage in the years indicated. In most cases, the final extension of the suffrage entailed the admission of women to the suffrage—as early as 1893 in New Zealand, but as late as 1948 in Belgium, 1954 in Colombia, and even 1971 in Switzerland. In three countries, the final step in making the franchise universal involved the grant of secure voting rights to ethnic and racial minorities: Indians (or First Nations, as they are now known) in Canada in 1960, Aborigines in Australia in 1962, and the African American minority in the United States in 1965, when the Voting Rights Act was passed.[9] In terms of the establishment

8. This is well illustrated by the October 2002 Iraqi election, in which the only candidate on the ballot was Saddam Hussein. See the BBC article, "Saddam 'wins 100% of vote'" available online at http://news.bbc.co.uk/2/hi/2331951.stm. Examples of authoritarian governments allowing elections are numerous. Certainly we could refer also to the old Soviet Union and various Soviet satellite states, such as East Germany. Sometimes the disconnect between elections and governance is more subtle, such as in Mexico under the Institutional Revolutionary Party (PRI) before the democratizing reforms of the 1990s.

9. The principle of universal suffrage was also violated by the United States, the United Kingdom, France, the Netherlands, and Belgium while these countries were colonial powers, because the inhabitants of their colonies lacked voting rights; by the three Allied Powers while they were occupying Germany

of universal-suffrage democracy—which is really a redundant term because, as stated earlier, universal suffrage is a sine qua non of democracy—the United States is not at the top, but only roughly in the middle of table 3.5. It is therefore more accurate and more modest to claim that the United States is the oldest country with a broadly representative government—which, however, did not become fully democratic until the 1960s.

4. How democratic is the US Constitution? Democracy requires adherence to the principle of "one person, one vote" but also to the principle of "one person, one vote, one *value*"—that is, all votes should have equal weight. In his book with the provocative title *How Democratic Is the American Constitution?* Robert A. Dahl (2001) identifies several antidemocratic elements in it and, in particular, the serious inequality in the value of citizens' votes that results from the equal representation of the fifty states in the US Senate. He points out that the vote of a resident of Nevada is worth about seventeen times that of a resident of neighboring California, and that the vote of someone in Connecticut is worth almost six times the vote of his or her neighbor in New York. "In the extreme case, the ratio of over-representation of the least populated state, Wyoming, to the most populous state, California, is just under 70 to 1." Dahl (2001: 49–50) argues that such inequalities in representation constitute "a profound violation of the democratic idea of political equality among all citizens."

Dahl recognizes that, in all federal systems, there is an inherent tension between the idea of equality of citizens and the special representation of states, provinces, and cantons that are the constituent

---

and Japan; and by post-1967 Israel, on account of its control over the occupied territories. Postwar control of conquered countries or areas is the least serious violation of the universal-suffrage standard because such control is meant to be temporary; the longer such control lasts, however, the more it creates a dilemma for democracy.

Further, in the contemporary United States, US citizens residing in territorial holdings such as Puerto Rico and Guam lack voting rights as they pertain to the Congress and the presidency. Residents of the District of Columbia have had voting rights for the presidency since the passage of the Twenty-Third Amendment in 1961 but have no voting member of the Congress.

Table 3.5. Establishment or reestablishment of universal suffrage in thirty-one democracies

	Year	Universal suffrage established		
		After transition from autocracy	At time of national independence	As final extension of suffrage
New Zealand	1893			X
Finland	1906			X
Denmark	1915			X
Austria	1918	X		
Netherlands	1919			X
Sweden	1919			X
United Kingdom	1928			X
France	1944			X
Italy	1945	X		
Japan	1947	X		
Belgium	1948			X
Israel	1948		X	
Germany	1949	X		
India	1950		X	
Colombia	1954			
Canada	1960			X
Australia	1962			X
United States	**1965**			**X**
Switzerland	1971			X
Greece	1974	X		
Portugal	1976	X		
Spain	1977	X		
Argentina	1980	X		
Brazil	1985	X		
Korea	1988	X		
Chile	1990	X		
Czech Republic	1990	X		
Hungary	1990	X		
Poland	1990	X		
South Africa	1994	X		
Mexico	2000	X		

Sources: Based on data in Karatnycky, Piano, and Puddington 2003; Inter-Parliamentary Union 1995; and Mackie and Rose 1991.

units of the federation. This special representation frequently means the over-representation of the smaller units and hence the under-representation of the residents of the larger units.[10] Dahl's criticism is therefore not so much that a degree of citizen inequality exists, but that this inequality is unusual and extreme in the United States. In most of our other federal democracies, the inequality is indeed more modest. We shall return to this topic in greater detail in our chapters on federalism (4) and legislative power (7).

5. *A constitution that allowed, then prohibited, slavery.* The Constitution of the United States is only one of eight that mentions slavery, and the only one that contained constitutional provisions that supported the "peculiar institution" that it then had to amend out of the document.[11]

In comparative terms, the eight constitutions that mention slavery in some capacity are those from Argentina, Brazil, Chile, Colombia, Japan, Mexico, South Africa, and the United States of America. Of these eight, four (Chile, Colombia, Mexico, and South Africa) contain a prohibition on slavery as an original constitutional right, with two (Chile and Mexico) also providing immediate emancipation for any foreign slaves who enter their national territories. Two constitutions (Brazil and Japan) make reference to slavery without any particular rights being defined. Japan's preamble simply asserts a "desire to occupy an honored place in an international society" and to "striv[e] for the preservation of peace, and the banishment of tyranny and slavery, oppression and intolerance for all time from the earth," while the Brazilian constitution speaks of preserving "documents and sites" of historical significance to runaway slave communities. The Argentina constitution provides both a prohibition of slavery and an emancipation proclamation: "The few [slaves] who still exist shall become free as from the swearing of this Constitution."

The US Constitution, on the other hand, has three references to legal slavery from its original 1789 incarnation (and the wording re-

10. However, as we shall see in ch. 4, it does not necessarily mean the completely equal representation of all units, regardless of population.

11. One could also argue that the British constitutional system had to amend itself to abolish slavery, as was done with the Slavery Abolition Act of 1834.

mains in the document). It is worth noting that the word *slavery* was not mentioned until it was abolished by the Thirteenth Amendment (the fourth reference to the institution of slavery in the Constitution), but the inclusion of the concept was quite clear. The first reference is in Article I, Section 2, Clause 3, which contains the infamous "Three-Fifths" compromise in which persons "bound to Service for a Term of Years" (that is, slaves) would count as three-fifths of a person in terms of taxes (which were then based on head count) and representation in the House of Representatives. The second reference is in Article I, Section 9, Clause 1, which prohibited the regulation of the "Migration or Importation of such Persons as any of the States now existing shall think proper to admit" (that is, slaves) until 1808. The third reference is to runaway slaves, which can be found in Article IV, Section 2, Clause 2, which states (in its entirety): "No Person held to Service or Labour in one State, under the Laws thereof, escaping into another, shall, in Consequence of any Law or Regulation therein, be discharged from such Service or Labour, but shall be delivered up on Claim of the Party to whom such Service or Labour may be due."

As noted, all of these clauses were made moot by the Thirteenth Amendment, which prohibited slavery and involuntary servitude.

All of this, however, does mark the US Constitution as having a unique place on this issue, which illustrates that political impasse over the slave issue at the framing and also underscores the degree to which historical sequencing (that is, when a constitution is written) can substantially influence the contents of that document (and the pathways its institutions are then set upon). Further, this aspect of the origins of the United States highlights why issues of race have been of great salience to the development of US politics, even to the present day.

Of course, it is not surprising that the bulk of the constitutions that mentioned slavery in one form or another (six out of eight) would be from the Americas, where the issue of slavery was a key component of both colonization and development. Along those lines, it is noteworthy that other cases in our study did utilize slavery, especially in colonial holdings. For example, the Dutch did not ban slavery in its colonies until 1863, and while slavery was outlawed in France during their revolution, it was restored in the colonies by Napoleon. Also noteworthy: The end of slavery in Brazil in 1888 marked the latest emancipation of slaves for countries in our study.

6. *A constitution that is difficult to amend.* All democratic constitutions contain provisions for their own amendment, and almost all of them make it more difficult to change the constitution than to enact or change ordinary laws. But they differ a great deal with regard to how flexible or rigid they are in this respect. Procedures for amending a constitution vary in their *numeric* thresholds for approval, as well as the institutional *complexity* of the process. Thus we have two dimensions, where the numeric dimension refers to "how many must agree," whereas the dimension of complexity refers to "who must agree."

On the numeric dimension, we find that constitutional amendment processes often require some sort of supermajority of the legislature, although not all do. The range of thresholds runs from an absolute majority (half plus one)[12] up to three-quarters. Many constitutions also require a certain number of legislators to be present (a quorum). Numeric thresholds that make approval of amendments more difficult can also be applied to referenda, which are votes by the public.

The second dimension, that of complexity, reflects the number of actors/veto gates in the process. In pure legislative supremacy in a unicameral setting, complexity is low, as the number of veto gates is one: the legislature itself. However, most amendment processes go beyond just the legislature. Some require multiple votes, forcing legislators to take responsibility twice for voting for change, such as in one of the procedures under the Colombian constitution. Others required two votes *and* an intervening election. Instead of one actor, a given legislative body, such a process includes three: the originating legislature, the electorate, and then a newly elected legislature chosen by those voters, who will likely have had their vote influenced by their views on constitutional reform. Other systems require a ref-

---

12. As distinct from an ordinary majority, which means more "yes" than "no" votes, which may be less than a majority of the members, due to abstentions.

erendum, which directly inserts the voters into the decision-making process, by having them vote for or against the proposed changes. Further, federal systems often include subunit legislatures or have referendum provisions that take account of the states or other units. For example, Switzerland requires a majority of voters nationwide and also majorities in a majority of subunits (cantons). The complexity of such procedures is such that the combination of subunits and a supermajority requirement can empower minorities to band together to block changes to the constitution. We tend to find that federal states have more complex processes for amending their constitutions, which are therefore typically more rigid than their unitary counterparts.

Figure 3.1 plots the constitutional amendment procedures (in some cases more than one, as is elaborated upon in the appendix) for our thirty-one democracies on these two dimensions. Some countries (such as India) have different processes depending on what part of the constitution is being amended. As the chart moves from the top left cell to the bottom right, the constitutions as plotted in the chart move from flexible to rigid.

The dotted diagonal line in the chart is the line of constitutional rigidity, moving from the least rigid (legislative supremacy with a 50 percent plus one process) to the most rigid (to a two-level approval process involving a referendum and a 75 percent threshold for passage). Of course, the most rigid arrangement within the confines of this model is a theoretical one, as none of our democracies have those provisions in place. Only one of our democracies fits in the most flexible category (Israel). In the past, New Zealand and the United Kingdom could also have been included in the least rigid category, but increasingly in both cases the referendum possibility has become the consensus position.

Among our thirty-one democracies, the United States is the only example of a constitution with a three-fourths supermajority requirement for all amendments. Indeed, it is only one of two cases that uses a three-fourths supermajority at all, as South Africa's constitution employs it for amending some of the foundational aspects of its constitution. The much more common supermajority, found in most (eighteen out of thirty) of our democracies, is the two-thirds

	1/2 + 1	3/5	2/3	3/4
Legislative Supremacy	Israel	*Brazil* [bi] Czech Republic [bi] *France$_2$* [bi]*	*Austria* [bi] *Germany* [bi] Hungary *India* [bi] Poland$_1$ [bi] Portugal South Africa$_1$ [bi]	*South Africa$_2$* [bi]
Double Vote	Colombia$_1$ [bi]			
Double Vote + Intervening Election		Greece	*Argentina* [bi]** *Belgium* Finland Netherlands	
Referendum Threat	Italy New Zealand Sweden UK [bi]	Chile$_1$ [bi] *Spain*	Chile$_2$ [bi] Poland$_2$ [bi]	
Referendum Requirement	Colombia$_2$ [bi] Denmark France$_1$ [bi]		*Austria* [bi] Japan [bi] Korea	
Two-Level Approval			*Canada* [bi] *India$_2$* [bi] *Mexico*	*USA* [bi]
Two-Level Approval w/ Referendum	*Australia* [bi] *Switzerland* [bi]			

More Complex (vertical axis, top to bottom)

Fig. 3.1. Constitutional amendment strategies and supermajority requirements in thirty-one democracies

Key: [bi] Indicates a bicameral legislature, meaning two votes are needed within the process. *Italicized* states are federal.

*Under France$_2$ the parliament votes in a joint session. So while the legislature is technically bicameral, this process requires only one vote (Article 89).

**In Argentina, the legislature indicates the need for amendment, but must call an elected assembly to deal with the actual amending.

majority—based on the idea that supporters of a constitutional change have to outnumber their opponents by a ratio of at least 2 to 1.

CONCLUSIONS

Constitutions are foundational documents wherein a polity can establish its basic institutional framework. Therefore, constitutions are quintessential examples of political engineering, which set the stage for the subsequent process of policy creation within a given state. Indeed, the rest of this book discusses various aspects of democratic governance that directly or indirectly grow out of the constitutions of our thirty-one cases.

Like the other institutional variables that we are analyzing herein, the US Constitution stands out in comparison to its counterparts in our other cases: It is the oldest and longest-lived of such documents. In these ways it is unique among our cases. It is also one of the shortest constitutions under study. In terms of its democratic quality, it has legitimate claim to being one of the oldest democratic constitutions, although when it comes to the full establishment of universal suffrage, its performance is less singular.

APPENDIX: CONSTITUTIONS WITH MULTIPLE AMENDMENT PROCESSES

Here is a listing of the specific processes noted in figure 3.1:

$Austria_1$: two-thirds of both chambers
$Austria_2$: two-thirds plus referendum for total revision
$Chile_1$: three-fifths of both chambers
$Chile_2$: two-thirds if amendment to Chapters I, III, VIII, XI, XII, or XV (Referendum Threat by president in both cases)
$Colombia_1$: Passed by 50 percent +1 by two consecutive regular sessions (no intervening election)
$Colombia_2$: Passed by 50 percent +1 of legislature and then submitted to referendum (25 percent of electorate must participate for measure to pass)
$France_1$: 50 percent +1 of both chambers followed by a referendum

France$_2$: three-fifths of parliament convened in congress

India$_1$: two-thirds of legislature

India$_2$: Two-level requirement if changes affect:

    a. Article 54, Article 55, Article 73, Article 162, or Article 241, or

    b. Chapter IV of Part V, Chapter V of Part VI, or Chapter I of Part XI, or

    c. any of the Lists in the Seventh Schedule, or

    d. the representation of States in parliament, or

    e. the provisions of this article (that is, Part XX, 368)

Poland$_1$: two-thirds in the Sejm, 50 percent +1 in the senate

Poland$_2$: Amendments to Chapter I, II, or XII can also be submitted to a referendum

South Africa$_1$: Other amendments require a two-thirds vote in the National Assembly and six of nine (two-thirds) of the National Council of Provinces

South Africa$_2$: Section 1 and Subsection 74 require a three-fourths vote in the National Assembly and six of nine (two-thirds) of the National Council of Provinces

CHAPTER 4

FEDERALISM AND DIVISION OF POWER

As noted in chapter 2, one of the most profound choices made at the Philadelphia Convention was that concerning the relationship between the states and the central government. The political exigencies of the day were such that not only was a complex choice on the table, but it was such that they were forced to invent a new type of division of power that we now know as *federalism.* So fundamental was this issue that the proponents of the Constitution identified themselves as the Federalists as they advocated that the states ratify the proposed document. This innovation was one that would eventually be embraced by many countries, including thirteen of the democracies in our study (see table 4.1).

THE INSTITUTIONAL OPTIONS

What options were available to the Philadelphia conventioneers and, by extension, what options exist in theoretical space for the arrangement of relationships between localities and the central government? In terms of basic institutional design, there are four options open to a group of political engineers faced with the task of taking a set of units and establishing a basic governing system over them. These options are, in decreasing order of centralized authority: a *unitary state,* a *federal state,* a *confederal state,* and no state at all (that is, dissolution—the units all go their own way). These arrangements have to do with how much authority the center has vis-à-vis the subunits. In a unitary state, policy-making authority is concentrated in the center, and whatever autonomy the subunits have is as a result of delegation from that center: It is a system wherein

Table 4.1. Population (2011) and area of unitary and federal countries

Country	Population	Area (km²)
Unitary states (18)		
Japan	127,368,088	377,915
France	65,630,692	643,427
United Kingdom	63,047,162	243,610
Italy	61,261,254	301,340
Korea	48,860,500	99,720
Colombia	45,239,079	1,138,914
Poland	38,415,284	312,685
Netherlands	17,067,369	41,543
Chile	16,730,632	756,102
Greece	10,781,459	131,957
Portugal	10,767,827	92,090
Czech Republic	10,177,300	78,867
Hungary	9,958,453	93,028
Sweden	9,103,788	450,295
Israel	7,590,758	22,072
Denmark	5,543,453	43,094
Finland	5,262,930	338,145
New Zealand	4,327,944	267,710
Median	*13,756,046*	*255,660*
Federal states (13)		
India	1,205,073,612	3,287,263
United States	**313,847,465**	**9,826,675**
Brazil	205,716,890	8,514,877
Mexico	114,975,406	1,964,375
Germany	81,305,856	357,022
South Africa	48,810,427	1,219,090
Argentina	47,042,984	2,780,400
Spain	42,192,494	505,370
Canada	34,300,083	9,984,670
Australia	22,015,576	7,741,220
Belgium	10,438,353	30,528
Austria	8,219,743	83,871
Switzerland	7,655,628	41,277
Median	*47,042,984*	*1,964,375*

Source: CIA *World Factbook.*

power flows down from the center to the subunits. All democratic unitary states have at least a local (municipal) level of elected government, and several of them also contain an intermediate level that is elected, usually known as provinces or departments. However, in unitary states, the subnational governments are not guaranteed the right to make final decisions over any policy area.

A federal system may be defined most simply as one with multiple levels of *sovereignty*. To be sovereign is to be legally empowered to make binding decisions. So in a federal political system—which we can also term a *federation*—not only is the national government sovereign, but there is also a level of sovereign intermediate government in territorial entities typically known as states or provinces. In a federal system, ultimate sovereign power resides in the central government, but there exists also a range of policy questions upon which the intermediate-level governments hold sovereignty, implying that in these areas, the central government is constitutionally barred from overturning the decisions taken at the intermediate level.

Another way to look at these concepts in the light of the framework discussed in chapter 1 and outlined in figure 1.1 is to think of how the three power arrangements (unitary, federal, and confederal) work in terms of principal-agent relationships. In a democratic unitary system, the people as principals delegate their power to their agents in the central government, which then has a hierarchical relationship with subunit governments. In such an arrangement, the subunits do not independently make policy, but simply administer the policies created and handed down by the central government. In a federal system the citizens as principals delegate to both the central and subunit governments, whose relationship is defined in a nonhierarchical fashion. In confederal systems the central government is an agent of the subunits, and there is no direct connection between the citizens and that government. Instead, they delegate to the subunits, which then delegate to the central government.

The lines of authority in a federation are outlined schematically in figure 4.1. Using the same symbolic notation as we introduced in chapter 1, we see solid lines with arrows at their endpoints indicating the direction in which authority flows, and thick bold lines with arrows on both ends referring to transactional relationships—that is, bargaining between constitutionally independent actors. Starting at

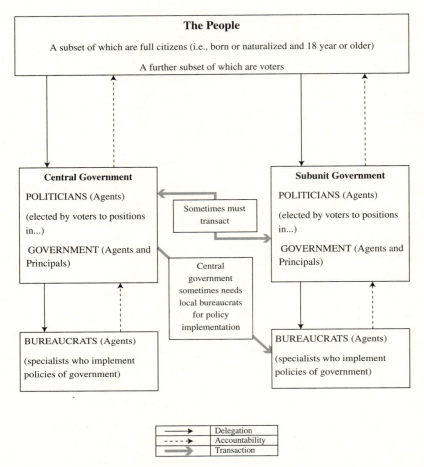

Fig. 4.1. Basic principal-agent relationship under federalism

the top, we find (as in figure 1.1) that if the country in question is a federal democracy, the electorate is the source of authority. Through the act of voting, and mediated through the rules of the electoral system (chapter 5), voters delegate authority to both the national politicians and politicians in the subunit (state, province) in which they reside. That is, all voters are simultaneously members of the national electorate and of the electorate of their subunit. In the context of political systems with a presidential structure, such as the United States, this means in practice that every voter is able to vote for the national executive (president), national legislators (representatives and senators), as well as the state executive (governor) and state legislators.[1] Both the national and subnational governments have their own respective bureaucracies, which implement the policies enacted by elected politicians.

Although it is conventional to speak of the national (central) and intermediate (subnational, that is, state) governments as being different "levels"—and we will adopt this phrasing for convenience as well—they are depicted in figure 4.1 as being side by side to make an important point that is critical for understanding how federal and unitary systems differ. In any system that meets the definition of being federal, there are policy areas in which the subnational governments make binding decisions, which are not subject to being overturned by the national government. Thus in these policy areas, the national government is unable to impose its will on the units, which results in a transactional relationship between the national and unit governments (hence the horizontal depiction of relations between them). A significant amount of policy making in federal systems consists of national legislation that offers *incentives* to the unit governments to adapt their policies to be consistent with national preferences. Such a relationship is transactional and stands in contrast to what we see in unitary systems, where the national government has the legal authority to simply impose its preferences through legislation that is binding on the provincial or departmental governments. In addition, as also depicted in figure 4.1, much policy implementation in federal systems requires the cooperation of the national and unit bureaucracies. Because these bureaucracies are agents of different principals, again this sort of policy making is transactional: The national government is unable to dictate how state bureaucrats do their job. Indeed, in some federal systems, subunit governments have to cooperate with central government policies in terms of implementation. This can manifest in a variety of ways, which include implementation, design, and budget. For example, central governments often utilize state-level bureaucracies

1. The terms used for state legislators vary across states, but typically they are members of the assembly and senators. All state legislatures are bicameral, with the exception of Nebraska.

as the point of distribution for a policy, such as using county health departments to manage and distribute the Supplemental Nutrition Assistance Program (SNAP) in the United States (or the fact that interstate highways are constructed and maintained by state departments of transportation). In some policies subunits may be afforded leeway in how a program is put into practice (although within set parameters), such as with the Temporary Assistance for Needy Families (TANF) program in the United States, a poverty assistance program sometimes colloquially referred to as "welfare." In that situation, US states have leeway to determine factors such as eligibility and specific benefits. Subunits can also influence policies via fiscal inputs. In the previously noted programs in the United States, states provide some of the funding and therefore influence the policies in that fashion as well. More dramatically, a study of federal countries by Stepan (2004b: 330) notes that in Argentina and Brazil, fiscal powers over central government policy are so strong at the subunit level that they amount to a veto power.

These transactional relationships depend on the very existence of distinct policy areas in which the unit and central governments enjoy sovereignty. Naturally, the boundaries between these sovereignties are subject to dispute, and they may evolve over time. Thus there must be some means of identifying which decisions rest with which level of government, and a means for sorting out and resolving disputes. The remainder of this chapter will discuss the various constitutional features that exist for protecting the units from encroachments by the center, and vice versa. Some of this sorting out is left to the political institutions themselves, for instance, bargaining between the first and second chambers of the legislature or among and within political parties. Often, however, conflicts over jurisdictional matters are left to the judicial branch, as we will discuss in our chapter on courts.

So far we have contrasted federations to unitary systems, noting that the latter lack the transactional relations that typify federal systems, whereby the central government and intermediate governments have their own areas of sovereignty. So what of confederal systems? In these, sovereign power flows "upward" from the subunits to the central government, which is typically limited in scope. Confederacies are arguably not viable models for actual states, especially in the modern era. Indeed, Madison noted multiple historical examples in *Federalist 18, 19,* and *20* of the problems associated with this form of government. The closest example we have at the moment is the European Union, wherein the member states retain ultimate sovereignty, although that discussion is beyond the scope of our study.[2] Finally, if subunits cannot find a way of coexisting in some capacity, dissolution of the federation is an option, as in the case of the peaceful breakup of Czechoslovakia into the Czech Republic (one of our thirty-one democracies) and Slovakia in 1993 (not included in the study).[3]

The US founders were well acquainted with three of these options, two of which they rejected from the beginning: dissolution of the union, and what the authors of *The Federalist Papers* called "consolidation," that is, what we today would call the creation of a unitary state. A third option, that of confederation, also lacked appeal, as it was the failure of governance under the Articles of Confederation, the first constitution of the United States, which brought the founders to Philadelphia in the first place. As noted in chapter 2, there was a formal proposal made to reform the confederal arrangement under the Articles (that is, the New Jersey Plan), but it was ultimately rejected. As such, they needed innovation to create a fourth

2. The European Union has its own parliament, which would seem to meet one of the core criteria for federalism: Voters wherever they live in the EU have the right to vote both for their country's politicians (the governments of Britain, France, Germany, etc.) and for European-level politicians. However, the EU lacks its own executive that is either directly elected by European voters or accountable to the European parliament. Instead the executive is comprised of delegates of the member-state governments. There is a distinct European bureaucracy, but the enforcement of decisions made by the European institutions remains with the member-state governments. It is this last point that makes the EU fundamentally not a federation: Binding authority remains with the member states.

3. Often the breakup of multinational states is violent, such as with dissolution of Yugoslavia in the 1990s or Sudan in 2011. Indeed, the end of the Cold War led to a dramatic example of dissolution, as the Soviet Union went from one single state to fifteen separate states. However, none of these cases is the breakup of a *democratic* federation, and Stepan (2004a) makes a convincing argument that no authoritarian system can be considered meaningfully federal.

option, which they did in the form of federalism. The government under the Articles was one in which each of the states was coequal, that is, each had one vote in the Congress (even if the different states sent different-size delegations) regardless of the population of the state. Further, normal business under that system required a supermajority of votes, nine of thirteen, and unanimity to alter the Articles. As such, the system was one in which the feeble powers of the central government were impossible to deploy effectively because it was quite easy for a minority to thwart the process (as discussed in chapter 2 and as outlined by Madison; see box 2.1). Clearly, then, the national government under the Articles of Confederation lacked sovereignty in a meaningful sense. It lacked national-level institutions that were agents of a national electorate, which is, as figure 4.1 indicates, required for a federation. Instead, the national institutions were constitutionally subordinate to the political institutions elected within each of the separate states.

It is important to understand that while a major purpose of federalism was the maintenance of the states as political entities with an important degree of political autonomy within the union as a whole, the basic goal of the move from confederalism to federalism was the strengthening of the central government of the United States, by endowing it with a source of authority separate from that of the sates. As such, while contemporary US political debates about federalism are often about states' rights in the system, the purpose of creating what Madison called an "extended republic" was to create a central government strong enough to govern the union of states as a whole and to subordinate the states to that central government in policy areas reserved by the new Constitution to the national government.

WHY FEDERALISM?

At this point, we have established the options available in terms of the relationship between the central government and its subunits, and we have sketched out how authority patterns vary among unitary, federal, and confederal systems. Now we turn to a consideration of why designers of a constitution for a given country might, as a general proposition, choose federalism. Therefore, we shall turn to an examination of the specific institutional characteristics of federations. A classic reason—in the sense of having been the justification for the US federal design itself—is that separate political entities may already exist and "come together," as Stepan (2004a) put it. That is, if existing sovereign units decide to build a common government to subsume some of their separate authorities, they may establish a federal balance of power to preserve some of their existing sovereignty even as they create a larger polity. While this was certainly the case in the United States, it would be only partly or not at all accurate as a description of most of the other federal systems. Some federal systems—notably Belgium, India, South Africa, and Spain—were unitary states at one time and later transformed themselves into federations as a result of political decisions taken in the national legislature or a constitutional assembly. Stepan refers to this pattern as "holding together," to signify that a political decision to guarantee sovereign powers to the subnational level was made as a way to provide distinct subnational groups, such as geographically concentrated ethnic groups, incentives to remain within the larger country.

In fact, size and ethnic diversity are very strongly linked to federalism. By size, we mean here both in population and area. In fact, figure 4.2 shows that all countries that are exceptionally large in one or both dimensions are federal. The figure shows a country's population on the horizontal dimension, and its area on the vertical dimension. Federal countries are shown with one symbol, the solid square, while unitary systems are shown with two other symbols (as discussed in more detail in the next section). The data on which the graph is based are provided in table 4.1, and show that the median population of our federal systems is approximately 47 million, while the median size of our unitary states is much smaller, approximately 14 million. Measured by territorial extent, the median federal system is almost ten times the size of the median unitary state (1,964,375 square kilometers versus 255,660).

In figure 4.2, the more a country is located toward the upper right, the more it is large in both dimensions, while the more it is located toward the lower left, the smaller it is in both dimensions. The dashed curve in the graph separates the set of countries that are very large

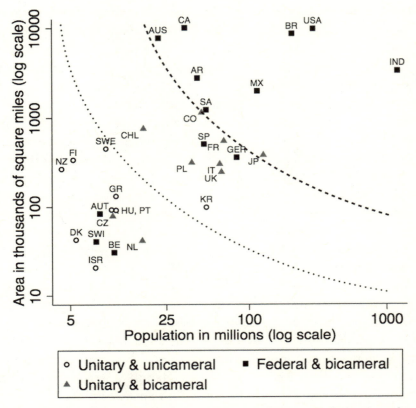

Fig. 4.2. Relationship between size (population and area) and division of powers

Key: USA, United States; AR, Argentina; AUS, Australia; AUT, Austria; BE, Belgium; BR, Brazil; CA, Canada; CHL, Chile; CO, Colombia; CZ, Czech Republic; DK, Denmark; FI, Finland; FR, France; GER, Germany; GR, Greece; HU, Honduras; IND, India; ISR, Israel; IT, Italy; JP, Japan; KR, South Korea; MX, Mexico; NL, Netherlands; NZ, New Zealand; PL, Poland; PT, Portugal; SA, South Africa; SP, Spain; SWE, Sweden; SWI, Switzerland; UK, United Kingdom.

in at least one dimension, all of which are federal. A case like Japan, which is very large in population, is nonetheless much smaller in area that any of the countries on the other side of the dashed curve. (Japan is also an unusually homogeneous society.) The dotted curve then roughly differentiates those smaller countries that are mostly unicameral as well as unitary, from those unitary systems that have bicameral legislatures yet unitary divisions of power. We will discuss the distinction between unicameral and bicameral systems further in the next section of this chapter, and then more fully in chapter 7. For now, the important observation is that bicameralism tends to be associated not only with federalism—indeed, all the federal systems are bicameral—but also with those unitary systems that are large in one dimension—such as Japan (large population, middle-size area) and Chile (middle-size in area, but small in population).

While most federal systems are large in both area and population, a glance at figure 4.2 shows that there are some federal systems mixed in among the mostly unitary smaller countries (Austria, Belgium, and Switzerland). On the other hand, none of the unitary states are as large, territorially speaking, as the median federal state. The one that comes closest is Colombia (1,138,914 square kilometers) and it is worth noting that it had a phase of experimentation with federalism in the nineteenth century. Six unitary states have populations close to or greater than the median for federal states (Colombia, France, Italy, Japan, Korea, and the United Kingdom),[4] but each of these is below the median federal system in area.[5]

Two of the federal systems that are small in both population and area—Belgium and Switzerland—are excellent examples of the use of federalism as a means to grant local autonomy to regionally concentrated ethnic or linguistic minorities. While these countries may be small, they have clearly distinct ethnolinguistic regions that are able to constitute local majorities in specific subnational units. Much the same can also be said about several of the large federations that likewise have subnational units where national minorities constitute either local majorities or at least much larger minorities than in the federation as a whole, including Canada, India and South Africa.

Although US state boundaries were never set with ethnic representation in mind, some national minorities constitute far greater shares of the population of specific states than they do of the US population as a whole. For instance, African Americans comprise just more

4. Colombia, a unitary state, has a population that places it just below the median for federal systems.
5. Only Colombia has an area more than one-third that of the federal median. (Colombia's area is about 58% of the median federation).

than 12 percent of the US population, but more than 25 percent of the population of six states.[6] Native Americans comprise less than 1 percent of the US population, but more than 4.5 percent of seven states.[7] Hispanic/Latino Americans comprise about 12.5 percent of the US population, but more than 25 percent in four states.[8] Federalism permits minorities potentially to enjoy greater political influence over a state's politics than they might be able to exercise at the national level.

INSTITUTIONAL CHARACTERISTICS OF FEDERALISM

We have already indicated one necessary defining characteristic of federalism that is institutional in nature: the presence of a constitution that establishes dual levels of sovereign governments. Various institutional properties then follow as a means to put the principle of federalism into effect. Those institutional properties are:

1. independently elected subnational and national governmental institutions;
2. a constitution that guarantees sovereignty to the subnational governments and provides some distribution of responsibilities between national and subnational; and
3. institutions to represent subnational preferences within national political institutions.

The first two criteria were already discussed earlier, and shown in figure 4.1, where we indicated that in federal systems, voters elect both national and subunit governments, which exist in a "transactional" relationship with one another, rather than having the na-

6. Mississippi (37.1%), Louisiana (31.5%), Georgia (29.7%), Maryland (28.7%), South Carolina (28.3%), and Alabama (26.2%). In addition, African Americans comprise 54.4% of the population of the District of Columbia, but as we noted below, DC residents have limited political representation. Source: US Census Bureau (2006–2008 estimates).

7. Alaska (13.4%), New Mexico (9.3%), South Dakota (8.4%), Oklahoma (6.7%), Montana (6.1%), North Dakota (5.3%), and Arizona (4.5%). Source: US Census Bureau (2006–2008 estimates).

8. New Mexico (42.1%), California (32.4%), Texas (32.0%), and Arizona (25.3%). Source: US Census Bureau (2000 census).

tional government hold all sovereignty. Many unitary systems meet the first criterion (and some meet the third as well), but by definition they do not meet the second. If a given political system does not meet all three of these conditions, it is not federal.

In unitary states, then, only the national government is sovereign, and any policy responsibilities exercised by subnational governments are contingent on national law and, as a result, may legally be taken away by a change in national law. Similarly, in confederations, only the units are meaningfully sovereign, and the government of the confederation itself enjoys no direct democratic connection to voters in the broader confederation (whether directly or through being responsible to a democratically elected central legislature). One of the reasons unitary systems allow, at least in principle, the national government to take away local or provincial governments' policy-making responsibilities is not only that there is no constitutional guarantee of a division of power, but also that there is usually no mechanism to represent the preferences of subnational electorates, or the regional governments themselves, in the central policy-making institutions.

We now turn to the principal means by which such interests are represented in federal systems—through a second chamber. We already noted, with respect to figure 4.2, that bicameralism tends to be associated with countries that are large and especially those that are federal. We discuss bicameralism in greater length in chapter 7. Now we turn to a more detailed discussion of why federalism goes with bicameralism, and of variations among federal systems in the ways in which they structure their second chambers.

As noted in chapter 2, bicameralism with equal representation of the states in the second chamber was one of the great compromises of the US Constitution-drafting process. Whereas the smaller states favored the so-called New Jersey Plan, which would provide for equal representation of the states in a unicameral federal congress, the larger states favored the Virginia Plan, which called for representation based on each state's population. This division of preferences over institutional design is quite natural and rational, in that the delegates to the Constitutional Convention from smaller states feared that their states would be outvoted by a legislature dominated by representatives of larger states. On the other hand, larger states' delegates objected to equal representation, as it would dilute the representation of the big states. The so-called Great Compromise, crafted at the Constitutional Convention in 1787, was to have a bicameral legislature with one chamber based on each of these principles. Thus the United States has a House of Representatives (first chamber, also called the lower chamber) where each state has a number of representatives based on its population, and a Senate (second chamber, also called the upper chamber) where each state has an equal number of senators regardless of its population. In other words, representation for each state in the first chamber is approximately proportionate to population, while the second chamber over-represents the smaller states. Similar compromises are common in other federal systems, as we shall see.

All thirteen of our federal democracies are bicameral. While figure 4.2 shows that many unitary systems are also bicameral, as we shall see in more detail in chapter 7, there is a notable difference between bicameralism in federal and large unitary systems. The constituencies of second-chamber legislators tend to be drawn very differently in federal and unitary systems. The role of the second chamber in a federal system is to represent the subnational units, whether or not equally. None of our unitary bicameral systems has a second chamber with equal representation for provinces (or other units),[9] and many do not even have their subnational units and second-chamber constituencies coincide in any way. The equal representation of the states in the second chamber is, of course, the classic "federalist" compromise that we see in the United States. However, as we shall see shortly, not even all federal systems share this feature.

FEDERALISM AND FISCAL DECENTRALIZATION

One of the typical justifications for federalism is that it allows regional specialization in policy. Separate regional governments may

9. The Dominican Republic (a democracy not among our thirty-one countries) is among the rare unitary systems in which the subnational units are equally represented in a second chamber.

decide, through their own internal democratic processes, to provide different mixes of policies than do others. They may even compete with one another to attract business investment and citizens themselves, who may be drawn by a regional unit's specific mix of taxes, public services, and other policy characteristics. This kind of specialization and competition is less likely to be feasible in unitary states because the local governments have far less autonomy and most of their policy choices are significantly constrained by the national government.

A more immediate requirement for regional policy specialization than whether the system is federal or unitary is the availability of revenue. Almost any policy requires revenues to carry out, and countries vary widely on the share of revenue raised by the subnational levels, compared to the central government. In table 4.2 we see the various levels of government for twenty-six cases and the revenues they raise both as a function of the percent of GDP and what shares each level receives as a percentage. It is immediately evident that the degree of revenue centralization is closely related to the unitary-federal distinction. The median share of revenue raised by the central government is 93.22 percent in the seventeen unitary systems, and 78.74 percent in nine federal systems.[10] The shares in unitary systems range from 68.04 percent (Sweden) to 99.09 percent in the most centralized (Greece). Among the federal systems, the United States, at 66.32 percent of revenues raised by the central government, is below the median for federal systems but higher than the two most decentralized federal systems on the list: Canada (53.29 percent) and Switzerland (59.15 percent). Two of the federal systems in which the share of revenue raised by the central government is at or above the median, and thus more akin to the unitary systems, are also relatively new to the game of democratic federalism. Belgium and Spain were once unitary states. Belgium began a process of federalization only in the 1970s, and Spain somewhat later than that. In general, the strength of federalism is linked very closely to the ability of subunits to collect revenue as well

10. This difference of means easily meets standards of statistical significance.

Table 4.2. Tax revenue in twenty-six democracies (1990–2010 averages)

	As a percentage of GDP			Share		
	Central	State	Local	Central	State	Local
Unitary systems (17)						
Netherlands	39.05%		1.26%	96.87%		3.13%
France	38.78%		4.72%	89.15%		10.85%
Hungary	38.18%		1.86%	95.35%		4.65%
Italy	36.94%		4.63%	88.86%		11.14%
Czech Republic	35.86%		0.78%	97.87%		2.13%
Finland	34.98%		9.74%	78.22%		21.78%
United Kingdom	33.27%		1.55%	95.55%		4.45%
Denmark	33.18%		15.29%	68.45%		31.55%
Israel	33.12%		2.41%	93.22%		6.78%
Sweden	33.00%		15.50%	68.04%		31.96%
New Zealand	32.38%		2.01%	94.16%		5.84%
Poland	30.92%		3.60%	89.57%		10.43%
Greece	30.49%		0.28%	99.09%		0.91%
Portugal	28.85%		1.50%	95.06%		4.94%
Japan	20.04%		7.11%	73.81%		26.19%
Chile	18.59%		1.34%	93.28%		6.72%
Korea	18.36%		3.91%	82.44%		17.56%
Median	*33.12%*		*2.41%*	*93.22%*		*6.78%*
Federal systems (9)						
Belgium	40.39%	1.40%	2.07%	92.07%	3.19%	4.72%
Austria	38.72%	1.56%	2.22%	91.11%	3.67%	5.22%
Spain	26.45%	4.20%	2.94%	78.74%	12.50%	8.75%
Germany	25.61%	7.90%	2.80%	70.53%	21.76%	7.71%
Australia	22.61%	4.86%	0.93%	79.61%	17.11%	3.27%
Canada	18.44%	12.96%	3.20%	53.29%	37.46%	9.25%
United States	**18.08%**	**5.40%**	**3.78%**	**66.32%**	**19.80%**	**13.87%**
Switzerland	16.75%	6.90%	4.67%	59.15%	24.36%	16.49%
Mexico	16.16%	0.36%	0.18%	96.77%	2.16%	1.08%
Median	*22.61%*	*4.86%*	*2.80%*	*78.74%*	*17.11%*	*7.71%*

Note: Data were unavailable for the five excluded cases.

Source: OECD Fiscal Federalism Network, http://www.oecd.org/tax/federalism.

as their share of said revenue relative to the other portions of the country.

US FEDERALISM IN COMPARATIVE PERSPECTIVE

Even if the United States was the first federal system, its institutions and political practices are atypical in some respects. We now turn our attention to a comparison of US and other variants of federalism.

1. Equal representation of states with widely divergent populations. The principle of equal representation in the Senate is enshrined in the US Constitution. In fact, it is the only feature of American government that the Constitution's provision on amendments (Article V) explicitly says cannot be subject to amendment. If the units of a federation are not too disparate in size, equal representation may not be politically significant. However, if the largest state is very much bigger than the smallest, and the population is concentrated in one or a few states, then equal representation of states implies highly unequal representation of voters. Consider that the ratio of population size between the largest American state, California, and the smallest, Wyoming, was about 66 to 1 at the 2010 census. Yet in the Senate, their representation is, of course, 1 to 1, given that each has two senators. It is worth reiterating that this is precisely the intent of the federal bargain institutionalized in the Great Compromise for the original thirteen states—to have one chamber of Congress representing the states and another representing the population. Of course, in the House of Representatives (lower house), California, with fifty-three seats as of the 2010 census, and Wyoming, with one seat, are represented far more closely to their shares of the national population.[11] This disparity of popular representation is worth putting in both historical and cross-national perspective. Historically,

11. Nonetheless, even in the House, Wyoming remains over-represented, due to every state's guarantee of one representative no matter its population. California has 53 representatives; to give it the 70 that would be needed to provide a fully proportionate share would require a larger House. As we see in the chapter on legislatures, it was formerly the case that the US House size periodically increased; however, it has been fixed at 435 since 1910.

the ratio of largest to smallest states in the United States has increased greatly. It was only 12.7 to 1 when the Great Compromise was reached, or about 18 percent as disparate as it is in the early twenty-first century.

A good way to compare federations to one another and also to compare the United States of the early twenty-first century with that of the late eighteenth century is to construct an "effective number" of federal units by both population and Senate representation. We then can compare this effective number to the actual number of units. The effective number gives us a weighted index of how concentrated some quantity is. It weights the states' contribution to the index by their own shares, which is to say each share is squared. The squares are then summed, and the inverse (reciprocal) of this sum yields the "effective" number. The effective number, first introduced by Laakso and Taagepera (1979), is now a standard measure used by political scientists in analysis of party vote and seat shares, and we will use it in this way in chapter 5. To illustrate how the effective number works, consider a hypothetical federation consisting of three states with equal populations; for this federation, the effective number of states based on population is 3.0. If, instead, one of the states had two-thirds of the nation's population, another had 23 percent, and the smallest of the three had the remaining 10 percent, then the effective number of states would be only 1.97. The smaller effective number compared to the actual number indicates that the federation's population is concentrated, rather than equally distributed across the states.

We can perform the same calculation on states' shares of seats in a legislative chamber. Comparing the effective number of states by population with the actual number of states gives us a sense of how concentrated the population is across the units of the federation. Comparing the effective number of states in the Senate to the effective number by population gives us a clear idea of how closely Senate representation mirrors the distribution of the population across states. Throughout this discussion, we will refer to the calculation based on population as N_{fed}, signifying "effective number of units in the federation," and the calculation based on Senate representation as N_{sen}, or "effective number of units in the Senate."

Table 4.3. Actual and effective number of units in federal systems

Country	Number of units[a]	Effective number of units by population (N_{fed})	Effective number of units by seats in the second chamber (N_{sen})
United States	**50[b]**	**22.75**	**50.00**
Mexico	31[b]	18.38	30.58
India	28[b]	13.53	17.73
Brazil	26[b]	11.17	27.00
Switzerland	26	12.67	24.60
Argentina	23[b]	5.72	24.00
Spain	17	9.72	11.64
Germany	16	8.78	15.02
Canada	10+3	4.25	7.11
Austria	9	6.92	7.09
South Africa	9	6.98	9.00
Australia	6+1[b]	4.40	6.62
Belgium	3	2.22	2.00
Median	*17*	*8.78*	*15.02*

Notes:
[a] Indicated as number of states, provinces, or other principal units, plus number of other territories with any legislative representation (if greater than zero), but not including the capital territory, if any.
[b] Separate capital territory (all with legislative representation, except District of Columbia in the United States).

In table 4.3, we report the effective numbers of units in both the federation and its second chamber for each of the federal systems in this book. We can see immediately that the US population is quite concentrated, such that the effective number, N_{fed} (22.75) is less than half the actual number of states (50). The effective number of states in the Senate, N_{sen}, is, of course, 50, because every state is represented equally in the second chamber. The data from the other federal systems show that some federations have even more concentrated populations than the United States, notably Argentina, where the effective number of provinces (5.72) is less than a quarter the actual number (23). Like the United States, Argentina represents its states equally in its senate, as can be seen by a figure for N_{sen} that is equivalent to the actual number of units (provinces plus a special capital district). Brazil's concentration of population is similar to that of the United States, and likewise its states (and capital district) are equally represented in their senate. Argentina and Brazil are the only federations in the set of countries considered in this book that have second-chamber representation of the population more unequal than the United States has.[12] Only Switzerland comes close among the industrialized states, though in Switzerland some of the smallest cantons are actually considered "half-cantons" and thus have less representation in the upper chamber than the full cantons.

On the other hand, several other federations have an effective number of units in their second chambers that are much closer to the effective number of units in the federation. What this means is that, contrary to the concept the founders of the US Constitution agreed to in the Great Compromise, these federations provide fewer seats in their second chambers to the smallest states than to the largest. Consider the example of India, where the effective number of states in the federation is less than half the actual number, similar to the United States. The ratio of largest to smallest states in India is, however, vastly greater than in the United States, at more than 300 to 1. Rather than provide equal representation to these highly unequal states, Indian second-chamber representation is somewhat proportional to state population, ranging from twelve to eighty-six members per state, resulting in a value for N_{sen} that is actually closer to N_{fed} than it is to the actual number—the opposite pattern from that seen in the United States. Several other federations provide second-chamber representation that is even closer to the units' shares of the

12. Argentina and Brazil, but especially the former, also stand out in providing their smaller states over-representation in the first chamber as well, whereas the United States comes very close to providing perfect proportionality of House seats to state populations. See Samuels and Snyder 2001 for a discussion of malapportionment in first chambers.

population than India does. Austria and Belgium have almost perfect proportionality of unit representation in the second chamber.

Two federations deviate somewhat from the principle of representing their units in the second chamber. In Mexico, the senate has three senators for each of the thirty-one states and the capital district, thus resembling the US (and Argentinean and Brazilian) models of equal representation. However, the Mexican senate also has another thirty-two national senators, or one-fourth of the total.[13] This provision leads to a value of N_{sen} (30.58) that is slightly less than the number of units (31).[14] In Spain, some senators are directly elected within the provinces, but these are not the primary units of the federation.[15] The primary units are the Autonomous Communities, most of which consist of more than one province and have additional senators, appointed by the parliament of the Community.[16]

The federal systems can be compared at a glance in figure 4.3, which graphs the ratio of actual units to N_{fed} on the horizontal axis, while the vertical axis shows the ratio N_{sen} to N_{fed}. By graphing our data in this way, we are able to see at a glance how the United States

13. These are elected in a single national district, proportional to political parties' shares of the nationwide votes (i.e., the sum of all votes cast for senatorial tickets in each of the states).

14. For Mexico, we calculated Nsen as follows: First, we calculated the percentage contribution of each unit to the election of national senators (each unit's share of the national population multiplied by 31. Then we added this result for each state to the number of state-based senators (always 3) to arrive at an "effective" number of senators for each state, which ranges from 7.3 for the largest state (Estado de México) to 3.14 for the smallest (Baja California Sur). This effective number of senators for each state then serves as the basis (out of the total 128) for calculating the effective number of units in the senate.

15. The Spanish constitution does not identify Spain as a federation; however, it qualifies in every definitional aspect that we employ in the chapter. The same can be said for South Africa.

16. Provinces predate the establishment of Autonomous Communities. Therefore, whereas Spain's federation would be classified as "holding together" in Stepan's sense, the provinces engaged in a process of "coming together" to establish the larger Communities that form the basis of federalism in Spain.

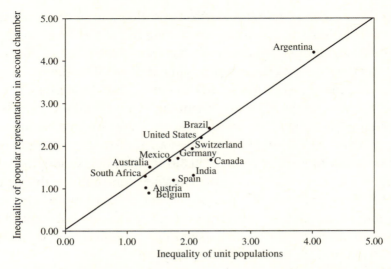

Fig. 4.3. Relationship between population concentration and second-chamber representation of units in federal systems
Key: The horizontal axis graphs the ratio of actual units to N_{fed}; the vertical axis shows the ratio N_{sen} to N_{fed}.

compares to other federations in two of the core features of such systems: how equal the units are to one another in population, and how equal they are in representation. The closer a country comes to the upper right of the space, the more it offers equal representation despite highly unequal populations of its units. The more it is in the lower left, the more the federation approaches equal-sized units. Any case that falls on the diagonal line has adhered to the institutional principle of the Great Compromise: unit equality in the second chamber, regardless of population. (Those that are above the diagonal are those that have capital districts that are also represented, which we return to later.) The federations that are below the diagonal are those in which the units are not equally represented.

At a glance, we can see that Argentina employs equal representation in its senate despite having a population that is highly concentrated in just a few of its provinces, and we can also immediately identify a set of federations that have not adhered to the equal-representation principle of the Great Compromise—including Canada and India and the others that fall well below the diagonal line.

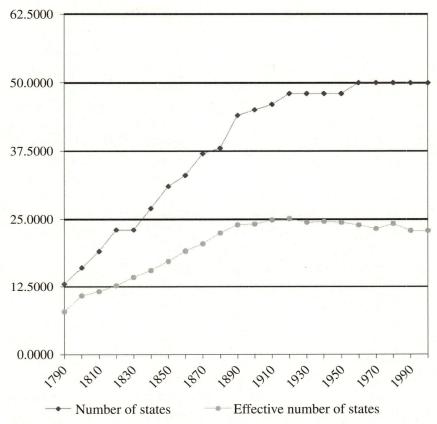

Fig. 4.4. Actual and effective number of US states over time

Only Brazil and Switzerland join the United States and Argentina as federations with a ratio of actual to effective number of states greater than 1.75 in which the ratio, N_{sen} to N_{fed}, is likewise greater than 1.75. In other words, these four federations combine unequal-sized states with equal representation of those states in the second chamber. The other federations either have much less skewed population distributions or more proportionality of unit representation in the second chamber, or both.

As we noted, this equal representation of unequal states is one of the immutable features of the US Constitution, which raises the question of whether the framers who compromised on this fixed equality of states in the Senate possibly could have imagined how much the divergence of state populations would grow over time. As we can see in figure 4.4, the gap between the actual and effective number of states has indeed grown significantly over time. At the first federal census, the effective number of states in the union (7.9) was only about 40 percent less than the actual number (13). Since 1960, the effective number has been no greater than half the actual number. Since 1980 the effective number has actually fallen somewhat, as the largest states have grown much faster than the smallest ones. It is interesting that equal representation of widely divergent state populations has not become a political issue in the United States. The principles of American federalism, including equal representation in the Senate, are deeply rooted in American politics, but Senate representation could emerge as an issue in the future as the disparity of populations continues to expand, as it almost certainly will do.[17] The original balance at the founding, when the idea of equal representation of the states was set into the Constitution, becomes more unrepresentative over time. As we have seen here, some other federations—notably Canada and India—trade off to some degree the "representation of units" principle in order to approach more closely the "one person, one vote" principle of democracy.

   2. Absence of representation of the capital and other territories. In some federations, the national capital is located within its own territory, rather than within one of the states or provinces. For instance, the US capital, Washington, is contained within the District of Columbia, rather than within either Virginia or Maryland, the two states that ceded territory to create the capital district. Five of our other federal systems also have special capital districts: Argentina, Australia, Brazil, India, and Mexico. However, the United States is unique in not granting the residents of its capital territory voting representation in the national legislature. The residents of Washington, DC, have a *nonvoting* delegate in the House of Representatives and neither voice nor vote in the Senate. Thus DC residents are

17. The most important of the Founding Fathers with respect to the design of US institutions, James Madison, was originally an advocate of representation of the states according to their share of the national population, as we discussed in ch. 2.

deprived of representation despite being more numerous than the residents of Wyoming, and being close in number to those of Alaska and North Dakota.[18] The matter of the federal capital's nonrepresentation in Congress is sporadically an issue in the United States and is typically framed as a question of whether the District of Columbia should be granted statehood.[19] Among all of our federations, however, the US capital has the smallest percentage of its population in the national capital, by far. Only 0.2 percent of the US population lives in Washington, DC. The next lowest shares for federations that have special districts for their capitals are 1.2 percent for Brasília (Distrito Federal), Brazil, and 1.6 percent for Canberra, Australian Capital Territory.[20] The smallness of Washington, DC, relative to the nation's population as a whole may explain why the issue of representation for its residents does not loom larger in the national debate.

Similarly, many federations have other territories that are not granted the status of a state or province, often because they are noncontiguous or otherwise remote from the population centers of the nation, sparsely populated, inhabited largely by indigenous groups, or some combination of these factors.[21] Examples include the Northwest

18. Only since 1964 have DC residents been entitled to vote for president.

19. Another option that is also discussed is the opposite of statehood: retrocession of the land north of the Potomac River back to Maryland save for a very small district in and around the National Mall where most of the buildings of the federal government reside. Such a process would allow the currently disenfranchised citizens living in the District of Columbia to vote for House and Senate members and in presidential elections as citizens of Maryland. There is precedence for such a move, as the land originally ceded to the District by Virginia was returned to Virginia, including Alexandria, in 1847 (basically all the territory originally given to the District south of the Potomac). A variation of this option was proposed in Congress in 2004, which would have granted citizens of the District voting rights as part of Maryland without formal retrocession (H.R. 3709: District of Columbia Voting Rights Restoration Act of 2004).

20. At the other end of the scale, about 38% of Argentina's population lives in Buenos Aires.

21. The United States is unique among our federations in having noncontiguous units (excluding islands close to the mainland) that are fully incorporated into the federation: Alaska and Hawaii.

Territories, Nunavut, and Yukon in Canada; Northern Territory in Australia; and six territories in India, including the Andaman and Nicobar Islands. In many federations, some such territories have legislative representation.[22] However, no US territory has either a voting representative in the House of Representatives or any delegate to the Senate or a vote in presidential elections (although some of them are included in the major parties' presidential nomination processes). US territories include the Commonwealth of Puerto Rico, which at more than 3.7 million residents, is larger than almost half (twenty-four) of the states (and only slightly smaller than Oklahoma).[23] US territories also include several smaller units: American Samoa, Guam, the Northern Mariana Islands, and the US Virgin Islands.[24] The largest of these, Guam, has just shy of 160,000 residents.[25]

3. Concurrent national-subnational elections versus staggered calendars. Because both subnational and national elections must be held in federal systems, the question of the electoral calendar arises. If many states hold their own legislative or executive elections in between elections for the national legislative or executive elections, the state elections may serve as informal bellwethers of support for the national parties. If, on the other hand, all states hold their elections at the same time as national elections, obviously this

22. In Australia, e.g., the Federal Capital and Northern Territories have half the representation of a state in the federal senate.

23. Based on the 2010 US Census.

24. Surprisingly, given a lack of representation in US federal elective institutions for these territories, the integration of the party system extends to all of them except Puerto Rico. While local parties or independents are prevalent in the other territories, Democrats and Republicans contest territorial elections.

25. Each of the US territories listed has a nonvoting delegate to the House of Representatives, as entitled under a federal law that mandates such a delegate to any territory with more than five thousand residents. Federal law also allows any territory with more than sixty thousand residents to apply for statehood. Each listed territory meets that threshold as well, but given that all, other than Puerto Rico, are much smaller than the smallest existing state, these territories would be unlikely to be considered seriously for statehood. The question of statehood for Puerto Rico, on the other hand, is very much a live issue, as is the opposite position: full independence.

bellwether phenomenon can't exist; moreover, there may be less political distinctiveness of the two levels of the federation. Whether
unification of the national and subnational calendars favors the na-
tionalization of regional politics or the regionalization of national
politics depends on a factor we discuss subsequently, which is the
nature of the party system. First, however, let us see how the United
States compares to other federal systems in the extent to which national and subnational elections occur separately.

Our federal systems vary substantially on this dimension. In the
United States, of the forty-eight states that have governors with four-
year terms, thirty-five elect their governors at the midterm of the
federal president's term (2006, 2010, and so on). Ten elect their governors at the same time as the president (2008, 2012, and so on). The
remaining four hold their gubernatorial elections in odd-numbered
years: Kansas and Louisiana in the year before a presidential election, New Jersey and Virginia in the year after. Two states, New
Hampshire and Vermont, have two-year gubernatorial terms with
elections both in presidential-election years and at the presidential
midterm. As for legislative elections, because all states and the US
Congress hold elections biennially, federal and state legislative elections always coincide, except in the four states that have elections
for state offices in odd-numbered years.

The electoral calendar in the United States is thus somewhere
in the intermediate range in terms of the unification of state elections, both with one another and with national elections. The highest degree of unification would be if all national and state or provincial elections occurred on the same day. Brazil is the one case
with complete unification of the federal and state electoral calendar. Every four years, voters vote for federal president and congress
members and their state governor and legislative assembly on the
same date.[26] At the opposite extreme, every subnational unit could
hold its elections on its own schedule, never coinciding with either
another unit or with the national elections. This pattern is typical of
Canada, where election dates rarely coincide. It is approximated in

26. Elections for local governments are held on a common day throughout
Brazil, but separately from other elections.

Germany, where between federal elections in 1998 and 2002, fifteen of the states held state elections on fourteen different dates, while one[27] held elections concurrently with the two federal elections. India and Mexico also have distinct calendars, though often with several states having elections concurrent with the federal elections or on interim dates on which several states vote. In Spain, most of the autonomous communities have their elections on a single date separate from federal elections, but a few—notably the Basque and Catalonian regions (the largest)—have their own dates. Thus there is a wide variation among our federal systems in the degree to which their electoral calendars are unified, with the United States closer to the unified end of the spectrum, but not the most unified.

4. Integration of the party system. The integration of the party system refers to the extent to which the same parties compete across the federation, in both national and subnational elections. Parties may vary in their strength across the subnational units, but if the party system is integrated, the same parties run and win representation in both national and subnational legislative elections in all states or provinces. The United States is quite unusual among federal systems in this respect.[28] The Democratic and Republican Parties contest elections in all states, and in no state is one of the parties so dominant that there has not been recent alternation in its state governorship. In some of the very small states that have only one congressional representative, the same party might regularly win the seat, but the other party typically contests it. Moreover, distinct state parties are very rare in the United States. Only Alaska has a distinct party—the Alaskan Independence Party (AIP)—which has been competitive in several consecutive state elections. The AIP even elected its candidate, Walter Hickel, to the state governorship in 1990. The only other states that recently have had governors who were nominated by neither the Democratic nor the Republican Party are Connecticut (Lowell Weicker, nonpartisan, 1990) and Minnesota (Jesse "The Body" Ventura, Reform Party, later Independence Party,

---

27. Mecklenburg-Pomerania.

28. The party system has been less integrated in the past—especially before the Civil War, when there were distinct subsystems.

1998). These are the only recent exceptions to the rule that the US party system is fully integrated at the national and state levels.

This high level of integration is not found in most other federal systems, although some, such as Australia, Germany, and Mexico, come close. In each of these countries the party system is highly integrated, in that the same major national parties contest elections in all states (though all are not necessarily competitive in all states). Australia and Germany each have at least one party that competes only in one or a few states—the Christian Social Union in Bavaria, Germany, and the National Party in some Australian states—but in these cases the party is in an essentially permanent alliance with one of the national parties in federal elections.

Spain and India represent the most unintegrated party system in our set of federal democracies. In Spain, there are two national parties (the Socialist and Popular Parties) that are competitive in most of the regions, while in India, one party (Congress) is national in scope and another major party (Bharatiya Janata) competes in most states. However, both countries have numerous parties that are specific to a single subnational unit, and often these regional parties are major parties in their own state or regional assembly. In six of the nineteen autonomous communities of Spain, at least one regional party also obtains representation in the national parliament; frequently, one of the Basque or Catalan regional parties will provide support in parliament for a minority cabinet of one of the two big national parties (see chapter 8). Many state parties are represented in India's national parliament as well, and in both countries these parties often hold the balance of power between the two major national parties, effectively determining which one of them will be in government.[29]

The Canadian party system lies somewhere in between the highly integrated US and unintegrated Indian and Spanish examples. The three major national parties—Conservative, New Democratic, and Liberal—compete in all provinces, and except in Quebec, they are

29. Both India and Spain are parliamentary systems, though in India large coalitions often contain several state parties, while in Spain it is typical for a single-party minority government to form, with regional parties offering support from outside the cabinet.

the only parties that regularly win seats in the federal parliament from any province. However, in addition to Quebec parties,[30] there is a Saskatchewan Party that has formed the government in that province twice and a Yukon Party that is active in that territory. Very small province-specific parties exist in a few other provinces. None of these parties competes in federal elections.[31] In addition, even though it was for decades only the third party nationally, the New Democratic Party has long been one of the two major parties in several provinces. Thus there is a high degree of regional party diversity in Canada, though more party-system integration than we see in India and Spain.

Whether a party system is integrated or not matters for several reasons. For example, distinct subnational parties may have a stronger incentive than subnational chapters of national parties to seek to extract resources from the center as a means to build their own political bases. In more integrated party systems, on the other hand, the national scope of the parties implies a balance of interest within the parties in seeking to please national and subnational constituencies. It is also typical in federations with integrated party systems for units governed by a given party to affect the national reputation of the party and even to serve as recruitment grounds for national candidates who may run on the claimed success of their policy implementation in a state or province. The integration of the party system is also likely related to the extent of separatist tendencies within a federation. For example, Canada's province of Quebec has held two referenda on separation from Canada, though they were defeated. Spain has an active and violent separatist movement based in the Basque territories, as well as movements seeking greater autonomy in various other regions. India has numerous separatist movements. Of course, these countries do not have separatist movements because

30. Parti Québécois in provincial elections and Bloc Québécois in federal elections. The latter party lost most of its seats in the 2011 election, although it remains active.

31. Additionally, in the Northwest Territories and Nunavut territory, there are no parties in provincial elections, but the national parties do contest the single seat each territory has in the federal parliament.

their party systems are not integrated; in fact, the causal path may well run in the opposite direction. Nonetheless, if distinct subnational parties gain the upper hand over national parties, the federal balance may become more difficult to sustain in the face of these centrifugal pressures.

CONCLUSIONS

Federalism provides an arena of regional political competition and policy formation that is distinct from the arena of national politics. As we saw in this chapter, just fewer than half of our thirty-one democracies are federal. The federal systems tend to have a lower share of revenue collection in the hands of the central government, which at least potentially provides an opportunity for distinct jurisdictions to engage in experimentation and competition in policy in a way that is less feasible in a unitary state. We saw that federal systems are always bicameral, with the second chamber structured to represent the units of the federation. Nonetheless, the United States model of equal representation of the subnational units in the second chamber is not followed by all federal democracies, with several providing fewer seats for the smallest units in order to compromise the federalist principle of unit representation somewhat to approximate more closely the democratic principle of one person, one vote. These are contradictory principles in any federation that has states of widely divergent populations, and all federal systems need to strike some balance in them in order to be both federal and democratic.

We saw that the degree of integration of the party system and the coordination of the electoral calendar are significant for the degree of distinctiveness of subnational politics. Those principles of federalism that emphasize the sovereignty of the separate units are most strongly manifested with separate calendars of elections and relatively unintegrated party systems, such as in Canada and India. Those principles of federalism that stress the coordination of the separate units within one national polity are strongest with concurrent elections and integrated party systems. It is perhaps somewhat surprising, then, that the United States has one of the most coordinated electoral calendars and the most integrated party systems, given the primacy placed on the states in American politics. Recall that the United States has one of the lowest shares of central-government revenue collection (though not as low as Canada), as well as equal representation of highly unequally sized states in a powerful "federalist" second chamber. How can the United States have all of these decentralizing tendencies despite electoral coordination and party-system integration? The answer probably lies in distinctive features of US politics that we will discuss in later chapters. For instance, US parties are notably weaker and more locally organized than parties in most other democracies in this book, a product partly of the presidential form of government and partly of the way legislators are elected. None of our other democracies combines a presidential executive with single-member district legislative elections and federalism, as we shall see. In the context of all of these institutional features that tend to fragment political power, perhaps what is surprising is that the party system is so integrated. In this context, it could be that without coordination of the electoral calendar there would be much less coordination of states' distinct interests at the federal level than what we see in practice. On the other hand, the much stronger parties associated with parliamentary democracy in countries such as Canada, Germany, and India might threaten subnational sovereignty and the development of distinct regional parties were it not for the separate electoral calendars that allow state politics to remain a mostly separate arena even in the context of strong parties. This discussion thus highlights the ways in which different components of the larger political system fit together, and sets the stage for us to continue our discussion of these other components.

CHAPTER 5

ELECTIONS AND ELECTORAL SYSTEMS

E xcept in very small communities, democracy necessarily means *representative* democracy in which elected officials make decisions on behalf of the people. How are these representatives elected? This indispensable task in representative democracies is performed by the electoral system—the set of methods for converting citizens' preferences into decision-making authority for members of the legislative, executive, and, sometimes, judicial branches of government. In other words, the electoral system, that is, the rules used to translate votes into elected office, is *the* fundamental basis of the principal-agent relationship between voters and politicians. First, it is the means by which the authority of voters is transferred to politicians, making them the agents of voters. Second, it is the method by which politicians are later held accountable to the voters, since elected politicians and their parties must regularly return to ask for reaffirmation (or suffer rejection) at election time (see figure 1.1).

While constitution writing is the most macro-level manifestation of political engineering that we have, one of the key areas within a given system that is directly amenable to specific legislative changes (and sometimes constitutional ones) is with electoral rules. Changing an electoral system is not an easy task, given that in a democratic setting such changes usually require the acquiescence of persons elected by the existing electoral rules and therefore predisposed for self-interested reasons to oppose change. Still, as Sartori (1968) noted, "Electoral systems are the most specific manipulable instrument of politics." He did not mean they are easy to change, but that the dimensions of a country's political culture and issues are not things that can be "engineered," while the electoral system can be.

Later on in this chapter, we will discuss some cases in which established democracies did change their electoral systems in fundamental ways. As we will see below, the nature of the electoral rules can have specific and important effects on the behavior of both voters and politicians and therefore on the composition and functioning of government.

INSTITUTIONAL OPTIONS

What were the options open to the Philadelphia conventioneers in regards to this issue of elections? On the one hand, the exact question of an *electoral system* (that is, a set of rules used to determine how seats become votes) was not a major topic of conversation (or, indeed, much of a conversation at all) in Philadelphia. However, we can still examine basic theoretical options that exist before considering how the United States compares to our other cases. There were two key choices that had to be made. The first was between *direct democracy* and *representative democracy.* The second was about the electoral system itself.

A Republic Not a Democracy?

It is sometimes stated that the United States is a republic and not a democracy, and often *The Federalist Papers* are used to back up that claim.[1] However, what does the claim mean? First, it is important to understand that a *republic,* in its most basic definition, deals with a government that does not have a monarch.[2] Hence, when the US

---

1. Indeed, Dahl notes that Madison himself is responsible for much of the confusion on this count, as the republic vs. democracy "distinction had no basis in prior history" before Madison gave the words distinct definitions in *The Federalist Papers* (Dahl 1998: 16). For a more extensive discussion, see appendix A of Dahl 2001. Of course, any discussion of this topic has to take into account the historical evolution of the standards by which democracy is judged. See also our discussion in ch. 3.

2. Even more fundamentally, we can look back to Plato's *Republic,* which focused on the notion of government that governed on behalf of the common interest, rather than the private, personal interests of the ruler.

Constitution states in Article IV, Section 4 that "The United States shall guarantee to every State in this Union a Republican Form of Government," it means that there will be no establishment of a hereditary ruling class and that the national government would make sure that was the case in the states as well. Second, the most significant issue worth underscoring is the fact that it is a non sequitur to claim that a republic and a democracy are distinct regime types, because the words are, for our purposes, roughly synonymous.

Indeed, if we are going to base this discussion on the words of Madison, we need only turn to *Federalist 39* to see that Madison himself was concerned more with definitions than with what label was being used. In that essay, he listed a number of states (Holland, Venice, Poland, and England) that had been called "republics," and yet he notes that "These examples, which are nearly as dissimilar to each other as to a genuine republic, show the extreme inaccuracy with which the term has been used in political disquisitions" (Madison, Hamilton, and Jay 1987: 254). In the same essay, Madison goes on to define a republic as "a government which derives all its power directly or indirectly from the great body of the people" (255)—a description that fits the general parameters of the democratic model we laid out in chapter 1.

If we look at the juxtaposition of the specific terms *democracy* and *republic* within *The Federalist Papers,* we see that the fundamental issue had its origins in the distinction between direct and indirect (or representative) democracy, that is, do the people govern directly themselves, or do they do so indirectly, via elected representatives? A good place to start such a discussion is to note that in the Greek, the word *demos* can mean "the people," and the word *kratos* means "rule," so that when the words are combined (*demos* + *kratos*) we get the English word democracy.[3] At its simplest form, democracy means rule by the people. Of course, the reality is that there is little

3. For a more complete discussion see Blackwell 2003: 3 (available online at http://www.stoa.org/projects/demos/article_democracy_overview?page=3&greek Encoding=). Blackwell also provides a detailed description of democracy as it existed in ancient Athens, which differs significantly from our contemporary understanding.

simple about such a process. Who, for example, qualifies as part of "the people," and how do they rule?

At least in theory it is possible for a group of persons to directly govern themselves. A small enough system could function by having all its members come together to discuss and vote on the direction of that system. However, in larger systems (such as countries), such a process is a practical impossibility. It is true that in some of our cases there are limited amounts of direct democracy, that is, wherein the people are directly consulted on governing decisions. The best example would be Switzerland, where it is possible that a given law could be presented to the populace for an up or down vote. However, this is a rare mechanism, and even in the Swiss case is not one in which the people directly govern on a day-to-day basis. So if a country is to be governed by the demos, but not directly, what is the alternative? It is, as noted at the beginning of this chapter, via representative democracy, wherein the voters choose, on a regular basis, those who get to make the authoritative decisions for said country.

How did Madison see this dichotomy? In *Federalist 14* he wrote, "In a democracy the people meet and exercise the government in person; in a republic they assemble and administer it by their representatives and agents" (Madison, Hamilton, and Jay 1987: 141).[4] As such, it can readily be seen that what we call "democracy" in the current era is not the same thing that Madison was referring to in the late eighteenth century. Rather, since the advent of the first wave of democratization (as discussed in chapter 3), the notion of democratic governance has been one of representative democracy. Hence we can see that what Madison called a "republic" is synonymous, as a general category, with the contemporary notion of representative democracy (which we typically just call "democracy"). To actually have such a system requires a process by which those representatives are chosen, and kept responsible to, the citizenry. This fact leads us to the next question: What electoral system do we choose?

A key fact about the word *democracy* that is worth keeping in mind is that the word, as Dahl wrote, "refers to both an ideal and an actuality" (1998: 26). Any discussion of democracy in the United States (or really anywhere) has to keep in mind this tension between

---

4. See also *Federalist 10* in Madison, Hamilton, and Jay 1987: 126.

ideal and reality (not to mention conflicting visions of what the ideal ought to resemble).

Choosing an Electoral System

As noted earlier, the Philadelphia conventioneers did not discuss electoral rules, per se, but did assume that members of the House of Representatives would be selected by popular vote. This fit Madison's notion of a republic, from *Federalist 39*, that this part of the government was to be chosen directly by the people.[5] The exact process was left to the states to determine. The lack of a serious debate over the electoral system of the early United States likely owes itself to the fact that the country was entering essentially uncharted territory. In any democracy founded in the contemporary era, electoral-system choice is a prominent feature of the debate. Indeed, in some long-standing democracies, notably Japan and New Zealand, wholesale "reengineering" of the electoral system has taken place as recently as the mid-1990s; Italy had two major changes between 1990 and 2006, and some other counties have undertaken smaller but still significant changes to their electoral systems.

The room for potential variation within electoral systems is vast,[6] but the most fundamental choice is between two broad options: *majoritarian* and *proportional* systems. This distinction reflects two fundamentally different principles regarding what the role of elections is meant to be: (1) Majoritarian systems reflect the premise that elections should produce clear winners and losers, and advantage large parties over smaller ones; (2) proportional systems reflect the premise that all parties, small as well as large, should have a percentage of seats in the legislature roughly equal to their percentages of the votes. The United States is, as we shall see, among a minority of our democracies that use majoritarian systems. Before comparing

5. Of course, the rest were to be chosen indirectly: the Senate was to be chosen by state legislatures, the president via the Electoral College, and the Supreme Court via presidential appointment and Senate approval.

6. An extensive literature has developed on this topic and includes Diamond and Plattner 2006, Farrell 2011, Gallagher and Mitchell 2005, Lijphart 1994, Norris 1997, Taagepera 2007, and Taagepera and Shugart 1989.

the countries on the systems they use, however, it is necessary to introduce just a bit more detail about how these basic systems work, as well as other types of electoral system.

Most majoritarian electoral systems start with *single-seat districts,* meaning that each legislator is elected from his or her own district. One means of determining the winner in such districts, as in the US House,[7] is by *plurality.* This means the winner is the candidate with the most votes, even if that candidate has less than half the total votes cast.[8] There are other types of majoritarian systems, as we shall see, but the plurality system in single-seat districts is the most common.

In proportional systems, on the other hand, districts contain more than one seat, and those seats are usually allocated not immediately to individual candidates but first to *lists* of candidates. Each party (or alliance of parties) submits a list, and a mathematical formula is applied to the votes cast for competing lists in order to establish a number of seats for each party that corresponds closely to its percentage of the votes cast in the district. Once the number of seats each party has won has been determined, then parties that have won seats elect candidates in order off their respective lists.[9]

The most important factor affecting how proportional the allocation of seats to parties will be is the district magnitude, abbreviated M, which is how many seats there are per district. As we noted earlier, most majoritarian systems use single-seat districts, which means $M=1$. However, in order to have proportional representation (PR), it must be the case that $M>1$, that is, that the system uses multiseat districts in order to make it possible to divide the seats in a district among two or more parties. In general, the higher the M, the more proportional the result. Box 5.1 shows how both magnitude and

7. In most states, although there are a few exceptions, such as Georgia, which requires an absolute majority.

8. This system is also known variously as "first past the post" (FPTP) or "winner take all."

9. This may be done either from "closed" lists, in which the party has preordered the list, or the candidates on the list may be ordered according to "preference votes" cast for them within the list. This is a distinction that will not concern us further here. For details, see Shugart 2005.

BOX 5.1. PROPORTIONAL REPRESENTATION AND DISTRICT MAGNITUDE

Scholars have frequently noted that a critical factor in the degree of proportionality of proportional representation (PR) systems is district magnitude–the number of seats elected from a district. Regardless of which of several mathematical formulas for PR is used, the general rule is that higher district magnitude promotes greater proportionality. Thus one of the main factors promoting lower proportionality of some PR systems is the use of small districts, as in the case of Spain (where the average district has around seven seats, although a few are much larger) or Chile (where every district elects only two).

Here we describe the workings of one of the most common of several PR formulas and demonstrate how district magnitude affects proportionality. The formula we will use is called D'Hondt, after the Belgian mathematician who invented it in late the nineteenth century. D'Hondt works as follows: First, arrange the parties by their vote totals and determine which is the largest. This party gets the first seat (of course). Then divide its votes by two. See if this party's votes are still greater, even after dividing by two, than those of the second largest party. If they are, then the largest party also gets the second seat. If not, then the second seat goes to the second party. The process continues, with the general rule that at each stage of the count, always divide the votes of the party that just received a seat by $s + 1$, where s is the number of seats it has won so far. Continue until all M seats have been allocated.

Let us take a simple example in which there are 100 voters and five parties (labeled A through E); the largest has 38 votes, the second 31, and the remaining parties have 17, 9, and 5, respectively. Table 5.1 demonstrates the process of allocating seats under D'Hondt, with the numbers in parentheses indicating the number of the seats allocated across all parties at each step.

Table 5.1. How D'Hondt works (and illustrating how magnitude matters)

Divisor	Party A	Party B	Party C	Party D	Party E
1	38 (1)	31 (2)	17 (4)	9 (9)	5 (18)
2	19 (3)	15.5 (5)	8.5 (10)	4.5	2.5
3	12.7 (6)	10.3 (7)	5.7 (15)	3	
4	9.5 (8)	7.75 (11)	4.25	2.25	
5	7.6 (12)	6.2 (14)	3.4		
6	6.3 (13)	5.17 (17)			
7	5.4 (16)	4.43			

Table 5.1. (*continued*)

M=3	2 (66.7%)	1 (33.3%)	0	0	0
M=9	4 (44.4%)	3 (33.3%)	1 (11.1%)	1 (11.1%)	0
M=18	7 (38.8%)	6 (33.3%)	3 (16.7%)	1 (5.6%)	1 (5.6%)

As we can see, party A wins the first seat, because it has the most votes. If M=1, that is, if we have a single-seat district system, we are done! Thus D'Hondt reduces to the plurality rule if there is only one seat. However, if M>1, we need to divide party A's votes by two (s+1, where s=1). Now, to allocate the second seat, see if party A's votes, after division, remain larger than those of party B. Clearly they do not, as party B has 31 percent of the vote, whereas 38/2 = 19. So party B wins the second seat, and its votes are divided by two. (This result, each of the two largest parties winning one seat, is typical of the two-seat districts used in Chile.)

For a third seat, we need to see who has more votes at this stage: the third party (C) or either of the two parties that won its first seat already (A and B). As the table shows, party A has 19 votes remaining, which is more than party C (17 votes), so the third seat in the district goes to party A. Now party A's votes will be divided by three, because it has won two seats. The process continues until we have filled all seats in the district.

At the bottom of the table, the seat totals for each party are indicated for three hypothetical district magnitudes: 3, 9, and 18. Also indicated, in parentheses, are the percentages of seats for each party that won a seat, which can be compared directly to their votes (out of 100). It is immediately apparent that when M=3, the result is not very proportional at all, because the largest party has won two-thirds of the seats in the district despite less than 40 percent of the votes. Yet this is considered a PR system; after all, if M=1, meaning plurality rule, party A would have won 100 percent of the seats. Thus splitting three seats 2 to 1 among the two largest parties is indeed relatively proportional, with the low district magnitude being the limiting factor.

If district magnitude is increased to 9, it is immediately evident that proportionality increases. Now the largest party has 44.4 percent of the seats, which means it is still over-represented, but much less so; a total of four parties now split the seats, meaning many more voters are represented.

Finally, when M=18, each of the five parties wins at least one seat, and the over-representation of party A is reduced to a small degree (38.8 percent of seats on 38 percent of votes).

This example demonstrates clearly how district magnitude shapes proportional-ity: With more seats allocated in a district, seat percentages more closely reflect vote percentages. By the same token, reducing district magnitude advantages the largest parties, and making it as small as it can get means that only the one largest party wins any representation, giving us the plurality system in a single-seat district.

While invented by a Belgian mathematician for the purpose of allocating seats in a district to parties, the identical formula was actually invented earlier by Thomas Jefferson. The difference is that Jefferson invented it for the purpose of determining how many seats each of the US states would send to the House of Representatives, based on states' populations. Likewise, Daniel Webster created his own system for seat allocations, and it was the same as another divisor-based electoral formula, the Sainte-Laguë method (which uses different divisors than D'Hondt but functions that same basic way as the process outlined in table 5.1). Over the years, both the Jefferson and Webster methods have been used to allocate seat distributions for the US House of Representatives,[a] which demonstrates that while, as we have stressed in this chapter, the founders of the US Constitution did not consider the question of different electoral systems for distributing seats to parties, they did encounter the mathematically identi-cal puzzle of apportioning seats to states.

NOTE

a. Currently, the United States uses yet another divisor method, the Huntington-Hill method, to allocate seats. The Hamilton-Vinson method has also been used. For more information, see "The History of Apportionment in America," at http://www.ams.org/samplings/feature-column/fcarc-apportion2, as well as "The House of Representatives Apportionment Formula: An Analy-sis of Proposals for Change and Their Impact on States," at http://www.fas.org/sgp/crs/misc/R41382.pdf.

one common mathematical formula used in PR systems work (the D'Hondt method in table 5.1). Other factors that limit proportional-ity are *thresholds,* which define a minimum percentage of votes a party must win in order to obtain seats, or, less commonly, *bonus* provisions, which automatically give the largest party or alliance extra seats beyond their proportional share.

We have so far sketched out the basics of plurality and propor-tional systems. We now consider briefly some other types of systems, some of which are used for some offices in the United States, as well as for the national legislature in some other countries. Each of these is described in more detail in the appendix to this chapter; we offer only a general sketch here. First, a majoritarian system might be designed in such a way as to make it likely that the winner will have an actual majority (that is, more than half) of the votes, instead of only a plurality. There are different ways to do this. One is to require a second round (a "runoff") in case no candidate obtained a majority in the first round of voting. These Two-Round systems (TRS) are used for the French National Assembly and in some places in the United States, including Georgia for US Congress and for local elections in many states. Another way to make a majority more likely is to use "ranked choice" ballots, in which voters may indicate which candidate is their first choice, and then also which candidates are their second and third (and so on) choices, in case their more preferred candidate lacks the votes to be elected. Systems of this sort are known as the Alternative Vote (AV) or Instant Runoff, and are used for Australia's House of Representatives and for some local elections in the United States. (The appendix to this chapter includes an explanation of ranked-choice voting.)

As we noted previously, the plurality system in districts electing a single legislator (M=1) involves voting for candidates, whereas proportional systems require multiseat districts (M>1) and usually voting for lists. However, it is possible to have majoritarian systems that use multiseat districts (M>1) and lists of candidates; the most prominent example of this rare system is the US Electoral College for choosing the president, and hence we shall discuss it in chapter 8. There are also systems with M>1 and voting solely for individual candidates instead of party lists. For decades, until a change of the system in the 1990s, the most prominent example was Japan, where the Single Non-Transferable Vote (SNTV) was used: Most districts had a magnitude (M) of three to five legislators, the voter could vote for just one candidate, and the winners were the top-M candidates (regardless of party). SNTV and similar systems, sometimes termed *semi-proportional* are in use in some locales in the United States, as we will discuss in a later section. Multiseat districts and candidate voting can also be used with ranked-choice ballots in a form of proportional representation known as the Single Transferable Vote (STV), which is explained in the appendix to this chapter. The most famous example of STV is Ireland, which is not one of our thirty-one democracies; STV is also used in the United States in some local elections as well as for the Australian Senate.

The final class of electoral systems we need to consider are "mixed-member" systems, which have dual sets of districting: Every voter is represented simultaneously in a single-seat district, usually decided by plurality, and a multiseat district where PR is used.[10] As explained in the appendix to this chapter, these systems can be either fully proportional or quite majoritarian, depending on how the rules relate the single-seat districts and the PR lists to one another. If the relationship between the two components of the system is such that the PR-list seats are allocated to compensate parties that do not win many single-seat districts, the system is Mixed-Member Proportional (MMP), as in Germany and, since 1996, New Zealand. If the two sets of districts are decided independently, the resulting system results in the single-seat component of the system being relatively dominant over the outcome, giving us Mixed-Member Majoritarian (MMM), as is the case in Japan since 1996. Details of how these two types of mixed-member systems work are explained in the appendix to this chapter.

Table 5.2 summarizes the electoral systems of our thirty-one democracies according to two primary dimensions, whether voting and seat allocation are based on candidate votes or voting for party lists. Other critical features are also noted in each primary cell. The mixed-member systems are indicated at the bottom of the table, because they combine elements of both candidate and list voting, as noted previously. We can see that the United States joins only six other countries in using a single-seat district system for its legislative elections, including three others that currently use plurality: Canada, India, and the United Kingdom. Among our democracies, there are few examples of candidate-based systems in multiseat districts, although Japan until 1993 was a prominent case. Eighteen of our thirty-one democracies, or 58 percent, use party-list proportional

10. In addition, the voter normally has two votes, one for a candidate in the single-seat district, and one for a party list. However, in Mexico and, until 2005, Korea, there is a single vote that counts for both a candidate and the party that nominated the candidate.

Table 5.2. Electoral systems for legislative elections in thirty-one democracies

	Candidate-based: votes cast and seats allocated solely to candidates	*Party-based: seats allocated to lists before being allocated to candidates on those lists that win seats*

Single-seat districts (M=1)	Plurality
	    Canada
	    India
	    New Zealand to 1993
	    United Kingdom
	    United States
	Two-round system
	    France[a]
	Alternative Vote (ranked-choice ballots)
	    Australia House
		(not logically possible)

multi-seat districts (M>1)	Single Non-Transferable Vote
	    Japan to 1993[b]
	Proportional representative via Single Transferable Vote (ranked choice ballots)
	    Australia Senate[c]
		Party-list proportional representation
		    Argentina
		    Austria
		    Belgium
		    Brazil
		    Chile
		    Colombia[d]
		    Czech Republic
		    Denmark
		    Finland
		    Greece[e]
		    Israel
		    Italy to 1992 and since 2006[e]
		    Netherlands
		    Poland
		    Portugal
		    South Africa
		    Spain
		    Sweden
		    Switzerland

Notes: Table excludes mixed-member systems: MMP is used in Germany and New Zealand (since 1996); MMM in Hungary, Korea, Mexico, Italy (1994–2001), and Japan (since 1996).

[a] Rule is majority-plurality; if no candidate wins more than half the votes in the first round in a district, any candidate who obtains votes equivalent to more than 12.5% of registered voters may advance to a second round, at which a plurality suffices.

[b] SNTV is still used for part of Japan's second chamber.

[c] Most voters cast a vote "above the line" for a party, rather than ranking candidates, resulting in nearly a list system in practice.

[d] Before 2003, Colombia used a list system that was functionally the same as SNTV.

[e] Bonus-adjusted PR, whereby PR is applied only after the largest party or alliance has been awarded a block of seats (in Italy, since 2006).

representation (PR) systems. This count included two—Greece and Italy—that use Bonus-Adjusted PR, which provide an automatic surplus for the largest party or alliance before the proportional formula is applied.[11]

It is clear from table 5.2 that political engineers looking to design an electoral system have a wide menu from which to choose. In this light it is even more striking that there was no debate about specific means of electing legislators at the founding of the US democracy. Of course, as we have stressed, the reason for this lack of debate lies in how early the US system was founded; most of the choices were simply unknown at the time. By the late nineteenth century, and especially after the middle of the twentieth, many newer democracies had extensive debates about electoral systems. There are, in particular, two prominent cases of fundamental electoral-system change in the 1990s: Japan and New Zealand.

In Japan, the post–World War II democracy featured one dominant, but internally factionalized, party, the Liberal Democratic Party (LDP). The electoral system was SNTV. After years of dissatisfaction with the failure of elections in Japan to give voters clear options, including the possibility of an alternation in power, the LDP actually split over the issue of political reform in 1993. As a result of negotiations involving both the LDP and the opposition, which now included former factions of the LDP, the electoral system was changed to MMM. While the LDP continued to win the next few elections, the changed system produced one of the desired changes to Japanese politics, as a viable alternative emerged in the form of the Democratic Party of Japan (DPJ). The DPJ defeated the LDP in the 2009 election. The MMM system had helped bring about this result due to the dominance of the single-seat districts, in which voters were presented with a clear choice between one candidate of the LDP and one of the DPJ, unlike the earlier SNTV system, in

11. Under current rules as of 2013, Greece awards forty of three hundred seats to the largest party, then allocates the rest proportionally among all parties clearing a 3% threshold. In Italy, the largest party or pre-electoral alliance is guaranteed at least 55% of the seats (nationally in the first chamber, region-by-region in the Senate).

which the main choice was among multiple candidates of the one dominant party, the LDP.[12]

In New Zealand, there was a change from plurality to MMP in the mid-1990s. For decades, New Zealand politics had been dominated by two major parties, much like US politics; in New Zealand the main parties were Labour on the center-left and National on the center-right. However, in the 1970s and 1980s, third parties began to get increasing numbers of votes. Yet, due to the advantage that plurality in single-seat districts confers on large parties, these smaller parties usually won at most one or two seats. In 1978 and 1981, elections under the plurality system resulted in two consecutive "spurious majorities": Labour won the most votes, but in both elections National won the majority of seats.[13] When Labour finally won a parliamentary majority in 1984, it appointed a Royal Commission on the Electoral System. This commission proposed that New Zealand adopt a Mixed-Member Proportional (MMP) system in order to afford better representation. Despite hesitation by the two big parties, finally in 1992 and 1993 referenda were held, in which the public endorsed a move to MMP.[14] In elections since 1996, the changed system has brought dramatic changes to New Zealand politics, by allowing several smaller parties to win seats in close proportion to their votes, and introducing an era of multiparty coalition governments. We will discuss some of these consequences in more detail in later chapters. Having now seen the variety of electoral systems across our thirty-one democracies and considered how two democracies have reengineered their electoral systems when the previous systems were perceived as not working well, we now turn to a set of features on which we compare US elections to those of our other thirty democracies.

12. The LDP returned to power in the 2012 election.

13. Under plurality in single-seat districts, it is not the percentage of votes that parties win that determines their seats, but simply the number of districts in which they have a candidate who earns more votes than any other candidate. As we note below, spurious majorities have also occurred in the US House.

14. For an overview of the process of reform in New Zealand, see Denemark 2001.

US ELECTIONS AND ELECTORAL SYSTEMS
IN COMPARATIVE PERSPECTIVE

A lengthy list of twenty-two important differences between the American electoral system and the systems of all or most other democracies can be identified, but several of these can be described in relatively brief terms.

1. A highly decentralized electoral system. Most unitary democracies have uniform rules for elections at each level; even local elections tend to be conducted under the same rules in every part of the country. Federal systems sometimes allow more variation, with the constituent subunits of the federation—states, provinces, *Länder,* and cantons—having the power to determine the rules at the state and lower levels. This is especially true in the United States, where the states can and do use different election rules, and where cities and counties also often have the freedom to determine their own methods of election for different local offices.

What is highly unusual in the American case, however, is that even for national—congressional and presidential—elections many crucial rules are determined by the states. For elections to the House of Representatives, the districts are determined by state authorities— usually the state legislatures, but sometimes bipartisan or nonpartisan commissions. Other issues, such as the format of the ballot and the type of voting technology also vary among the US states (and sometimes even within states).

The only comparable situation occurs in Switzerland, but only with regard to the second chamber, modeled after the US Senate, to which each canton elects two representatives.[15] Here the cantons have complete freedom to determine the electoral system, the timing of the election, the terms of office, and whether popular elections or election by the cantonal parliament will be used. In practice, all cantons have four-year terms for their representatives, and all use

15. At different times in Swiss political history, three cantons were split into six so-called "half-cantons." With few exceptions, these half cantons operate like regular cantons, but one exception is that they have only one representative in the Council of States, half of the representation that the other cantons have.

direct popular elections (which, in two small cantons, take the form of a show of hands in the annual citizens' assemblies instead of a secret ballot). Most cantons elect their representatives to both chambers at the same time, but four elect their second-chamber members in the year before the first-chamber election. All except one use the majority-runoff system; the exception is the canton of Jura, which uses proportional representation.

2. *A large number of elective offices.* In the United States, there are three kinds of national elections: presidential, Senate, and House of Representatives elections. As table 5.3 shows, only six of the other democracies have the same three types of national elections: five Latin American democracies—which, like the United States, have presidential and bicameral systems—and semi-presidential[16] and bicameral Poland. All of the other democracies have only two or merely one national election. Five elect both their president and one legislative chamber by direct popular vote: four European countries and Korea. Seven countries—six parliamentary democracies and Switzerland[17]—have popular elections for both chambers of the legislature. And in more than a third of our democracies—twelve out of thirty-one—the only national election is the election of the first or only chamber of the legislature.

The contrast between the United States and most other democracies is even greater below the national level. At the state and local levels, judges are also frequently elected in addition to legislative and executive officials. Furthermore, not only the chief executives, like governors and mayors, are popularly elected but also other executive officers, such as, in California, as many as six state officials in addition to the governor and lieutenant-governor: the secretary of state, attorney general, superintendent of public instruction, treasurer, controller, and insurance commissioner. No other democracy comes even close to the American system of directly electing very large numbers of legislative, executive, and judicial officeholders.

16. Semi-presidentialism is a hybrid type of executive, discussed in ch. 8.

17. As explained in ch. 8, the Swiss executive is selected by parliament but not responsible to it.

Table 5.3. Types of national popular elections in thirty-one democracies

	Presidential	First chamber[a]	Second chamber
Argentina, Brazil, Chile, Colombia, Mexico, Poland, **United States** (n=7)	X	X	X
Austria, Finland, France, Korea, Portugal (n=5)	X	X	
Australia, Belgium,[b] Czech Republic, Italy, Japan, Spain, Switzerland (n=7)		X	X
Canada, Denmark, Germany, Greece, Hungary, Israel, India, Netherlands, New Zealand, South Africa, Sweden, United Kingdom (n=12)		X	

Notes:

[a] Sole chamber in democracies with unicameral legislatures.

[b] Disregarding the few indirectly elected or appointed members of some second chambers; in the Belgian case, however, only slightly more than half of the members of the Senate are popularly elected.

3. Many levels of elections. Most democracies conduct elections at three levels of government: (1) the national level; (2) an intermediate level, such as regional, state, provincial, *Land,* cantonal, and so on; and (3) the municipal or local level. Since 1979, an additional level of election was added in countries that are members of the European Union when direct supranational elections to the European Parliament were introduced. After the enlargement of the European Union in 2004, all of the European countries except Switzerland among our thirty-one democracies are now EU members. Most American voters, however, elect officials for four to six, or even more, levels of government: national, state, county, municipal, and frequently special-function authorities, such as school boards, that may not coincide with other local jurisdictions. In 2007, there were 50,432 county and municipal governments, 13,051 school districts, and 37,381 special districts responsible for various local administrative functions. All of these entities have elected officials who run them.

4. *Short terms of office.* Many American elective officeholders tend to be elected for unusually short terms. At the national level, terms of office range from the six-year term of US Senators to the four-year presidential term and the two-year term of members of the House. In comparison with first, or sole, chambers of national legislatures in other democracies, as we will discuss in chapter 7 on legislative power, the two-year House term is uniquely short. A similar pattern prevails at the state level. Most governors and state senators serve four-year terms, but two governors (those of New Hampshire and Vermont) and senators in twelve states are elected for only two years. However, forty-four states elect members of their first chambers to two-year terms (Council of State Governments 2003: 113, 199). At the local level, 56 percent of mayors have four-year terms, but 37 percent have two-year terms, with most of the remainder having one-year terms (Hajnal and Lewis 2003). At the local level, term lengths of city council members vary from one to six years. Terms of shorter than four years are rare in most other democracies.

5. *Inflexible timing of elections.* Members of Congress are elected for fixed terms of office, and elections therefore take place on a fixed schedule. This feature makes the House of Representatives belong to a minority of, mainly presidential, democracies. At lower levels of government in the United States, fixed election schedules are also the norm, but in this respect the differences between the United States and other democracies is not as great. Regional and local governments elsewhere are also usually elected for fixed, instead of flexible, terms, although some cases of flexibility in local elections also exist.[18]

6. *Prevalence of term limits.* At the national level in the United States, the president is term-limited, but all attempts by some states to impose terms limits on their US Senators and Representatives have been unsuccessful so far, as a result of Supreme Court rulings. At the state level, however, term limits have become very common,

---

18. For example, flexible elections can be found at the Länder level in Germany and the states of Australia vary in their legislative terms and whether elections are fixed or not.

not only for executive officials but also for legislators. Governors face a two-term limit in two-thirds of the states, and state legislators are term-limited in sixteen states (Council of State Governments 2003: 87, 199). Legislative term limits of any kind are extremely rare in our other democracies. The only major exception is Mexico where members of the first chamber can serve only one three-year term, and senators only one six-year term. Term limits for presidents in Latin America and elsewhere are common, however, as we shall see in chapter 8 on executives.

7. *Recall elections.* The recall is a special, and peculiarly American, procedure for the removal of elected officials and their replacement by newly elected officials. It allows a relatively small number of voters to petition to remove an official before the expiration of his or her regular term, and to force a new election for the office in question. This device does not exist at the national level in the United States, but several of the states and many local governments have adopted it. The best-known example is the recall of California Governor Gray Davis and his replacement by Arnold Schwarzenegger in 2003. However, it is used infrequently at either level; important reasons are that the number of signatures that have to be gathered is often forbiddingly high and that many legislative terms are already short anyway. Nevertheless, the complete absence of recall elections in our other democracies still means that we have yet another striking contrast between American political institutions and those elsewhere.

8. *Many referendums (at the state and local levels).* A referendum allows a direct vote by the electorate on proposed laws or constitutional amendments. The United States occupies an unusual place in two respects. It belongs to the small minority of democracies in which a *national* referendum has *never* been held, although national referendums are also quite rare in most other democracies except Switzerland. What is more important, however, is that many states in the United States, especially in the western region of the country, use the referendum with great frequency at both the state and local levels. This means that the only two cases of the widespread application of the referendum in our thirty-one democracies are the United States and Switzerland (Butler and Ranney 1994).

9. Frequent elections. As a result of several of the characteristics mentioned earlier—the large number of elective offices, many levels of elections, short terms of office, direct primary elections, recall elections, and frequent referendums—elections have to be held very often in the United States: on average, two to three times per year. The only country with even more frequent dates on which elections and referendums are conducted—about six or seven times per year—is Switzerland. All other democracies have far fewer election days in any given year: only once a year or less often.

10. Concurrent elections and long ballots. There would have to be many more election days in the United States if each individual election and referendum were scheduled on a separate day. However, the number of election days is held to a reasonable, if still large, number by holding many elections and referendums concurrently—that is, on the same day. This practice necessitates the so-called long ballot—a ballot on which as many as forty or fifty choices have to be made in some states. The United States is the only country in the world to use such long ballots. All other democracies, including Switzerland, usually hold only one election or referendum, or at most two or three, on a single day.

11. Low voter turnouts. In sharp contrast to the wide range of opportunities for electoral participation—many elective offices and relatively short terms of office, as well as many referendums at many levels—the actual turnout at elections in the United States is unusually low. For example, if we look at the 1990–2010 period, voting age turnout was below 60 percent in three out of five presidential elections and was below 40 percent for all congressional midterm elections (that is, nonpresidential years) during that time period.

Table 5.4 presents the average turnout figures in national elections in the 1990–2010 period for our thirty-one democracies. In all cases, the basic measure is the number of voters as a percentage of the voting-age population. This is a more accurate measure of turnout than actual voters as a percentage of registered voters, because voter registration procedures and reliability differ greatly from country to country. In the United States, turnout figures based on the number of registered voters are particularly misleading because so many eligible voters are not registered to vote. In some countries, however, the number of registered voters may actually be higher than the voting-age population as a result of the failure of the electoral register being kept up-to-date and of deaths and movements of voters from one district to another not being properly recorded.

The table reports the turnout for elections that are most decisive in determining control over the national executive. In the case of parliamentary democracies, this means the election of the first or only chamber of the national legislature. In the seven presidential democracies, including the United States, this means presidential elections; turnout in legislative elections is often lower, if elections are held on different dates (as with midterm elections in the United States and Mexico, and all legislative elections in Korea). In semi-presidential systems (Austria, Finland, Poland, and Portugal), where there are presidential elections but executive power is also dependent on the outcome of legislative elections held on different dates, we must make a judgment as to which is the more decisive election. For Austria, Finland, and Portugal, there is little question that we should use the legislative elections, because most of the time the executive is either a coalition or is held by a party other than that of the president. For Poland, and especially France, the political process is dominated by the contest for the presidency, and thus these are the elections we report. (Semi-presidential systems and coalition governments are explained in detail in chapter 8.)

The turnout rate in the United States since 1990 is the fourth lowest among our thirty-one democracies: 57.28 percent, as shown in table 5.4. Switzerland has the lowest voter turnout at 37.47 percent. Most (twenty-six) of the other democracies have turnouts above 60 percent: between 60 and 70 percent in seven countries, between 70 and 80 percent in thirteen countries, and between 80 and 90 percent in six countries.

The low level of turnout among American voters can be explained in terms of three factors, some of which are unusual characteristics of democracy in the United States, which we have mentioned earlier. First, the United States uses a disproportional electoral system: plurality in single-seat districts for congressional elections, and the even more disproportional plurality in multiseat districts in the Electoral College (see chapter 8). As table 5.4 shows, turnout generally

Table 5.4. Average voter turnout (as a percentage of the voting-age population) in national legislative or presidential elections[a] in thirty-one democracies, 1990–2010

	Voter turnout (%)	Plurality elections	Compulsory voting
Italy	86.12		X[b]
Belgium	86.11		X
Greece	84.17		X
Australia	82.52		X
Denmark	82.36		
Sweden	80.69		
Brazil (pres.)	79.57		X
Finland (pres.)	78.59		
Korea (pres.)	78.14		
New Zealand	78.13		
Spain	77.91		
Argentina (pres.)	77.07		X
Israel	76.85		
Austria (legis.)	76.29		
Czech Republic	76.25		
Netherlands	74.72		
France (pres.)	72.98		
Germany	71.82		
Portugal (legis.)	71.68		
Chile (pres.)	69.06		X
South Africa	65.68		
Japan	65.07		
United Kingdom	64.34	X	
Mexico (pres.)	63.05		
India	61.33	X	
Hungary[c]	60.26		
Poland (pres.)	58.51		
United States (pres.)	**57.28**	X	
Canada	57.14	X	
Colombia (pres.)	44.61		
Switzerland	37.47		
Median	*74.72*		

Notes:

[a] For countries with popular elections for both the first (or sole) chamber of the national legislature and the president, the higher of the two average turnout percentages is shown in the table, and the type of election that resulted in the higher turnout is indicated in parentheses after the country's name.

[b] Compulsory voting until 1994.

[c] Data through 2006.

Sources: Based on data collected by the International Institute for Democracy and Electoral Assistance in Stockholm (www.idea.int/vt).

tends to be lower in the four countries that currently use a plurality electoral system than elsewhere. Unlike PR systems, plurality has a tendency to reduce voter interest because of the "wasted vote" problem: voters who favor a party that is not competitive in their district (or that is assured of victory) may have little incentive to vote. PR systems, by contrast, allow more voters to see their vote as effective, and give parties incentive to mobilize voters even in areas of the country in which they are weak. Even MMM and bonus-seat systems provide such incentives, despite typically offering smaller parties less representation than a PR system would.

A second explanation is that countries where voting is compulsory—that is, where voting is not only a right but also a duty—tend to have relatively high voter turnout rates, although the typical penalty for not voting is merely a small fine, similar to a fine for a parking violation, and although these fines are imposed on only a small fraction of the nonvoters. Table 5.4 shows that most of the countries with compulsory voting are among the democracies with the highest turnouts. The top four, for example, all have compulsory voting (although Italy abandoned compulsory voting in 1994), and six of the seven compulsory voting cases are above the median (75.49 percent), with Chile being the lone exception below. It should also be pointed out that the United States is for once *not* exceptional in this respect: It is among the majority of our democracies with optional voting.

Third, an important explanation is voter fatigue caused by the frequency of elections and the large number of choices to be made in the United States. One of the few countries in our set of thirty-one democracies with even lower turnouts is Switzerland—which is also the country with even more election days than the United States.

12. Felon disenfranchisement. Calculating voter turnout rates in terms of actual voters as a percentage of voting-age population solves the problem of the unreliability and noncomparability of the numbers of registered voters in different countries, as discussed earlier. However, it introduces a new problem: Voting-age population numbers include ineligible voters—non-citizens and, in several countries, felons—and excludes citizens who live abroad who are eligible to vote in national elections in most countries. Non-citizens present the greatest problem. One study of American voter turnout uses the measure of "voting-eligible population" instead of voting-age population, and it estimates that when ineligible non-citizens are excluded, the turnout rate in the 2000 election goes up by 4.5 percentage points (McDonald and Popkin 2001: 966). Exactly comparable figures are not available for other countries, but especially the larger West European democracies have roughly similar or only slightly lower proportions of non-citizens in their resident populations.[19] Excluding non-citizens would increase several turnout percentages in table 5.2 by about 2 to 4 percentage points. It should also be pointed out that if we added the 4.5 percentage points to the US turnout rate of 57.28 percent in table 5.4 for an adjusted total of 61.78 percent, and if we made the unrealistic assumption that no adjustments are necessary for other democracies, the United States would still have the seventh lowest voter turnout in the table. Adjusting for ineligible felons and overseas citizens makes a much smaller difference. In fact, the two adjustments cancel each other out in the United States: Excluding felons increases the turnout percentage by 0.7 points, and including overseas citizens decreases it by 0.7 points (McDonald and Popkin 2001: 966).

Table 5.5 categorizes the different ways that our democracies treat the voting rights of prisoners and ex-felons. The United States is the only country in our set of thirty-one democracies in which ex-prisoners may be *permanently* disenfranchised. Actual practice varies from state to state. Two states, Maine and Vermont, are like the most permissive eleven countries in Table 5.5 and allow even current prison inmates to vote, but four states permanently bar all ex-felons from voting, and seven others permanently bar certain cat-

19. Compared with the 8.0% of non-citizens among the voting-age population in the United States in 2000 (McDonald and Popkin 2001: 965), the percentages of non-citizens among the total population—roughly, although not exactly comparable to the US percentage—in several European countries for which data are available in recent years, ranging from 1999 to 2003, are as follows: Austria 8.9%, Germany 8.9%, Greece 7.3%, France 5.6%, Sweden 5.3%, Denmark 4.9%, Netherlands 4.3%, United Kingdom 4.2%, Norway 4.1%, Italy 2.2%, and Finland 2.0% (Migration Policy Institute 2004).

Table 5.5. Prisoner voting rights in thirty-one democracies

Canada, Czech Republic, Denmark, Finland₁, France, Israel, Poland, South Africa, Sweden, Switzerland (n=10)	Prisoners allowed to vote
Australia, Austria, Germany, Greece, Italy, Japan, Netherlands, Spain (n=8)	Some prisoners denied vote based on length of sentence, or type of crimes committed
Argentina, Brazil, Hungary, India, Poland, Portugal, United Kingdom (n=7)	Prisoners do not have voting rights
Belgium,[a] Chile, Colombia, Finland₂[a], Mexico, New Zealand[a], **United States**[b] (n=7)	Prisoners have no voting rights, and voting rights may be restricted after term served, based on crime committed or length of term

Notes: Laws vary by state in the United States, but forty-eight deny prisoners the right to vote (Maine and Vermont allow prison voting). Thirty states deny voting rights to those on probation, and thirty-five deny the vote to parolees. Four permanently bar ex-prisoners from voting, and seven others restrict certain classes from voting. States that allow ex-prisoners to vote typically require extensive legal/bureaucratic processes for voting rights to be restored.
[a] Disenfranchisement for a limited time only in cases of those convicted of voter buying and selling (Fellner and Mauer 1998: 17).
[b] Permanent disenfranchisement possible.
Sources: Based on data in Rottinghaus 2003: 22–25, and Sentencing Project 2007: 8 and 2012: 3.

egories of felons (Rottinghaus 2003: 31). These laws constitute an especially serious denial of voting rights for two reasons. One is that the United States imprisons many more of its citizens—and therefore also has many more ex-prisoners—than most other countries (see table 10.11 and the discussion in chapter 10). Second, the high American imprisonment rate disproportionately disenfranchises members of ethnic and racial minorities and socioeconomically disadvantaged groups. Indeed, according to the Sentencing Project, a Washington, DC, think tank, in 2012, while 2.4 percent of the total population has been disenfranchised due to imprisonment, 8.3 percent of all African Americans had been.[20] Further, "Given current

20. See http://www.sentencingproject.org/map/map.cfm#map.

rates of incarceration, three in ten of the next generation of black men can expect to be disenfranchised at some point in their lifetime. In states that disenfranchise ex-offenders, as many as 40 percent of black men may permanently lose their right to vote" (Sentencing Project 2012: 1).

13. Strong class bias in voter turnout. There is a general tendency toward class inequality in voter participation in modern democracies: More privileged citizens—those with higher incomes, greater wealth, and better education—turn out to vote in greater numbers than less privileged citizens. This tendency becomes stronger as the overall level of voter turnout declines, and, as expected, it is especially strong in the United States, where voter turnout is very low. Election surveys have found that in presidential elections—the highest-turnout elections in the United States—since the 1950s, turnout among the college-educated has been more than 20 percentage points higher than among the population as a whole, whereas turnout for people without a high school diploma has been about 20 percentage points lower—a participation gap of about 40 percentage points; in the 2000 presidential election, the gap was 44 percentage points (Freeman 2004). A similar gap of 37 percentage points has been found in studies of Switzerland, the other Western democracy with extremely low overall turnout rates (Linder 1994: 95–96).

14. Prevalence of plurality and majority-runoff electoral systems. While the plurality method of election is prevalent at the national level, the decentralized nature of American election laws means that other methods are sometimes employed at the state level. Specifically, Two-Round systems are common in some states, especially at the local level. Generally these systems are the *majority-runoff* method, in which if the first round does not produce a majority, there is a second round in which only the top two candidates are eligible.

Plurality and majority elections are usually conducted in single-seat districts but can also be conducted in multiseat districts, or at large (meaning jurisdiction-wide, without a division into districts). For elections to the US House of Representatives, single-seat districts are mandated by congressional statute. State legislative elections are usually also conducted in single-seat districts. At-large elections used to be the rule in American cities, but they have become less common, especially under the pressure of court decisions, because, combined with plurality or majority rule, they make it very difficult for minorities to gain any representation. Democracies that use PR at the national level almost always use PR for lower-level elections as well.

15. Use of other systems alongside plurality/majority. Democracies that mainly use plurality and majority systems often also make use of other electoral methods for certain elections. The clearest case is Australia, where the Senate, which is about as powerful as the first chamber, is elected by PR (STV, but most voters use a party-vote provision rather than rank candidates).[21] In the United Kingdom various forms of PR are used for regional elections: in Northern Ireland (STV), Scotland (MMP for the Scottish Parliament and STV for local offices), and Wales (MMP for the Welsh Assembly). Elections for the British members of the European Parliament are by list PR. France uses PR for its European Parliament elections.

The United States is unique in the application of a much wider variety of nonplurality and nonmajority elections, especially at the local level—another illustration of the decentralized nature of American electoral arrangements. Several jurisdictions have used candidate-based rules in multiseat systems, including the Single Non-Transferable vote (SNTV), as was formerly used for the first chamber of the national legislature in Japan (see the appendix to this chapter). SNTV has been adopted for some local offices in Alabama, for example.[22] Other systems with candidate-based allocation and multiseat districts include the *limited vote* and the *cumulative vote*. Under the limited vote, the voter has more than one vote, but fewer than the number of seats being contested. It is used in some local elections in the eastern region of the United States, especially in

21. For the Australian Senate, a voter who wants to rank candidates must rank all the candidates on the ballot—a formidable challenge. Thus most vote "above the line," meaning accepting the rankings determined by the party of their choice. However, in the Australian Capital Territory and Tasmania, voters must vote for candidates (but need not rank all those on their ballot).

22. See Grofman 1999.

Connecticut and Pennsylvania. Under the cumulative vote, a voter is allowed to cast as many votes as there are seats being contested, but it is possible to cast more than one vote for one candidate. This system was used for more than a century (1870–1980) to elect the first chamber of the Illinois state legislature (in three-seat districts). The cumulative vote is now commonly used for local elections in the South, and its use has been increasing in recent decades. For instance, at least forty school districts and fourteen city councils in Texas are elected by this method, and they all adopted it during the 1990s. These systems—SNTV, the limited vote, and the cumulative vote—are sometimes called "semi-PR" systems because, while not assuring proportional results, they do make it easier for minority parties and for ethnic and racial minorities to be elected than do plurality or majority systems. True PR, always of the STV form, has also been used in the United States, but only to a limited extent: City councils were elected in the past by STV in about two dozen American cities, including New York City, Cincinnati, and Boulder, but only Cambridge, Massachusetts, currently uses it for city council elections. STV is also currently in use for school board elections in New York City and Minneapolis. In addition to these cases of STV, which require the use of ranked-choice ballots (see the appendix to this chapter), there are also some cities that use ranked-choice ballots to elect their mayors or other officials, resulting in the Alternative Vote system—commonly referred to as Instant Runoff Voting (IRV) in the United States. Examples include the mayors of Oakland and San Francisco, California.[23]

16. Very little criticism of the plurality method of election. In most of the other countries that rely on the plurality method for national elections, and particularly in the United Kingdom and Canada, this method has become a highly controversial issue. This was also the case in New Zealand, which, as we saw, abandoned plurality in favor of the MMP form of proportional representation, spurred by the plurality system having generated spurious majorities in 1978 and 1981. Major concerns in Canada have been the severe regional

23. Jurisdictions using STV and IRV are provided by the Center for Voting and Democracy (http://www.fairvote.org/).

imbalance in the support of the large parties, as well as swings in seats that have been far greater than swings in national vote shares of parties—both features that have been made worse by plurality elections. As noted at the previous point, several jurisdictions in the United Kingdom now use types of PR, and the coalition government formed after the 2010 election agreed to hold a referendum on whether to move to the Alternative Vote for the House of Commons. The referendum took place in 2011, but voters rejected the change. In the United States, however, it was not until the 1990s that an advocacy group, the Center for Voting and Democracy, became active, promoting systems such as STV and IRV. Although these systems have been adopted in a few jurisdictions in recent years, there is essentially no debate about changing the electoral system for congressional elections (as well as state legislative elections).

The plurality system has not been free of anomalous outcomes in the United States, yet the electoral system itself has not come under significant criticism. Spurious majorities—one party winning the most votes, but a different party having a majority of House seats—occurred once in the main period of our study, in 1996. In addition, there was a spurious majority in the 2012 House election, and there were four others since the early twentieth century: 1914, 1942, 1952, and 2012.[24] Some of these results can be attributed to political gerrymandering, although as Chen and Rodden (2013) note, much of it is the result of "unintentional gerrymandering" because of the geographic concentrations of some partisans (specifically of Democratic voters).[25] Such outcomes, however, rarely cause much in the

24. Some counts also include 2000 as an election with a spurious majority. Since there is no central voter-counting institution in the United States, different sources end up with different vote totals. For example, the Federal Elections Commission shows a spurious majority in the House in 2000, but not 1996, and one gets different results by looking at the records of the Clerk of the House.

25. For more on this, see Matthew Shugart, "Spurious majorities in the US House in Comparative Perspective" at http://fruitsandvotes.com/?p=6513, and John Sides, "Votes and Seats: What Made the 2012 Election Different" at http://themonkeycage.org/2012/11/12/votes-and-seats-what-made-the-2012-election-different/.

way of debate, and what debate it does stir is narrow in scope. Here, the contrast with one of our comparison countries, New Zealand, is noteworthy, given that the spurious majorities there in 1978 and 1981 contributed to the eventual replacement of the plurality system with Mixed-Member Proportional.

17. Relatively proportional election results. Several reasons may be advanced for the lack of significant opposition to plurality in the United States. One is that it has not produced disproportional results to the same extent as in the other plurality and majority countries. Disproportionality refers to the degree to which the seat shares won by parties deviate from their vote shares.[26] Table 5.6 shows the values of disproportionality (to the first or only chamber of the legislature) for each of our thirty-one democracies. The countries are listed in increasing order of disproportionality, so that the most proportional system is at the top of the list. The second column of the table also indicates the type of electoral system used in these elections; in cases where there has been a fundamental change of the electoral system, only the most recent system as of 2010 is included. Generally, PR countries achieve the greatest electoral proportionality, and the systems that are dominated by single-seat districts, the least. Previously we noted that PR systems are sometimes designed with features that limit proportionality: small district magnitude, high thresholds, or bonus provisions that award the largest party or alliance additional seats beyond its proportional share. Systems that have relatively high disproportionality due to provisions of this sort are indicated in the table.[27] It is noteworthy that all of the cases

26. Disproportionality is measured according to the index devised by Michael Gallagher (1991). It measures the total percentage by which the over-represented parties are over-represented (which is, of course, the same as the total percentage of under-representation) but adjusted in such a way that large deviations between the parties' vote and seat shares are counted more heavily than small deviations. When voters have more than one vote—for instance, in Germany, where voters cast both a vote for a party list and a vote for an individual candidate in a single-seat district—the parties' vote shares are based on the party-list votes.

27. In some cases, those systems marked as "PR-high threshold" may have thresholds similar to other systems not so indicated (e.g., 5% in Germany). The

Table 5.6. Electoral disproportionality in first-chamber elections in thirty-one democracies, 1990–2010

	Electoral disproportionality (%)	Electoral system
South Africa	0.30	PR
Netherlands	1.02	PR
Denmark	1.37	PR
Sweden	1.57	PR
Israel	1.89	PR
Austria	1.94	PR
New Zealand	2.75	MMP[a]
Switzerland	2.97	PR
Finland	3.12	PR
Germany	3.17	MMP
Brazil	3.32	PR
Belgium	3.60	PR
United States	**3.92**	**Plurality**
Colombia	4.32	PR[b]
Italy	4.67	Bonus-Adjusted PR[c]
Portugal	5.27	PR
Spain	5.45	PR-low M
India	5.90	Plurality
Czech Republic	6.08	PR-high threshold
Argentina	6.36	PR-low M
Chile	6.93	PR-low M (M=2)
Greece	7.03	Bonus-Adjusted PR
Mexico	8.16	MMM
Poland	8.41	PR-high threshold
Australia	10.40	Alternative Vote
Hungary	10.97	MMM
Korea	11.36	MMM
Canada	12.14	Plurality
Japan	12.28	MMM[d]
United Kingdom	16.07	Plurality
France	19.53	Majority-Plurality

Notes:

[a] 1996–2008 only.

[b] 2006 and 2010 only (after move from SNTV).

[c] 2006 and 2008 only; from 1994 to 2001, the system was MMM and disproportionality averaged 8.31.

[d] 1996–2009 only.

of PR that have disproportionality greater than that of the United States have features that make their PR "impure" by design, whereas those that use either a single nationwide district (and thus very high magnitude, such as M=120 in Israel and M=150 in the Netherlands) or that have predominantly high-M districts (for example, Finland) or other features meant to maximize proportionality (for example, nationwide compensation in South Africa and Denmark) do indeed have much lower levels of disproportionality than the United States. The German system of Mixed-Member Proportional (MMP) likewise has a relatively low degree of disproportionality, as has the similar MMP system adopted in New Zealand in 1996.

By contrast, the systems that are plurality, Majority-Plurality (France), or Mixed-Member Majoritarian (MMM) all have high levels of disproportionality, with one striking exception—the plurality system in the United States. With a disproportionality index value of 3.92, the United States has much less disproportionality than the next plurality case we find as we look down the list (India, at 5.90) and far less than the other two plurality cases (Canada, 12.14; United Kingdom, 16.07).[28] The MMM systems also have high values of disproportionality, and the Majority-Plurality system in France is by far the highest of all thirty-one democracies (19.53).

In those countries other than the United States that use plurality, majority, or MMM systems, the high degree of disproportionality is usually caused by two factors: (1) the over-representation of the largest party and under-representation of the second largest party, and (2) the fact that many smaller third parties are severely under-represented or fail to win any representation. The second cause of electoral disproportionality is largely absent in the United States because of its strict two-party system, in which third parties generally win no seats but do not win many votes either. Because the first

---

difference in the impact of a threshold on disproportionality lies in whether there is a substantial vote wasted on parties that fail to clear it. There often is in Poland, e.g., making the system rather disproportional, whereas in Germany relatively small vote shares are cast for below-threshold parties.

28. New Zealand's plurality system averaged a likewise high 14.74 in elections from 1978 to 1990.

explanation does apply to American congressional elections, these elections do not yield perfect or even near-perfect proportionality, but not a high degree of disproportionality either. A further explanation is the impact of the unique American institution of direct primary elections, which have been a crucial factor in shaping and maintaining the strict two-party system (as we will discuss further in chapter 6).

18. Little concern (or knowledge) about electoral disproportionality. Another reason why the plurality single-member-district system has largely escaped criticism in the United States is that the degree to which party-seat shares correspond with party-vote shares arouses little popular interest. Newspapers report the votes received by party candidates in individual districts, but will ordinarily not bother to add these up for all of the districts together. When elections are held in other plurality and majority countries, the overall degree of disproportionality of the results usually receives considerable attention. For instance, in Britain and Canada the election-night TV news and the newspapers and popular Web sites all report national vote totals by party, making the disproportionality obvious. Moreover, without reporting of national vote totals, the occurrence of the occasional spurious majority—which is itself a major breach in proportionality—goes mostly unnoticed. While the degree of disproportionality of US congressional elections is lower than in other plurality systems, it is not so low that it deserves to be disregarded. Yet it is, in fact, largely ignored by the media; politically interested citizens, let alone the public at large, are virtually unaware of it. One at least partial justification of this neglect lies in a distinctive feature of US parties that we will discuss at length in chapter 6: both the Democratic and Republican parties are nonhierarchically organized, which permits ideological tendencies that might otherwise result in separate parties to operate within one of the mainstream parties. If such tendencies ran as separate parties, disproportionality would inevitably rise and might gain popular notice.

19. Tuesday voting. With very few exceptions, American elections are held on Tuesdays. Most other democracies conduct their elections on Sundays or on a weekday that is declared a holiday. The only other country with a preference for Tuesday voting is Denmark.

Mondays are preferred by Canada, Wednesdays by the Netherlands and South Africa, and Thursdays by Korea and the United Kingdom. Because of India's large size, its parliamentary elections are held on different days, usually weekdays, in different parts of the country (Massicotte, Blais, and Yoshinaka 2004: 103–15; Katz 1997: 234–35).

All other factors being equal, weekend or holiday voting appears to produce higher voter turnout than weekday voting—by approximately 6 percentage points. We could therefore add Tuesday voting to the seven other explanations for the unusually low voter turnout in the United States discussed earlier. However, some doubt on the efficacy of weekend voting has been cast by recent research showing that changing from weekday to weekend voting, or the other way around, has no measurable effect on turnout (Franklin 2004: 144–45).

20. From highly unequal to highly equal election districts. A persistent problem in electoral systems based on single-seat districts is malapportionment—districts that are unequal in terms of population or number of voters. Compared with the other countries, using plurality and majority systems, the United States presents two contrasts. Before the 1962 Supreme Court decision in *Baker v. Carr,* election districts were unusually unequal. As a result of this and subsequent decisions, the opposite extreme has come about: Districts have become equal with an almost perfect mathematical precision.[29] The only significant malapportionment that remains is the over-representation of the smallest states, which are guaranteed at least one representative in the House in spite of their (too-) small populations and the inevitable rounding up or down due to the fact that seats have to be whole numbers.[30] In many other countries that

29. For instance, Southern California, with more than half of the state's population, used to be represented by only six state senators, while the other Californians could elect thirty-four senators. The Supreme Court's 1964 decision in *Reynolds v. Sims,* which mandated equal legislative districts for both state houses, including state senates, therefore introduced a change of monumental proportions.

30. For instance, two states entitled to 3.8 and 4.2 seats respectively are both likely to be allocated four seats—which means that the first will be over-represented and the second underrepresented.

use single-seat districts, such big changes have not occurred, because regular redrawing of boundaries has tended to keep districts roughly, but not precisely, equal—both at the national and lower levels of government. A glaring exception is India, in which the last redistricting was based on a census in 1971 (Heath, Glouharova, and Heath 2005) and the same boundaries have been used through at least 2009, despite major population shifts.

Aside from India, the other countries that use single-seat districts tend to have greater discrepancies in the population sizes of their districts, usually because of the conflicting requirements that their districts be drawn not only as equally as possible but also in such a way that local boundaries are respected as much as possible.

Some PR systems also have some degree of malapportionment. This can occur, for example, when provinces or states serve as electoral districts with varying district magnitude, but there is a minimum or maximum magnitude for each district that prevents the number of seats per district from being proportional to population. PR means that the seats are allocated proportional to votes by parties (or as proportional as the magnitude allows), but PR does not guarantee that the total number of seats is proportional to the district population. PR systems with significant malapportionment include Chile (both chambers), where all districts have a district magnitude of two, but differ considerably in population. Even PR systems that have varying district magnitudes across districts sometimes have substantial malapportionment; that is, the magnitudes do not vary as much as they would if the ratio legislators to voters was the same in all districts. Examples include Argentina and Brazil and, to a lesser but still significant degree, Spain.

Two PR countries, Israel and the Netherlands, use nationwide elections without separate districts—and therefore also without any malapportionment whatsoever. Several others have compensatory national allocation that mostly washes away any district-level malapportionment (for example, the MMP systems of Germany and New Zealand and the pure PR system of South Africa).

21. Partisan and pro-incumbent redistricting. Even if the malapportionment question is solved, the problem of *redistricting* remains. That is, even if all districts contain the same number of both legislators elected (that is, they are all of the same magnitude, as with single-seat districts in the United States) and voters, there is still the question of what the boundaries of those districts will be. In the United States, a particular feature of boundary delimitation is "gerrymandering," defined as the drawing of district lines for political advantage. This gerrymandering may be done for the advantage of a majority party that controls the redistricting, or for the "bipartisan" purpose of maximizing the reelection chances of incumbents of both major parties.[31]

Compared with the other countries with plurality and majority systems, the American redistricting process is much more political in both of these respects. Most other countries have neutral commissions to draw the district boundaries. These exist in some American states as well, but the usual pattern is for the state legislatures to be in charge. In contrast with the activist stance of the courts with regard to redistricting on the grounds of malapportionment and discrimination against racial and ethnic minorities, they have been much more reluctant to intervene on the grounds of partisan or pro-incumbent gerrymandering—which is, of course, a much more difficult problem to diagnose and remedy than the relatively simple question of ensuring that districts have substantially equal numbers of voters or residents. David Butler and Bruce Cain (1992: 128) express the uniqueness of American democracy in the following words: "There is a notable contrast between, on the one hand, the rigorous regard for numbers [that is, the strict adherence to equal districts] and the high politicization of the United States and, on the other hand, the more statistically relaxed approach but the lower politicization" of other countries using single-seat districts.

22. Frequent legal challenges to election rules. It is highly unusual for a new districting plan adopted by a state legislature and signed by the governor *not* to be challenged in the courts on various

---

31. The term *gerrymandering* refers to the drawing of electoral districts in a way that favors a particular person, party, or group and the boundaries are usually drawn in a visually and geographically distorted fashion so as to include the intended blocs of voters. The term comes from a political cartoon published in the early 1800s that lampooned a district drawn in Massachusetts when Elbridge Gerry was governor.

grounds. In other democracies, disputes concerning election rules may also end up in the courts. One example is the election law written for the first parliamentary election in newly unified Germany in 1990, which was declared unconstitutional by the Constitutional Court, and which had to be rewritten to meet the court's objections. The German Constitutional Court again ruled against certain provisions of the electoral system, and attempted fixes by parliament, invalid in 2008 and 2012. But such judicial interventions are much less frequent in other countries than in the United States.

This last, twenty-second, characteristic of the American electoral system can be seen as a counterpart to the first characteristic discussed in this chapter: the highly decentralized system of elections in the United States. Decisions concerning election rules of all kinds are widely dispersed among government authorities—not only from the federal to the local level, but also among legislative, executive, and especially judicial authorities.

CONCLUSIONS

Elections are central to democracy, and the electoral system is a critical factor in the link in the delegation chain between voters and their elected representatives. As we have seen, there is wide variation in electoral systems among our thirty-one democracies, with most of them using some form of proportional representation, based on party lists, rather than the US-style system of plurality election of candidates competing in single-seat districts. This dominance of plurality and sometimes other candidate-based systems in the United States can be attributed to the country's early establishment of democratic institutions. As we have noted, it is striking that there was no debate about electoral systems at the Philadelphia Convention; thus the "choice" of candidate-based rules was really not a choice at all but rather something that was taken for granted.

Several of the differences between the United States and other democracies can be attributed to the uncommon mix of federalism and presidentialism. Specifically, factors like the long ballot and frequent elections are due to the specific nature of American federalism. Likewise, some of the variation in the system (such as the recall) is the result of differences in state constitutions. Other factors, like the set electoral calendar, are the direct result of presidentialism.

Other differences, like Tuesday elections, are idiosyncratic, while those like felon disenfranchisement or the strong class bias in turn-out are reflections of the political culture. An interesting aspect of the politics of the electoral system is that there is essentially zero interest in electoral reform, despite some innovation taking place at the local level in a few jurisdictions. Public discourse regarding electoral rules is largely nonexistent outside issues like redistricting, which is itself a matter of discussion driven primarily by the comparatively unusual (though certainly not unique) use of candidate-based elections, taking place in single-seat districts.

APPENDIX: EXAMPLES OF VARIOUS ELECTORAL SYSTEMS

The text of this chapter describes in general terms some of the main electoral system types, and in box 5.1 we saw how one common proportional representation formula works and how district magnitude affects degrees of proportionality. Here we offer an overview of several other systems, including the Single Non-Transferable Vote, the Alternative Vote (also known as Instant Runoff), the Single Transferable Vote, and mixed-member systems.

Single Nontransferable Vote

The Single Non-Transferable Vote, or SNTV, is a simple extension of candidate-based rules, like plurality in single-seat districts to a multiseat district (see table 5.2). As with plurality, the voter continues to have one vote, which is cast for a single candidate. Also as with plurality, votes cast for a candidate can increase the election prospects of only that candidate, meaning there is no process by which two or more candidates of the same party can share votes (as they do with list PR systems, where seats are allocated first to parties, or with the Single *Transferable* Vote, as explained below). In fact, while a party can win more than one seat, because M>1, if it has two or more candidates, they are in direct competition with each other, as well as with candidates of other parties.

Table 5.7. SNTV in Japan: Two actual district results from the 1990 election

Candidate	Party	Aichi, district 4; M=4; Total votes: 662,510 Votes (%)	Won?	Candidate	Party	Wakayama, district 1; M=3; Total votes: 363,408 Votes (%)	Won?
Kawashima Minoru	CGP	151,968 (22.9)	Yes	Nakanishi Keisuk	LDP	109,964 (30.3)	Yes
Ito Eisei	DSP	134,793 (20.3)	Yes	Sakai Hiroichi	CGP	71,652 (19.7)	Yes
Sugiura Seiken	LDP	125,688 (19.0)	Yes	Kishi Hachiro	JSP	68,976 (19.0)	Yes
Urano Yauoki	LDP	116,470 (17.6)	Yes	Noma Tomoichi	JCP	64,699 (17.8)	No
Inagaki Jitsuo	LDP	112,537 (17.0)	No	Tamaoki Hiroyasu	LDP	48,117 (13.2)	No
Omura Yoshinori	JCP	21,054 (3.2)	No				

Japan used the Single Non-Transferable Vote from 1947 through 1993. Table 5.7 shows examples of two actual district races from the 1990 election, to show how SNTV works and the challenges it poses to a party that seeks to win more than one seat.

SNTV is simply a "top-M" system, where M is the district magnitude; that is, if there are four seats in the district, the candidates with the four highest individual vote totals win the seats. This means that a party wins a number of seats equivalent to how many top-M candidates it has, regardless of the total number of votes won by the party's candidates collectively. A party that may be attempting to win two or more seats must take care not to have its votes either (1) spread out among too many candidates, or (2) overly concentrated on one. That party is best off if it can collectively decide on the optimal number of candidates to run in the district and then seek to have each candidate win an approximately equal number of votes. If it has too many candidates, it may lose a seat it otherwise could have won—if only one of the candidates had not run and that candidates' voters had voted for its other candidates. If its candidates' vote totals are overly unequal, it also may fail to win as many seats as it could have won, if some of the votes for the most popular candidate had been cast for a trailing candidate instead.

All candidates running in these two districts are shown. The party names are: CGP, Clean Government Party (Komeito); DSP, Democratic Socialist Party; JCP, Japan Communist Party; JSP, Japan Socialist Party; LDP, Liberal Democratic Party.

Both districts show a common feature of Japanese elections under SNTV: One party, the Liberal Democrats (LDP) runs multiple candidates, whereas other parties often would run only one per district (except in their few regional strongholds). The LDP was Japan's ruling party from its formation in 1955 until 1993 (when a coalition of other parties replaced it in government). It could maintain its majority only by seeking to elect two or more of its candidates in most districts. The district magnitude was usually three, four, or five. The smaller parties, on the other hand, tended to play it safe: Nominating only one candidate meant avoiding the risk of having its vote spread across too many candidates and possibly electing none.

The first example is from district 4 in Aichi Prefecture, where the district magnitude was four (M=4). The LDP's candidates together had 53.5 percent of the vote—a clear majority. Nonetheless, the party elected just two out of the four candidates it ran. In most other electoral systems, when M=4, a party with more than half the votes would be likely to win three of the four seats—especially when, as is the case here, no other party has even a quarter of the votes. (Recall from box 5.1. that small magnitudes tend to yield disproportional results, such as 75 percent of the seats on 53.6 percent of the votes, with M=4.)

The vote totals of the three LDP candidates show clearly that the party was aiming to equalize the votes across its candidates and thus elect all three. Indeed, the vote totals are almost equal, with their third candidate (Inagaki) having almost 90 percent of the votes of the party's first (Sugiura). Yet even this amazingly high degree of equalization was not good enough, as two other parties each concentrated all their votes on a sole candidate and won the district's first two seats, while the LDP's third candidate just missed winning a seat.

The second example comes from district 1 of Wakayama Prefecture. Here there are three seats (M=3). The LDP ran two candidates, and together they won 43.5 percent of the vote. The LDP elected one candidate, while its second candidate came in fifth place and hence was not elected. If the system were D'Hondt PR, the LDP would have won two of the three seats, because its combined vote was more than twice that of the second largest party (the CGP). Under SNTV, the LDP's problem was that its candidates' vote totals were too unequal: Nakanishi won more than twice as many votes as his party colleague. The LDP could have elected both of them if only 20,860 of Nakanishi's voters (less than 20 percent of his personal total) had voted for Tamaoki instead, pushing the latter candidate's vote total up into third place in the district, ahead of the votes of the one JSP candidate, Kishi.

Alternative Vote (Instant Runoff)

The Alternative Vote typically retains the single-seat districts of the plurality rule but is designed to encourage the election of a majority-supported candidate. Unlike two-round rules, which require a runoff election between two leading candidates to ensure a majority, the Alternative Vote starts with ranked-choice ballots. That is, voters may select not only their first-choice candidates, but also their second choice, third choice, and so on. Instead of eliminating trailing candidates and having voters vote again in a second round to determine a majority, as with Two-Round systems, there are multiple rounds of counting to determine who has won. It is this feature that leads to this system's other name, Instant Runoff.[32]

The counting proceeds as follows. The first count determines whether any candidate has obtained a total of first-choice votes equivalent to at least 50 percent plus one vote—a majority. If so, then, of course, the count is complete and we have a winner. However, if there is no candidate with a majority of first-choice votes, the candidate with the lowest number of first-choice votes is eliminated. The ballots of the eliminated candidate are now transferred to the candidate that these voters had marked as their second choice. If these

32. There are other formulas that might be considered "Instant Runoff" aside from the Alternative Vote, but we shall consider only the latter here. For reviews, see Grofman and Feld 2004 and van der Kolk 2008.

votes have put one of the remaining candidates over the 50 percent mark, we have a winner. If not, the process is continued, eliminating the remaining candidate with the lowest vote total and transferring that candidate's votes to the voters' second-choice candidate. This process of sequentially eliminating weak candidates and transferring their votes to their voters' second choice continues until some candidate reaches 50 percent plus one (or all ranked-choice ballots have been used). Whenever a voter's second choice has already been eliminated on an earlier count, the third choice comes into use, and so on.

We can look to the United States for an example of AV—the 2010 election of the mayor of Oakland, California (where they call it "ranked-choice voting"). In that contest, ten candidates were on the ballot, plus there was an option for a voter to write in some other candidate. In the initial count, as we see in table 5.8, no candidate had the requisite 50 percent plus one of the first-preference votes. Don Perata had a large plurality over Jean Quan, leading 33.73 percent to 24.47 percent. However, Perata's lead left him far short of a majority and thus required the reallocation of votes based on the second preferences of the voters whose first-choice candidate was unpopular and thus eliminated. Third preferences come into play only if a voter's top two choices have been eliminated.[33] This process started with the reallocation of the write-in vote, which was the lowest total for any option on the ballot. The question was, What other preferences did the voters who cast write-in ballots have? We can see from the table the distribution of the second choice for those voters went to varying degrees to all candidates (for example, the initial first place candidate, Perata, gained thirty-two votes, and the tenth-place candidate, Arnold Fields, gained five). Obviously, this first reallocation did not put any candidate over the majority quota, so a further count was needed. The process continued in multiple counts, always eliminating the candidate in last place following the previous reallocation and transferring the votes from that candidate to voters' second- (or, where necessary, third-) ranked choice.

33. In Oakland, voters may give up to three ranked preferences. By contrast, in elections to the Australian House of Representatives, voters are required to rank every candidate on their ballot.

Table 5.8. An example of the alternative vote, the 2010 election for mayor in Oakland, California

	Count 1: Original vote		Count 2: First reallocation			Count 9: Penultimate reallocation			Count 10: Final result		
Don Perata	40,342	33.73%	32	40,374	33.80%	+3,277	45,465	40.16%	+6,407	51,872	49.04%
Jean Quan	29,266	24.47%	33	29,299	24.53%	+3,378	35,033	30.94%	+18,864	53,897	50.96%
Rebecca Kaplan	25,813	21.58%	18	25,831	21.62%	+5,244	32,719	28.90%	−32,719	0	0.00%
Joe Tuman	14,347	12.00%	10	14,357	12.02%	−15,462	0	0.00%	0	0	0.00%
Marcie Hodge	2,994	2.50%	5	2,999	2.51%	0	0	0.00%	0	0	0.00%
Terence Candell	2,315	1.94%	1	2,316	1.94%	0	0	0.00%	0	0	0.00%
Don Macleay	1,630	1.36%	6	1,636	1.37%	0	0	0.00%	0	0	0.00%
Greg Harland	966	0.81%	2	968	0.81%	0	0	0.00%	0	0	0.00%
Larry Lionel "LL" Young Jr.	933	0.78%	6	939	0.79%	0	0	0.00%	0	0	0.00%
Arnold Fields	733	0.61%	5	738	0.62%	0	0	0.00%	0	0	0.00%
Exhausted by over votes	355		1	356		+45	461		+65	526	
Write-In	268	0.22%	−268	0	0.00%	0	0	0.00%	0	0	0.00%
Under votes	2,306		0	2,306		0	2,306		0	2,306	
Exhausted ballots	0		149	149		+3,518	6,284		+7,383	13,667	
Continuing ballots	119,607	100.00%		119,457	100.00%		113,217	100.00%		105,769	100.00%
TOTAL	122,268		0	122,268		0	122,268		0	122,268	

Note: Exhausted ballots are those in which, at a given count, there are no further preference that can be transferred; hence such ballots are excluded from the final result. *Over votes* are those that contain more marks than are permitted (for instance, marking two candidates as first choice). *Under votes* are ballots cast that have no marks for any mayoral candidate. *Continuing ballots* are those that include ranked preferences for further candidates who have not yet been eliminated.

We do not have space to show all ten counts, so we now jump ahead to the ninth count, at which the candidate who was in fourth place, Joe Tuman, was eliminated.[34] We can see that he had 15,462 votes (his original 14,347, plus votes transferred in prior reallocations from eliminated candidates). The table shows that a plurality (5,244) of these votes went to the third-place candidate, Rebecca Kaplan, and another 3,378 went to Quan. However, there was still no majority among the three remaining candidates. Thus in the tenth count, Kaplan was eliminated. A clear majority of her votes (18,864 of 32,719) transferred to the second-place candidate, Jean Quan (and only 6,407 to Perata), giving Quan more than half the votes in the final count.

Quan was able to win the office even though she started the process in second place, because she was the second (or in some cases, third) preference of enough of the voters that originally cast ballots for other candidates. That is, she had a broader base of support than Perata, who could not extend his base far enough beyond the initial third of the electorate that supported him as a first choice. In fact, Quan and Kaplan had both campaigned by asking for first-choice votes, of course, but importantly, each asking her voters to give the other their second preferences.[35] We also saw that Tuman's voters were more likely to favor either Kaplan or Quan over Perata (in the ninth count). In this way, both Quan and Kaplan could campaign individually for mayor yet avoid splitting the pool of votes of those who preferred either of them over Perata.

SINGLE TRANSFERABLE VOTE

The Single Transferable Vote (STV) operates like the Alternative Vote, except that $M > 1$. The first step is to determine a quota, which is a number of votes sufficient to guarantee that a candidate wins a

---

34. The entire process can be viewed online at http://www.acgov.org/rov/rcv/results/rcvresults_2984.htm.

35. "Jean Quan Wins Oakland Mayor's Race," *San Francisco Chronicle,* November 11, 2010. Available at http://www.sfgate.com/bayarea/article/Jean-Quan-wins-Oakland-mayor-s-race-3166295.php.

seat. A commonly used quota is the Droop quota, named after its nineteenth-century British inventor, Henry R. Droop. The formula is:

$$q = [V/(M+1)] + 1,$$

where V is the number of valid votes, and M is the district magnitude. The reason this quota is useful for allocating seats to candidates is that it identifies the smallest number of votes that only M candidates could obtain. It should also be noted that this is the exact same quota that is used in the Alternative Vote: let M=1, and the formula tells us that a candidate wins the seat if he or she has won V/2 plus 1, in other words a majority of the votes. For M=1, half the votes plus one is clearly the smallest number of votes that only one candidate could obtain, because if we set the quota as one vote less, we could have two candidates with exactly V/2. Thus the Droop quota for STV is simply the generalization of the majority quota to any situation in which more than one seat is to be allocated.

As with the Alternative Vote, the count under STV proceeds in steps whereby first it is determined whether any candidate or candidates obtained the quota. If all *M* seats have not been filled based on quotas, then the process of transferring votes begins and is similar to what we saw for AV. Only now we are also going to transfer surplus votes—the votes that any winning candidate has obtained that are above the quota. These are transferred to the marked second-choice candidate of these voters; they might put another candidate over the quota, in which case another seat is filled. If there are still seats unfilled, then the process of sequential elimination described for the Alternative Vote begins: The weakest candidates are eliminated, one by one, and their votes are transferred to the candidates their voters indicated as their second choices (or third, if the second choice has already been either eliminated or elected; fourth if the third has been elected or eliminated, and so on). The process continues until all seats are filled.

We use an example from the subnational level in Australia to illustrate how STV works. Australia, like the United States, has two major parties—Liberals on the center-right and Labor on the center-left. In addition, it has a Green Party that has become a significant third party recently. Our example comes from the 2008 legislative election in the Australian Capital Territory (ACT) and specifically from the district called Ginninderra, which includes a part of the city of Canberra. With a district magnitude of five and 60,049 votes cast, the quota is calculated as:

$$q = [60,049/(5+1)] + 1 = 10,009$$
(ignoring digits after the decimal point).

This is the vote total that will guarantee election. Candidates with less than this number of votes to start with will be elected only if they can obtain sufficient second (and third, and so on) preferences from other candidates who are eliminated as the counting proceeds.

The table below shows the first-preference vote totals of thirteen of the twenty-seven candidates who ran in this district in 2008. It shows all the candidates of the three parties that each won at least one seat. It is noteworthy that each of the two big parties, Labor and Liberal, nominated five candidates. However, the third party, Green, nominated only two. In this way the Greens were minimizing the risk that all of their candidates, if they had run as many as five, might have vote totals too low to remain in contention in later rounds, when they could pick up votes from other parties' eliminated candidates. Not splitting votes is critical for a small party; in fact, as the table shows, the combined vote for Greens (8,350) was less than the quota. Hence one of their candidates could win only by obtaining not only most of the other Green candidate's second preferences, but also ranked preferences from voters of candidates of other parties. In addition to the candidates of the three largest parties, the table also shows an independent (not party-affiliated) candidate who had a higher vote total than several of the candidates of major parties. In fact, the independent, Mark Parton, had one of the five highest vote totals yet did not win one of the five seats. We will explain why.

It is immediately evident from the table that one candidate, John Stanhope of Labor, has a vote total greater than the quota, and hence is elected. Stanhope, having been elected on the first count, has 3,452 surplus votes (his initial vote of 13,461, minus 10,009). We do not show all steps of the counting process for reasons of space, but from

Table 5.9. Results of Australian Capital Territory Legislative Assembly, 2008 for district of Ginninderra, via Single Transferable Vote, District magnitude: 5, Total votes: 60,049, Quota: 10,009

Party	Candidate	First preference votes	Share of total vote	Share of quota	Elected? (order)	Count on which elected
Labor	**John Stanhope**	**13,461**	**0.224**	**1.34**	**Yes (1)**	**1**
	Mary Porter	**3,719**	**0.062**	**0.37**	**Yes (4)**	**49**
	Adina Cirson	2,797	0.047	0.28	No	—
	David Peebles	2,711	0.045	0.27	No	—
	Chris Bourke	1,431	0.024	0.14	No	—
(party total)		*24,119*	*0.402*	*2.41*	*2*	—
Liberal	**Alistair Coe**	**5,886**	**0.098**	**0.59**	**Yes (3)**	**45**
	Vicki Dunne	**4,237**	**0.071**	**0.42**	**Yes (5)**	**51**
	Andrea Tokaji	2.553	0.043	0.26	No	
	Jacqui Myers	2,460	0.041	0.25	No	—
	Matthew Watts	1,547	0.026	0.15	No	—
(party total)		*16,683*	*0.279*	*1.67*	*2*	—
Green	**Meredith Hunter**	**6,104**	**0.102**	**0.61**	**Yes (2)**	**42**
	James Higgins	2,246	0.037	0.22	No	—
(party total)		*8,350*	*0.139*	*0.83*	*1*	—
Independent	Mark Parton	3,785	0.063	0.38	No	—

Note: Fourteen other candidates are not shown.
Source: http://www.elections.act.gov.au/elections_and_voting/past_act_legislative_assembly _elections/2008_election/distribution_of_preferences \.

the detailed information released by Elections ACT, it was possible to determine that just more than one-third of this surplus transferred to another Labor candidate, Mary Porter, who would eventually be elected, as well. Most of the rest of Stanhope's surplus transferred initially to the other Labor candidates; when they lacked sufficient votes to reach the quota, these candidates' votes transferred third or later preferences to Porter. In other words, Labor voters were able to use their ranked-choice ballots to combine their efforts toward electing two candidates of their party, despite the fact that one of them

(Stanhope, with 22.4 percent of the total first-preference vote) dominated the field of candidates while their next most popular candidate (Porter, with 6.2 percent) trailed in sixth place overall on the first count. Thus ranked-choice ballots prevented Labor voters from wasting their votes on account of their candidates having unequal vote totals, in the sort of situation we saw can happen in the SNTV example.

The one Green Party winner was the second candidate to be elected, but did not obtain the quota until the forty-second round of counting. To obtain the quota, this candidate, Meredith Hunter, picked up small numbers of votes in each count from other minor-party candidates who are not shown in the table. However, critically, she also obtained a bloc of 333 votes from one of the Labor candidates, Adina Cirson. In other words, there were some Labor voters who actually preferred to see a Green elected if their preferred Labor candidate did not have a strong-enough following to win a seat.

What about Mark Parton, the independent candidate who ranked fifth overall in first-preference votes in a five-seat district, but was not elected? Why was he not elected, and were his voters' votes wasted? To the first question, we can answer that he was not elected because he lacked allies among the other candidates—like Perata in the Oakland AV example earlier—from whom preferences might have flowed. For the second question, we can answer no, because the ranked-choice ballots permitted his voters to redirect their votes to other candidates. Parton was not eliminated from contention until the forty-fourth round of counting. By this time, his vote total had grown from its initial 3,785 votes to 5,690, as a result mainly of transfers from other independent candidates who were eliminated. He also picked up a few hundred votes from eliminated Liberal and Labor candidates, indicating that there were some voters for candidates of the two big parties who actually liked Parton more than they liked other candidates from the party of their first choice. Parton ultimately was eliminated because Porter (Labor) and Vicki Dunne (Liberal) had pulled ahead in intermediate rounds of counting, so it became necessary to distribute Parton's votes. Interestingly, they split among three remaining candidates of the big parties. About 14 percent of them went to Porter, thus helping her go over the quota and be elected, while about 38 percent of them split between Dunne and another Liberal candidate, Alistair Coe (who had started the counting in third place overall), helping put both of these candidates over the quota as well. Thus we can see that the block of voters who placed the independent Parton in fifth place initially with 6.3 percent, or about .38 of a quota, were able to assist the election of candidates of the big parties that they preferred over others. That is, some of this independent candidates' voters "leaned" toward Labor, others toward Liberals—and toward different Liberals. They were able ultimately to see a preferred candidate among these parties benefit from their votes when their first-choice independent was not sufficiently popular to win the quota required to guarantee election.

The final result is relatively proportional in partisan terms, in that Labor (40.2 percent) and Liberals (27.9 percent) each won two of the five seats, while Greens (13.9 percent) won one seat. It is important to note that the result is relatively proportional only because most voters gave their second and other preferences to candidates of the same party as their first preference. Unlike in a list system (see box 5.1), it is ultimately the choice of voters to decide which candidates should benefit from their votes when their first choice is unable to be elected. Moreover, unlike plurality in single-seat districts or SNTV, relatively few votes are wasted by being cast for candidates out of the running or due to voters being split among multiple candidates. On the other hand, the result is not fully proportional, because of a rather low district magnitude (box 5.1) and because, as we saw, not all voters keep their ranked preferences within the same party as that of the candidate of their first choice.

Mixed-Member Systems

In a mixed-member system, there are two overlapping "tiers" of districts. What this means is that every voter is represented simultaneously in a candidate-based tier and a party-list tier. The candidate-based tier, also known as the *nominal tier,* usually consists of single-seat districts, where plurality determines the winners, whereas the party-list tier employs proportional representation, sometimes nationwide and other times in regional multiseat districts. In most mixed-member systems, the voter has separate votes in each tier—one for a candidate, and the other for a party.

There are two principal types of mixed-member system: Mixed-Member Majoritarian (MMM), as is currently used in Japan, and Mixed-Member Proportional (MMP), as used in Germany and New Zealand. They differ in how the list tier is related to the nominal tier. When the system is MMM, the allocation of seats to party lists proceeds *independently* of how many seats each party has won in the nominal tier. When it is MMP, the list seats are allocated to parties to *compensate* for seats won in the nominal tier. That is, with MMP, if a party has been over-represented in the nominal tier, relative to its party-list vote percentage, it will receive relatively few party-list seats; if a party has been under-represented in the nominal tier it will receive additional seats from the list tier to bring its overall total into proportion with its party-list votes.[36]

The following tables use examples from actual elections in New Zealand and Japan to illustrate how MMP and MMM, respectively, work.

In the New Zealand election of 2008, the National Party won just less than 45 percent of the vote. It won the single seat in each of forty-one districts around the country. As is often the case with plurality in single-seat districts, this is a highly disproportional result: 58.6 percent of the seventy districts in the nominal tier. Because National was over-represented in the nominal tier, and because MMP awards the list seats in a compensatory manner, this party obtains only 17 list seats, ensuring that its total, 58, is approximately proportional overall: its 58 seats are 47.5 percent of the total 122, which

---

36. Systems of partial compensation are also possible, as in the mixed-member systems of Hungary since 1990 and Italy from 1992 to 2001. Both systems should be considered MMM because list *seats* are not allocated in a manner dependent on nominal seats won; rather list *votes* are adjusted to reduce disproportionality, but only somewhat. The systems are still dominated by those parties or alliances that are large enough to win many single-seat districts. By contrast, the number of nominal-tier seats a party wins has little or no bearing on its overall seat total when the system is MMP.

Table 5.10. MMP in New Zealand election of 2008

Party	% votes (party list)	Districts won	List seats	Total seats	% seats
National Party	44.7	41	17	58	47.5
Labour Party	33.8	21	22	43	35.2
Green Party	6.7	0	9	9	7.4
New Zealand First Party	4.0	0	0	0	0.0
Act New Zealand Party	3.6	1	4	5	4.1
Maori Party	2.4	5	0	5	4.1
United Future Party	0.9	1	0	1	0.8
Jim Anderton's Progressive Coalition	0.9	1	0	1	0.8
Others	3.0	0	0	0	0.0
Total		70	52	122	

is a minor degree of over-representation.[37] By contrast, Labour, with 33.8 percent of the party vote, had won only 21 nominal-tier seats. Thus it was allocated more list seats than National because it needed more compensation in order to reach its proportional share. Its total 43 seats is 35.2 percent, close to its party-vote percentage.

Now consider the smaller parties. The Green Party, with 6.7 percent of the list votes, had these votes spread too thin to be the largest in any one district. Yet due to the compensatory feature of MMP, it won 9 seats, all off its party list. For the remaining small parties, we have to consider New Zealand's thresholds: a party must win 5 percent of the party vote or at least one single-seat district to be eligible for compensation. (Germany's MMP has a similar alternate

37. Most of the over-representation that we will see for all parties stems from the fact that 7% of the list votes were cast for parties that did not qualify for seats according to thresholds discussed later.

threshold: 5 percent of the list votes or three single-seat districts.) Thus the New Zealand First Party received no seats, because it failed to meet either of these thresholds. However, four other parties won at least one district, and thus have representation. Of special interest here are two of these parties. The Act New Zealand Party, whose 3.6 percent of the party-list vote was sufficient to elect five members, given that it also won a district and hence cleared one of the threshold provisions. The Maori Party won five districts, which is two more than it would have had out of the usual 120 seats of the New Zealand Parliament, based on only 2.4 percent of the list vote. As a result of this party's over-representation just from the nominal tier, additional seats are added to the Parliament in order to compensate the other parties. These seats are called "overhang seats." (Germany's MMP also has a provision for overhang seats, or *Überhangmandate,* as they are known in German.) This discussion of the smaller parties helps underscore the "mixed-member" nature of MMP. On the one hand, it is essentially as proportional as a system

Table 5.11. MMM in Japan (2009)

Party	% votes (party list)	Districts won	List seats	Total seats	% seats
Democratic Party of Japan (DPJ)	42.4	221	87	308	64.2
Social Democratic Party	4.3	3	4	7	1.5
People's New Party	1.5	3	0	3	0.6
Liberal Democratic Party (LDP)	26.7	64	55	119	24.8
New Komeito	11.4	0	21	21	4.4
Communist Party	7.0	0	9	9	1.9
Your Party	4.3	2	3	5	1.0
Others	1.9	7	1	8	1.7
Total		300	180	480	

Note: The DPJ, Social Democrats, and People's New Party contested the single-seat district in alliance; the LDP and New Komeito likewise had an alliance for the single-seat districts.

of nationwide PR would be, given the use of nationwide compensation; on the other hand, four parties that would have had no seats under pure PR, given the 5 percent threshold, in fact do have seats, due to having sufficient concentration of support to win one or more of the single-seat districts that make this a mixed-member form of PR.

As for the Japanese MMM system, we can understand its mechanics by looking at the national results of the 2009 election.

It is immediately clear that this is a majoritarian variant of a mixed-member system, fundamentally different from the MMP system we saw in New Zealand. Note that the DPJ has close to half of the list seats (87/180, or 48.3 percent),[38] despite the fact that it has a very significant over-representation coming from the nominal tier. Thus, far from compensating other parties for the DPJ's success at winning single-seat districts, the allocation of list seats proceeds without regard to the outcome in the nominal tier. The noncompensatory allocation of the list seats is further demonstrated by the third largest party, Komeito, which won no single-seat districts. This party's 21 seats are a proportional share of the list tier only (21 of 180 is 11.7 percent); this is in contrast to the MMP system, where the similarly placed Green Party won its proportional share not merely of the list tier but of the entire legislature despite likewise winning no single-seat districts.

These examples show how MMM is a system in which the overall outcome is dominated by the single-seat districts, rewarding parties that perform well in this tier. MMP, by contrast, is an overall proportional system, in which the main criterion determining a party's seats is its share of the party-list votes, as would be the case if all seats were allocated to party lists by PR.

38. Japan's list-tier seats are allocated in several regional multiseat districts (as indeed are seats in many PR systems), rather than nationwide. That several of these list-tier districts have relatively small magnitudes accounts for the over-representation of the largest party in the list tier.

CHAPTER 6

POLITICAL PARTIES, ELECTION CAMPAIGNS, AND INTEREST GROUPS

F
reedom of association for the purpose of aggregating and representing interests of citizens is a key right that is central to representative democracy. If we think back to figure 1.1, we will recall that politicians in democracies must act as agents of the citizens. However, millions or even thousands of citizens are not able to spontaneously act as principals over their democratic agents. They must act through organizations, which collectively act to represent the views of groups within the citizenry. The two basic ways in which citizen interests are aggregated and represented in the democratic process are *political parties* and *interest groups.* Political parties, by definition, are organizations that are formed in democracies for the purpose of nominating and electing candidates to governmental office. Interest groups, on the other hand, are formed around narrower purposes, such as seeking to advance economic and social policies of benefit to their group.

Before we can have political parties and interest groups to represent the preference of groups of citizens in government, we must have a prior condition met: the existence of fundamental political rights, such as speech, association, and petition of government. Without these it is impossible for persons, united by common interests, to band together and seek political influence.

This chapter explores these two key actors as central components in the overall functioning of democratic politics. The way parties, interest groups, elections, and electoral systems are organized has a major impact on the operation of the other institutions of government, as we have already shown on a number of occasions in previous chapters. We have also already pointed out repeatedly that

American political institutions differ in many respects from those in most other democracies. These differences are especially striking as far as political parties and elections are concerned.

BASIC DEFINITIONS

Political parties are groups of individuals who coalesce under a common label and offer candidates to compete for votes in elections. The presumed goal of political parties is to affect policy outcomes by winning office and functioning in government. It should be noted that in some cases political parties may never win office and yet are still attempting to influence policy by presenting candidates and therefore being part of the public debate surrounding the campaign process; simply by presenting candidates under an organizational label, they meet the definition of being political parties. The usage of a common label is a key ingredient in our definition because the label acts as a signal to voters as to the general policy orientations of the party in question. Thus the label facilitates collective action because voters who sympathize with the goals of the party can use the label to orient their behavior, in particular making choices at election time. In order for the label to work, it must communicate at least rudimentary information regarding the policy preferences of those running for office under its name. As such, we would expect that seeing labels like "Republican," "Democrat," "Green," "Libertarian," and so on communicates basic political information to the voter. Such communication is simplistic and incomplete, to be sure, but is substantially more useful than having only the names of candidates with no information about how they are or are not associated with other candidates and officeholders.

Not only do parties help organize elections, but they also are collective actors who must assume responsibility for forming legislative majorities to pass legislation, and in parliamentary systems they also must form the government (that is, select a prime minister and cabinet). We say that parties ultimately bear responsibility for government because voters have the right, at regular intervals, to reward or punish a party at the ballot box in accordance with the public's perception of a given party's performance in office. This relationship is fundamentally part of the principal-agent relationship outlined in chapter 1, and it is the very essence of representative democracy as discussed in chapter 5. Indeed, political parties and elections are at the heart of modern representative democracy. Parties provide the main link between citizens and policy makers. A famous statement made roughly seventy years ago by political scientist E. E. Schattschneider, but still often cited today, is that "modern democracy is unthinkable save in terms of parties" (1942: 1).

By *interest group* we mean an association of persons organized together for the purpose of attempting to influence government behavior. Interest groups can accomplish this task through a variety of actions, including *lobbying* (direct contact with members of government in the hopes of persuading them concerning policy outcomes), *electioneering* (helping to elect or defeat specific candidates or parties), or by trying to influence public opinion in various ways. Interest groups tend to be more narrowly focused on specific policies or policy areas than is the case with political parties, and they do not contest elections by presenting candidates under their label.

While all democracies have interest groups, there are also substantial differences in these groups, both within each country and across countries. Within countries, interest groups obviously differ a great deal with regard to the issues they embrace, how broad or narrow the interests are that they represent, the size of their memberships, the extent of their financial resources, and whether they mainly engage in direct and low-profile contacts with political decision makers or also use public demonstrations and protest as indirect pressure tactics.

Interest groups, as noted earlier, act as agents of various segments of the population who wish to see certain policy outcomes from government. One manifestation of this activity is *issue advocacy* in which a group focuses on a specific policy topic or set of topics. A classic illustration of this in the United States would be the National Rifle Association (NRA). Such groups attempt to influence policy outcomes at various levels of government as well as provide support to specific candidates in elections.

Another important manifestation of interest group activity is the degree to which groups represent economic interests in the society, and the key issue here is the manner in which labor and management are represented in a given country. Interest groups that represent the key constituencies of labor and management tend to be organized and to function in quite different ways in different democracies. The distinction that is commonly used by political scientists is between *pluralist* and *corporatist* interest-group systems. Pluralism can be described as a free-for-all competition among multiple independent groups; corporatism means a high degree of coordination and "concertation" among a smaller number of groups (which are larger in membership than in pluralist systems) that are formally allied or federated with each other. These large interest groups (such as labor unions) then negotiate with management groups and the government. More specifically, corporatism and pluralism are contrasting interest-group systems in four respects. In corporatist systems (1) interest groups are relatively large in size and relatively small in number; (2) they are further coordinated into strong national peak organizations; (3) the leaders of the peak management and labor organizations regularly consult with each other and with government representatives; and (4) the aim of these consultations is to arrive at so-called tripartite pacts—comprehensive national agreements that are binding on all three partners (labor, management, and the government) in the negotiations. Interest group pluralism can be recognized by the opposite characteristics: (1) a multiplicity of small interest groups; (2) the absence or weakness of peak organizations; (3) little or no tripartite consultation; and (4) the absence of tripartite pacts. Pure pluralism and pure corporatism are rare, and most interest-group systems can be found somewhere on the continuum between the pure types.

INSTITUTIONAL OPTIONS

The notion that more freedom leads to more interests being expressed was inherent in Madison's basic theory of faction and was well expressed in *Federalist 10* when he wrote, "Liberty is to faction what air is to fire" (Madison, Hamilton, and Jay 1987: 123). Indeed, Madison's basic theory of faction forms the basis for both political parties and interest groups in the modern sense, even though he did not directly foresee the evolution of either in the form that we understand them. In terms of basic institutional parameters, we would expect that democratic constitutions would provide some type of basic protections for citizens to create and join groups, express views in public, and make preferences known to government. These are all central pillars of democracy, and they are concretized in parties and interest groups.

Unlike questions such as whether a state should be federal or unitary, presidential or parliamentary, or even what the electoral rules will be, political parties and interest groups are less a feature of a constitutional/legal order as they are a result. This is to say that while political engineers create the parameters under which parties and interest groups form, they do not directly create parties or interest groups. Returning to the principal-agent relationship demonstrated in figure 1.1, the citizenry needs a link between its position as principal, selecting and holding accountable its agents in government. Voting is a central component of that chain, and parties (and the candidates they nominate) are the vehicles by which the voters invest their votes, and if enough voters are amassed, specific members of given parties serve in government. Likewise, between elections, interest groups are a mechanism by which interested citizens can communicate (via lobbying, for example) with their agents in government. Further, all of these groups form in the context of the prevailing social and cultural order.

To refer back to the earlier Schattschneider quote, parties have become a mainstay of modern democracies. They are an organizational mechanism that groups of citizens use to influence who represents them and how. Interestingly, the notion of political parties as defined here did not occur to the authors of *The Federalist Papers*. This is especially ironic given that the conflict between Federalists and Anti-Federalists formed a protoparty system that fits the definition provided earlier, as one label indicated a pro-Constitution position and the other the opposite. From there, a nascent party system would form around the Hamilton-Jefferson split in early American politics, with the former using the label "Federalist" and the latter the label "Republican" (which would eventually evolve into the modern Democratic Party). If we look, for example, at *Federalist 10,* we see that Madison foresaw a system of various factions linked to local constituencies and interests. He thought that such local factions would ally with others as needed on a specific legislative issue, not foreseeing the idea that a majority of seat holders would band together to control the legislature for a given term. *The Federalist Papers* themselves can also be seen as an early act of electioneering, a common interest-group technique in modern democracies, insofar as they tried to use specialized knowledge to foster a particular political point of view and to use the public dissemination of that knowledge to influence the public.

The issue of the development of political parties in the United States and in all representative democracies over time is an excellent example of the degree to which political engineers cannot always be expected to fully understand the consequences of their designs. The authors of the US Constitution did not fully anticipate political parties in the modern sense. Of course, as noted in the comparative section later, it has become fairly standard for constitutions to at least acknowledge the right of citizen to form parties, even if little else is said about the form and function of said parties.

Beyond the mere existence of specific parties operating in a given polity, a critical question for how democracy functions is, How many parties compete for and win elected offices? When speaking of multiple parties operating in a given polity, we are referring to the *party system* in that polity. Typically, party systems are described in terms of the number of parties of significance operating in the system, for example, a two-party system or a multiparty system. The number of parties shapes the menu of options available to voters as they make their choices in elections, and it also shapes the number of organizations, representing different interests, that must transact in the process of making public policies. These transactions may include two or more parties forming legislative majorities to pass laws or, in parliamentary systems, forming cabinets. Further, the more parties that are able to win seats in the legislature, the more the number of veto players tends to increase (as described in chapter 1). Parties in situations of legislative or executive coalitions often have to transact with one another to allow a given veto gate to be opened (for example, passing legislation through a legislative chamber).

Counting parties is not as straightforward a process as it might immediately seem. A raw count of parties participating in elections, for example, would indicate that the United State has a multiparty system, as it is typical for ballots in the United States to feature Libertarians, Greens, and so forth, alongside the Republican and Democratic Parties. However, as is well known (and will be further discussed later), the United States has a strikingly stable "two-party system." It might seem that a remedy to the counting problem is simply to ignore parties that do not win political office. However, that approach is not especially useful, either. For example, in the British House of Commons elections of 2010, eleven parties won seats. Yet, describing the British party system as a eleven-party system, or even as a multiparty system, would distort the actual reality of the situation, which is that there are two very large parties in the United Kingdom (Labour and Conservatives), one small party (Liberal Democrats) and eight microparties that won an average of 3.5 seats each out of a chamber of 650. This system is sometimes called a two-and-a-half-party system. As such, a counting method is needed by which we can discuss party systems in a way that captures various constellations of parties descriptively and allows for systematic comparison across countries and specific elections.

The standard measure used by political scientists is the "effective number of parties" (Laakso and Taagepera 1979). It is a measure that tells us the number of parties in a system while taking their relative sizes into account. The measure can be used both in terms of the number of parties in a legislature as well as in the electoral arena. For example, if a legislature has two parties each with exactly half the seats, the effective number is 2.00. If one party is considerably stronger than the other, with, for instance, one having 70 percent of the seats and the other 30 percent, the effective number is 1.72—in accordance with our intuitive judgment that we are moving away from a pure two-party system in the direction of a one-party system. Similarly, with three exactly equal-size parties, the effective number is 3.00, but if one of these parties is weaker than the other two, the effective number of parties will be somewhere between 2.00 and 3.00.

The identical measure can be calculated instead on the basis of the percentages of the vote collected by the different parties instead of the percentages of their seats. To distinguish between the two, we shall use the phrases "effective number of *legislative* parties" and "effective number of *electoral* parties."[1] Table 6.1 contains the effective number of legislative and electoral parties for our thirty-one democracies for legislative elections between 1990 and 2010. The countries are listed in ascending order of effective number of legislative parties. A comparative discussion of the table, including the relationship to electoral systems, which are also indicated in the table, is contained in the next section of this chapter.

Unlike most of the items under discussion when speaking of political engineering, the number of political parties in a system is not set by simply declaring in a constitution (or in regular laws) how many parties there will be, although many of our democracies do have explicit support for the existence of parties in their constitutions. Many constitutions assert that party formation is a basic right, and they often even note roles that parties may play in the organization of national politics.

Fundamentally, the number of parties in a given system is dependent upon a variety of other factors in the institutional setting as well as the cultural context in which a given democracy operates. For example, the electoral process used in a system (as we discussed in chapter 5) influences the number of parties that will seek office. Other factors also include political culture and issue dimensions generated by that culture (Lijphart 1999: 78–89, Taagepera and Shugart 1989: 92–98). For example, in almost every country, parties divide to some degree on basic socioeconomic questions, but other issues may be prominent and may lead to the formation of additional parties. For instance, religion, ethnicity, language, and other issues can support distinct parties.

1. The equation for computing the effective number of legislative parties (N) is: $N = 1/(\Sigma s_i 2$) in which s_i is the seat proportion of the i-th party. In order to calculate the effective number of electoral parties, substitute v_i (the vote proportion of the i-th party) in the above equation. In this case, *i* is a variable to capture the number of parties with seat (or vote) shares (e.g., if there are three parties with seat shares, we have to take into account S_1, S_2, and S_3 in the calculation). See Laakso and Taagepera 1979; Lijphart 2012: 63–67; and Taagepera and Shugart 1989: 77–91 for a complete explanation.

Table 6.1. Effective numbers of legislative parties in the first (or only) chamber of national legislatures and effective numbers of electoral parties in first (or only) chamber elections in thirty-one democracies, 1990–2010

	Effective number of legislative parties	*Effective number of electoral parties*	*Electoral system*
United States	**1.98**	**2.18**	**Plurality**
South Africa	2.11	2.13	PR
Australia	2.28	3.04	Alternative Vote
United Kingdom	2.32	3.38	Plurality
Greece	2.35	2.83	PR-bonus
Spain	2.54	3.11	PR-low M
Japan[a]	2.61	3.66	MMM
Portugal	2.64	3.16	PR
Korea	2.72	3.83	MMM
France	2.78	5.68	Majority-Plurality
Hungary	2.78	4.42	MMM
Canada	2.88	3.87	Plurality
Mexico	3.13	3.43	MMM
Argentina	3.31	4.06	PR-low M
New Zealand[a]	3.35	3.68	MMP
Austria	3.45	3.71	PR
Germany	3.70	4.20	MMP
Czech Republic	3.87	5.12	PR-high threshold
Italy[b]	4.07	4.76	PR-bonus
Sweden	4.15	4.45	PR
Denmark	4.72	4.94	PR
Poland	4.73	6.90	PR-high threshold
Finland	5.06	5.82	PR
India	5.42	6.60	Plurality
Switzerland	5.48	6.22	PR
Netherlands	5.51	5.77	PR
Chile	5.97	6.85	PR-low M (M=2)
Colombia[c]	6.30	6.78	PR
Israel	6.58	7.37	PR
Belgium	8.14	9.56	PR
Brazil	8.74	9.93	PR

Notes:
See chapter 5 for electoral-system terminology.
[a] Current system since 1996 only
[b] Current system, 2006 and 2008 only.
[c] Current system, 2006 and 2010 only.
Sources: Calculations by Royce Carroll, Arend Lijphart, and Steven L. Taylor. Some numbers also from Michael Gallagher's Web site (http://www.tcd.ie/Political_Science/staff/michael_gallagher/ElSystems/).

Like with political parties, the exact nature of an interest-group system is not the type of issue that is set, directly, by the Constitution. Rather, the basic institutional order created by constitutions helps determine the incentives for interest-group formation, as well as the type and number of groups that may emerge. Likewise, specific rights and privileges enshrined in the Constitution will also have an effect in this area of political behavior. As with political parties, the protection of certain basic rights, like the rights to free association, to petition government for redress of grievances, and to free speech all sum to create an environment where groups would emerge to seek to pursue their own interests before government.

US PARTIES, ELECTION CAMPAIGNS, AND INTEREST GROUPS IN COMPARATIVE PERSPECTIVE

In this section we shall focus on ten distinctive features of the American party system, including partisan competition and election campaigns, and four distinctive features of US interest groups.

1. A constitution that does not mention parties. The United States is not alone in its lack of mention of parties in its Constitution. However, it is part of a distinct minority. Of our twenty-nine democracies with written constitutions, twenty-three make mention of political parties either in terms of the role played by parties in organizational politics and/or in terms of the rights of citizens to form parties. Many constitutions, in fact, underscore the importance of political parties to democratic governance, such as that of Argentina, which states in Section 38, "Political parties are basic institutions of the democratic system."

The United States joins Belgium, Canada, Denmark, Japan, and the Netherlands as countries whose constitutions fail to mention parties. All, however, do explicitly affirm the rights of citizens to freely assemble and to associate with like-minded citizens, both of which are essential rights needed for the functioning of parties. It is worth noting that of the six constitutions that lack mentions of parties, four are old constitutions, with the US Constitution dating to the eighteenth century and those of Belgium, Canada, and the Netherlands dating to the nineteenth century. Indeed, if we consult table 3.2 we see that these are the four oldest constitutions among the twenty-nine cases. It is also interesting to note that these constitutions were written during that era when political engineers were still in the process of fully understanding the essential role of parties. Along those lines we should note that while Denmark's current constitution dates to 1953, that country's experience with constitutionalism dates to the nineteenth century. Most of these are also short constitutions, with only those of Belgium and Canada exceeding ten thousand words (see table 3.3) which would naturally preclude too many details.

2. A strict two-party system. The most important and distinctive characteristic of the American party system is its extreme bipartism. The United States has the most stable and well-defined two-party system in our study. While there have been (and remain) a plethora of third parties in the United States, they tend to share a common characteristic: They rarely win many votes, let alone offices within the government. In a few states, especially New York,[2] there are significant third parties, but in the vast majority of the states and at the national level, the Democrats and Republicans reign supreme without serious challenge by third parties. It is highly unusual for members of Congress to be elected under a third-party label. For example, the 111th Congress (2009–2011) had zero third party members in the House of Representatives, and the Senate had only two independents: Bernard Sanders of Vermont and Joseph Lieberman of Connecticut (and both caucused with the Democrats).[3]

If we refer back to table 6.1, which lists the effective number of legislative and electoral parties in our thirty-one cases, we can see that the United States is the only case in which there is an effective

2. And even the New York example is in many ways the exception that proves the rule, since major candidates can be the nominee of both a mainline major party and a minor third party. For example, John McCain was the 2008 presidential nominee in New York of the Republican, Independence, and Conservative Parties. So, on the one hand, there are far more third parties in New York than in most states; on the other, part of this is a function of unusual nomination rules that can link small and large parties.

3. Sanders was an independent member of the House from Vermont from 1991 to 2007 and was elected to the Senate in 2006. Lieberman was a Democrat until his defeat in the 2006 Democratic primary. He went on to win reelection against the Democratic nominee running as an "Independent Democrat."

number of legislative parties less than 2.0 (1.98, to be exact). Further, the United States is only one of three cases with an effective number of electoral parties less than 3.0 (2.18, to go along with South Africa's 2.13 and Greece's 2.83). An effective number barely below 2.0 for legislative parties indicates that there are only two parties with seats, one of which has a small majority over the other (on average). And the effective number of 2.18 in House elections shows that very few votes are cast for candidates other than Democrats and Republicans.

What accounts for this unique position of the United States? One reason is the use of the plurality electoral system in single-seat districts (as discussed in chapter 5), which makes it hard for small parties to win seats, and which in turn makes voters—who do not want to "waste their vote"—reluctant to vote for minor party candidates. This is obviously not a complete explanation, however, because the other three plurality countries are not at the top of the list. The United Kingdom is near the top, in fourth place, but Canada is only in twelfth place and India is number twenty-five, near the bottom of the list.[4]

A more complete explanation can be approached by comparing the effective numbers of parties with the electoral systems, which are indicated in the right column of table 6.1. We can see that other majoritarian systems offer similar advantages to large parties and discriminate against small parties: Australia (Alternative Vote), France (Majority-Plurality), and the Mixed-Member Majoritarian (MMM) systems of Japan, Korea, and Hungary all have an effective number of legislative parties less than 3.0. We now see that there is a clear, but still obviously not perfect, link between electoral systems and numbers of parties: The majoritarian systems tend to be at or near the top of the list, and the PR countries toward the bottom.[5] Recall that

4. In Canada and India, the plurality system also favors the larger parties, but the presence of regional parties, especially in India, means that in any given region, sometimes parties other than the larger national parties are locally dominant.

5. The association would be even stronger if we used pre-electoral alliances to count the effective number of "parties" in Chile (where two-seat districts have led to the formation of two large alliances, each of which presents a joint list in every district) and India (where the two main national parties have

the table is sorted by the effective number of *legislative* parties. When we look at the effective number of *electoral* parties, the impact of the majoritarian systems becomes even clearer. For instance, the United Kingdom, Canada, and especially France all have substantially higher values for electoral parties than for legislative. In the case of France, the difference between effective numbers of electoral and legislative parties is particularly dramatic: 5.68 and 2.78, respectively. This difference reflects many parties running in the first round, but the two-round process winnowing most district contests to just two parties.[6] Likewise the plurality systems in the United Kingdom and Canada under-represent the many small parties, whose votes contribute to increasing the effective number of electoral parties, but which win relatively few seats and thus have less impact on the legislative figure.

What about the unexpectedly low effective numbers of parties in several PR countries at the top of the list? South Africa's 2.11 legislative parties make it look like an almost pure two-party system, but, in fact, South Africa's party system can be described more accurately as a multiparty system with a dominant party, the African National Congress, which has been able to win around two-thirds of the votes and seats in the four democratic elections held so far. The one weakness of the effective-number-of-parties equation is that it makes such a system look like a two-party system. In the 2009 election, for instance, the African National Congress won 264 out of 400 seats (66.0 percent); three parties won 65, 30, and 18 seats each (16.76, 7.5, and 3.0 percent); and nine smaller parties won from 4 to

---

alliances with various regional parties, and each alliance presents only one candidate per district). We follow the convention in using the parties themselves, rather than the alliances, in our calculations. However, a very strong case can be made that the alliances should be used. If we did so, the effective numbers of legislative and electoral parties, respectively, in the 2009 elections in these countries would be 2.17 and 2.56 in Chile and 2.92 and around 4.1 in India.

6. In the French two-round legislative elections, parties beyond the top two are eligible to participate in the runoff (if they obtain votes equivalent to at least 12.5% of the registered voters), but normally trailing parties withdraw their candidates in favor of their strongest alliance partner.

1 seats each. When we plug these numbers into the equation, the result is the deceptive number of 2.11 effective parties.

An additional and generally accepted explanation for the low number of parties in the United States is its presidential system of government. The fact that the presidency is the biggest political prize to be won and that only the largest parties have a chance to win it gives a considerable advantage to the larger parties in legislative elections, too. Once again, however, this is only a partial explanation. For instance, Brazil has a presidential system, too, meaning that the lowest and highest effective numbers of parties are both systems where the biggest political prize is an elected presidency! Several other presidential systems have notably higher effective numbers; in fact, the next lowest figures for electoral parties are in the three-four range (Mexico, 3.43; Korea, 3.83). However, only the United States uses a highly majoritarian method of electing its presidency, too: *multiseat plurality in an electoral college*. As we explain in chapter 8, this system is even more unfavorable to participation by small parties than the direct plurality election of presidents in Korea and Mexico.

3. Systemic (and systematic) use of direct primary elections for nominations. Primaries take the selection of candidates for elective office out of the hands of the party organizations and their formal membership and give it to the entire electorate (or at least a large self-selected subset thereof). The first distinctive characteristic of primaries is that they allow any voter who declares himself or herself to be a member of a party to vote in that party's primary. This "membership" often entails the requirement that a voter be preregistered[7] as a member of a particular party (the *closed* primary), but it can also mean deciding one's party membership on the day of the primary election (the *open* primary).[8] The second crucial characteristic of primary elections is that they are imposed on the parties by the state and are conducted by public officials, that is, they are not

7. The length of time between the preregistration and the vote varies from state to state.

8. Before 2000 another option was available, the blanket primary, in which voters could change their partisan preference office to office without any public declaration whatsoever.

adopted voluntarily by the parties and run by party organizations (Ranney 1981: 86).

Primaries affect parties internally, by making them nonhierarchical. What primaries do is to deprive parties, as organized entities, of their vital role in nominating candidates, and by extension, weaken the disciplining authority of party leaders. Furthermore, primaries require candidates in the same party to compete with each other for the voters' support and encourage these candidates to stress their differences. In the United States, primaries are the near-universal method for the selection of candidates to national legislative office (as well as state level offices)—a pattern that was already clearly established by the 1950s.[9] The United States is clearly unique in this respect.

Primaries are central to the previous item on our list, as they help solidify the two-party system in the United States. The pressures leading to the formation and persistence of third parties in other countries using plurality electoral systems, such as Canada and the United Kingdom, tend to be absorbed by the more flexible nature of the Democratic and Republican Parties in the United States. Direct primary elections contribute a great deal to this pattern. It is much more attractive for dissidents from the mainstream of the two parties to try to gain office by running in one of the two major parties' primaries than to establish or join a minor party. Two examples illustrate this fact.

The first is Texas Congressman Ron Paul, a Republican who also ran for his party's presidential nomination on several occasions. Representative Paul was a Republican member of the House for three stints, first from 1976 to 1977, then 1979 to 1985, and again from 1997 to2013. Between those times in office Paul also ran for president as the Libertarian Party's nominee. Further, Paul is well known for identifying with libertarianism; however, both his successful runs for Congress were under the Republican label. Why might this

9. The system for selecting presidential candidates for the two major parties is also linked to primaries, but it is too complex to simply classify as being nomination by primary election and, further, was not institutionalized until the early 1970s. Presidential primaries are further discussed in ch. 8.

have been the case? Paul clearly determined that his strategic advantage, given the nature of electoral competition in the United States, was to compete for the nomination of one of the major parties in the primaries and then be one of the two viable candidates in the general election. Had he run for the House as a Libertarian, he likely would have lost to a Republican.

A second and more comprehensive example of this nature would be the emergence of the Tea Party faction of the Republican Party in 2009–2010. The Tea Party arose out of discontent with the economy and the policies of President Barack Obama as well as with the Republican Party establishment. However, instead of forming a new political party to challenge the prevailing duopoly, the Tea Party adherents sought nomination in the Republican primaries (save for one case in Nevada[10]). There were a number of high-profile primary fights across the country in 2010 in which Tea Party–backed candidates beat more established Republican politicians, with perhaps the most prominent examples being in Delaware, Kentucky, Utah, and Nevada.[11]

The fundamental point thus is that the primary process allows for party factions to fight it out for control of individual candidacies, and perhaps the party as a whole, from within the nomination process and in a direct appeal to voters in a way that has to be done via third-party formation in other democracies.

Selection procedures in other countries are sometimes referred to as primaries but fail to conform to one or both of the criteria noted earlier. For instance, so-called primary elections in Israel and Belgium are restricted to formal dues-paying party members and are conducted by the parties themselves rather than by the electoral authorities. Other democracies in our study have seen the selective

10. In addition to a Tea Party–favored candidate, Sharron Angle, winning the Republican nomination in Nevada in 2010, another candidate, Scott Ashjian, was able to gain access to the ballot as the Tea Party of Nevada candidate (noted as TPN on the ballot).

11. For a rundown, see the Associated Press: "A look at the Tea Party's primary season wins" online at http://www.salon.com/2010/09/15/us_tea _party_wins/.

usage of primaries that are open to the public and that do not require fees to be paid (for example, Mexico and Colombia), but there is no other party system in the world where nomination via primary is a constituent element of party behavior. Essentially all candidates who run in partisan elections in the United States are selected via primary elections in a way that is unique, even if the prevalence of primaries and primary-like structure have been on the increase globally in the last decade or so.

4. Candidate-centered election campaigns. Not only is the nomination system in the United States candidate-centric (because primary elections are, by definition, about choosing specific persons to run, rather than about choosing parties), but the general-election campaigns for office are candidate-centric as well. Also, in contrast to some systems as discussed in chapter 5, candidates are directly offered up to voters, unlike most proportional representation systems, which offer lists of candidates and thus emphasize the party label.[12]

In American election campaigns, the focus of a given campaign is less on party label than on the views and personal characteristics of individual candidates. Primary elections are elections *within* parties, and hence the party label is completely neutralized. Similarly, nonpartisan elections (discussed further later) were introduced to reduce the significance of partisan affiliations in local politics and have largely succeeded in doing so. With the partial exception of presidential election campaigns in other democracies, the party label is always much more important than the qualities of the individual candidate in these countries.

A key illustration of the candidate-centered nature of US politics versus one that is party-centered is the fact that party leaders have no control of the usage of party labels. To be a Democrat or a Republican simply requires a declaration by the given candidate or of-

12. Even in "open" lists, where candidates compete for votes within their parties' lists (e.g., in Brazil, Finland, and Poland), the fact that seats are allocated based on collective party totals tends to emphasize the "team" aspect of the party organization.

ficeholder.[13] As such, politicians can easily change party affiliation as suits their needs. While not an everyday occurrence, it happens frequently enough to underscore the lack of party control over their so-called members.[14]

5. Nonhierarchical parties. As the previous two points have illustrated, party leaders in the United States lack control over (1) nominations and (2) usage of party labels; therefore they also lack control over (3) the content of given campaigns. These factors add up to parties that are not hierarchical insofar as party leaders lack the tools needed to direct the behavior (for example, campaigns, legislative votes, and so on) of their members. This means that when party leaders attempt to pass specific legislation, they often must negotiate with their members (that is, make bargains) rather than enforce party discipline from the top down. Likewise, party leaders cannot enforce unified campaign themes on their candidates.

Another factor that makes for weak party hierarchy is presidentialism. In parliamentary systems, reasonably disciplined parties are the norm because their ability to control the executive depends on their acting collectively. Parliamentary systems, as we will discuss in some detail in chapter 8, most closely preserve the basic hierarchy

13. A key example would be the switch in 2001 of Senator Jim Jeffords of Vermont, who changed his party affiliation from Republican to being an independent that caucuses with the Democratic Party. This was quite significant given that Jeffords's switch was enough to move the partisan control of the US Senate from Republican to Democratic hands. The Senate elected in 2000 was split fifty–fifty in terms of the two caucuses, and the rule that allowed the Republican vice president (Dick Cheney) to cast a tie-breaking vote meant that leadership of the chamber went to the Republicans. Jeffords's switch lowered the Republican's seat total to forty-nine, allowing the Democrats to assume control of the chamber for the remainder of the 107th Congress. There were also a number of party switches after the 1994 midterms, when the Republicans gained control of both chambers of Congress. For example, Senator Richard Shelby of Alabama and Ben Nighthorse Campbell of Colorado switched from the Democrats to the Republicans.

14. Party switching by legislators is far more common in, e.g., Brazil and Korea.

we sketched in figure 1.1, in the sense that there is a single chain of principal-agent relationships connecting voters to legislators to the executive. Thus it makes sense that parties in parliamentary systems would tend to be hierarchically organized themselves, given that they nominate candidates, organize the legislature, and seek to appoint their leaders to the cabinet (Samuels and Shugart 2010). By contrast, in presidential systems, legislators often find themselves having "competing principals" (Carey 2009), dividing their loyalties between the executive and legislative "branches" of their party (Samuels and Shugart 2010). When we consider the impact separated legislative and executive powers have on parties, and then add to it the other major factors that we have already discussed—primaries and candidate-centered elections—it becomes clear that parties in the United States lack a single center of authority, which is another way of saying they are nonhierarchical.

Although there are no precise comparative indicators of party hierarchy available, it is unlikely that parties anywhere else in our set of countries are as fully and consistently nonhierarchical as they are in the United States. We do have other cases of relatively fluid party lines, notably Colombia (also a presidential system). We also have the case of Japan, a parliamentary system in which parties have continuing internal factions, even in the years since the extremely candidate-centered Single Non-Transferable Vote electoral system was replaced, as discussed in chapter 5. Under the Mixed-Member Majoritarian system, Japanese parties have become more hierarchical, as demonstrated in a major intraparty fight over postal-service privatization in 2005. The party divided over the issue, and Prime Minister (and Liberal Democratic Party leader) Junichiro Koizumi exercised his authority to dissolve the parliament, ran and won an election campaign on the issue, and afterward the party fell back into line behind his leadership. Clearly, he demonstrated how hierarchical parties can be under parliamentary government! Nonetheless, Japanese parties have continued to be notably more internally divided in subsequent years than is the norm for other parliamentary systems. Just as some important parties may diverge from the hierarchical norm of parliamentary government, so too are some parties in presidential and semi-presidential systems more hierarchical than we might expect from the more transactional nature of these constitutional types. Particularly, the party that holds the presidency at any given time is often quite hierarchical in, for example, France and Mexico (Samuels and Shugart 2010), where presidents often dominate their parties to degrees that no US president could even imagine. Examples of parties that do not closely adhere to the hierarchy of parliamentary government or the separated branches of presidential government remind us that parties, while shaped by the constitutional structure and the electoral system, are not fully determined by these institutions.

6. *An increasingly polarized party system.* The ideological span of the US party system is less than many of the other systems under study, in large part due to their being only two parties of any significance. Nonetheless, the differentiation between the parties has increased in recent years. Historically, not only were US parties nonhierarchical, they were also not polarized ideologically because of regional variations within the parties that diluted their ideological concentration. Specifically: the Democratic Party dominated the South regardless of the ideological disposition of the voters, candidates, or officeholders. Electoral contests in that region were, from the post-Reconstruction period (that is, roughly the 1870s) to the 1990s, between liberal Democrats and conservative Democrats (with Republicans essentially being reduced to the status usually reserved in the United States for third parties, that is, election losers). However, in a long-term process that came to fruition in the 1994 congressional elections, and which consolidated into the 2000s, conservative southern Democratic voters (and some officeholders) changed their identification to the Republican Party. This shift had the effect of making both parties more homogeneous ideologically speaking and, hence, causing far more polarization between the parties than had been the case. Recent studies have indicated that the parties have become more unified, in terms of legislative voting patterns, and that the ideological space between the parties has widened. This widening of the gap, which is what is typically meant by "polarization," has been an ongoing process since the 1970s, accelerated after 1994 (especially in the House), and further increased through the first two decades of the 2000s.

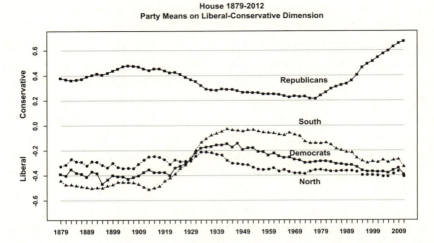

Fig. 6.1. Ideological distance of Republicans and Democrats in the House of Representatives over time
Source: Keith Poole, www.voteview.com.

These patterns are clearly evident in figure 6.1, which plots the mean position of each major party's members in the House of Representatives on a liberal-conservative scale developed by Poole and Rosenthal (1997 and 2007), based on members' votes on legislation. The farther a party's mean position lies toward the top of the graph, the more it leans to the conservative (right) side, whereas points near the bottom of the graph indicate a mean position that is more liberal (or left). The graph not only shows Republicans and Democrats as parties, but also breaks out Democrats according to South and North. The degree to which there used to be a centrist Southern Democratic component to the US party system is thus visible. However, this has now mostly vanished, and the great gap between the mean position of each party is evident in the most recent decades. Both parties have moved away from the center, but Republicans more so. While figure 6.1 shows polarization in the House, a similar process has also occurred in the US Senate.[15]

15. For further discussion, see Royce Carroll, Jeff Lewis, James Lo, Nolan McCarty, Keith Poole, and Howard Rosenthal's Web page that analyzes the DW-NOMINATE data set: http://voteview.com/blog/?p=284. We are grateful to

It is worth noting that this process of polarization has tended to make the United States more like many other democracies, especially in western Europe, in that it means parties are more distinct and focused on national issues, whereas in the past, US parties overlapped in their issue positions and were more internally divided. However, it is probably the case that the overall ideological spread of the two parties remains less than in many of our comparison cases, though measuring ideology across both countries and time periods is difficult (see point 7, subsequently).

To refer back to the previous discussion: The nonhierarchical, or bottom-up, nature of the parties means that the degree to which the parties are polarized or not is a function of the members themselves, not party elites or centrally enforced policy platforms. For example, before the partisan realignment that came about with the 1994 congressional elections, the parties were more ideologically amorphous, as noted earlier, because the result of the bottom-up nature of the parties meant that many conservative southern Democrats influenced the behavior of that party. Once those conservative southern Democrats switched to being conservative southern Republicans, this changed the nature of both parties. Such dynamics mean that factionalism within the parties can lead to changes on policy positions (bubbling from the bottom up), for example, the influence of evangelical candidates within the Republican Party in the 1980s and 1990s and, more clearly, the emergence of the Tea Party faction within the Republican Party in the 2010 election. Faction influence of this nature can be seen in the 2011 fight in the Congress over raising the federal debt limit. In that debate, Republican Party leader Speaker of the House John Boehner appeared willing to compromise with the Senate and the Obama administration on the legislation, but was initially blocked by the Tea Party caucus in the House of Representatives. The nonhierarchical nature of the party system was illustrated by the fact that Speaker Boehner had to negotiate with the Tea Party caucus and could not simply assert control over them, as is the case in more hierarchical party systems (as we typically see in European cases). The ability of Tea Party candidates to win

Professor Poole and his collaborators for granting permission to use a version of their graph here.

primary elections allowed them to, from the bottom up, influence public policy outcomes.

7. A narrow ideological spectrum (with a rightward tilt). Party programs and ideologies differ from each other in many respects in most democracies, but a universal contrast among parties in all democracies concerns their stands on socioeconomic or left-right issues—such as a strong versus weak governmental role in economic planning, support of versus opposition to the redistribution of wealth from the rich to the poor, and the expansion of versus the resistance to governmental social welfare programs. A striking characteristic of the US party system is that, despite some popular rhetoric to the contrary, the United States lacks a significant social democratic party, let alone a true Socialist or Communist Party. Rather, the Democrats and Republicans tend to occupy ideological space that is, in global terms, center to center-right (that is, pro-business and moderate on social policies). Additionally, it should be noted that the United States lacks electorally successful ultraright or extreme nationalist parties, its Green Party is not electorally relevant, and it lacks parties rooted in ethnic or religious minorities. Parties of at least some of these types are found in many of our other thirty democracies, accounting for their higher effective numbers of parties (table 6.1). As such, the general ideological space of American electoral and partisan politics remains, in comparative terms, narrow—recent polarization notwithstanding.

This narrow space with a rightward tilt can be illustrated by considering that the presence of some type of left-leaning party in the legislature is quite common in our other thirty democracies. Indeed, all of our other cases have at least minor, and often major, parties that are significantly to the left of the Democratic Party in the United States. Likewise, many cases in Europe have prominent and electorally successful right-wing nationalist parties. There has been a rise in the number of ultranationalist parties in Europe during the last two decades, such as the True Finns party in Finland, the National Front in France, the Party for Freedom in the Netherlands, and Jobbik in Hungary. These parties have views that are in reaction to the open borders of the European Union and are nativist in nature, if not xenophobic. In recent decades, parties rooted in environmental issues have arisen in many countries, such as Green Parties that are electorally significant and sometimes hold the balance of legislative power in Australia, Germany, and New Zealand. Other countries have parties that articulate specific regional interests, such as the Bloc Québécois in Canada, the Basque and Catalan nationalist parties in Spain, and numerous parties in India.

Some of our cases have members of their legislatures both from left and/or center left and the far right. Greece is perhaps the most extreme example, as in elections within the years of our study there have been members of the parliament elected from the Communist Party of Greece as well as from the protofascist Golden Dawn Party. In general, the US party system, at least in terms of parties capable of winning votes and seats, is limited to the relatively narrow ideological space occupied by the Republicans and Democrats.

8. Nonpartisan elections at the local level. An extreme version of candidate-centric politics can be found in the United States at the local level. About three-fourths of American cities and other local government bodies use ballots that, by law, ban the publication of the party affiliations of the candidates.[16] While a nonpartisan ballot does not guarantee a nonpartisan election, it clearly reduces the relevance of political parties in those races. In the past, many other countries also used ballots on which the names, but not the party affiliations, of the candidates were listed, but this is no longer the rule today. Moreover, it was more a relic of periods in which parties had not yet become important than a deliberate attempt to weaken parties, as it is in the United States. In this respect too, the United States occupies a unique position.

9. Very long election campaigns. In Britain, the national election campaign begins with the dissolution of the House of Commons and ends with the parliamentary election only about one month later. In most other countries, campaigns tend to last more than one month, but no other democracy has election campaigns that last as long as a year or sometimes longer, as it does in the United States. There are three reasons for this peculiarly American phenomenon. One is

16. Another example of nonpartisan elections is the election of the state legislature of Nebraska.

that primary elections necessitate an early start for campaigning by individual candidates. Second, primary elections usually take place at least two months, but usually much longer, before the general elections. Third, nonpartisan elections often use the majority-runoff method, with the runoff taking place at least two months, but also often considerably longer, after the first round of the election.

With regard to the presidential election process, a special reason is that the first primary in New Hampshire takes place roughly ten months before the actual election in early November, and that other states have been scheduling their primaries soon after the New Hampshire primary.[17] As we will see in chapter 8 on the presidency, eight other democracies have presidential elections that use the majority-runoff system and that therefore may require two rounds of elections, and Argentina's qualified-plurality method may also necessitate a runoff. But all these runoffs are held very soon after the first round: between three and five weeks in Argentina, Austria, Brazil, Chile, Colombia, Finland, and Portugal, and only two weeks in France and Poland. France also uses a two-round system for its National Assembly elections, and these are held just one week apart (Massicotte, Blais, and Yoshinaka 2004: 103–15).

10. Importance of private funds in election campaigns. In most countries, campaign funds are mainly party funds rather than funds raised and controlled by individual candidates. The American system of direct primary elections and nonpartisan elections as well as the candidate-centered nature of all election campaigns, including general election campaigns, makes the United States a clear exception to this pattern.

11. Multiple points of access for interest groups. Interest groups concentrate their activities and resources on the institutions and in-

17. In the 2008 electoral cycle, the state of Iowa held its nominating caucuses on January 3. Both Iowa and New Hampshire fiercely and jealously guard their status as the first caucus and primary, respectively, and have threatened to move their contests into December, if need be, to ward off other states trying to move their contests earlier. Indeed, state law in New Hampshire dictates that it is to be the first primary each cycle and has empowered its secretary of state to unilaterally move the primary as needed to maintain its status as first in the land.

dividual policy makers who have the power to make decisions on issues these groups care about. In fact, a good operational indicator of the relative power of different institutions and politicians in a given democracy would be the degree to which they are targeted by interest groups. Organized interest politics in the United States is highly dispersed because of several basic features of American democracy discussed throughout our study: the presidential system and separation of powers, the federal division of power, and the candidate-centric nature of American political parties, which makes for a high degree of independence and power for individual politicians. Most of our other democracies have parliamentary instead of presidential governments, unitary instead of federal systems, and disciplined instead of loosely organized political parties. In all these respects, the United States occupies an unusual position, and the dispersed nature of interest-group activity is a direct consequence of these unusual institutional and partisan characteristics.

Not only are there numerous access points within the political structure, since campaigns (and campaign fund-raising) are candidate-centric, there is also a lot of government in the United States that can be targeted for lobbying. As we noted in chapter 5, there is a large and complex federal government, as well as fifty state governments, which are divided into counties, municipalities, and various special districts. Depending on the issue of interest to a given group, this creates a large number of access points. Consider, for example, a group interested in environmental protection in regards to pesticides. Such a group might lobby the Congress regarding the legal usage of a specific substance nationwide, as well as the Environmental Protection Agency in regards to rules pertaining to that substance. They might also lobby state legislatures over issues such as building codes and the usage of chemicals in that context. They might find it useful to deal with city governments and local construction of drains and sewers as they pertain to runoff and the potential for the pesticide in question to find its way into local water supplies. They might also want to deal with a local mosquito control district and its application of the chemical. Indeed, the complexity of government in the United States can be staggering in terms of layers and scope. In this simple example we have a given group lobbying (1) the national legislature (which would actually be 1a and 1b, since the US Congress is bicameral), (2) a national bureaucracy, (3) a state legislature (in fact, 3a for the first state chamber, and 3b for the second state chamber, except in unicameral Nebraska), (4) local government, and (5) a special district. That's a lot of access points! And, further, there are more (like state and local bureaucracies) that could be added to our scenario. There are, therefore, a lot of incentives to group formation for the purpose of lobbying government in the United States.

12. *The strong influence of business interests on national policy.* In the United States, it is often said, pressure groups representing business and corporate interests exert extremely strong influence on national policy. To what extent, however, is this statement more valid for the United States than for other democracies? The answer can be given in two steps. First, it is probably true that interest groups generally have greater power in the United States than in other democracies as a result of the candidate-centric nature of American political parties (as lobbyist lobby individual legislators as well as party leaders). Where political parties are nonhierarchical, other political actors—and interest groups in particular—simply fill the "space" left open by strong party leadership. Second, business interests have benefited in particular from this open "space," because, as we shall show in the next several paragraphs, the American interest-group system is highly pluralistic and lacks the constraints imposed by the interest-group corporatism in many other countries, and because American labor unions are relatively weak as a result of their low and declining memberships and are unable to counterbalance the pressures exerted by business interests.

13. *A highly pluralistic interest-group system.* The United States clearly fits the general picture of free-for-all and uncoordinated pluralism as described earlier. There are a large number of mutually competitive groups, and tripartism is virtually unknown in the United States. The AFL-CIO looks a bit like a peak organization for labor, but it is really only a loose confederation that does not compare at all to the strong and unified labor union federations in countries like Sweden and Austria. Similarly, while there are strong national organizations representing business, manufacturing, and corporate interests—like the US Chamber of Commerce, the National Asso-

ciation of Manufacturers, and the Business Roundtable—there is no single peak organization that can speak for these interests. But where exactly does the American interest-group system fit on the continuum between pluralism and corporatism? The pluralism scores in table 6.2, which are listed in ascending order, have a theoretical range of zero to four with the higher the number, the more pluralistic the system. The observed range for our democracies runs from 0.38 for Austria, as our country with the most corporatistic interest-group system, up to Canada's 3.17, which is our most pluralistic system. As we can see, the United States is not the most pluralistic country, but with a value of 2.88, it is among the most pluralistic (along with a number of other Anglosphere states).

14. Low levels of membership in labor unions. An aspect of the pluralism-corporatism contrast that deserves separate attention is the degree to which workers are members of labor unions. Corporatism requires that union leaders can speak and act on behalf of labor, but this works optimally only if most workers are members of labor unions. What is often called "union density"—the percentage of employed wage and salary workers who are members of unions— has generally declined in the industrialized democracies in recent decades. Table 6.3 provides the data for twenty-five of our thirty-one countries, specifically those who are members of the Organisation for Economic Co-operation and Development (OECD) and for whom data were available. These data are supplemented in table 6.4, which contains more limited information for our other six cases (the tables are split because of differing data sources that are, therefore, not fully compatible).

Table 6.3 provides both the average union density for these cases from 1990 to 2008 as well as the most recent figures (2008). The figures over time are useful to get a fuller picture of unionization during the recent past. We can also see that uniformly for our cases, the 2008 figures are lower (in some substantially so) than the average. Indeed, there has been a global decline in union membership across countries in the last several decades.[18]

18. For more on this topic, see Scruggs and Lang 2002, whose article title asks, "Where Have All the Members Gone? Globalization, Institutions, and Union Density."

Table 6.2. Interest-group pluralism in thirty-one democracies

Austria	0.38
Sweden	0.42
Finland	0.67
Denmark	0.88
Germany	0.88
South Africa	0.88
Switzerland	0.88
Netherlands	1.00
Brazil	1.13
Mexico	1.20
Belgium	1.33
Japan	1.38
Israel	1.50
Czech Republic	1.75
Australia	1.80
Colombia	1.80
Hungary	1.85
Poland	1.95
Italy	2.08
India	2.15
Chile	2.25
Portugal	2.62
Argentina	2.70
New Zealand	2.71
France	2.75
United States	**2.88**
Korea	2.90
Spain	3.04
United Kingdom	3.08
Greece	3.12
Canada	3.17
Median	*1.80*

Scale: 0–4, with the higher the number indicating more pluralism.
Sources: Lijphart 2012 and authors' estimates.

Table 6.3. Union density rates in twenty-five OECD democracies

	1990–2008 Average	2008
Sweden	79.1	68.3
Finland	75.4	67.5
Denmark	74.0	67.6
Belgium	53.2	51.9
Austria	37.9	28.9
Italy	35.9	33.4
Poland	33.1	15.6
United Kingdom	31.7	27.1
Canada	30.5	27.1
Greece	28.8	24.0
Czech Republic	28.5	20.2
Australia	28.1	18.6
New Zealand	26.5	20.8
Germany	26.1	19.1
Hungary	24.4	16.8
Portugal	23.4	20.4
Netherlands	23.0	18.9
Japan	21.8	18.2
Switzerland	21.1	18.3
Mexico[a]	18.3	17.4
Spain	15.7	14.3
Chile	15.1	13.6
United States	**13.4**	**11.9**
Korea	12.0	10.3
France	8.5	7.7

Note:
[a] Information for Mexico ranges from 1990 to 2005.
Source: OECD Database, http://stats.oecd.org/Index.aspx?DataSet Code=UN_DEN.

Table 6.4. Union density for six non-OECD[a] democracies

	Averages	*Most recent figure*
Argentina	N/A	37.6% (2006)
Brazil	N/A	20.9% (2007)
Colombia	26.8% (1991–1997)	28.7% (1997)
India	21.4% (1990–1998)	25.6% (1998)
Israel	N/A	35.0% (2002)
South Africa	53.6% (1990–1994)	39.8% (2008)

Note:
[a] Israel joined the OECD in 2010, and therefore no data was available in OECD data-bases used to construct this table.
Sources: International Labour Organization, and Hayter and Stoevska 2010.

As expected, the United States is near the bottom of the list, with an average union density of only 13.4 percent for the period under examination, but not in very last place, because France's 8.5 percent is even lower. The contrast is especially striking with the three Nordic countries, in which an average of more than 76 percent of workers belong to unions in those cases. Indeed, if we compare the United States to all of the other cases, it is only one of six countries in the table to have an average density of less than 20 percent (along with Mexico, Spain, Chile, Korea, and France).

CONCLUSIONS

Associations of political actors are essential for representative de-mocracy; without them, citizens could not collectively act as princi-pals over their government, lobby it, and hold it accountable. Never-theless, unlike issue such as what the electoral rules will be or what the relationship between national and subnational governments will be, constitutional planners do not directly create parties or inter-est groups, nor can they guarantee the number of parties or interest groups in a system. In other words, associational groups develop in response to the broader institutional environment rather than being a designed part of that environment.

The US party system, with its rigid bipartism, is especially noteworthy in our discussion in this book about how different the US democracy is, since parties develop in response to their political environment. It is also significantly different from most of the party systems under discussion because of the nonhierarchical organization of the parties and the commensurate significance of the candidates themselves. The weakness of party organizations is especially evident in the candidate selection process, where primaries are used to select the party's nominees.

Likewise, we can ask, Is the pluralistic nature of the American interest-group system related to other characteristics of the American political system? Peter J. Katzenstein (1985: 32, 157) argues that the institutional features of interest-group corporatism are complemented by a strong feeling of social partnership, which "mitigates class conflict between business and unions [and] integrates differing conceptions of group interest with vaguely but firmly held notions of the public interest." It contrasts with the "winner-take-all mentality" characteristic of interest group pluralism. Katzenstein points out that this difference in mentalities also shows up in the contrast between the competitiveness of majoritarian electoral systems and the inclusiveness of proportional representation. In this indirect way, therefore, a significant connection between interest group systems and electoral systems can be said to exist.

CHAPTER 7

LEGISLATIVE POWER

This chapter and the next two focus on the three essential aspects of governing power: the legislative, the executive, and the judicial; in other words, the power to make the laws, the power to put the laws into practice, and the power to interpret how those laws should be applied when disputes arise. This chapter examines the lawmaking power as manifested in the design of the Congress of the United States. In *Federalist 51*, Madison wrote, "In republican government, the legislative authority necessarily predominates." Indeed, in most of his theoretical writings, Madison focused heavily on the role of legislative power. If we think back to chapter 2, we will recall that the framers of the US Constitution spent most of their time at the Philadelphia Convention discussing the design of the legislature. The government of the United States under the Articles of Confederation had been based on a unicameral legislature, and the major plans presented to the conventions (for example, the Virginia and New Jersey Plans) used legislative design as their primary foundations (see the appendix to chapter 2). The key political compromise in Philadelphia revolved around the design of the legislature, specifically the Great Compromise that led to equal representation of the states in the second chamber of the Congress (as discussed in chapter 2). As such, the discussion of legislative power has a special place not only in democratic theory, but also in the political engineering of James Madison, and was central to the debate over the US Constitution.

In the case of representative democracy (that is, "republican government" in Madison's language), a legislature is the central political institution, as it functions as the main focus of representation and controls the basics of policy making. It is within the process of electing a national legislature that the electorate most directly exercises its role as the principal, sending its agents to the capital to make laws and oversee the functioning of government for a set amount of time and then holding them accountable at the next election. For this reason, it is impossible to conceive of representative democracy without an elected legislative body.

INSTITUTIONAL CHOICE SET

When discussing the design of legislatures, there are a series of specific choices that can be made in terms of how the institution is structured, including how it represents the population and how it functions. We focus here on the basic structure of the legislature with some further discussion of representation. By structure we mean its basic constitutional "architecture" or, more specifically, whether it is unicameral or bicameral, and if bicameral, how those chambers interact, which dictates how many veto gates there may be within the legislature, as well as how hard it may or may not be to open those gates. By representation, we mean how its members are selected and what that means for representing constituents. There is also the fundamental question of how many seats will be in the chamber.

Legislatures may be structured to be either unicameral or bicameral, that is, to have one chamber or two.[1] In the early development of legislative bodies, such as the British Parliament, two chambers were created to allow for different types of representation. The House of Commons developed as a representative body of shire and borough interests, while the House of Lords represented clergy and the hereditary, title-holding class. Some modern second chambers have origins of this nature. Typically, these second chambers do not have as extensive an ability to veto the first chamber as has the US Senate (more on the power relationships between chambers to come).

1. Indeed, there is no reason, from both a theoretical and historical perspective, that a legislature could not have more chambers. For example, the South African apartheid constitution of 1983 called for a tricameral structure. However, the norm is for a legislature to have either one or two chambers.

In the modern context, bicameralism is typically adopted by federal states (as we discussed in chapter 4) so as to allow one chamber to represent the general population and another chamber to represent the interests of the subunits (recall figure 4.2). If there are to be two chambers, the next question becomes the relative powers of the two chambers and their interrelationship. To approach this question, we can think of two dimensions of bicameralism (Lijphart 2012). The first is the *symmetry* of the powers of the first and second chambers; that is, do they have equal powers, or is one chamber (usually the first) much stronger than the other? The second dimension is the *congruence* of the constituencies of the two chambers; that is, are they elected in the same way, or differently?

When a legislature has two chambers, the most fundamental question is, To what degree are the chambers equal in their legislative powers? In a perfectly *symmetrical* relationship, all legislative activity must pass both chambers in identical form and neither chamber can have an advantage in the process (that is, neither side has a final say by itself, nor are some types of bills, such as money bills, the domain of only one chamber). The other extreme is total *asymmetry*, wherein one chamber can make legislation by itself without regard to the views of the second chamber. There is also a middle ground wherein second chambers have mechanisms that are not full and direct vetoes but nonetheless can block legislation or, at least, force the first chamber to transact with it. Table 7.1 lists and categorizes the bicameral cases in our study, placing them in these three categories: asymmetry, medium symmetry, and high symmetry. The role each chamber plays in passing legislation is directly linked to the concept of veto gates, first raised in chapter 1: Each chamber that has a say over the passage of legislation is a veto gate insofar as each gate must be opened to allow legislation to pass through. In unicameral systems there is only one gate, and in bicameral systems there are two, but the difficulty of opening the gate in a given situation can vary.

How to properly understand these chambers can be tricky, because while the notion of asymmetry versus symmetry may appear dichotomous, in fact it is a continuum. For the purpose of classification, therefore, we have three categories: asymmetry, medium symmetry, and high symmetry. The two extremes are easy to understand: In asymmetrical cases, the second chamber is not a veto gate at all. In

Table 7.1. Strength of bicameralism in twenty-two democracies

Asymmetry (no second chamber veto) N=6	Medium symmetry (some limitations on second chamber veto) N=8	High symmetry (strong second chamber veto) N=8
Austria	Canada	Argentina
Belgium	Japan	Australia
Czech Republic	Germany[a]	Brazil
France	India	Chile
Poland	Mexico[b]	Colombia
Spain	Netherlands[c]	Italy
	South Africa	Switzerland
	United Kingdom	**United States**

Notes: Italics indicate federal cases.
[a] Second-chamber veto applies only to bills affecting the states.
[b] The Mexican second chamber lacks a veto over the budget.
[c] The Dutch second chamber has an absolute veto, but it lacks the power to amend bills.
Sources: Tsebelis and Money 1997: 50–52; Maddex 2008; and authors' assessments.

cases of high symmetry, both chambers are veto gates, meaning that every bill must pass both chambers in identical form. In the medium category the second chamber may be limited in terms of types of bills that it has power over, or its veto may be less than complete.

An example of the medium category would be the British case, where the House of Commons drafts and votes on all laws, while all the House of Lords can do is object to bills and cause a delay of up to a year, at which time the Commons can pass the bill without the Lords' consent.[2] This type of veto is referred to as a *suspensory* veto because instead of an outright block, it suspends action for a time. On the one hand, this is an asymmetrical power relationship, because ultimately the House of Commons wins. However, in practical terms, this is a real power because legislation is often time sensitive (sometimes because the policy problem is a pressing one, or the majority has a policy preference that it wants to enact without

2. The exact process is spelled out in the UK Parliament Acts.

having to wait a year). Hence, the ability to delay underscores that the relationship between the chambers is not as hierarchical as it may seem initially. Often instead it is transactional, and the government and Commons majority choose to compromise with the Lords majority. In other words, the Lords can close the veto gate, at least for a year, which can cause a reaction by the Commons to try to find a way to persuade members of the Lords to open that gate, which may require concessions by the majority in the Commons.

Also in these types of seeming asymmetrical relationships between chambers, such as in Canada, it may be that paper powers and behavior are not always in synch (a situation that can, therefore, change over time). It had been the practice of the Canadian Senate to defer to the first chamber; however, in recent years a change in partisan control of the chambers has caused the Senate to change its behavior and assert paper powers that it had not been in the habit of using in the past.

Since the behavior of a given legislative body is linked to the way that the chamber represents citizens, it stands to reason that different types of representation processes would lead to different types of legislative behavior. This is why the question of congruence or incongruence of the chambers in a bicameral system can matter. For example, in the German parliament, the first chamber is selected via the vote, with representation of the population being a combination of electoral districts and a national vote. The second chamber, however, consists of members named by the subunit (Länder) governments to represents those units. As such, this system is one of incongruence. Most of the federal cases are incongruent in this sense (see chapter 4 for more discussion of this topic). Some second chambers are, however, elected in a manner that makes them relatively congruent with the first chamber. One common source of moderate incongruence is the use of a different electoral system in the two chambers, or a similar electoral system but with different-size districts and other variations of the sort we discuss in chapter 5. Further, as we shall see later in this chapter, chambers of bicameral legislatures often have significantly different sizes.

As noted in chapter 6, the electoral rules of a given country will influence the number of parties in a given party system. The number of parties is quite important to understanding legislative activities, as legislatures typically operate under majority rule. This is true for the passing of legislation (although sometimes other rules may apply, as we will see later), but also for organizing the internal operations of the legislature. Majorities are further (and especially) relevant in parliamentary systems where the legislature selects the executive. If a legislature is dominated by a two-party system with a clear majority party, as has historically been the case in the United Kingdom (an average effective number of legislative parties of 2.32 from 1990 to 2010—see table 6.1), then issues like government formation and legislation are relatively straightforward. However, in countries like Israel, which has a true multiparty system (an average effective number of legislative parties of 6.58), the formation of operating majorities can require substantial interparty negotiations. As such, we can see the intersection of several key institutional variables here: electoral rules, the legislature, and (in some cases) the selection of the executive branch (more on this in chapter 8). An increasing number of parties within a legislative chamber tends to make internal decision making and agreement more difficult. The earlier notion of opening the veto gate is relatively easy if there is a unified majority in a given chamber that holds the keys to that gate. However, if opening the gate requires the agreement of multiple parties within a legislative coalition, then individual parties or factions within that coalition may be able to be veto players, who withhold their consent to open the veto gate unless granted some concession. In other words: If it takes 50 percent plus one of the legislature to vote to pass legislation through the chamber, but no one party controls this majority on its own, then two or more parties must engage in interparty transactions in order to arrive at a decision to open the gate and thus pass a bill or take some other action. Such transactions are especially critical in parliamentary systems with multiparty coalitions that must work together for the government to function, a point discussed in chapter 8.

THE US CONGRESS IN COMPARATIVE PERSPECTIVE

The US Congress differs in many respects from the legislatures of the other democracies that we analyze in this book. The most important distinction when compared to most of our other democracies is that Congress has no role in the selection of the executive[3] and no role in removing it, except in extraordinary circumstances (impeachment for "high crimes and misdemeanors"). Of course, the reason for this distinction is that the United States has a presidential form of government, in which the executive authority originates and survives in office separately from the legislature. These themes are discussed in chapter 8 on the executive.

This section details nine specific areas in which the United States is unique, or near unique, in comparison to our other thirty democracies.

1. Symmetrical bicameralism for legislation. The US Constitution created a bicameral legislature with a second chamber at least as powerful as the first. As noted earlier, one way to look at bicameralism is the question of whether the two chambers share the same legislative power (are symmetrical) or have different power (are asymmetrical). The federal bargain in the United States calls for the two chambers to be coequal, meaning their powers are symmetrical. All legislation must be approved by both chambers in identical form before being sent on to the president for approval (or veto). Notably, this symmetry applies to the federal budget, which is not the case in all federal systems. For example, in Mexico, the expenditure side of the budget must pass only the first chamber (while revenue bills, like all other legislation, must pass both houses). This perfect symmetry of legislative power in the US case places it in the minority in this study. See table 7.1 to see the types of symmetry in our bicameral cases. The symmetrical nature of the Congress means that each chamber is a key veto gate within the policy-making process. No policy can be passed without the consent of both chambers.

3. It should be noted that if no candidate receives an absolute majority of the electoral vote, then the House of Representatives chooses the president. This has only happened twice: in the election of 1800, when there was a tie, and 1824, when four candidates split the vote. While the framers thought that Congress would often have to select the president (see *Federalist 66* and *68,* in Madison, Hamilton, and Jay 1987), it basically only worked out that way twice, and one of those (the 1800 example) was the result of poorly written rules in Article II of the Constitution, regarding the election of the president and vice president that were changed by the 12th Amendment to the Constitution.

2. Some asymmetry favoring the second chamber. While the most important part of the relationship between chambers is the question of power over legislation, there are other functions performed by legislative chambers. Interestingly, in some ways, the Senate is even more powerful than the House of Representatives. This is unusual, in a comparative sense, as typically any discussion of asymmetry favors the first chamber. For instance, only the Senate has the authority to ratify international treaties (by a two-thirds vote) and only the Senate confirms (or rejects) the president's cabinet nominees and other federal officeholders, including federal judges and Supreme Court justices. In the area of treaties and appointments, then, the two chambers are asymmetrical, but in favor of the second chamber. The other bicameral and presidential systems in the Americas—federal Argentina, Brazil, and Mexico and unitary Chile and Colombia—all share this asymmetry, having some exclusive powers for their senate. Outside the Americas (and presidentialism), asymmetrical (or, at least, weakly symmetrical) bicameralism is common and almost uniformly means the second chamber is the weaker of the two (although as noted earlier, the degree of weakness varies).

Thus the US second chamber is significantly more powerful than those of several other federal systems. Not only must all bills, including expenditures, pass it as well as the first chamber, but also it has special powers. Notably, however, even if all federal systems have second chambers to represent the interests of the units of the federation, few of those second chambers are as powerful as the US Senate.

3. Supermajority requirement in the Senate versus majoritarianism in the House. Debate in the United States Senate is governed by the idea that individual members of the chamber are allowed to speak on a given matter as long as they wish, with debate only ending if, as per Senate Rule XXII (the cloture rule), three-fifths of the chamber agrees to do so. The requirement that debate can only end with a vote of sixty senators means that many bills are never brought to a vote. The traditional notion of a filibuster is that of talking a bill to death, that is, endless debate by a given senator or group of senators in the hopes of creating such a massive delay that the Senate will agree to kill the given bill. This type of filibuster is associated in the public consciousness with the classic film *Mr. Smith Goes to Washington,* starring Jimmy Stewart. A key historical example of an extended debate in the hope of defeating legislation came in an attempt to block the Civil Rights Act of 1964, which lasted fifty-seven working days.

Modern usage of the filibuster mechanism has evolved to the point that actual floor debate need not take place to block a bill from a vote. The known disposition of a sufficient number of senators to vote against cloture is normally sufficient to block a bill, and hence creates a de facto supermajority requirement for all legislation to escape the Senate (save the budget, which by law cannot be filibustered).[4] Indeed, the process is such that even one single senator can attempt to block legislation by signaling a willingness to filibuster a bill, an action known as a hold. As such, the Senate has increasingly run on the principle of a supermajority requirement since the early 1970s.

As Koger (2010) discusses, the notion that that US Senate should function under supermajority requirements is not a function of constitutional design or intent. Rather, it is an example of how the evolution of the internal rules of a given institution can change over time and have profound systemic effects. Not only can senators use these powers on legislation, but they can also place holds and threaten filibusters on appointments to the federal courts and to the executive branch.

Supermajority rule in the US Senate is even more significant when one considers the nature of representation in the body (recall our discussion in chapter 4, and especially table 4.3 and figures 4.3 and 4.4). Since each state is allotted two seats regardless of its population size, it is possible for senators representing both a minority of the Senate and a substantial minority of the population to block ma-

---

4. The Congressional Budget Act of 1974 forbids the filibustering of budget resolutions and also allows for a majority vote on bills that reconcile budget matters between the chambers. This is done by creating a time limit on such matters. However, this does not mean that individual spending bills cannot be filibustered. Budget resolutions set spending guidelines, but the actual appropriations and spending of money is handled in separate legislation, which can be filibustered,

jor legislation. Indeed, if the twenty-one smallest states in terms of population banded together, they would have forty-two votes in the Senate and would represent 11.21 percent of the population of the states. This fact is considered problematic in terms of the representative function of the Senate (at least vis-à-vis the population) and underscores an example of incongruence in representation between the two chambers. Proponents of the supermajority requirements also note that since a majority of states (twenty-six) can be formed from just 17.7 percent of the population, the supermajority requirement can also serve as a protection against small-state dominance of the chamber. Of course, supermajority mechanisms are typically deployed not as a result of state-level politics, but because of ideological/partisan goals.

These rules and procedures make a determined minority of forty-one senators into a formidable veto player within the US system, as without the consent of those senators, the veto gate that is the Senate cannot be opened. This requires internal transactions between the majority and the minority in the Senate; nothing of the sort is required in the House, where majority rule prevails. As we noted in chapter 6, using the filibuster rule is increasingly the behavior of the minority party in US politics, given the increasingly polarized nature of the parties.

The two chambers of the United States Congress are symmetrical in terms of legislative power, and so the necessity to have a supermajority in the Senate is extremely significant in terms of understanding the legislative process in the United States (as we will illustrate in a case study in chapter 10), and it is unique in this regard vis-à-vis our other democracies.

4. A first chamber with a fixed size. We would expect that the legislatures of small countries would be smaller than those of large countries, and, as a general rule, that is indeed the case. In the US House of Representatives, each state is allotted a number of representatives based on its population, with the proviso that each state must have at least one representative. We might also expect that a country's legislature would tend to grow with its population. That is also generally true, but the United States recently has been an aberration. After having been increased in size periodically over the first century following its establishment, the House of Representatives has mostly remained fixed in size, at 435 members, since 1912.[5] After each census, every ten years, the House must be *reapportioned,* which means that the number of seats per state must be determined based on the updated population information. Given that the size of the House is fixed, with each reapportionment, some states lose one or more House seats, even if they have gained population compared to the previous census. For instance, after the 2000 census, New York and Pennsylvania each lost two seats and several other states each lost one seat, in order to allow faster-growing states like California, Florida, Nevada, and Texas to gain seats. If, instead of being fixed, the size of the House were allowed to grow periodically, it would be possible to add seats to the fastest growing states without taking seats away from states with slower growing (but not decreasing) populations. Prior to 1912, new members were typically added to the House after each census.

Some of our other democracies likewise have fixed sizes. For instance, Israel's Knesset has been fixed at 120 seats since the state was created in 1949. The Tweede Kamer of the Netherlands has been fixed at 150 since 1956, and had been fixed at 100 for several decades before that. Finland has had the same number of legislators in its Eduskunta even longer than the United States has had in its House: 200 members ever since the first election in independent Finland in 1907. On the other hand, most countries adjust their legislature's size every few decades, and at least one, the United Kingdom, has increased the size of its House of Commons at almost every election.[6] Not all movements are upward; Belgium, Colombia, Italy, and Japan are among the very few countries to have decreased the size of their first chamber in the 1990s. Table 7.2 shows the sizes, in terms of seats, of the legislatures of thirty-one democracies.

5. This number was originally established in the Apportionment Act of 1911. There were temporary increases when Alaska and Hawaii were admitted as states in 1959, but after the 1960 census, seats were reapportioned and the House returned to 435 members.

6. In 2005, however, the size of the House of Commons was reduced slightly.

Table 7.2. Size (in seats) of legislative houses in thirty-one democracies (as of 2010)

	First or only chamber	Second chamber	Ratio of sizes (second to first)
United Kingdom	650	741	1.14
Italy	630	315	0.50
Germany	*622*	*69*	*0.11*
France	577	343	0.59
India	*545*	*250*	*0.46*
Brazil	*513*	*81*	*0.16*
Mexico	*500*	*128*	*0.26*
Japan	480	242	0.50
Poland	460	100	0.22
United States	***435***	***100***	***0.23***
South Africa	*400*	*90*	*0.23*
Hungary	386		
Spain	*350*	*264*	*0.75*
Sweden	349		
Canada	*308*	*105*	*0.34*
Greece	300		
Korea	299		
Argentina	*257*	*72*	*0.28*
Portugal	230		
Czech Republic	200	81	0.41
Finland	200		
Switzerland	*200*	*46*	*0.23*
Austria	*183*	*63*	*0.34*
Denmark	179		
Colombia	165	102	0.62
Australia	*150*	*76*	*0.51*
Belgium	*150*	*71*	*0.47*
Netherlands	150	75	0.50
New Zealand	122		
Chile	120	38	0.32
Israel	120		

Note: Federal cases are in *italics*.

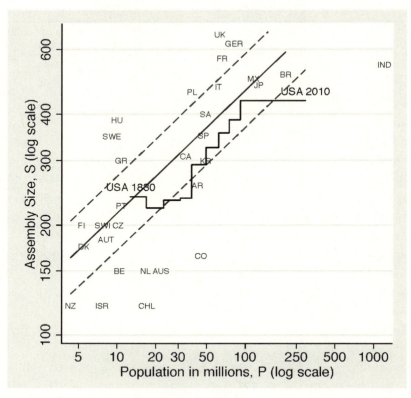

Fig. 7.1. Assembly size and population

What size is the right size? Figure 7.1 plots the size of national assemblies (sole or first chambers) against population. The solid diagonal line in the figure shows the "cube-root law" prediction, derived by Taagepera (1972; see also Taagepera and Shugart 1989), based on a deductive model that assumes that a legislature's size is set to balance the needs of members to communicate with their constituents and with one another. If we think of Taagepera's cube-root law as expressing an approximately optimal size for a given country's legislature, and the dashed lines in the figure as showing a range of relatively modest deviations from the optimum for any given population, we can see that some countries have legislatures that are surprisingly small or large. Nonetheless, the fit of the cube-root law to the data is remarkably good, especially when we consider that none of the decisions in these countries on assembly size was likely taken after consulting a political science text![7]

A glance at figure 7.1 shows that the United States is among the countries with a significantly smaller House than the cube-root law would predict. This is not surprising, of course, given that the size has been fixed since 1912, and the US population has more than tripled since then. The figure also shows the trend over time in the United States, since 1830. It is clear that up until the US population reached about 185 million (in the 1960s), the size of the House had remained no smaller than the cube root of half the population since the time of the Civil War. However, the size of the House around the turn of the twenty-first century is equivalent to the cube root of less than a third of the population.

The US House is not short of the cube-root prediction by as much as the Chilean Chamber of Deputies, but it is quite a bit smaller than what the cube-root law would imply as optimal. Several European countries have assemblies that are much higher than the cube-root estimate. In fact, the 435 members of the US House would be about "optimal" for Germany, whereas the largest assembly among our twenty-nine democracies, the UK House of Commons, with around 650 members, would be consistent with the cube-root law if it were serving a nation the size of the United States.

The size of the House of Representatives is not currently a political issue in the United States; however, two trends could eventually come together to place the idea of periodic increases in the size of the House back on the agenda: (1) states with slower-growing populations continuing to lose seats with subsequent reapportionments, and (2) an increasing malapportionment as the smallest states continue to have 1/435 of the House representation, even as they fall further and further below that share of an expanding national population.

7. If we run an Ordinary Least Squares (OLS) regression on logarithms of our thirty-one countries' populations and assembly sizes, the coefficient on population is .293 (with R^2 of .52); however, the constant term, which theoretically should be zero, is .26 but utterly insignificant. Rerunning without the constant yields a coefficient of .328, or almost exactly the expected one third.

What about second chambers? There is no reason why they should necessarily be related to national population, because their purpose is usually defined as representing some other constituency. For instance, the size of the Senate in the United States (and also in Argentina, Australia, Brazil, and Mexico) is simply the product of the number of states times the equal number of senators constitutionally mandated to each state. It is notable that there is only one exception to the rule, visible in table 7.2, that a country's second chamber is always smaller than its first chamber, the United Kingdom. The United States thus has one of the smaller second chambers relative to is first chamber (100/435 = .23), but not as small as Germany's (69/603 = .11). The table also shows for each bicameral system the ratio of the size of its second chamber to that of its first chamber. The mean ratio for federal systems is about .34, whereas for unitary systems it is .53. The difference is statistically significant.[8] This is probably due to the common practice in federal systems of having some small fixed number of second-chamber members per subunit (see chapter 3), which naturally keeps the size of the second chamber small. By contrast, in unitary systems, the basis of representation is usually not subunits, and so there is less reason to limit their size, even if the norm nonetheless is that they are considerably smaller than first chambers.

In considering relative sizes of chambers, two points about other major English-speaking democracies, one federal and the other not, are of interest. First, in federal Australia, the constitution (Article 24) specifically states that the first chamber shall have a number of representatives "as nearly as practicable, twice the number of senators"—probably the one case of a mandated ratio between a country's two chambers. Second, in the United Kingdom, when a bill was submitted to Parliament in 2012 to change the appointed second chamber to mostly elected, it proposed cutting its size to around 450. While this would still be larger than half the size of the House of Commons, if it were enacted it would bring the United

---

8. It is significant with about 98% confidence; even if the anomalous case of the United Kingdom, the only case with a ratio greater than one, is ignored, the difference (changing to .34 and .46) remains significant (at just under 95%).

Kingdom in line with the norm of second chambers being smaller than first chambers.

5. Short terms of office for members of the House of Representatives. The two-year term of office for US representatives is uniquely short. The first or only houses of the legislatures of all of our other thirty democracies have longer terms. This is shown in the first column of table 7.3. Only three of the other legislative chambers have three-year terms: in Australia, New Zealand, and Mexico. The unicameral Swedish parliament also had three-year terms from 1970 to 1994, but reverted to four-year terms from 1994 on. All of the others have four-year or five-year terms. In other words, most of the other chambers have terms that are at least twice those of members of the US House of Representatives. The most common term length, in twenty of our democracies, is four years. Five-year terms are found in the United Kingdom and some former British colonies, in addition to France and Italy.

These are usually maximum terms—in twenty-three of our thirty-one democracies, as table 7.3 shows—and premature dissolutions of

Table 7.3. Terms of office of members of the first or only chambers of national legislatures in thirty-one democracies

Country	Terms of office (years)	Fixed or maximum?
United States (n=1)	2	Fixed
Australia, New Zealand (n=2)	3	Maximum
Mexico (n=1)	3	Fixed
Austria, Belgium, Czech Republic, Denmark, Finland, Germany, Greece, Hungary, Israel, Japan, Netherlands, Poland, Portugal, Spain, Sweden (n=15)	4	Maximum
Argentina,[a] Brazil, Chile, Colombia, Korea, Switzerland (n=6)	4	Fixed
Canada, France, India, Italy, South Africa, United Kingdom (n=6)	5	Maximum

Note:
[a] Argentina has staggered terms, with half of the chamber coming up for reelection every two years.

the legislatures in parliamentary systems may shorten them considerably. The actual average for the other thirty democracies is somewhere between three and four years—still much longer than the two-year term served by members of the US House of Representatives.

In sharp contrast to their colleagues in the House, US senators serve very long, six-year terms—in fact, also longer than any of the first chambers listed in table 7.3. However, the appropriate comparison here is not with first chambers but with second chambers elsewhere, and, in particular, with the eleven other second chambers whose members (or almost all of whose members) are elected by direct popular vote; the other democracies have either unicameral legislatures or second chambers that are largely elected indirectly. Table 7.4 provides the figures. Terms vary from a relatively short maximum term of four years in Poland to the long, and fixed, eight-year terms in Brazil and Chile. The US Senate's fixed six-year term is actually also the median term for the twelve elected second chambers—and therefore not exceptional.

The longer terms of second-chamber members in the United States and some other countries are accompanied by staggered terms. That

Table 7.4. Terms of office of members of directly elected second chambers of national legislatures in twelve democracies

Country	Terms of office (years)	Fixed or maximum?
Poland (n=1)	4	Maximum
Colombia, Switzerland (n=2)	4	Fixed
Italy (n=1)	5	Maximum
Australia (n=1)	6	Fixed[b]
Argentina,[a] Czech Republic,[a] Japan,[a] Mexico, **United States**[a] (n=5)	6	Fixed
Brazil,[a] Chile[a] (n=2)	8	Fixed

Notes:
[a] Indicates staggered terms.
[b] The Australian Senate can be dissolved, but the conditions for dissolution are difficult to meet.

is, not all members of the second chamber are elected at the same time, meaning that elections occur more frequently than would be implied by simply looking at the term length. In fact, of the eight countries shown in table 7.4 with terms of six or more years, only in Mexico are all senators elected at the same time. Thus longer terms and staggering are both common in second-chamber elections; by contrast, among our thirty-one democracies, there is only one with staggered first-chamber terms: Argentina, where half the seats are up for election every two years.

Staggering of second chambers takes two basic forms. Either just a portion of the districts (states or provinces, in the case of the federal systems) can elect second-chamber members at any given election, or just a portion of a district's seats can be renewed at any given election. The United States, Argentina, Chile, and the Czech Republic follow the first form of staggering, whereas Australia, Brazil, and Japan follow the second. For instance, in the United States Senate, there are elections in about one-third of the states every two years, and because each of the two senators per state is elected separately, every state has a senate election in two out of every three elections. In Argentina, all three of any province's senators are elected at the same time, but each senate election takes place in only one-third of the provinces. In Brazil the term is eight years, but every state elects alternately one or two of its three senators every four years. Similarly, in Australia, every three years each state elects six of its twelve senators.[9]

6. Inflexible timing of congressional elections. Whether terms of office are fixed or maximum terms affects the actual length of time that legislators serve, but its more important effect is on the timing of elections. Because congressional terms of office in the United States are fixed, elections occur on a fixed schedule. This pattern differs from that of most other democracies where the first or only chamber has a flexible (maximum) term, and where elections may

9. The exception is in the rare case of a dissolution of the senate, in which case all twelve seats must be filled, half from each state for the full six years and the other half for only three years. The capital and Northern Territory have only two senators each, and all are renewed every three years.

happen before the formal end of the term; in fact, in some countries, such as the United Kingdom, parliamentary elections frequently take place about a year before the end of the maximum term. Of our thirty-one first chambers, twenty-three have flexible terms, and only eight, including the United States, have fixed terms. Seven of the eight countries with fixed-term elections are presidential systems, which foreshadows an important theme of chapter 8 on executive types: A very definitional feature of the presidential system is fixed terms. Parliamentary systems, on the other hand, generally allow for the possibility of early elections, although it is possible for parliamentary systems to have fixed terms, as well. For instance the coalition government in the United Kingdom after the 2010 election legislated practically fixed election dates.[10] The eighth democracy out of our thirty-one that has fixed terms is Switzerland, which is neither parliamentary nor presidential (as will be discussed in chapter 8).

The pattern of most of our democracies having variable terms is reversed when we turn our attention to second chambers. Ten of twelve second chambers have fixed terms. However, this is largely a function of the presence of six presidential systems among the twelve democracies with directly elected upper houses. All six have fixed-term second chambers, as do two parliamentary systems—the Czech Republic and Japan—and Switzerland, which has a hybrid system of government.[11]

7. Election by plurality in single-seat districts. Democracies use many different systems for the election of their national legislatures, and there is no electoral system among these that is exactly the same as that in another country. However, electoral systems can be grouped

10. There remain contingencies under which an early election can occur, hence we continue to indicate the term as "maximum" in table 7.3 Critically, it is no longer at the discretion of the prime minister to "advise" the monarch to dissolve the House of Commons. Some Australian states and Canadian provinces, as well as Norway (not one of our cases), all of which have parliamentary systems, have fixed term lengths.

11. Australia's Senate terms are almost fixed, though there are contingencies in which the chamber can be dissolved.

in broad categories (as discussed in chapter 5). The most important contrast is between majoritarian and proportional systems. In most majoritarian systems, the country is divided into election districts, each of which elects one representative to the legislature. The most common election rule in majoritarian systems is the plurality rule: The candidate with the most votes wins, even if he or she garners less than a majority of the total vote. As table 7.5 shows, the United States (with minor exceptions, as noted in chapter 5) is one of four democracies using the plurality method for first-chamber elections. Two other countries, Australia and France, also use majoritarian systems in single-seat districts, but with the Alternative Vote (using ranked-choice ballots) and two-round Majority-Plurality, respectively; see chapter 5 for details. Plurality and other majoritarian systems favor large parties, because it is very difficult for minority party candidates to win a sufficiently large number of votes to secure election. In contrast, proportional representation (PR) systems use multiseat districts in which seats are allocated to parties in rough proportion to the votes that the parties receive. The other categories of systems noted in table 7.5 are PR systems that have a bonus for

Table 7.5. Electoral systems for first or only chambers of national legislatures in thirty-one democracies

Canada, India, United Kingdom, **United States** (n=4)	Plurality
Australia (n=1)	Alternative Vote
France (n=1)	Majority-Plurality
Hungary, Japan, Korea, Mexico (n=4)	Mixed-Member Majoritarian
Greece, Italy (n=2)	Proportional representation with bonus
Argentina, Austria, Belgium, Brazil, Chile, Colombia, Czech Republic, Denmark, Finland, Germany, Israel, New Zealand, Netherlands, Poland, Portugal, South Africa, Spain, Sweden, Switzerland (n=19)	Proportional representation (PR; including Mixed-Member Proportional)

Note: Current systems as of 2010 are shown.

the largest party (Greece) or alliance (Italy since 2006) and Mixed-Member Majoritarian systems (as explained in chapter 5).

As table 7.5 shows, PR is by far the most common system for first-chamber elections among our thirty-one democracies; the American plurality system is not unique but is used in only three other countries: Canada, India, and the United Kingdom. When we add Australia and France to the category of majoritarian systems, the number of such systems increases to six out of thirty-one. The two categories of intermediate systems combine for another six countries that do not elect their first chambers solely via PR methods. Thus the total of all non-PR or not fully PR systems still amounts to a minority of about 38 percent of all of our countries, with the majority using PR systems. Obviously, if we count the two systems of PR with bonus with the PR category, then PR systems are even more dominant, amounting to more than two-thirds of the democracies.

8. Affirmative gerrymandering. The winner-take-all nature of single-seat systems favors majorities: not only partisan majorities, as discussed earlier, but also social groups such as ethnic and racial majorities, especially if they are not geographically concentrated. The problem is often even further exacerbated when plurality voting is used in multimember districts (plurality bloc voting), the polar type of which is an at-large plurality election, that is, a plurality election in a multiseat district that is the entire jurisdiction. In this case a group that might have been large enough to form the majority in a single seat constituency is submerged by voters of the majority group in a multiseat constituency. In the United States, the principal method to allow greater opportunity for minority electoral success within the framework of plurality-based elections is often called "affirmative gerrymandering" (this is sometimes called *majority-minority districting*). These types of districts normally involve drawing the lines in such a way that protected minority groups, such as African-Americans or Latinos, either constitute majorities in these districts or constitute a majority of the voters in a given party's primary electorate. In the former case, a unified minority community can be assured of electing the candidate of its choice; in the latter case, it can be assured of doing so if the minority candidate of choice wins the primary and then there is sufficient nonminority "crossover" voting among party identifiers in the general election to give that candidate a victory. Note that, in these instances, the way in which districts are drawn matters a lot.

Legally the creation of majority-minority districts is not required in the United States, but what is required are lines being drawn that do not have either the purpose or effect of diluting the voting strength of groups that are protected under the Voting Rights Act of 1965 and its subsequent renewals and extensions, for example, African Americans, Latinos, Asian Americans or Native Americans. Thus, for example, large and geographically concentrated minority groups may not have their voting strength fragmented over two or more districts in ways that make it hard or impossible to elect any minority candidates of choice when that same voting strength would have allowed them success had it not been dispersed. However, in some instances, attempts to provide minority representation have led to the drawing of noncompact districts with irregular boundary lines that pick up isolated pockets of minority voting strength, and US courts have become increasingly hostile to such districts. Nonetheless, US courts continue to protect geographically concentrated minorities against techniques that would fragment, submerge, or otherwise dilute their vote.

Affirmative gerrymandering, in the strict sense of drawing single seat districts with a majority minority population, is unique to the United States, but race-conscious districting is not. In some other countries there may be seats that are "reserved" for members of a given group. India, for example, sets aside about a fifth of its parliamentary election districts for the "scheduled castes" (untouchables) and "scheduled tribes." In these districts, only members of these groups are allowed to be candidates (although any citizen residing in these districts may vote). These set-aside seats guarantee that a member of the specified minority is elected. Another example is New Zealand, which has an alternative set of electoral districts for Maori voters (eligible voters can register to vote in either the Maori district or the standard one in which they reside).

However, methods to promote ethnic and racial minority representation are relatively rare. One reason is that in other multiethnic countries with majoritarian electoral systems, the ethnic minorities are regionally concentrated and are therefore often natural minorities in single-member districts: for instance, French-speakers in Canada, and Scots and Welsh in the United Kingdom. The more important reason is that most democracies use PR. PR gives minorities of all kinds—political, ethnic, racial, religious, and so on—a decent chance to be elected if the group is large enough.[12]

9. *Low Levels of Female Representation.* Apart from questions of minority representation in legislatures is the question of the ratio of males to females. Given that at least half of adults are female, it is worth considering the balance of gender representation in legislatures, which are, as noted earlier, the primary vehicle for representing populations in a democracy. Further, as with the earlier discussion of seats for minorities, it cannot be ignored that historically representatives have been, in any democratic setting, overwhelmingly from a dominant class, and that one constant across cases is that historically, males have been the politically dominant class. Given this fact, it is worth considering the degree to which legislatures have become more gender balanced, and how the United States compares with the other democracies.

Table 7.6 details the percentage of female legislators in first or only chambers in our thirty-one democracies in 2000 and 2010. Observations a decade apart gives us a sense of whether there has been any change in the number of women in legislatures. Indeed, we can see that there were gains across all cases, but that the level of increase has not been uniform. The United States, with 16.8 percent in 2010, is below the median of 22.1 percent, although it is not the lowest case.

Several factors come into play here. One is that we would expect that PR systems would be more likely to have higher incidences of female representation than in majoritarian systems, simply because

12. A rare PR case that provides for specific minority-related seats is that of Colombia. Instead of drawing special districts, Colombia provides for a parallel election in which seats are set aside for indigenous communities, Afro-Colombians, and other groups by allowing candidates to run for those seats in a national, parallel election in which voters must decide whether to vote in the main election in their district or to vote in the national election for the specific set-aside seats.

Table 7.6. Female representation in first or only chambers, 2000 and 2010, in thirty-one democracies

	% Female 2000	% Female 2010
Sweden	42.7	45.0
South Africa	29.8	44.5
Netherlands	36.0	40.7
Finland	36.5	40.0
Belgium[a]	23.3	39.3
Argentina[a, b]	26.5	38.5
Denmark	37.4	38.0
Spain[a]	28.3	36.6
New Zealand	30.8	33.6
Germany	30.9	32.8
Switzerland	23.0	29.0
Austria	26.8	27.9
Portugal[a]	17.4	27.4
Mexico	16.0	26.2
Australia	*23.0*	*24.7*
Canada	*19.9*	*22.1*
Czech Republic	15.0	22.0
United Kingdom	*18.4*	*22.0*
Italy	11.1	21.3
Poland	13.0	20.0
Israel	12.5	19.2
France[a, b]	*10.9*	*18.9*
Greece	8.7	17.3
United States	***12.9***	***16.8***
Korea[a]	5.9	14.7
Chile	10.8	14.2
Colombia[a]	11.8	12.7
Japan	7.3	11.3
India	*9.0*	*10.8*
Hungary	8.3	9.1
Brazil[a]	5.7	8.6
Median		*22.1*

Notes: Countries with majoritarian electoral systems (single-seat districts) are in *italics.*

[a] Legal quotas for female candidates.

[b] Constitutional requirements linked to gender and elections.

Source: The Quota Project (http://www.quotaproject.org/), and Women in Parliaments (http://www.ipu.org/wmn-e/arc/classif311210.htm).

PR systems make it easier for newer political actors to win seats. More parties typically win seats in PR systems (see chapter 6), and some of those may take the lead by nominating more women, and then other parties may follow. Moreover, because most PR systems involve parties submitting lists of candidates and electing more than one candidate off their lists (at least in the case of larger parties), it is feasible for a party to mix both women and men on its lists. By contrast, when there is only a single seat elected in each district, the party must select one from among various potential candidates, favoring more established politicians, which frequently means men. When we compare the countries in table 7.6, we see some tendency for PR systems to have higher rates of female legislators. For instance, in 2010, the thirteen countries with the highest rates are all proportional systems, although so is the lowest (see table 6.1 for a complete classification of electoral systems). The highest rate in a system of single-seat districts is Australia, which at 24.7 percent in 2010, was just more than the median. However, there are also some PR systems with low rates, including the lowest of all in both 2000 and 2010, Brazil.

Another factor that affects the representation of women is whether policies have been put into place to encourage political parties to place female candidates on the ballot. Two of our cases, Argentina and France, have constitutional provisions that promote female representation, although the efficacy of the provision in France is questionable. Likewise, a number of cases have laws that require a certain quota of candidates (typically between 30 and 40 percent) to be female. As the table demonstrates, the results of these laws have been mixed in terms of resulting in female legislators being elected—sometimes because these laws often do not require that parties nominate women for seats they are actually likely to win, only that they have a certain share of candidates, and sometimes simply because the sanctions for noncompliance are weak.

CONCLUSIONS

We can thematically break down these nine comparisons into three related concepts: the strength of bicameralism, the basic structure of the legislature, and representation.

The most striking of the three in terms of the United States in comparative perspective is the way its bicameralism functions. The fact that it has a bicameral legislature itself is not unusual, as twenty-two of our cases have second chambers. However, it is only one of seven that has a highly symmetrical relationship between the two chambers in terms of legislative powers. It is part of another minority of cases (one of six) that grants some asymmetry in direction of the second chamber (that is, in terms of approval of treaties and many executive appointments). The most significant difference, and one that the United States is alone in having, is the empowerment of the minority in the second chamber so as to increase the significance of the second chamber in the legislative process. In short, the nature of US bicameralism is such that it creates two strong veto gates through which all legislation must pass if it is to become law. However, while the first chamber operates under majority rule, meaning the only veto player of significance is the majority party (and factions thereof), since the second chamber operates under supermajority rules for most actions, the number of veto players increases. To get legislation passed in the US Senate usually requires the agreement not just of the majority party (and its factions), but of the minority party (or a faction thereof) as well. This is a key reason why policy making is frequently more difficult in the United States than in our other cases (and contributes to the general policy outcomes that will be discussed in chapter 10). Ultimately, the United States is unique in this area.

In regards to structure, the United States has some unique or near-unique characteristics. It shares basic characteristics with other presidential systems, including fixed terms and an inflexible electoral calendar. However, it does have a few noteworthy characteristics: a small (relative to population) first chamber with a fixed size as well as a very short term of office for the first chamber. Indeed, the two-year term for the first chamber is an area in which the United States is unique within our study. When we combine short terms with the long campaign cycle in the United States (as mentioned in chapter 6), it means that the legislative process overlaps with campaign season every other year. These factors (along with others also noted in chapter 6, such as candidate-centric fundraising) result in a near-permanent campaign for representatives.

CHAPTER 8

EXECUTIVE POWER

Executive power is the power to put into action that which the legislature has created. It encompasses not just a single official, such as a president, but also the cabinet and the various bureaucratic organs of the state. In this chapter we will first examine the basic choices considered by the framers, then move on to a broader description of executive power in contemporary democracies, and finally conclude with a list of differences between the United States and our other thirty democracies.

INSTITUTIONAL OPTIONS

As was noted in the previous chapter, the Philadelphia conventioneers focused most of their debate on the design and scope of the legislature. However, they also had to consider the shape of executive authority. They went into the convention with two models that they ended up rejecting based on experience. Their immediate experience under the Articles of Confederation was a legislature that lacked an actual executive. While there was a "president" of the Congress, it was a largely ceremonial role, and since one of the deficiencies of the Articles was its lack of executive power, this model was not to be emulated. Likewise they rejected the notion of a hereditary monarchy (although Alexander Hamilton did propose a plan that would have created an executive for life).

If we examine the actual proposals made at the convention (table 8.1), we see a number of possibilities: from a singular to a plural executive, and from one chosen by the legislature to one chosen by electors selected by the voters. There was also some debate in Philadelphia over the possibility of a popularly elected executive

Table 8.1. Five versions of the US executive at the Philadelphia Convention

Plan	Name of office	Term of office	Chosen by	Other aspects
Pinckney	President	Annual selection	Legislature	Candidates from either the legislature or general public
Virginia	National executive	Set number of years	Legislature	No definition of candidates
New Jersey	Federal executive (committee)	Set number of years	Legislature	Could not hold any other office
Hamilton	Governor	Life (on conditions of good behavior)	Electors (selected by people at the district level)	No qualifications listed
US Constitution	President	Four years (reelection possible)	Electors chosen at the state level	Separate from the legislature

(Madison 1987: 368–69). In the end we know that the final selection was a chief executive wholly separate from the legislature, to be selected by an indirect process.

Of course, these options do not encompass all that a modern constitutional planner needs to consider. The remainder of this section examines the concepts and interactions needed to understand the role of the executive in a representative democracy. The first subsection addresses basic roles (head of state versus head of government; the second addresses the question of whether legislative-executive relations are based on hierarchical or transactional relationships; the third deals with the issue of cabinets; and the last, with executive election.

Basic Roles

The executive is the branch of government charged with two overarching tasks. First, the executive, in the function of *head of state*, is supposed to embody the nation as a whole and represent it in international affairs. These are, of course, primarily ceremonial functions; more important are the political and administrative roles of the executive, which are handled by the *head of government.* Heading the government means overseeing the day-to-day administration of the government and making key political choices regarding policy options. The head of government presides over the *cabinet,* which is comprised of the officials, known as ministers or secretaries, who head the various departments—for instance, defense, finance (treasury), transportation, and so on. Democracies vary in whether the roles of head of state and head of government are held by different officials or combined in a single person. The head of state may be a purely ceremonial figure, sometimes even a hereditary monarch. In this case of the ceremonial head of state, the role of head of government is always separate and is typically known as a *prime minister.* In other systems, notably the United States, the head of state—the *president*—is popularly elected, and also serves as head of government. As we shall see, still other countries have both an elected president, who serves as head of state but may be more than just ceremonial, and a prime minister to head the government. Table 8.2 details the heads of state and government for our thirty-one democracies. The table indicates that nine of our thirty-one democracies have a head of state called "president" who is not popularly elected. These include parliamentary-selected presidents who also serve as head of government, as in South Africa and Switzerland; heads of state selected by the parliament (the Czech Republic, Greece, Hungary, and Israel); and heads of state selected by electoral colleges that are made up of members of the national legislature plus regional delegates (Germany, India, and Italy).

In considering the ways in which executive power is structured in a given polity, one of the most important questions concerns the ways in which the executive works with the legislature. The reason this is so important is that in many systems—though not in the United States—executive authority originates from political parties represented within the executive and survives in office only so long as it maintains the support of a majority of legislators. Moreover, whatever the rules for the origination and survival of executive authority, nearly all major policy changes must be approved by the

Table 8.2. Head of state versus head of government in thirty-one democracies

	Head of state	Head of government
Argentina	President	President
Australia	Monarch[a]/ Governor General	Prime minister
Austria	President	Prime minister
Belgium	Monarch	Prime minister
Brazil	President	President
Canada	Monarch[a]/ Governor General	Prime minister
Chile	President	President
Colombia	President	President
Czech Republic	President[b]	Prime minister
Denmark	Monarch	Prime minister
Finland	President	Prime minister
France	President	Prime minister
Germany	President[b]	Prime minister
Greece	President[b]	Prime minister
Hungary	President[b]	Prime minister
India	President[b]	Prime minister
Israel	President[b]	Prime minister
Italy	President[b]	Prime minister
Japan	Monarch	Prime minister
Korea	President	Prime minister
Mexico	President	President
Netherlands	Monarch	Prime minister
New Zealand	Monarch[a]/ Governor General	Prime minister
Poland	President	Prime minister
Portugal	President	Prime minister
South Africa	President[b]	President
Spain	Monarch	Prime minister
Sweden	Monarch	Prime minister
Switzerland	President[bc]	President
United Kingdom	Monarch	Prime minister
United States	**President**	**President**

Notes

[a] The monarch of Australia, Canada, and New Zealand are the same as that of England (currently Elizabeth II).

[b] Indicates presidency is not popularly elected. Note that this changed for the Czech Republic in 2012, but that is outside the scope of our study.

[c] The president of the Swiss Confederation is the presiding officer (but first among equals) of the seven-member Federal Council, and serves only a one-year term.

legislature, or may be vetoed by it. Thus we consider executive-legislative relations first among a series of variations in the origin and survival of executive authority.

Executive and Legislatures: Transactional or Hierarchical Relations?

In considering matters of the constitutional design of executive authority, a critical characteristic is the way in which a given system juxtaposes hierarchical and transactional relations. A hierarchy results when one institution is constitutionally or otherwise subordinate to another, whereas transactions result when two coequal actors must share power in order to accomplish their objectives. All democracies entail mixes of hierarchical and transactional relations, but in some systems one or the other tendency is more dominant. In regards to this basic interaction, think back to figure 1.1, which diagrams the basic relationship we are discussing here. The United States Constitution represents the dominance of transactional relations, whereas the British political system, before 2010 (as we shall see) represents the most hierarchical of relations. Most other systems have some combination of the two types of relationships.

If we start with the basic dichotomy of presidential versus parliamentary systems, we can see that the constitutional relationship of the executive and legislature is fundamentally different in the two types. Figure 8.1 depicts the two systems in their purest forms, where solid lines indicate hierarchical relations with arrows running from principals to agent. Bolded lines represent transactional relationships, with arrows at either end noting the coequal nature of the authority of the actors bargaining over and concluding these transactions. Note that the hierarchy is depicted such that the principals are superior in a vertical relationship to their agents, while the transactions are depicted horizontally, because they occur between coequals. In any democracy, by definition, the voters are the ultimate principals, as they make their choices as to who their representative agents will be via the election process. In the presidential form of government that typifies the United States, voters have at least two choices to make in national elections, because they elect

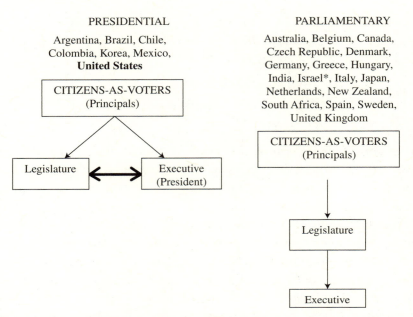

Fig. 8.1. Delegation and hierarchical versus transactional relations in presidential and parliamentary democracy
Key: Hierarchical relations are depicted with solid lines, with the arrows showing the direction of authority from principal to agent. Transactional relations are shown as a bold two-headed arrow.
*Israel had a hybrid system (directly elected prime minister) from 1996 to 2003.

both a legislature and an executive. Of course, there may actually be three choices, because the legislature may be bicameral with both chambers elected, as in the United States, and as we discuss in the chapter on legislatures; however, we ignore bicameralism in the figure for simplicity. In this constitutional design, the elected president is both head of state and head of government. In a parliamentary system, on the other hand, the voters elect only a legislature (which again, may be bicameral). Executive authority then depends on the outcome of legislative elections, and the executive remains in office only so long as it enjoys the *confidence* of the majority in the legislature. That is, it remains in office until a majority of legislators votes it out, or until it is defeated in the next election.

The relationship between the executive and legislature in the United States or other presidential democracies is transactional for two critical reasons. First, the executive and legislature have fixed terms, meaning that neither can dismiss the other when political disagreements arise. Second, both actors must cooperate to produce legislation, or else policy stasis results, with neither accomplishing its objectives (unless the objective is simply to say no to the other). In other words, the president has veto or other legislative powers so that he or she is, in a sense, another (unipersonal) "chamber" of the legislature, as well as the executive.

The relationship between the executive and legislature is hierarchical in the parliamentary system. What this means is that the executive—the prime minister and the cabinet that he or she heads—serves only so long as it enjoys the confidence of the majority in the parliament. If this majority is held by a single party, then we have the purest hierarchy that we can have in a democracy. In fact, while the cabinet is the agent of the majority party, the actual functioning of the political system is one characterized by *executive dominance* over the legislature. How can an agent dominate the principal to whom it should be subordinated? The answer lies in the dual role of the prime minister, who is not merely head of government but also *head of the majority party.* Because the party members in the parliament usually have no political interest in contradicting their own party leader on the most important legislative matters, prime ministers rarely suffer significant defeats in the parliament, lending an appearance of dominance: What they propose almost always passes.[1] Dominance is further reinforced because a majority party would seldom exercise its vote of no confidence against an executive that is made up of its own leadership, for to do so would be to invite political instability and possible loss of power to the opposition at a new election.

1. The flipside of this is that the prime minister rarely proposes a measure that he knows his own party is divided on, thus further decreasing the risk of an observed defeat, which would be politically embarrassing for the PM and for the party as a whole.

When there is no majority party in the legislature of a parliamentary system, the hierarchy of executive dependence on parliamentary confidence remains. However, now the policy-making process is complemented by a large dose of transactional relationships. The transactions that are most important are generally not, however, between the executive and legislative institutions, as in the presidential system. Rather, they are between separate political parties that must share power in order to govern, because in the absence of a majority, no one party can govern alone. In the case of a *coalition* cabinet, two or more parties divvy up cabinet positions and transact over the policy program of the government, as we discuss in more detail later. In other cases, when there is no majority party, one or more parties may form a *minority* cabinet, in which the parties sharing cabinet positions do not control a majority in the parliament. In this case, there is a transactional relationship between the executive and legislature or, more specifically, with one or more parties in the parliament that otherwise might be tempted to join an opposition-led no-confidence motion to bring down the minority government. We return to the composition of cabinets later, but first we must consider other forms of government besides presidential and parliamentary.

Figure 8.1 shows that our thirty-one democracies include seven presidential systems and eighteen parliamentary systems. What about the others? These six are hybrids of various sorts. One is the Swiss system, in which the leaders of multiple parties in the parliament constitute a power-sharing executive, much as in parliamentary systems. However, there is no procedure by which the parliament may vote no confidence, meaning that there is a stronger separation of powers between executive and legislature than there is in a parliamentary system. There was also a hybrid in Israel during the time period of our analysis: From 1996 to 2003, the Israeli prime minister was directly elected (like the head of government in a presidential system),[2] yet remained subject to parliamentary confidence. This experiment was widely considered to have been a mistake and was abandoned in favor of a return to the previous pure parliamen-

---

2. The head of state continued to be a president, elected by parliament, as had always been the case.

SEMI-PRESIDENTIALISM

Austria, Finland, France, Poland, Portugal

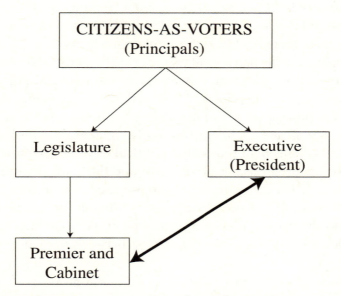

Fig. 8.2. Delegation in semi-presidential systems
Key: Hierarchical relations are depicted with solid lines, with the arrows showing the direction of authority from principal to agent. Transactional relations
are shown as a two-headed bold arrow.

tary system beginning in 2003 (Samuels and Shugart 2010: 179–90).
The more common hybrid form is the *semi-presidential* type, which
includes elements of both presidentialism and parliamentarism. Its
structure of authority is depicted in figure 8.2, and is represented
among our thirty-one democracies by Austria, Finland, France, Poland, and Portugal.[3]

3. This type of executive-legislative arrangement can be further broken
down into *premier-presidential* and *presidential-parliamentary.* In the former subtype, the prime minister and cabinet are constitutionally responsible
only to the legislative majority, whereas in the latter, the president has a
constitutionally granted right to dismiss a prime minister and cabinet (Elgie

In a semi-presidential system there is a popularly elected president, who serves as head of state. However, distinct from (pure) presidential systems like the United States, the president in a semi-presidential system is not constitutionally also the head of government. Instead there is a prime minister (or "premier") who is subject to the confidence of the legislative majority. In a semi-presidential system, then, there is a hierarchical relationship between the head of government and the parliamentary majority—exactly as we described for a parliamentary system. However, the president and prime minister may exist in some form of transactional relationship, depending on the precise constitutional allocation of powers.[4] France and Poland, as well as Finland until recently,[5] offer examples of systems in which the president is a central political figure. If the president is the most important leader of his party, and this party in turn dominates the parliament, then the prime minister may be politically— even though not constitutionally—subordinated to the president. This was the case in France in nearly all cases from 1965 to 1986[6] and again since 2002 (as well as at times between these periods).

2011; Shugart and Carey 1992, Samuels and Shugart 2010). All of the cases of semi-presidentialism included in this work are premier-presidential, except for Austria. However, specialists agree that Austria functions as if it were premier-presidential, (see Müller 1999; Samuels and Shugart 2010: 88–90) or even parliamentary (Lijphart 1994: 95). Other examples of presidential-parliamentary systems, with far more active presidents, outside of our set of democracies include Peru, the Russian Federation, and Taiwan.

4. In Korea, there is a position of prime minister; however, the constitutional system belongs to the presidential category, because the prime minister is not responsible to the legislative majority but rather serves at the pleasure of the president (Shugart 2005: 327; Elgie 2011: 26).

5. The Finnish president's powers have been reduced in recent years, both formally and informally. Formally, a constitutional reform in 1999 took away the president's power to dissolve parliament. Informally, the end of the Cold War reduced the salience of foreign affairs in Finnish politics. A head of state—especially a popularly elected one—can be expected to play a significant role in relations with other states, and given Finland's long border with the Soviet Union, foreign affairs was the main domain in which Finnish presidents played a prominent role.

6. The year 1965 was the first in which direct presidential elections were held under the French Fifth Republic constitution of 1958. The year 1986 was

Some of these presidents, including in France, have the right, under certain conditions, to *dissolve the parliament.* However, this power is not as formidable as it may seem, because it simply returns to the ultimate principal, the voters, the power to decide what the new parliamentary majority will be. This worked to the president's advantage in France in 1981, when, shortly after his own election, President François Mitterrand of the Socialist Party dissolved the conservative-dominated parliament, which the voters then replaced with a Socialist-dominated one, allowing Mitterrand to appoint a Socialist premier. However, a similar gambit failed miserably for Mitterrand's successor, conservative Jacques Chirac, in 1997. Hoping to consolidate and extend his allies' grip on the parliament, Chirac exercised his right of dissolution to hold an assembly election a year earlier than required. The voters responded by returning a majority for the left-wing bloc! As a result, Chirac was forced to accept the Socialist leader, Lionel Jospin, as premier. Periods such as these are known as *cohabitation,* defined as a president and premier from opposing parties, and the president's party not represented in the cabinet (Elgie 2011: 59–60, Samuels and Shugart 2010: 44–46). This concept of cohabitation is utterly different from what in the United States is called *divided government.* Superficially they are the same: The president and the legislative majority (either House or Senate in the United States) are from different parties. However, in the United States, even with divided government, the president remains the head of government with freedom to control the cabinet and exercise executive full authority. By contrast, under cohabitation, the cabinet is under the control of the legislative majority and not of the president. Later on we will discuss the distinctiveness of situations in which the president and legislature are held by different parties, as well as the composition of cabinets.

Single-Party Cabinets versus Executive Power-Sharing

As we noted, the president in a presidential system is by definition the head of government and has a fixed term of office. In

the first in which the party or alliance of parties that had elected the president did not also hold a majority of parliament (and, therefore, the premiership).

presidential systems, then, the cabinet's origin depends on choices made by the voters, who choose the head of government, as well as choices regarding cabinet appointments made by the voter's agent, the president. In parliamentary systems, on the other hand, the head of government is a prime minister who, along with the rest of the cabinet, serves only with the confidence of the majority in the legislative assembly. Thus the origin of the cabinet depends on the outcome of parliamentary elections and of transactions among leaders of different parties when none of them wins a majority. Similarly, the cabinet's survival in power depends on not losing parliamentary confidence. In semi-presidential systems, the president typically initiates the selection of a premier, but the president's choice, as well as whether the premier and cabinet remain in office, depends on the parliamentary majority.

In parliamentary or semi-presidential systems, if a single party holds a majority in the legislature, it almost always reserves all the seats in the cabinet for itself. If there is no single party with a majority, the result is either a coalition or minority cabinet, because two or more parties must transact in order to shepherd legislative proposals through the parliament as well as to maintain control of the executive.

As such, it is important to underscore that cabinet formation is fundamentally different in presidential systems than in parliamentary, or even semi-presidential, systems. While US presidents must gain legislative approval (as discussed in chapter 7) for appointments to the cabinet, and presidents in some other presidential systems (notably Brazil) negotiate cabinets with parties in the legislature, presidents do not depend on legislative support to remain in office, as do prime ministers. While presidents may choose to include members of other parties in their cabinet, such cabinet members are far less agents of their parties as is the case in parliamentary coalitions, and can always be dismissed by the president, whose term is fixed. Indeed, in the US case, the significance of party identification in the cabinet is so minimal that it is rarely discussed, and even when a cabinet member was identified with a party different from that of the president, it does not mean that the cabinet member has loyalties outside of his or her job within the administration. For example, President Barack Obama's first secretary of defense was Robert Gates, who had held that same job under President George W. Bush. That Bush was a Republican and Obama a Democrat really had no special bearing on Gates's role in that job.

In parliamentary systems, if no one party is in a position to form a government by itself, cabinets are formed as a result of transactions among parties. Often, two or more parties will form a coalition in which the leader of one of the transacting parties becomes prime minister, and leaders of some of the other parties that join the coalition will obtain other cabinet positions. Each of the parties that enter a coalition becomes a veto player, because the consent—or at least acquiescence—of each party is typically needed to enact a policy change. If a party determines collectively that it is unwilling to support some government policy, it can withdraw from the government, causing the need for a new coalition to form or perhaps resulting in early elections. However, a coalition partner will not just blithely bring down a government, because in doing so it risks losing influence over the next government that is formed or being blamed for creating a "crisis." Most disagreements among coalition partners are resolved through interparty transactions well short of coalition breakdown.

This relationship is captured in figure 8.3, which details a theoretical legislature with four parties, A, B, C, and D. In the figure, we follow the chain-of-delegation argument that relates back to the discussion in chapter 1 and to figure 1.1 but adds layers of detail. Specifically, blocs of voters, acting as principals (since they are citizens who hold ultimate power in a democratic setting), delegate to their agents, politicians, who are members of specific political parties who win seats in the legislature. For simplicity, we will assume a unicameral legislature. So the process of forming a government is one of assembling a transaction among separate agents of different blocs of voters that can come together to control the one veto gate. Thus we can speak of a coalition as two or more veto players controlling the single veto gate.[7] Each party is depicted on a left–right scale to

7. If the legislature is bicameral, and the second chamber has significant powers (see ch. 7), then there are also two veto gates. In such cases, coalition

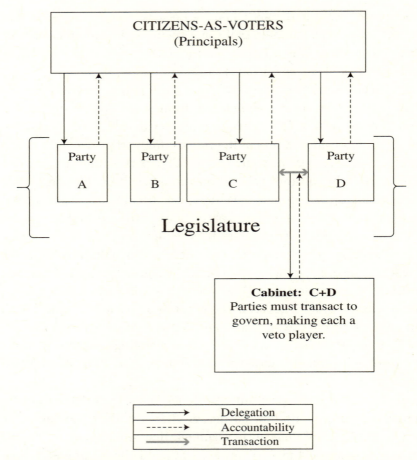

Fig. 8.3. Delegation and creation of veto players in a parliamentary system
Key: Solid arrows indicate delegation relationships, with the direction of the arrow showing the flow of authority from principal to agent. Dashed arrows indicate accountability of agents to principals. The two-headed arrow shows transactional relationship.

simulate different policy positions, and each box is a different size to indicate seat shares. In this example, parties C and D jointly have a majority of seats, and thus transacted to form a government, by which we mean the following:

---

formation may take account of the balance of parties in the second chamber as well as the first. This is the case, e.g., in Italy.

1. One of them (likely C, the largest party) provides the prime minister and some other ministers (secretaries, in US terms) of the cabinet, while the other party supplies other ministers (and perhaps a deputy PM).
2. The two parties compromise on policies, implementing some priority items of C and some of D, splitting the difference on other issues and agreeing to disagree on some issues that are especially contentious between the two parties. Usually the policies they agree to in their transaction are published in a coalition agreement, which becomes the program of the government.
3. Ongoing policy transactions take place between the parties, meaning primarily within the cabinet, where the ministers act as both specialists in the policy area (the "portfolio") to which they have been assigned, and as agents of their respective party.
4. This transactional relationship makes parties C and D veto players, because both have to agree to policies for them to be passed by the one veto gate (in this example, a unicameral legislature).

Now, it should be noted that other coalitions are possible, for example: A, B, and C in a three-party cabinet. However, this would create a more complex transactional relationship because three veto players would have to be satisfied. Certainly the ideological space encompassed by the three parties might make such transactions more difficult than in a two-party arrangement. Further, party A, being the most left-leaning of our hypothetical parties, might find a three-way coalition to be less attractive than waiting for a future election when maybe A plus B could win a majority of seats and transact in a two-party coalition of their own (without C). Yet another possibility would be a minority government, in which the largest party, C, governs alone, meaning that it has all of the cabinet positions. In such a case, it would be able to remain in government by alternately transacting with the party to its left (B) or to its right (D). Which outcome prevails would depend on the preferences of each party and its leaders and which option gives it what it considers its best payoffs from the transactions.[8] Box 8.1 has an example of two cases

---

8. By not taking cabinet positions, for instance, party D is not responsible for actions taken by the government that party D's voters dislike. However, it also has less influence over what those policies will be.

BOX 8.1. COALITION EXAMPLE: GERMANY 2005 AND 2009

In Germany in 2005, the election resulted not only in no party having a majority, but also neither of the most likely coalitions of parties having a majority. Due to the proportional electoral system (specifically, Mixed-Member Proportional or MMP; see chapter 5) in Germany, and the country's multiparty system, it is extremely unlikely for any single party to win a majority of seats. However, since the 1990s, there has been a general expectation that the country would be governed by either of two possible coalitions: a center-right bloc consisting of the Christian Democrats and Free Democrats, or a center-left formation of the Social Democrats and Greens.

Leading up to the 2005 election, the governing coalition consisted of the Social Democrats (SPD) and Greens. In the campaign, the two main options presented to voters were either a continuation of the incumbent coalition or a change to a center-right government. Table 8.3 shows the results of the September 2005 election. The SPD remained the largest party, with 222 seats. However, a majority required 308 seats, and even with the inclusion of the Greens' 51 seats, this formation was far short of being able to govern. The alternative government would have consisted of the two conservative parties, the Christian Democratic Union (CDU) and the Christian Social Union (CSU),[a] together with the Free Democratic Party (FDP, also referred to as the Liberals). These parties had combined for 287 seats, and so this coalition also would be short of a majority.

With neither of the two expected coalitions having majority support in the Bundestag (first chamber of the parliament), several rounds of interparty bargaining ensued, during which attempts at various coalitions were made. In order to form a coalition, each party that would join must agree to compromise some of the program

Table 8.3. Federal Republic of Germany election result, September 18, 2005

Party	% Votes	Seats
SPD	34.3	222
CDU	27.8	180
CSU	7.4	46
FDP	9.8	61
Left (Linke)	8.7	54
Green	8.1	51
Others	3.9	0

that it campaigned on. At the same time, it also will seek to get at least some of its key preferred policies included in any proposed coalition's joint program of government, in order to be able to show benefits to the coalition for those who voted for the party. The parties will also bargain over how many ministerial positions each party will obtain and which ones. Parties typically seek to obtain the positions that most closely match the policy areas of greatest concern for the voters and interest groups that make up their support base in the electorate.

There were negotiations about bringing the Green Party into the center-right formation. This was nicknamed by the press as the "Jamaica Coalition" because the colors of the various parties are those of the Jamaican flag: black (Christian Democratic), yellow (Free Democratic), and Green. The negotiations on this potential coalition, which would have had 338 seats, were reported to have lasted only an hour and half before breaking down. The policy gap between the Greens and the other two parties was just too great for the parties to find common ground. (One commentator joked that no one could imagine Angela Merkel in dreadlocks–a reference to the Christian Democratic leader and the Greens' support among younger and countercultural voters.)

Another possibility that was discussed was the "Traffic Light Coalition": red (SPD), yellow, and green. This combination, with 334 seats, also was not attractive to the various parties, because the FDP's policies are so distant from those of the other two. Theoretically, there could have been a "coalition of the left": SPD, Greens, and the Left Party. These parties collectively had won 327 seats, and all are certainly left of center in an ideological sense. However, the Left Party consisted of the former Communist Party of East Germany, which made it anathema to many mainstream voters, along with a faction that had defected from the SPD over the latter's enactment of reforms to the welfare state during the SPD-Green coalition government (1998–2005). For these reasons, the parties were politically incompatible despite superficial ideological affinities.

With none of these various combinations being viable, what finally resulted was a "Grand Coalition" consisting of the two big parties, the SPD and the CDU, plus the CSU. While the CDU/CSU block and the SPD normally oppose each other, they agreed to form a government together because each party preferred that possibility over taking in partners it and its voters saw as too extreme (Greens for the CDU/CSU, FDP or Left for the SPD). They also preferred the Grand Coalition over going to fresh elections, which would have been required had there been no government formed. Thus the Grand Coalition was no one's first choice, but it was the most viable option.

A formal agreement was reached in November. The parties produced a 130-page coalition agreement in which they detailed a series of difficult policy reforms, including increasing the Value Added Tax, raising the retirement age, and many others. At a news conference, the SPD leader commented, "None of us was prepared for a grand coalition—none of you either. We learned to make compromises."[b] Indeed, compromise is the essence of forming coalitions.

The Grand Coalition government was headed by Angela Merkel, the CDU leader, who assumed the position of chancellor, the equivalent of prime minister in the German case. The SPD, reflecting its status as the largest party, was able to bargain for a majority of the total number of cabinet ministries, after relenting on its initial demand for the chancellorship. The SPD also received several important posts, including the ministers of environment, finance, foreign affairs, health, and labor, as well as the position of vice chancellor. The CDU held other key positions, including defense, economics, and interior. Thus the transaction between the CDU/CSU and the SPD reflected the close balance of power between the two biggest parties in the parliament, with each party able to negotiate for itself key positions, while having to concede others to its partner.[c]

The government served the full four-year parliamentary term, and given its huge majority in the parliament, enacted several major policy reforms. In 2009, despite still being in government together, the CDU/CSU and the SPD each ran their separate campaigns, seeking an election outcome in which one could lead a government without the other. The CDU/CSU combined for 239 seats, and the FDP won 93; thus these parties were able to form a center-right coalition. Angela Merkel remained chancellor. This time, reflecting her party's much stronger position vis-à-vis its coalition partner, the FDP, the two conservative parties held around two-thirds of the cabinet ministerial posts, including defense, environment, finance, interior, and labor. Nonetheless, the FDP also received some important posts in the cabinet, including economics, foreign affairs, and health, as well as the vice chancellorship. Earning these positions out of the transaction with the stronger CDU/CSU reflected its pivotal position as a veto player without whom the Christian Democrats could not form the center-right government that they preferred. The SPD, meanwhile, became the largest party of the parliamentary opposition, waiting to make its case to the voters in the next election.

NOTES

a. The CDU and CSU are separate party organizations, but they do not compete with one another in elections. The CSU contests elections only in Bavaria, and the CDU runs in all other states.

b. "New Government Pact Finally in Place," Deutsche Welle, November 13, 2005, http://www .dw.de/new-government-pact-finally-in-place/a-1773778-1.

c. "Grand Coalition a Delicate Balancing Act," Deutsche Welle, October 11, 2005, http://www .dw.de/grand-coalition-a-delicate-balancing-act/a-1737942-1.

of coalition formation in parliamentary systems: Germany following two elections, 2005 and 2009.

As such, when there is no single party that can govern alone, the transactions in parliamentary systems are among the parties over the formation of the government (meaning its head, the prime minister, as well as the cabinet); transactions are ongoing over maintaining the government in office and compromising over policy—or alternatively, breaking it up early, likely leading to new elections. This stands in contrast to presidential systems, including the United States, where the government is headed by a president who has his or her own separately elected and fixed-term institution and is not dependent upon transactions among legislative parties. Presidents may choose to appoint cabinets containing members of parties other than their own, but the point is that this is their choice; unlike a prime minister, the president never has to transact in order to get into office, stay in office, or form a cabinet. Due to the separation of powers, transactions in presidential systems over policy enactment are between these separately elected institutions, each acting as a veto gate in the process and each sitting for a fixed term; policy in such systems can only be made when there is sufficient agreement across the institutions.

The question of whether cabinets are single-party majorities or are coalitions is crucial to parliamentary democracies, because it determines how many veto players must transact and agree to policy changes: the majority party alone or the two or more parties that together form a coalition. Minority governments are intermediate cases in which the party or parties in the cabinet do not collectively have the support of a majority in the parliament. Minority governments consisting of a single party sometimes are not greatly different in practice from single-party majority governments, because all members of the executive come from one party. However, given the hierarchical relationship between the parliamentary majority and the executive, which defines parliamentary democracy, a minority government is always subject to the threat of losing a no-confidence vote. The lower the probability of this happening—for instance, if the various opposition parties do not agree enough on policy to act together to replace the incumbent—the more the single-party minority government can resemble a single-party majority government.[9] Box 8.2 offers some examples of minority governments in Canada and New Zealand.

Table 8.4 shows the prevalence of different types of cabinets in our thirty-one democracies. The table actually contains thirty-two entries, because we show New Zealand twice due to the change in their electoral system (see chapter 5) from plurality to a proportional system. As intended by those who promoted this electoral system change, the result was a substantial difference in the types of cabinets that formed, as we shall subsequently discuss further. The country cases are sorted in descending order by the frequency of coalition cabinets, and then within any group having the same percentage, in decreasing order of the frequency of minority governments. The table also shows the median number of parties in the cabinets of parliamentary democracies and the median of all coalitions.[10]

In scanning table 8.4, we see that the United States is in a distinct minority of our democracies that have had no coalitions during our time period. Only Argentina and Mexico, two other presidential systems, and the parliamentary systems of Australia, Canada, New Zealand (pre-reform,) Greece, and Spain have been without coalitions;

9. On the other hand, a minority coalition more closely resembles any other coalition, due to the presence of two or more parties in the cabinet, and the necessity to transact also with a party or parties that are needed to win majority support in parliament.

10. Presidential systems are excluded from these two latter categories. First, they are excluded from consideration of minority governments because this concept is less meaningful in pure presidential systems. Unlike a coalition, which results from transactions with other parties that are akin to those that take place in a parliamentary system (Cheibub 2007: 73–86)—other than the fact that the president's position is not dependent on such transactions— minority governments may either result from situations similar to those in parliamentary systems or may be cases of divided government (discussed later). Second, presidential systems are excluded from consideration of the number of parties in cabinets because of difficulties obtaining the necessary data on all cases.

Table 8.4. Types of cabinets in thirty-one democracies, 1990–2010

Country	Coalitions	Minority governments	Mean number of parties in cabinet
Denmark	100.0%	100.0%	2.33
Belgium	100.0%	71.4%	4.70
Finland[a]	100.0%	40.0%	4.10
Netherlands	100.0%	16.7%	2.83
Israel[b]	100.0%	7.7%	5.42
Germany[c]	100.0%	0.0%	2.00
Italy	100.0%	0.0%	4.10
Brazil	*100.0%*	—	—
Chile	*100.0%*	—	—
Colombia	*100.0%*	—	—
Switzerland[b]	100.0%	—	—
France[a]	90.9%	9.1%	2.09
Hungary	88.9%	22.2%	2.10
Austria[a]	88.9%	11.1%	1.89
Poland[a]	85.7%	28.6%	2.57
Czech Republic	81.8%	36.4%	2.64
India[d]	80.0%	90.0%	—
New Zealand 2 (from 1996)	71.4%	71.4%	1.71
Japan	66.7%	33.3%	1.93
Sweden	42.9%	85.7%	2.29
Portugal[a]	37.5%	37.5%	1.38
South Africa	20.0%	0.0%	1.20
United Kingdom	16.7%	0.0%	1.17
Korea	*12.5%*	—	—
Spain	0.0%	80.0%	1.00
Canada	0.0%	37.5%	1.00
Greece	0.0%	12.5%	1.00
Australia[c]	0.0%	10.0%	1.00

(*continued*)

Table 8.4. (*continued*)

Country	Coalitions	Minority governments	Mean number of parties in cabinet
New Zealand 1 (to 1993)	0.0%	0.0%	1.00
Argentina	*0.0%*	—	—
Mexico	*0.0%*	—	—
United States	**0.0%**	—	—
Median (parliamentary)	*71.4%*	*22.2%*	*1.97*
Median (all)	*80.9%*		

Notes: Presidential systems are in *italics*.

Data on number of parties in cabinet was unavailable for India and omitted for presidential systems.

[a] Semi-presidential systems.

[b] Other hybrids: Switzerland (neither executive elections nor cabinet responsibility to parliament) and Israel, 1996–2003 (directly elected prime minister); if hybrid period is removed from Israeli calculations, 10% of governments are minority and average number of parties in cabinet is 4.6.

[c] In Australia the Liberal and National Parties are considered a single party, as are the CDU and CSU in Germany.

Sources: For parliamentary and semi-presidential systems, authors calculations based on the Parliament and Government Composition Database (ParlGov), available at http://www.parlgov.org/. For presidential systems and other countries not in ParlGov (India, Israel, and South Africa), compiled by authors from various sources.

in Spain, the norm is single-party minority governments,[11] a format that has also occurred a few times in Canada (see box 8.2). Three other countries have had 20 percent or fewer of their cabinets be coalitions: Korea (presidential) and South Africa and the United Kingdom (parliamentary). In the South African case, the first cabinet upon the transition to democracy (1994) included the former ruling National Party for about two years, but all subsequent cabinets have consisted only of the party that has won a majority in all elections since 1994, the African National Congress. In the United Kingdom,

11. As mentioned in ch. 4, these governments in Spain typically rely on one or more parties from one of Spain's subnational units (e.g., the Basque Country or Catalonia) for their parliamentary support.

BOX 8.2. EXAMPLES OF MINORITY GOVERNMENTS: CANADA AND NEW ZEALAND

CANADA

Given that Canada has a parliamentary executive and a plurality electoral system for the first chamber of Parliament, it is not surprising that most of the country's cabinets have been single-party majority governments. The term of Parliament is five years, but as in many parliamentary systems, elections can be called early (see chapter 7). Elections in Canada tend to happen about every four years. However, from 2004 to 2011 there was an unusual string of minority governments, as well as four general elections. The governments during this period always consisted of a single party, although one minority coalition was formally proposed but never took office. We can thus use the Canadian case as a window to understand how minority governments function.

As the 2004 election approached, the Liberal Party of Canada (LPC) was ruling in a single-party majority government. However, in the election its seat total was reduced to 135, several seats short of a majority in the 308-seat House of Commons. Paul Martin, the LPC leader, remained prime minister but now headed a minority cabinet. That is, all ministers in the cabinet were from the LPC, but because this party had less than a majority of seats, it could remain in office only so long as the other parties did not combine on a no-confidence vote against it. Two episodes during the tenure of this government demonstrate the dynamics of executive-legislative relations and interparty relations in a minority situation.

First, in May 2005, the third largest party in Parliament, the New Democratic Party (NDP), demanded some changes to the federal budget as the price of not joining with the rest of the opposition to defeat the government. In a parliamentary system, the vote on the government's annual budget is by definition a matter of confidence: If the government is unable to obtain "supply" (that is, a majority voting for its spending

Table 8.5. Canadian House of Commons election, 2004

Party	% Votes	Seats	% Seats
Liberal Party of Canada	36.7	135	43.8
Conservative Party of Canada	29.6	99	32.1
Bloc Québécois	12.4	54	17.5
New Democratic Party	15.7	19	6.2
Independents	1.3	1	0.3
Green Party of Canada	4.3	0	0

proposals), it must resign. In order to obtain NDP support, Martin offered increased spending on health care and other social policy priorities of the NDP. This deal complete, the NDP voted with the government, which remained in office.[a] Thus, here we can see how a transaction between a single governing party and one party outside the government resulted in both a change in policy and the survival of a government that by itself lacked a majority.

In November 2005, the opposition parties all combined to bring down the Martin government, which had been rocked by a scandal involving some LPC campaign finance practices. In a no-confidence vote, every party in the House other than the LPC–the Conservatives, the Bloc Québécois (BQ), and the NDP–voted against the government. As a result, Martin resigned and early elections were called. In January 2006, the new elections again resulted in no party with a majority, only this time it was the Conservative Party of Canada (CPC) that emerged with the most seats. It formed a single-party minority cabinet with its leader, Stephen Harper, as prime minister.

A little more than two years later in October 2008, Harper decided to call early elections (strictly speaking, they are called by the governor general, but this is only a formality). He expected that he could improve his party's standing in Parliament, perhaps even winning a majority. Thus, for the third time in less than four years, Canada had elections. And for the third time, no party won a majority.

In the 2008 election, the CPC remained the largest party but was again short of a majority. In response to the outcome, the other parties began to negotiate over an alternative government that might replace Harper's government when the newly elected Parliament convened. The LPC, NDP, and BQ signed an agreement in which there would have been a coalition government consisting of ministers from both the LPC and NDP. The BQ would have agreed to support it, without having any ministers in the government.[b] The various parties shared a belief that Harper's failure to win a majority of seats for his party indicated he had lost the legitimacy to continue his minority government, and they argued that his economic policies did not offer sufficient

Table 8.6. Canadian House of Commons election, 2006

Party	% Votes	Seats	% Seats
Conservative Party of Canada	36.3	124	40.3
Liberal Party of Canada	30.2	103	33.4
Bloc Québécois	10.5	51	16.2
New Democratic Party	17.5	29	12.0
Independents and others	5.6	1	0.3

Table 8.7. Canadian House of Commons election, 2008

Party	% Votes	Seats	% Seats
Conservative Party of Canada	37.6	143	46.4
Liberal Party of Canada	26.2	76	24.7
Bloc Québécois	10.0	50	16.2
New Democratic Party	18.2	37	12.0
Independents	0.7	2	0.6
Green Party of Canada	6.8	0	0

stimulus for the slumping economy (at the outset of the world economic recession). The BQ, which runs and wins seats only in Quebec (as discussed in chapter 4), argued that Harper was shortchanging the province in terms of federal transfers of funds.

Had this coalition been formed, it would have been a first for Canada since the Second World War. It would have been a three-party transaction establishing a two-party minority coalition, with the third party (the BQ) offering "outside" support—that is, support on confidence and supply votes in the House despite having no cabinet representation. However, Harper responded immediately by requesting (and obtaining) a temporary closure of Parliament and by denouncing the proposal as a coalition of "socialists and separatists."[c] By the time Parliament reconvened, the LPC had changed its leader, due to internal disagreements about the wisdom of the coalition (particularly its reliance on BQ support). The LPC, under its new leadership, made a new transaction with Harper and the CPC, by which the latter would agree to present regular fiscal reports to Parliament.[d] This minor agreement between the largest party (CPC) and the largest opposition party was enough to allow Harper to continue as prime minister, still heading a single-party minority government.

Later the LPC announced it was no longer satisfied with the minimal concessions it had obtained from Harper. Without the assurance of LPC support against a no-confidence vote, and with a supply vote due, Harper turned to the NDP and transacted with it by offering an increase in Employment Insurance spending.[e] This was an important issue to the labor-affiliated NDP, due to the high degree of unemployment during the recession. It may seem like an implausible transaction, inasmuch as it involved a Conservative government and its most left-wing opponent in Parliament. However, it was mutually beneficial because for Harper and the CPC, it ensured their minority government would remain in power, while for the NDP it gave them a policy concession that they could claim to have delivered to their constituents.

Finally, in May 2011, following a no-confidence vote by all the opposition parties against Harper, another early election was called—the fourth election in just under

Table 8.8. Canadian House of Commons election, 2011

Party	% Votes	Seats	% Seats
Conservative Party of Canada	39.6	167	54.2
New Democratic Party	30.6	102	33.1
Liberal Party of Canada	18.9	34	11
Bloc Québécois	6.0	4	1.3
Green Party of Canada	3.9	1	0.3

seven years. This one produced a majority for the CPC, restoring–at least for now–a single-party majority government.

NEW ZEALAND

A second example of minority governance comes from New Zealand. As noted in chapter 5, the change of the electoral system from plurality before 1996 to Mixed-Member Proportional since then has resulted in regular coalition or minority governments. The minority governments in New Zealand have differed in a key respect from those we saw in Canada: instead of shifting transactions with different parties in Parliament, depending on the policy issue, those in New Zealand have tended to have written "confidence and supply" agreements with one or more parties in Parliament. This creates a more formalized and ongoing transactional relationship between the minority government and its support party or parties. A good example comes from the government led by Helen Clark, leader of the Labour Party, following the November 1999 election.

In this election, Labour and its prospective coalition partner, a left-wing party known as the Alliance, came up just short of a majority of seats. In order to ensure support in Parliament, Clark signed an agreement under which the Green Party (seven seats) agreed to support the Labour-Alliance coalition cabinet on confidence and supply measures, in exchange for policy consultations.

There was one especially contentious policy issue that arose during the life of this government. A Royal Commission was established by the government to study the issue of genetically modified (GM) food crops and to propose whether the government should lift a moratorium on the importation of such plant materials. The commission concluded in 2001 that GM foods should be allowed. The government agreed and announced a plan to lift the moratorium in 2003. The Green Party was implacably opposed to this proposed policy change, and as it was a veto player, due to the government's dependence on its votes, its stance raised the possibility that the government would not survive if it pushed ahead with its plans. However, an election was due before the 2003 planned lifting of the moratorium, and Clark decided to move it up a few months.

In the July 2002 election, the Greens made the GM issue a priority and said they would not support any government that would lift the moratorium.[f] Labour, meanwhile emphasized other issues but also made it clear that it intended to go ahead with the Royal Commission recommendations. The election could be said to have produced a win for both the Greens and Labour. Both saw their seat total increase.[g] However, clearly Labour and the Greens were no longer compatible, as the Greens had made it apparent that they would not support a Labour minority government unless it dropped its plans to lift the moratorium. Clark ended up forming a minority cabinet again, only this time with the support of a center-right party, United Future, which demanded very few policy concessions in exchange for supporting the government on confidence and supply.[h] The Greens, meanwhile, announced they would go into opposition rather than support a government committed to a policy that they and their voters strongly disagreed with.

The example of minority governments in New Zealand shows multiple parties transacting with one another in order to jointly achieve the majority needed both to avert potential no-confidence votes against the government and to allow the veto gate of Parliament to be opened for passing policy. Unlike in the Canadian case, in New Zealand minority governments have tended to sign "confidence and supply" agreements with one or more other parties in Parliament. These agreements allow the government to be assured of the support party's votes on confidence votes and the budget, and allow the smaller party to obtain some policy concessions. They do not commit the smaller party to vote for the government's policies in areas not covered in their agreement, if the smaller party disagrees with the government policy, as we saw with the Green Party in GM policy. In this way, if we look back to figure 8.3, we can see that parties seek to balance maintaining accountability to the block of voters who

Table 8.9. New Zealand Parliamentary election, 1999

Party	% Vote	Seats	% Seats
Labour Party	38.7	49	40.8
National Party	30.5	39	32.5
Alliance	7.7	10	8.3
ACT New Zealand	7.0	9	7.5
Green Party of Aotearoa New Zealand	5.2	7	5.8
New Zealand First Party	4.3	5	4.2
United New Zealand	0.5	1	0.8

Table 8.10. New Zealand Parliamentary election, 2002

Party	% Votes	Seats	% Seats
Labour Party	41.3	52	43.3
National Party	20.9	27	22.5
New Zealand First Party	10.4	13	10.8
ACT New Zealand	7.1	9	7.5
Green Party of Aotearoa New Zealand	7	9	7.5
United Future New Zealand	6.7	8	6.7
Jim Anderton's Progressive Party	1.7	2	1.7

delegated to them their votes at the last election, on the one hand, while transacting and compromising to pass legislation through the veto gate, on the other hand.

NOTES

a. The government also needed to negotiate with one independent–nonpartisan–member of Parliament in order to ensure a majority. Exactly what the independent might have obtained in the transactions was not clear, but the vote on the NDP-supported budget amendment was dramatic, and its outcome was uncertain until one of the last of the independents stood up to cast his vote for the amendment, resulting in a tie vote in the Parliament. The speaker of the House cast the tiebreaker in favor of the government, which thereby survived. A timeline of the 2004–2006 Parliament is available at http://www.cbc.ca/news/background/parliament38/index.html.

b. The agreement called for eighteen Liberal and six NDP ministers of cabinet, with the BQ committed to supporting the cabinet for at least eighteen months, http://www.cbc.ca/news/canada/story/2008/12/01/coalition-talks.html.

c. "Harper Says Dion in Bed with Socialists and Separatists," *Western Star,* December 1, 2008.

d. "Ignatieff Puts Tories 'on Probation' with Budget Demand," CBC, January 1, 2009, http://www.cbc.ca/canada/story/2009/01/28/ignatieff-decision.html.

e. "NDP to Prop up Tories to Pass EI Changes," CBC, September 16, 2009, http://www.cbc.ca/canada/story/2009/09/16/ndp-election-tories.html.

f. See "Greens Given GM Warning," *New Zealand Herald,* March 6, 2002.

g. The Alliance ceased to be relevant, and its ex-leader, Jim Anderton, won only two seats heading his new Progressive Coalition, which committed to remaining in coalition government with Labour.

h. The main concessions that UF received were a Commission on the Family, which would vet–but not necessarily block–government policies for their compliance with supporting families, and a commitment to consider building a new highway to bypass a congested part of UF leader Peter Dunne's district. As of 2012, the Commission on the Family had been reduced to a single member with little policy influence, and the road had not yet built, despite UF having been a support party to every government during this time period.

all governments had been single-party majority until 2010, when no party won a majority in a House of Commons election and the Conservative and Liberal Democratic Parties formed a coalition.[12]

In eleven of our democracies, or 35 percent of them, all governments have been coalitions. These eleven include three of our presidential systems (Brazil, Chile, and Colombia), as well as several parliamentary systems. In all, we find that the median rate of coalitions is 80.9 percent across all countries and 71.4 percent in the parliamentary systems. In addition, we see that minority governments, while not especially common overall (22.2 percent is the median across the parliamentary systems), are very common in a few countries: 100 percent of governments in our time period in Denmark, between 80 and 90 percent in India, Spain, and Sweden, and more than 70 percent in both Belgium and post-reform New Zealand. The latter country is particularly significant, given that it is a case of "reengineering" (see chapter 5), having undergone a major change in its electoral system. Under the old system of plurality in single-seat districts, all governments were single-party majority.[13] Under the Mixed-Member Proportional system first used in 1996, the percentages of both coalitions and minority government have gone from 0 to 71.4 percent. (There have been both majority and minority coalitions, as well as single-party minority cabinets; box 8.2 discusses some examples of New Zealand's minority coalitions.)

In the column that shows the mean number of parties in the cabinet of parliamentary or semi-presidential systems, we see variation from 1.00 in the five nonpresidential cases that have had no coalitions, to more than 4.00 in Belgium, Finland, and Italy, and more than 5.00 in Israel; the median across the parliamentary cases is 1.97. The number of parties in a cabinet is a good guide to how many veto players there are at a given time, because normally all the

---

12. The only other time in the entire post-WWII period when a single party did not obtain a majority of seats was in February 1974. At an election in October of that year, a majority again resulted.

13. Table 8.3 includes only two such governments under "New Zealand 1"; however, all governments of the post-WWII era were likewise single-party majority.

coalition partners must agree to open the legislature's veto gate and enact a policy. (If the coalition is also a minority government, then the number of veto players may be at least one more than the number of parties in the government). Thus this column of table 8.4 suggests highly complex policy-making transactions are required in several countries, but that the median for all parliamentary systems is not so complex: Around two parties as veto players is typical.

As for the hybrid systems, all of our semi-presidential systems (Austria, Finland, France, Poland, and Portugal) normally have coalition governments. Some of them, like Portugal, have occasional single-party majority or minority governments, and France has had several governments that were dominated by one party but that contained members from other parties. Switzerland, also a hybrid but without an elected president, has had only coalition governments. So did Israel during its brief hybrid phase. As we mentioned already, even some pure presidential systems, notably Brazil, Colombia, and Chile, have frequent coalitions. It is important to recall, however, that when there are coalitions in presidential systems, they are of a fundamentally different character from those in parliamentary or even semi-presidential systems, because they are always subordinate to the elected head of government, the president.[14] Thus, the United States has an unusual cabinet format when compared to our other democracies in two senses: first, in having single-party governments, which table 8.4 has shown are not the norm; second, in having membership in those governments determined by the president, regardless of whether the president's party has a majority in either house of Congress.[15]

14. A good example of the dominance of the president, and her own party, comes from Brazil. The cabinet of Dilma Rousseff after her election in 2010 had twenty-seven members, thirteen of whom were from her Workers Party (PT), while just five were from the Party of the Brazilian Democratic Movement (PMDB). This imbalance of cabinet positions did not reflect the relative strengths of the parties in the legislature, as is normally the case in a parliamentary coalition. The two parties had almost equal shares of legislative seats, but the cabinet reflected the control of the PT over the most crucial seat: the presidency.

15. Since 2002, French governments have become much more subordinate to the president. This was the first year in which the president was elected

Election

How, then, are executives selected? As we have noted earlier, if the system is parliamentary, then the selection process is done within the legislature as an internal action of either the majority party or the majority coalition. If, however, we are dealing with a presidential or semi-presidential system, the executive needs to be chosen by the electorate.

We can start with the question of whether the election of the president is to be a direct or indirect process. An indirect election is one in which there are some type of institutional intermediaries between the electorate and those who select the president. The US Electoral College is such a mechanism. Voters in the United States do not actually vote for the presidential candidate of their choice (even if the ballot upon which they vote makes it appear that they are so doing). Instead, they vote for a slate of electors who are pledged to vote for the candidate who wins the plurality of votes in the given state.[16] Those electors then assemble in their state capitals in December to cast their electoral votes, which are, in turn, not counted officially until the new Congress convenes in January; as such, the president of the United States is formally elected by the electors, not the citizens of the United States. While the process is indirect, the electors do not also serve as legislators, preserving the separation of origin of the executive and legislature.[17]

In direct elections, the voters vote for the candidate of their choice directly (rather than voting for intermediaries). Direct elections can be single events, where the candidate who receives the most votes wins (that is, plurality elections, as discussed in chapter 5), or can be processes that require a specific percentage to win and may require voters to return for a second round if no candidate receives the

---

immediately before the legislature, and both for five-year terms. This change would tend to greatly increase the chances of a pro-presidential majority and make the president more dominant than before over all the parties in a coalition (Samuels and Shugart 2010: 175–79).

16. Save in Maine and Nebraska, as we will explain later.

17. This contrasts with the electoral colleges in Germany (known as the Federal Assembly) and India, in which sitting legislators comprise a large bloc of the electors.

requisite percentage of the vote in the first round. Most two-round systems require an absolute majority (that is, 50 percent plus one), but some systems use a *qualified plurality,* wherein a candidate can win in the first round sans gaining an absolute majority, but only by surpassing a specified threshold (for example, 40 percent) or margin requirement. The only such case among our set of democracies is Argentina, where victory requires a plurality of at least 45 percent or else at least 40 percent if the runner-up trails by at least 10 percentage points. Otherwise there is a runoff between the top two. Rules such as these forestall electing presidents with small pluralities but acquiesce to the mathematical likelihood that a second round is likely not necessary if a candidate can achieve a large plurality, but not quite an absolute majority, in the first round.

THE US EXECUTIVE BRANCH IN COMPARATIVE PERSPECTIVE

In this section we detail nine ways in which the United States is different (if not unique) in comparison to our thirty other democracies. Of the nine differences, the first three deal with the structure of the office in regards to term, reelection, and emergency replacement. The next four deal with the nomination and election process. The last two deal with the question of the transactional relations between the executive and the legislature.

In presidential systems, as we have noted, the popularly elected head of government must transact with a separately elected legislature, which, like the presidency, has a fixed term of office. Thus a further area of variation among such systems is in the relative bargaining weight that the president has vis-à-vis the legislature. This bargaining weight is principally affected by two factors, the president's constitutional powers and his partisan powers. Constitutional powers means the formal authority over legislation granted the president in the Constitution. Partisan powers refers to the degree of support that the president has in Congress, both from the majority or opposition status of the party and from the likelihood that he will obtain legislative support from his own party. Thus, while all presidents in a given country have the same constitutional powers (bar-

Table 8.11. Presidential terms of office in twelve democracies with popularly elected presidents

	Terms of office (years)
Argentina, Brazil, Chile, Colombia, **United States** (n=5)	4
France, Korea, Poland, Portugal (n=4)	5
Austria, Finland, Mexico (n=3)	6

ring changes in the Constitution itself), a given president's partisan powers depends on how well his party performs in congressional elections, as well as how much influence he has in his own party.

1. The four-year presidential term of office. As discussed in chapter 6, one of the most striking characteristics of the House of Representatives in comparative perspective is its very short term of office—only two years. Likewise, the four-year presidential term of office is short in comparison with that of other popularly elected presidents, but neither unique nor a great deal shorter. The majority of our cases with popularly elected presidents (the presidential and semi-presidential systems) have terms longer than four years (seven of twelve have terms of either five or six years). Table 8.11 shows that Argentina, Brazil, Chile, and Colombia have four-year terms, too. This increase in company that the United States has with other four-year terms is recent, as Argentina (1995), Brazil (1994), and Chile (2006) only recently changed to shorter terms.[18] There was one prominent case of even longer terms: French presidents were elected to extraordinarily long terms—seven years—until a constitutional reform cut it to a more typical five years starting in 2002.

2. Term limits. In the United States, while the term may be short, presidents are eligible for immediate reelection. Thus a given president may serve for eight years. As table 8.12 shows, some presidential

18. The dates refer to the year in which the first president with the shortened term was elected. Previously, Argentina's and Chile's terms were six years, and Brazil's was five.

Table 8.12. Presidential term limits in twelve democracies with popularly elected presidents

	Term limits
	One term, then . . .
Korea, Mexico (n=2)	Lifetime limit
Chile (n=1)	Eligible after one interim term
	Two terms, then . . .
Brazil, Colombia, Poland, **United States** (n=4)	No reelection
Argentina, Austria, Finland, Portugal (n=4)	Eligible after one interim term
France (n=1)	No limits

Source: Based on data supplied by John M. Carey.

systems place stricter limits on how long a president can serve, by either limiting the president to a single term or allowing a second term but only after the passage of an interim term. Colombia has a limit of two four-year terms as well, but prior to the constitutional reform of 2003, presidents had been limited to one four-year term.[19] France is the only country among our set in which the president can be reelected without any limits. When we combine the information on terms of office with that on term limits, it is clear that the actual consecutive length of time that a US president can serve—up to ten years,[20] though more realistically, eight—is actually longer than in most of the other countries. For instance, Korea and Mexico have five-year and six-year terms of office respectively, but these terms also represent lifetime limits.

19. Under the rules of the 1886 constitution, nonconsecutive reelection was permissible. The 1991 constitution forbade all reelection until the 2003 reform was adopted.

20. A US president who has served two years or less of a term to which another person was elected (e.g., because the elected president dies or resigns) is eligible for two more terms, meaning one person may theoretically serve for up to ten years.

These variations in maximum tenure reveal that there is a trade-off between the length of a given term and the presence of term limits. With the notable and really striking exception of France—where the term length used to be seven years and reelection is unrestricted—presidents who can be reelected to consecutive terms usually are those whose terms are shorter. In fact, the recent changes to shorten the terms of presidents in Argentina and Brazil were both taken as compromises between the opposition and supporters of presidents who sought the right to run for reelection. Thus the trade-off we are referring to was embodied in constitutional compromise: potentially longer total tenure for any given president, but more frequent presidential elections. Similarly, over the years various proposals have surfaced in the United States for lengthening the presidential term—usually to six years—and these have almost always been linked to a proposal to ban reelection.[21]

3. Vice presidency versus early election to fill a vacancy in the presidency. In the United States, the position of vice president exists but has a limited role except in the event that the president dies, resigns, or is removed from office.[22] In that case, the vice president takes over as president, serving the remainder of the term for which the departed president was elected. Most other countries with elected presidents do not have a vice presidency. In fact, only Argentina, Brazil, and Colombia have the position of vice president. In other cases, if the presidency is vacated, an interim president is appointed (typically from congress), either to fill out the term, or until early elections are held. In these cases, unlike in the United States, even though the presidency has a fixed term, presidential elections could come early in the unlikely event that a president leaves office prematurely. In most cases, if there is an early election,

21. For an overview of this topic, see Neale 2009. See also Buchanan 1988 and Cutler 1980.

22. In fact, the vice president's only constitutional duty is to preside over the Senate and cast a vote only in the event that the votes of senators are tied. Vice presidents rarely attend the Senate, unless there is a high probability of a very close vote on a matter of great importance to the president or his party. Any other administrative role performed by a vice president is purely at the discretion of the president.

the president elected simply fills out the remainder of the original term, thereby returning elections to their regular schedule. However, in France, early presidential elections reset the clock, giving the new president a full term, as has happened twice: when President Charles de Gaulle resigned in 1969 after less than four years of his (then) seven-year term, and when President Georges Pompidou died in 1974, less than five years into his seven-year term.

4. *Indirect election.* The United States is now unique among countries with elected presidents in having those elections be indirect. Presidential elections in the United States are popular, in that voters select a presidential candidate after a public campaign by the candidates, but they are indirect, in that the ultimate selection takes place via the *Electoral College.* In direct elections, the candidate is elected who obtains the most votes, either in a single-shot election or in a runoff. Of the twelve countries with popular presidential elections—both presidential and semi-presidential systems—only in the United States is it possible for the candidate with the most votes in the final round of popular voting to lose out in favor of a candidate with fewer popular votes. Of course, this is what happened in 2000, when Al Gore obtained more votes than George W. Bush, but the latter candidate—after a lengthy series of recounts in the state of Florida and a ruling by the US Supreme Court—was determined to have obtained more electoral votes. In the Electoral College, each state has a voting weight equivalent to its total number of representatives and senators. States are free to choose their method for allocating their own electors—they do not even have to hold popular voting, although all do. Forty-eight of the fifty states, plus the District of Columbia, award all of their electoral votes to the candidate with the plurality (that is, most votes) in the state.[23]

We see in table 8.13 that the United States has not always been alone, as two other countries among our sample used electoral colleges in the recent past; both changed to direct election in the early 1990s. Argentina's, like that of the United States, was "federalist," in

23. In Maine and Nebraska, two electoral votes are awarded to the candidate who wins the statewide plurality, and the others are awarded to the winner of the plurality in each congressional district.

Table 8.13. Elected president: Method of election

Indirect election (electoral college)		Direct election	
Federalist	Partisan	Plurality	Majority runoff
Argentina (before 1995)	Finland (before 1994)	Colombia (before 1991)	Austria
United States		Korea	Brazil
		Mexico	Chile
			Colombia (after (1991)
		Qualified plurality	Finland
		Argentina[a]	France
			Poland
			Portugal

Note
[a] The qualified-plurality rule in Argentina stipulates that the leading candidate is elected on the first ballot if he or she wins either (1) at least 45 percent of the total vote, or (2) at least 40 percent of the total vote if the second-ranked candidate is at least 10 percentage points behind; if the leading candidate does not meet either of those conditions, there is a runoff between the top two candidates.

that it weighted the representation of states (provinces in Argentina) in the electoral college such that less populous states were over-represented relative to their share of the national population. The candidate who obtained a majority of the total number of votes cast by electors—who assemble only in their states and not as a national body, providing a further federalist element—is elected. The electoral college of Finland, on the other hand, was "partisan" in that electors were elected much like legislators. Candidates for elector campaigned as individuals as well as representatives of a party promoting a specific presidential candidate, and the electoral college assembled as a single body, deliberated, and was empowered to take multiple ballots, if necessary, to produce a winner.

The other eleven democracies with popularly elected presidents all use direct elections. As table 8.13 shows, most—eight out of twelve—use the majority-runoff method: If no candidate wins a majority of votes in the first round, a second election is held between the top two candidates. Korea and Mexico use the plurality method (as did Colombia until 1991), in which the candidate with the most votes wins even if he or she does not have a majority of the votes. Argentina uses a method that may be termed "qualified plurality," which can be seen as intermediate between plurality and majority-runoff. (The note in table 8.13 explains the details.) The use of run-off methods—whether majority or qualified-plurality—is a means of preventing the possibility that a president is elected against the wishes of the majority of voters. Often under plurality rules, the candidate with the most votes is well short of 50 percent. In such cases, it is not necessarily the case that the majority is unhappy with the result, but the risk of a majority-disapproved candidate is greater to the extent that the race is very close, or the largest party is relatively more extreme ideologically than the others. For instance, in Korea all presidential elections since the return to democracy in 1987 have been won with less than 50 percent of the vote, and those of 1998 and 2002 were decided by less than 2 percentage points. The Mexican presidential election of 2006 was won by a candidate, Felipe Calderón of the National Action Party, with 35.89 percent of the votes and a runner-up who trailed the winner by just more than half a percentage point (35.33 percent).[24] It is possible that some of these elections could have turned out differently if a runoff between the top two had been required. In the United States, the use of plurality rule, in indirect elections, is even more extreme, as we see next.

5. *Extreme multimember district plurality and barriers to small-party participation.* What makes the American system of electing presidents even more unusual is that the Electoral College is elected by plurality in districts (the fifty states and the District of Columbia), many of which have very large magnitudes; as we will recall from chapter 5, the magnitude of a district denotes the number of representatives (electors in the case of the Electoral College) to be elected in the district. District magnitude has a strong impact on election results both in proportional representation (PR) systems

24. And in 2012 a president elected with under 40% proved not to be a one-time event, as the PRI candidate, Enrique Peña Nieto, was elected with about 38%.

and in plurality systems (as well as other majoritarian systems like majority-runoff and the Alternative Vote), but in opposite directions: Increasing the district magnitude in plurality systems entails greater disproportionality and greater advantages for large parties. This is in stark contrast to the effect under PR, where increasing district magnitude results in greater proportionality and more favorable conditions for small parties (see box 5.1).

A similar hypothetical example for plurality is that in a particular area the election contest is between Democrats and Republicans and that the Democrats are slightly stronger. If this area is a three-member district, the Democrats are likely to win all three seats. However, if the area is divided into three single-member districts, a Republican candidate may well be able to win in one of the districts and hence win one of the three seats. When the district magnitude is increased further, disproportionality also increases. Imagine if the US House were elected state by state, using plurality, and, as is the case with the Electoral College, voters had to vote for an entire ticket rather than having the option to pick and choose candidates of different parties. If this were the case, then a party could beat the runner-up by a very thin margin yet would get all of the states' seats—for instance, all fifty-five in the case of California! This is precisely the system used in the Electoral College, and it is what can make a single close state contest so contentious as was the case in the struggle to determine which party's candidate had won Florida's twenty-five electors in 2000. It is also one critical reason why parties other than Republicans and Democrats rarely are significant in presidential elections, as we will discuss further.[25]

The combination of indirect election, high district magnitude, and plurality rule ensures that the number of candidates competing in presidential elections is sharply lower in the United States than

25. It is sometimes said that Maine and Nebraska award their electors proportionally, but this is incorrect. In Maine in 1992, e.g., Bill Clinton won all four electoral votes despite winning well under 50% of the votes, because he won the plurality in each congressional district as well as statewide. With PR, Clinton would have won two electors, and George H. W. Bush and H. Ross Perot would have won one each.

Table 8.14. Effective and actual numbers of candidates in presidential elections, 1990–2010

Election method	Effective number of candidates		Actual number of candidates with more than 2% (avg.)
A. Electoral college	*Popular vote*	*Electoral vote*	
Federalist			
Argentina (1989)	2.55	2.07	3.0
United States	**2.28**	**1.85**	**2.6**
Partisan			
Finland (1988)	3.93	3.53	5.0
B. Direct election	*Popular vote*		
Plurality			
Colombia (1990)	3.17		4.0
Korea	2.79		3.8
Mexico	2.98		3.7
Average	*2.98*		*3.83*
Qualified plurality (using votes and candidates from first round)			
Argentina	3.48		4.0
Majority runoff (using votes and candidates from first round)			
Austria	2.20		3.3
Brazil	2.70		4.2
Chile	2.64		4.0
Finland	3.99		5.3
France	6.43		9.0
Poland	3.48		5.4
Portugal	2.30		3.8
Average	*3.39*		*5.00*

in most other countries that hold presidential elections. Table 8.14 shows that effective number of candidates and the actual number of candidates (ignoring those with less than 2 percent of the vote), averaged over all the elections held in each country between about 1990 and 2010. We see that the effective number of candidates over this time period has averaged 2.28 in the United States, which is the lowest of any of our cases save Austria's 2.20.[26] The actual number of candidates is lower than anywhere else. Compare the majority runoff elections, where the effective number averages 3.39 and the actual number winning at least 2 percent averages 5.00 (in the initial round). These systems encourage additional candidates to run, and voters to support them, because (1) it may be unclear at the outset which two will be the top two, implying competition among three or more parties for runoff slots, and (2) smaller parties can demonstrate their support in the first round and then form alliances with one of the remaining candidates for the runoff. The second round also makes it possible for a candidate to have won the most votes in the first round but lose the runoff, when voters for other, eliminated, candidates prefer the candidate who initially placed second. In other words, the plurality winner is not necessarily majority-preferred, and having the second round ensures that a majority-*disapproved* candidate is not elected.

As table 8.14 shows, direct plurality elections tend to have less fragmented competition than the majority-runoff elections, given that the plurality rule by definition means victory to the largest: The effective number of candidates averages 2.98, and the actual candidates winning more than 2 percent of the vote averages 3.83. What is particularly interesting, however, is that even direct-plurality election tends to produce participation by a larger number of significant parties than we see in US presidential elections. This reinforces the

26. It is worth noting that though Austria's president on paper appears quite powerful, it is in reality mostly a ceremonial position. The 2010 elections were also especially noncompetitive, with the incumbent (Heinz Fischer) winning almost 80% of the vote in the first round. Even given the nature of the position and its less-than-competitive recent contest, Austria still averages more actual candidates (3.3) than does the US (2.6).

point we made previously about the impact of multiseat plurality rules being even more disproportional than single-seat plurality. When presidential elections are by direct plurality, we have a nationwide election for a single seat, and hence parties other than the top two can collect votes wherever in the country they have support, and potentially even win with less than 50 percent of the vote—or even less than 40 percent, as in the Mexican case we referred to previously. By contrast, the multiseat plurality election of electors in the United States means that a third party would have to win the *largest share* of votes in several states to have any realistic chance of winning. Thus the campaign for selecting the president is basically restricted to participation by large parties in the United States more than in the other countries. As a result, there is less injection of the viewpoints of smaller parties into the most important national political debate.

The disproportionality of the US Electoral college is clear from table 8.14, where we see that the effective number of candidates, when measured by their shares of the electors is only 1.85, which is even lower than when measured by votes (2.28).This contrasts with the lesser reductions in Argentina, and especially Finland, where electors were allocated via PR, and thus smaller parties could form coalitions to participate in the choice of a president.[27] The 1992 US presidential election, which featured an unusually strong third candidate, demonstrates the difficulty a candidate who is not from one

27. The Argentine case implies that some of the deterrence effect is not plurality allocation of electors but the need for a majority of electors to elect a president. In both Argentina (pre-1995) and the United States, if there is not a majority of the electors for one candidate, then the final selection devolves to Congress. Thus there is little incentive for parties to seek electoral votes if they have no chance at a majority. This was so even in Argentina, where the electors were allocated to candidates by proportional representation. Nonetheless, the effective number of candidates in the United States would be much lower than for Argentina if we took into account elections from before 1990, given that doing so would diminish the impact of the two elections in which H. Ross Perot ran unusually strong for an independent or third-party candidate.

In Finland, on the other hand, where their former electoral college was elected via proportional representation *and could take multiple ballots among the electors themselves*, participation by smaller parties was high.

of the two established parties has, on account of the use of state-by-state plurality in the Electoral College. Democrat Bill Clinton, Republican George H. W. Bush, and independent H. Ross Perot split the popular vote 43 percent–37 percent–19 percent. But the electoral vote split 370–168–0.[28] That is, Clinton won more than two-thirds of the electors, despite much less than half the votes. It is easy to see why the Electoral College, as employed in the United States, generally discourages many small parties from even entering—if they cannot win electoral votes, they can have no direct influence[29] on the final selection of the president.

6. Regionalized competition for president and over-representation of small states. A further consequence of both the federalist nature of the Electoral College and the use of plurality rule in large multi-member districts is the regionalization of presidential electoral competition. For instance, media commentary about presidential campaigns routinely refers to "red states" and "blue states," meaning those which are likely to give their entire slate of electoral votes to the Republican or Democrat, respectively, regardless of the margin of victory.[30] A small number of states is likely to be decisive in any given election year, as relatively small swings of the popular vote in

28. The last time a candidate in a US presidential election outside of the two major parties won electoral votes was in 1968, when George Wallace won forty-six electoral votes by winning Alabama, Arkansas, Georgia, Louisiana, and Mississippi. Before that, in 1948, J. Strom Thurmond, running under the State's Rights label, won thirty-nine electoral votes by winning Alabama, Louisiana, Mississippi, and South Carolina, and in 1960, there were fifteen unpledged electors selected. In recent elections we have seen "unfaithful electors" (i.e., electors who vote contrary to the plurality of voters in their states) cast protest votes in the Electoral College. Specifically, in 1988 an elector (from West Virginia) cast one electoral vote for Lloyd Bentsen (the Democratic nominee for vice president) and likewise a 2004 elector (from Minnesota) cast a vote for John Edwards. In 2000, an elector from the District of Columbia abstained rather than vote for Al Gore, as a symbolic protest against the Supreme Court's ruling in *Bush v. Gore.*

29. Only indirect influence, in the sense that their presence in the race can tip the statewide plurality in some states to a majority-disapproved candidate.

30. This practice started in the 2000 presidential elections and has become a staple of the US political vernacular since—going even beyond presidential politics.

a few states can shift the outcome in the Electoral College and hence determine the presidency. Under a direct-election procedure, attention would be unlikely to focus on swing states (and, within them, crucial voting blocs), because the goal would be to win a *national* plurality (or majority or qualified plurality, depending on the rules), rather than to amass a majority of electoral votes. Note again that it is not the Electoral College alone that is responsible for this regionalization, but the fact that each state gives its entire electoral-vote contingent to one candidate, with the winner determined by plurality.[31] For instance, if electors were awarded proportionally, small vote shifts in specific states would be much less decisive in the final outcome.

In the United States the electoral-vote winner may not be the popular-vote winner, because the percentage of electoral votes in each state is only roughly proportional to the population of the state. No state has less than three electoral votes, or about 0.56 percent of the total, because each state has a number of electoral votes equal to its representation in the House and Senate combined. Some of the states that have just three electoral votes have far less than 0.56 percent of the national population, with the greatest discrepancy being that in Wyoming (0.18 percent of the population).

We can calculate an *advantage ratio* for each state by simply dividing its share of the total electoral vote by its share of the national population. These ratios range from about .85 for California and Texas to 3.18 for Wyoming. In other words, California's weight in electing a president is only 85 percent of its contribution to the national population, while Wyoming's is more than three times as great as its population. Figure 8.4 plots each state's advantage ratio against its population (based on population estimates from 2002 and the Electoral College apportionment, which were effective in 2004

31. It is possible for a second candidate to obtain one of the four electors in Maine or Nebraska because these states do not use *statewide* plurality; this happened for the first time in 2008, when Democrat Barack Obama won the most votes in one congressional district in Nebraska and hence one of the state's electors, while Republican John McCain won the statewide plurality and hence the other four electors.

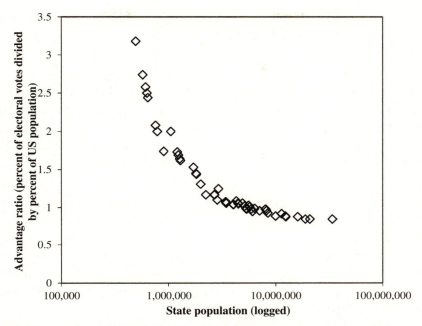

Fig. 8.4. Relationship of state population to over- or under-representation in the US Electoral College

and 2008). It shows very clearly how the smallest states are significantly over-represented. Only states with around 5 million population have an Electoral College weight about equal to their share of the population. There are thirteen states with an advantage ratio greater than 1.5. Together, these states hold 4.7 percent of the population, but cast 9.1 percent of the electoral votes.

Because no other country currently elects its president via an electoral college, no other country has electoral rules that regionalize the contest.[32] Regionalized competition prevails in Korea because

32. As noted earlier, Argentina, although emulating the federalist nature of the US Electoral College, used proportional representation to allocate each province's electors among the candidates. This proportionality somewhat mitigated the very high malapportionment of their electoral college itself. While the smallest provinces were more over-represented in Argentina than are the smallest states in the United States, no province could deliver its entire voting weight to one candidate.

the parties have distinct regional bastions; however, regions are not weighted in the final outcome (other than by their turnout), because the election is direct.

7. *Primary elections.* A primary is an election between two or more candidates of the same party, in advance of the general election, and it is used as a means of nominating that party's candidate for office. The United States uses a series of state-level primaries and caucuses[33] to nominate its major party candidates, who then compete for the presidency. Rules vary by state as to whether only voters who identified an affiliation with a given party when registering to vote may vote in that party's primary. As we noted in chapter 6, the United States widely uses primary elections to nominate candidates for most elected offices. The widespread use of primaries to nominate candidates by the major parties is a feature unique to the United States, although some countries have used primaries in a limited fashion. Table 8.15 shows that some Latin American parties have used primaries on a limited basis during our period of study.

Not only is the United States the only one of our democracies that has used the primary process consistently for its major party nomination for decades, it is also unique in the sense that it uses a state-by-state and indirect process. The US presidential nomination process is indirect because primaries select convention delegates—a partial analogue to the electors in the general-election phase.[34] Additionally, there remains no national vote in the primary process, but rather a sequence of state-level contests (often and increasingly with groups of states voting on a common day) that inevitably gives

33. Some hold party caucuses, where voters gather, deliberate, and select delegates pledged to specific candidates who obtain a minimum share of the caucus-goers support. Typically, caucuses receive much lower participation rates than primary elections. The most famous example of caucuses are those of Iowa, which are traditionally held before any of the other states hold their primary elections.

34. One difference is that the party conventions allocate states' voting power more proportionally than does the Electoral College (proportionate to votes for the respective party's presidential candidate in the state in past elections). The convention delegates further differ from presidential electors in that they are deliberative, at least in principle.

Table 8.15. Countries and parties that have held presidential primaries, 1990–2010

Country	Parties and dates
Argentina	FREPASO (1995) FREPASO-UCR (1999) UCR (1995, 2003)
Brazil	Worker's Party (2002)
Chile[a]	Concertación alliance (1993, 1999, 2001, 2005, 2009)
Colombia	Conservative Party (2010) Liberal Party (1990, 1994, 2006, 2009) Green Party (2010) PDA (2006, 2009)
Mexico	PAN (2005) PRI (1999, 2005)
United States	**Democratic, Republican, and some minor parties**

Note:
[a] In 2005 a primary was planned, but the withdrawal of one of the two candidates led to its cancellation. In 2009 a regional contest was held, and the substantial victory of the eventual nominee was large enough to preclude any further voting.
Sources: Siavelis and Morgenstern 2008; additional detail provided by Mark P. Jones and Peter M. Siavelis (personal communications).

greater weight in the ultimate selection of a nominee to voters in some states than in others. By contrast, other countries that have held presidential primaries have generally done so in a direct national vote. A partial exception to direct national primaries was found in Mexico's then-ruling Institutional Revolutionary Party in 1999. In that case, the election was held on the same day throughout the country, but the decision rule was that the candidate who won pluralities in the most congressional districts would be the party's nominee, even if that candidate did not have the plurality of the national popular vote.[35]

35. Because congressional districts are drawn to equalize population but not necessarily PRI voters across districts, this process effectively gave greater weight to localities where the party was weaker relative to other parties. Given that the party was going to face a tough general-election battle, a process that encouraged candidates to reach out to voters outside the party's strongest

The closest case to the United States in regards to using regional primaries was Chile in 2009, when one regional contest was used by the Concertación to nominate its presidential candidate.[36]

A concluding note on US primaries in comparative perspective, is that despite the lack of proportional representation (PR) mechanisms in US national elections, proportional representation rules are commonly used to allocate delegates in statewide contests. In fact, PR (albeit with very high thresholds) is required in all states by the rules of the Democratic Party, usually partly within congressional districts and partly statewide. In the Republican Party, some states use PR and others use plurality, either in congressional districts or statewide. Thus presidential primaries, especially for Democrats, are the one arena in which many Americans vote under PR rules.

8. Relatively weak constitutional powers over legislation. In the United States, the presidency is provided one constitutional power over legislation: the right to veto a bill passed by Congress, which then requires two-thirds of each house to override. It is this veto—combined with the fixed terms—that guarantees a transactional relationship between the executive and the legislature, because neither branch can accomplish a legislative agenda without the consent of the other. Assuming differences in preferred policy outcomes, either the two branches come to a negotiated agreement over the shape of a bill, or one side backs down and accepts the other's version, or else no legislation is passed. Contrast this with what happens in a parliamentary system, where the head of government—the prime minister—can be removed via a vote of no confidence if the legis-

---

congressional districts may have assisted the nomination of a more-appealing candidate over the candidate of the traditional party machinery. As it turned out, the winner of the most congressional districts also had the most votes nationwide—and then lost the general election.

36. On April 5, 2009, there was a regional primary in the Maule and O'Higgins regions of Chile between Eduardo Frei and José Antonio Gómez. Because Frei's margin of victory was more than 20%, no additional contests were held and Frei won the nomination. This was the first time this type of procedure was used (personal correspondence with Peter M. Siavelis). If Chile had engaged in a region-by-region process, this would have been the closest analogue to the US system among our cases.

lative majority disagrees over policy priorities with the executive. Thus the US president is in a strong position to say no to the legislature's majority but at the same time in a weak position in that he has few levers to exercise in order to push the legislature into action in support of his agenda.

Contrast the US presidency's formal powers to those of other elected presidents, shown in table 8.16. As can be seen at a glance, almost all presidents in presidential systems have at least the veto, but among our seven cases, five have more than the veto. Four of the presidencies in our set of countries are constitutionally given unilateral powers, by which we mean the right to enact decrees with the force of law. For example, in Brazil, the president may legislate on a wide range of policy matters by emitting a "provisional measure," which is effective for sixty days. After that time, it lapses, although presidents often reissue lapsed measures. Congress may reject a provisional measure by passing countervailing legislation, and here is where the veto power comes in. Notice from table 8.16 that the Brazilian president's veto has a lower threshold to override than that of the United States: an absolute majority, rather than two-thirds. However, this is actually not as weak as it may appear, as the Brazilian veto is based on a majority of all members, whereas the United States is based on two-thirds of members present and voting. What this means is that a determined congressional majority in Brazil could prevent a provisional measure from remaining in effect, but given that the Brazilian congress is often fragmented and has a high absentee rate, in fact the congress is not well equipped to block the president's use of unilateral measures. Generally, then, the unilateral powers permit the president of Brazil to play the leading role in promoting his agenda to a degree that a US president can only dream of. Nonetheless, really significant policy changes usually require statutes or even constitutional amendments, so congress is still a check on even the unilateral powers of the Brazilian president.

Another case of unilateral powers is Argentina, where presidents may issue what are known as "decrees of necessity and urgency," which take effect immediately. Given the president's much stronger veto, these are even harder to overcome than Brazilian provisional measures. They also do not expire after a set period.

Table 8.16. Powers of popularly elected presidents

Presidential system	Veto (override)	Unilateral	Integrative
Argentina	x[p] (2/3)	x	
Brazil	x[p] (50% + 1)	x	x
Chile	x (2/3)		x
Colombia	x[p] (50% + 1)	x	
Korea	x (2/3)	x	x
Mexico	x (2/3)		
United States	**x (2/3)**		
Semi-presidential system			
Austria			
Finland			
France			
Poland	x (3/5)[a]		
Portugal			

Notes:
[a] First chamber alone (Sejm) need to override.
[p] "partial" (or item) veto allowed.
Sources: Shugart and Carey 1992; Tsebelis and Alemán 2005; and respective national constitutions.

It should be noted, also, that not all vetoes are equal. Not only are there different thresholds by which legislatures can override a given veto (which affects a given president's potential for success), but three of our cases (Argentina, Brazil and Colombia) allow for a partial (or item) veto. As Shugart and Carey note, partial vetoes "increase presidential power dramatically" because "congress cannot present large legislative packages to the president. Which effectively force the latter to accept pork projects or other objectionable amendments . . . in order to pass desired legislation" (1992: 134). However, with the partial veto, a president can target specific elements of a given legislative package, while allowing the rest to pass into law.

Table 8.16 also shows that there are three cases of presidents with "integrative" powers. We borrow this term from Cox and Morgenstern (2001), who use it to refer to powers that allow the president to control the agenda of congress. These are different from unilateral powers, which allow the president to make policy without even consenting with congress (though legislators may subsequently reverse a unilateral act, with varying degrees of difficulty). Integrative powers allow the president, for instance, to establish a maximum spending level, which congress can cut but not increase. Other integrative powers establish that in specific policy areas, the congress may not initiate legislative change but must wait for the president to do so. These powers thus give the president a powerful role in shaping policy change, especially when combined with veto power (Chile and Korea) or with both veto and unilateral powers (Brazil). With only the veto power, then, the US presidency is considerably weaker in constitutional powers than at least five of the other seven presidencies in presidential systems. The powers of the Mexican presidency are the most comparable to that of the United States. Strikingly, none of these constitutional powers over legislation apply in semi-presidential systems, except for the veto wielded by the Polish president.

9. *Moderate partisan powers due to the prevalence of "divided government" and modest discipline.* A president can be said to enjoy high partisan powers if his party commands a majority of seats in congress and if he himself commands the party, such that its legislators regularly vote with the president. If a president has very high partisan powers, he does not need constitutional powers to dominate the legislative agenda. At the extreme of high partisan powers, the congressional majority would become subordinated in a hierarchical relationship with the president. Such a situation existed in Mexico before the long-ruling PRI lost its majority in 1997 and then lost the presidency three years later.

In the case of the United States, presidents frequently do not have a majority. As we noted in chapter 6, parties in the United States are nonhierarchical, which means that not only do their own legislative leaders not command their parties but neither does the president, typically. Thus presidents must transact with congressional leaders, even of their own party, or with individual members. The term *divided government* is commonly used to describe the situation in the

United States in which the Congress (or at least one house) is controlled by a majority party distinct from the party of the president. Divided government is actually the norm in the United States. In our primary period of analysis for this book, 1990–2010, both houses have been controlled by the president's party only for eight and one-third years out of twenty-one. Specifically, the Democrats have enjoyed unified government from 1993 to 1995 and from 2009 to 2011, and the Republicans for a portion of 2001 and then from 2003 to 2007.[37] Under these conditions, neither party can be said to be able to "form a government," because while the president is free to appoint a cabinet of his choosing, he has no control over the agenda of the legislature. All he has is the veto with which he can prevent his opponents in the legislature from passing laws he dislikes (unless they can muster the two-thirds needed to override him).

Given the effective supermajority requirements in the Senate for passing major legislation (except the budget) that we discussed in chapter 8, even unified government is not all that it is cracked up to be in the US system. Only a president with both a unified government and a sixty-vote margin for his party in the Senate could be said to have a truly unified government. This is an unusual situation and has only happened once in the period under analysis, and even then it was for only a portion of 2009. The Democratic Party's sixty-vote majority in the Senate was lost when Senator Ted Kennedy of Massachusetts died. Kennedy was replaced by a Republican (Scott Brown) in the subsequent special election.

A single-party majority opposing the president is rare in our other presidential systems. However, it is also not common in other presidential systems for the president to have a copartisan majority. The

37. Note that years of control start and end in the January after an election, hence 1993–1995 covers a twenty-four-month period starting in early January of 1993 and ending in early January of 1995. In 2001 the Senate was a fifty–fifty tie, with the fact that Vice President Richard Cheney was the Republican leading to a tiebreak vote to allow the Republicans control. However, Senator Jim Jeffords of Vermont switched his party affiliation from Republican to Independent (who caucuses with the Democrats) effective in May of 2001, which shifted control of the Senate to the Democrats and ended a brief period of unified government.

more common situation is for the president's party to be the largest in Congress but short of a majority, necessitating the formation of coalitions to pass legislation, and the use of whatever constitutional powers the president has at his disposal in order to put his stamp on the legislative output.

It is worth comparing what happens in the absence of a pro-presidential majority in the legislative assembly in presidential and semi-presidential systems. As we noted, opposition majorities—so-called divided government—are typical in the United States. Our other country with significant experience with opposition majorities (though usually coalitions, not a single party) is France, a semi-presidential system. As discussed earlier in this chapter, France has had periods of "cohabitation," when the parliamentary majority, and hence the premier and cabinet, were controlled by a party or alliance opposed to the president. Because, as we saw in table 8.16, the French president has no veto, decree, or integrative powers; in a situation of cohabitation, he is actually much weaker than a US president under divided government. A French president lacks the ability to shape the policy output of the government, except to the extent that he can shape the political complexion of the government itself. Obviously, he cannot shape it when it depends on a parliamentary majority opposed to him. In Poland, on the other hand, where we have also had brief periods of cohabitation—for instance from 1993 to 1995, when Lech Wałęsa was president but an opposition alliance of the SLD and other parties controlled the parliamentary majority—the president retained policy influence through his veto. The Polish system thus can be said to have both "cohabitation" (sometimes a premier and cabinet opposed to the president) and "divided government" (understood as the ability of the president to exercise a veto against the legislative majority). Finally, it is also worth considering whether divided government is akin to minority government in parliamentary systems, which we saw represents just more than a fifth of governments in those countries (table 8.4). Superficially, they are similar: an executive of a party that has only a minority of seats in the legislature (or at least one chamber, if bicameral). However, here is where the similarity ends. US presidents under divided government face a situation in which a party other than their own has the majority; a prime minister, by contrast, would never be in such a position, because when the majority shifts from one party to another, the prime minister also shifts to the new majority. It is the separate election and fixed term of the US executive institution that allows presidents, along with the cabinets they choose, to remain in office when they are opposed by a majority in the House, Senate, or both.

CONCLUSION

We have seen that the United States is unusual, though not unique, in having a presidential form of government. Among the thirty-one democracies included in this comparative study, a large minority of them have an elected president, and of those, seven are fully presidential systems. In terms of the structure of the office, the US executive has a shorter term of office, allows for immediate reelection (but only once), and has an elected emergency replacement (the vice president). All of these are features that place the US presidency in the minority of our presidential and semi-presidential democracies, but none of these are especially significant in terms of the way the office operates.

Pure presidentialism is significant for our understanding of executive power in the United States, insofar as it makes the executive a veto gate controlled by one player (the president), and this means that for a president to successfully see a legislative agenda passed, it is necessary to transact with the other veto gates, that is the two chambers of Congress (or, specifically, with the veto players within the chambers who determine when to open the congressional gates). This is to be contrasted with prime ministers who usually have all the veto players with which they need to transact represented within their own cabinet: Either the party that the prime minister heads is the only veto player (in the case of a single-party majority government) or the veto players are the parties in coalition with the prime minister's party.[38] Presidentialism, therefore, is a key component for understanding policy making and presents a very different set of in-

---

38. The exception would be in a minority government, in which the prime minister may also have to transact with one or more parties that are not in the

stitutional parameters than is the case in the parliamentary systems (or even semi-presidential systems, depending on the powers of a given president in those cases) in our study.

In terms of truly unique features of the US executive, we can look to the method of election. No other country systematically uses primaries to nominate the major party candidates, nor does any country use an electoral college or other indirect method to elect a president.[39] These features, along with the plurality system to elect electors from multiseat districts, diminish the incentives for third-party candidate to participate in the process, which further cements the two-party system discussed in chapters 6 and 7.

---

cabinet, but that potentially could join with other noncabinet parties in a no-confidence vote.

39. Not counting the mostly ceremonial presidents in some parliamentary democracies, such as Germany and Israel.

CHAPTER 9

Judicial Power

Judicial power, the power to adjudicate disputes over application (and sometimes the very meaning) of the law, is the third main power of governments. The judicial branch is responsible for ensuring the rule of law and thus is critical for democracy. In this chapter, we shall see that the judiciaries of our thirty-one democracies vary in the extent to which they are charged with enforcing the law as written and/or serving as a check on the executive and legislative branches.

Discussing judicial power can become complicated, because unlike executives, where there is one central figure to discuss, or legislatures, where there is an obvious chamber (or chambers) to study, judicial power is diffused among a larger number of actors situated at multiple locations. This diffusion of actors is made even more complicated in federal systems in which there may be parallel judicial systems in operation. While our focus in this chapter is primarily systemic (for example, common law or code law) or at the peak institutional level (that is, supreme or constitutional courts), the conversation also ranges into lower levels of the judicial systems.

THE ROLE OF COURTS IN DEMOCRACIES

Before entering into a discussion of the institutional options open to constitutional planners regarding judicial power, let us consider for a moment the specific functions that courts perform in a democratic setting.

As a general proposition, courts perform a basic role as the institution of mediation between parties who have disputes over the law, whether that be a judgment over whether a given citizen has broken a criminal law or whether a particular civil law needs to be applied in a dispute between two citizens. Courts also have to perform an interpretative or at least clarifying role in the application of laws that may have policy implications (of course, the latitude for interpretation depends on the nature of the legal system, as we will see later). Beyond this concrete function courts perform key system functions in democratic states. To wit: maintenance of the rule of law (and, indeed, of the constitutional order) as well as an institutional means by which to help ensure minority protections.

A key concept in democratic states is the rule of law, the idea that the society is governed by a set of known rules that apply equally and fairly to all citizens. This is to be contrasted with systems in which rules are arbitrary and in which powerful actors can avoid following said rules. Further, in a democratic setting, the expectation is that the laws are made by a known, public, and predictable set of rules that define and constrain public action, and that this process is linked directly to elections. If we think back to figure 1.1, a basic assumption of democratic governance is that the rules created by the agents of the people would be put into practice. A judiciary that is sufficiently independent from other political actors, and that is respected by those actors (that is, will respect its rulings), helps ensure that the law does, in fact, rule. So while most discussions and analyses of democratic governance focus more heavily on the elected offices of the government, the role played by courts in preserving rule of law and protecting the basic political rights and processes enshrined in constitutions are vital for successful democratic governance. Indeed, the ability of courts to function in this way is seen as an important institutional milestone in the development of democracy.[1]

Courts also serve a specific and special function in constitutional systems, since they are often charged, at least at the highest levels,

1. See, e.g., Diamond 1999: 11–12, 111–12, as well as Carey and Howard 2004 in terms of the general issues. Also see Ungar 2001 as an example of the examination of the importance of establishing rule of law in the context of democratization.

with interpreting the appropriate method of application, if not the very meaning, of the constitution. In most cases, the only means by which constitutional questions can be settled is via the courts, and democratic constitutions typically make provisions for such processes. Consider that constitutions are the highest laws in the land, and courts are charged with settling disputes over the law. As such, the highest courts in democratic cases are normally assigned the logical role of being the arbiter over issues concerning the meaning and application of the constitution. That role becomes especially salient when constitutions contain statements of fundamental rights, as most democratic constitutions do. Hence, courts that have the power to interpret and enforce such basic rights are essential guardians of the rights of the citizenry.

This role as constitutional arbiter can also have important implications for protecting the rights of citizens as individuals or as members of minority groups. A key example in US history would be *Brown v. Board of Education* (1954), which allowed for the application of the Fourteenth Amendment's guarantee of equal protection under the law to desegregate public schools, despite substantial support for the policy of segregation.[2] Such issues illustrate a key tension in democratic governance. On the one hand, democracy is government by the people, and in most cases we expect the majority (or sometimes the plurality) to rule. However, democracy also respects the rights and privileges of individuals. For example, free speech and free association are fundamental rights that are essential to democratic governance, and they cannot be subject to a majority

2. Polling was less prolific in that era than is the case now, making exact measurements of public sentiment difficult. However, a Gallup Poll taken after the Brown decision was issued showed 55% national support (see Gallup, "Race and Education 50 Years After *Brown v. Board of Education*," online at http://www.gallup.com/poll/11686/race-education-years-after-brown-board -education.aspx). However, we do know that regional opposition to desegregation was high. "In 1959, 72% of white Southerners objected to even a few blacks in white schools" (Frankenberg, Lee, and Orfield 2003: 16). At a minimum, even if there was majority support for ending segregation, that support was not overwhelming and certainly was not enough to result in a national policy change via the legislature.

vote. Hence, there is a need for parameters (for example, constitutional declarations of rights) and institutions (for example, courts) that can intervene to protect individual rights in the face of majority constraints on those rights.[3]

Some constitutions even allow for individual citizens to make direct appeals to courts based specifically on questions of individual claims of rights violations.

For example, the Polish constitution, in Article 79 states: "Everyone whose constitutional freedoms or rights have been infringed, shall have the right to appeal to the Constitutional Tribunal." Other examples of specific examples of constitutions that cite the courts as having specific roles in protecting individual rights include, but are not limited to, those of Colombia and South Africa.

As such, courts are quite central to democratic governance, even if they are not directly chosen by elections and even though they are not directly responsible to the citizens. Of course, it is worth remembering that judges are selected and held accountable by democratically elected actors, although the exact processes vary from case to case, as we will see in the next section.

INSTITUTIONAL OPTIONS

If we start with the US framers, we find that of the three elements of government, judicial power was the one with which they spent the least amount of time debating and formulating. We can see this in a variety of ways, not the least of which being that Article III of the US Constitution is the briefest and least detailed of the three major articles that define the US government. Two other facts underscore this point. First, the shape and scope of the federal court system beyond the Supreme Court was left to the Congress to define (see Article I, Section 8, Clause 9, and Article III, Section 1). Second, the most significant power of the Supreme Court of the United States, the power of judicial review, was not explicitly defined in the text

3. This problem was a central feature to John Stuart Mill's essay "On Liberty" and is a key debate within democratic theory. In the context of court actions and judicial review, see a theoretical discuss in Dworkin 1990.

of the Constitution itself, but rather was asserted by a court ruling in *Marbury v. Madison* (1803), although the Supremacy Clause in Article VI does provide some textual basis for the power.[4] Indeed, in *Federalist 78,* Hamilton called the judicial branch "the weakest of the three departments of power" and the one that "will always be the least dangerous to the political rights of the Constitution." However, he also noted in that same essay the vital need of a judicial branch that could protect the Constitution from an overreaching legislative branch.

Some basic nomenclature must be dealt with before a full discussion of courts can ensue. There are two basic types of courts, *courts of original jurisdiction* and *courts of appeal.* As the name suggests, courts of original jurisdiction are where trials begin (either criminal or civil cases). Appeals courts typically exist in the form of an intermediate level and a final court (or courts) of appeal. The highest courts of appeal are often called supreme courts (although sometimes those courts also have original jurisdiction in some types of cases). Court systems are further complicated in federal states, as there are usually parallel court systems that exist at the sub-unit and national levels.

The most important distinction between judicial systems is that between *civil law* and *common law* traditions, and that will be our starting point. As we shall see, some countries have borrowed from both traditions (with admixtures of traditional or customary law as well). Nonetheless, civil law, which derives from continental European notions about the role of the law and judges, is fundamentally different from the Anglo-American tradition of common law. Civil-law (also known as code law) systems have origins in Roman legal traditions and are oriented toward an administrative application

4. The Supremacy Clause in Article VI states that "Judges in every State shall be bound" by the Constitution, federal laws, and treaties. This provides, therefore, for some sort of judicial review of state laws. There is no similar provision made, however, for federal laws. The Supreme Court first applied this power in *Ware v. Hylton* (1796), over half a decade before *Marbury v. Madison* (1803) established judicial review of federal laws. See Benedict 2006, chap. 6, esp. 107–12 for a discussion.

of law to specific situations, as contrasted with the interpretative paradigm applied in the common-law tradition. In civil-law systems the laws are rigorously and systematically codified, and the job of the judge is to establish the facts of a given case to determine how that code should be applied in a given civil or criminal matter. In common-law systems the laws are not codified but rather are linked to specific statutes. In this system judges rely on established precedents (that is, what has been ruled on before on a given topic) and their own interpretative skills (and the higher the court, the more significant the role of interpretation).

Civil law is the more common type of legal system globally, with common-law systems being dominant in countries heavily influenced by English colonialism. Common law is based on the process of the establishment of precedence via the interpretation of laws by judges over time. The role and significance of the judge is enhanced under a common-law system because they are expected to try and figure out what the law means, rather than just applying it. It is worth noting, however, that some observers, such as Grossman and Epp, point out that the differences between these two types of law are becoming less stark: "Over the past century the two traditions increasingly have converged in practice. Legislation is now the source of much law in the common-law countries, and the principle of legislative supremacy is widely acknowledged if not always adhered to" (1995: 680).

A key question for the role of courts is whether or not they have the power of *judicial review*. Is the judiciary, or some organ within it, empowered to overturn acts of the national legislature, executive, or state governments on grounds that they do not conform to the constitution? The notion of judicial review is that the constitution, as the highest law of the land (and the locus, typically, of the basic rights of citizens) needs a privileged position from which to operate, and, therefore, the creation of a high court entrusted with this task may be necessary to make sure that the constitution is applied, even in the face of majorities that might have legislative priorities that might conflict with constitutional principles. In this way, the notion of constitutional rights and judicial review can be seen as contradicting majority will, but at the same time ensuring minority protections that are essential for democracy to function (such as freedom of the press and speech for unpopular ideas or freedom of religion). There is obviously also a strong logic *against* the notion of judicial review: Shouldn't such vital decisions as the conformity of law to the constitution be made by the elected representatives of the people rather than by an appointed and frequently quite unrepresentative judicial body?

There are two basic types of judicial review, if we look at the concept comparatively: concrete and abstract.[5] Concrete review takes place in the context of a dispute over the law once the law has been enacted and a case in controversy arises, while abstract review is the assessment of a law's constitutionality before it is enacted. The US process is the quintessential example of concrete review, while countries that have more recently adopted judicial review, such as in post–World War II Europe, have established processes that allow for the review of laws prior to the their application. Interestingly, James Madison's Virginia Plan (discussed in chapter 2) contained a model for abstract review, although it was not adopted. Madison's draft envisioned an institution that would have been called the "Council of revision," and it would have been empowered "to examine every act of the National Legislature before it shall operate" and veto it if it saw fit.[6]

There was an attempt, early in the history of the United States, to acquire advisory opinions from the Supreme Court, that is, advice from the Court to other segments of the government on their actions before actual dispute arose over the actions of government. The Washington administration requested that the Supreme Court provided advice on a list of matters in the summer of 1793, and Chief Justice John Jay responded by citing separation of powers as precluding such advice being provided to the executive from the judiciary. Underscoring that the Court viewed itself at the time as one

5. For a discussion, see Stone Sweet (2000: 44–45), who also classifies direct citizen appeals over rights violation as a third type of judicial review.

6. This council would have consisted of the executive and members of the judiciary, See the eighth clause of the Virginia Plan, online at http://avalon .law.yale.edu/18th_century/vatexta.asp.

that rendered only, in the language of our discussion here, concrete rulings, Jay informed the Washington administration that the Court was one of "last Resort."[7] In those democracies that have established judicial review, there is a divergence between those that combine the role of constitutional tribunal and of the highest appellate court into one body, usually called the "supreme court," and those that divide these roles into separate institutions. A constitutional tribunal is an institution charged with enforcing the higher status of the constitution, relative to laws and other government acts. The appellate process is the ultimate resolution of all ordinary legal disputes, whether they involve the government or not and regardless of whether they raise constitutional controversies.

The concept of a separate constitutional tribunal arose first in civil-law countries, for the obvious reason that civil law does not traditionally see a role for judges to be charged with invalidating legislation. Indeed, the regular courts in civil-law systems are expressly *not* oriented toward interpretation, up to the highest levels of the court system. High (or supreme) courts in civil-law systems are often called, after the French model, *courts of cassation.* These courts exist to ensure that the laws are uniformly applied through the court system in conformity with the law as codified. Such a role does not allow for the ability to deal with constitutional issues and their interpretation, hence the need to create a special, and separate, high court to address those types of questions. An additional reason was that it offered the compromise of a kind of "limited" judicial review between the two logics for and against the basic principle of judicial review. In practice, however, separate constitutional courts have usually not accepted a limited view of their responsibilities and have been at least as assertive in applying judicial review as other supreme courts. Germany's Federal Constitutional Court is a prime example of such a highly activist separate constitutional tribunal.

7. See Casto 2002 for a detailed discussion of the matter that inspired the request and the response of the court. Jay's letter can be viewed online at http://research.archives.gov/description/5956319. See also *Harvard Law Review* 2011.

The first separate constitutional tribunal was created in Austria in the 1920s, and the idea subsequently spread to many other continental European countries. By the late twentieth century, new or revised constitutions in Latin America, ex-Communist Europe, and South Africa were among those developing separate constitutional tribunals. Separation of constitutional and appellate functions is unknown in common-law countries. Of course, some common-law countries do not have judicial review at all, but even those that do, always lodge the function in their supreme court.

Another institutional variation is whether a given country has separate or unified federal and subunit court systems. In a federal system, there are separate legal systems at both the national and state (or provincial) levels. In fact, as we discuss in chapter 4 on federalism, the very definition of a federal system is one in which there is some degree of sovereignty in separately elected subnational governments. The manifestation of this sovereignty is the capacity of the subnational governments to make their own laws, subject to constitutional review at the national level to ensure conformity to the accepted division of national and state responsibilities. In federal systems, the question of who reviews the conformity of state acts to the federal law and constitution is clear—it is the federal courts (including the constitutional tribunal, if there is one). However, the question of who adjudicates disputes regarding state law has been answered differently in different federations. Not all federal systems have this dual structure of subunit and national courts. For instance, in Canada, individual provinces have their own courts only for very limited legal jurisdictions. The most important legal cases arising from either provincial or federal law play out within provincial branches of the federal court system.

A final institutional factor is the question of how judges and justices should be appointed. The selection of judges and justices is closely related to their tenure in defining how "independent" the courts will be. For instance, if judges were appointed and dismissed at the whim by the executive, obviously we would not expect them to rule contrary to the executive's wishes.

Georgakopoulos (2000) identifies two basic choices in terms of the method of appointing judges: career judges and recognition judges. Career systems function along a civil service model, wherein a person sets out to be trained for the bench and then has to pass examinations to qualify for the position. Once appointed to the bench the individual judge can work her or his way up through the ranks form trial courts to, potentially, the supreme court during a career. In recognition systems, the move to the bench is one done after being recognized for excellence or potential in another, likely legal, career. In such a system a person is nominated to serve on the bench likely by a political actor, such as a president, prime minister, or minister of justice, and if confirmed by whatever process exists in a given country, moves from an existing career to a new career as a judge. In such cases, formal training for the judiciary is not part of the process. Box 9.1 details the basic difference between the two systems.

A growing institutional trend, especially in career judicial systems (but not limited thereto) has been the development of judicial councils to oversee the operations of the courts, and often to function as appointment bodies.[8] Garoupa and Ginsburg (2008: 21) identify the following "three important competences" of judicial councils:

1. housekeeping (budgets, material resources, operations);
2. appointment; and
3. performance evaluation (promotion, discipline, removal, and so on).

According to their study, this institutional innovation began to take off in the 1940s with a steady trend of inclusion in constitutions written since that time, and this trend exists across various geographical areas of the world (26–27). This general trend is true within the group of countries under examination in our study, with seventeen employing some version of this structure.[9] Table 9.1 lists the countries and codes them for strength of the council in each case.

8. Depending on the situation, the judicial council may make a list of recommendations from which some other actor chooses, a singular recommendation that is a de facto nomination, or it may make the appointment directly.

9. Additionally, India created such a body via the Judicial Standards and Accountability Bill of 2010. Its establishment and operation lies outside the scope of this study, however.

BOX 9.1. CAREER VERSUS RECOGNITION JUDICIARIES

A *career judiciary* includes the following key features:

1. Judges are initially appointed to junior positions (for example, trial courts or assisting other judges).

2. Judges are promoted to senior positions based on performance (usually by review of bureaucratic, rather than political, bodies).

3. Tenure is not attached to a particular position but to the entire career.

4. Lateral transfers (from one court to another) are allowed.

5. Appointment and promotion are typically conducted by bureaucratic bodies and are less political (although not necessarily apolitical) in comparison to recognition systems.

A *recognition judiciary* contains the following key features:

1. Judges are selected after an initial career in another (likely legal) profession.

2. Judges are not usually promoted, and when they are, it is via a new political appointment (for example, from a district court to a court of appeals).

3. Tenure is attached to a specific appointment.

4. This general process tends to rely on other actors from elective portions of the government (for example, executives and legislators) and therefore tends to be more political.

Source: Adapted from Georgakopoulos 2000

Perhaps the closest to the ideal type of a career judiciary would be that of France, where aspiring judges attend schools dedicated to the topic and who then take specialized examinations in order to obtain jobs. Promotions to higher courts are achieved via positive performance evaluations, and all judges in France are trained at the École Nationale de la Magistrature.

While all judicial selection processes are influenced by politics, recognition systems tend to be more driven by partisan and ideological concerns than career systems, given that the main decision-making actors are elected politicians rather than technocrats.[10] The United States is the quintessential recognition system, as the Constitution does not dictate any type of formal legal training for

10. Volcansek 2006, e.g., discusses the partisan political nature of the Italian judiciary, which is a career system.

Table 9.1. Judicial councils in seventeen democracies, coded for roles/powers

Argentina	3
Belgium	2
Brazil[a]	1
Colombia	3
France	3
Germany	2
Greece	3
Hungary	1
Israel	2
Italy	3
Mexico	3
Netherlands[a]	1
Poland	2
Portugal	3
South Africa	3
Spain	2
United Kingdom[a]	2

Notes: The coding follows Garoupa and Ginsburg 2008: 37–39, and the key is as follows: 1 = administrative functions only; 2 = involvement in appointments; and 3 = roles in both appointment and discipline, removal or promotion of judges. The code for Argentina changed from 2 to 3 based on authors' reading of the Argentine constitution. Additional coding beyond original work is as follows: for Germany (Federal Court of Justice 2010, and German Judiciary Act), Netherlands (Garoupa and Ginsburg 2011), South Africa (Du Bois 2006), Spain (World Bank 2001), and the United Kingdom (Malleson 2006, Paterson 2006, and Garoupa and Ginsburg 2011).

[a] These cases are relatively new. Brazil had a council of this type in the late 1970s during the authoritarian period, but it was done away with in the democratic constitution of 1988. A new council was created via a 2004 constitutional amendment. The Netherlands council was the result of a 2002 reform; and the United Kingdom council was created via the Constitutional Reform Act of 2005.

justices. Despite the lack of a formal process or review body, there has emerged a set of established norms and expectations. For example, while there are no formal qualifications to hold a position on the US Supreme Court, in recent decades there has been a high expectation that candidates would have significant appellate court experience or some other high-level legal background (such as being a legal scholar or serving in some significantly high level in terms of the Justice Department). There is also an assumption that the potential justices will have attended elite-level law schools. If we look back to the Warren Burger Court forward (Chief Justice Burger came to the bench in 1969), we find that twelve of sixteen justices have been federal appeals court judges and that ten have law degrees from Harvard or Yale (with two from Stanford and one from Northwestern). The derailment of President George W. Bush's 2005 nomination of Harriet Miers is an instructive example, as she did not conform to these expectations.[11]

On the other hand, there is also a strand of thought in the United States that persons with a nonlegal background might be advantageous from time to time. Earl Warren, the chief justice from 1953 to 1969, had served as governor of California prior to his appointment to the bench by President Eisenhower, with his main judicial/legal experience being a stint as California's attorney general. Of course, while such notions are bandied about from time to time (in 2010, for example, Senator Patrick Leahy, D-VT, opined on *Meet the Press,* "I wish we could have some more people outside the judicial monastery"), as noted earlier, they have not actually been put into practice for over half a century.[12] Speculation concerning the possible nomination of nonjudicial politicians, such as former New York Governor

11. Miers was White House counsel at the time of the nomination and had served as president of the State Bar of Texas as well as having been in private practice at a large Dallas law firm. However, her lack of experience as a judge or legal scholar led to widespread criticism of her nomination. She eventually withdrew her name from consideration.

12. Leahy made the comment on the April 11, 2010, edition of the program. A transcript and video can be found online at http://video.msnbc.msn.com/meet-the-press/36388829#36388829.

Mario Cuomo and Senator/Secretary of State Hillary Clinton, illustrate this point.

THE US JUDICIAL SYSTEM IN COMPARATIVE PERSPECTIVE

Having examined the role of courts in democratic settings and having detailed the major options open to political engineers on this topic, we can turn to looking to the US court system in comparative perspective. The US judiciary is often seen as one of the strongest in the world, in that not only does it enforce laws passed by Congress, but it also is a constitutionally coequal branch that sometimes overturns a law on the grounds that it conflicts with the Constitution, which is higher than any ordinary law. In addition, given the federal structure of the US system, the judicial branch also regulates relations between the national and state governments, occasionally overturning acts of the latter that may exceed the authority of state governments.

1. A common-law system. The US legal tradition is rooted firmly in the common-law tradition that derives from England. Common law ascribes a greater role for the judge in shaping "the law," understood not only as written statute texts, but also evolving precedents that stem from individual cases adjudicated in similar situations over time. Civil law, on the other hand, tends to see judges as part of the bureaucracy, administering the law and ensuring compliance with it. It thus places the judiciary in a more cooperative relationship with the executive branch than does common law.

The US legal system is unmistakably part of the common-law tradition, inherited from England. In the United States, however, with its separation of executive and legislative powers and its federal structure, the common-law notion of judges as independent of the executive extends even further, into a role as part of the system of checks and balances. Table 9.2 details the types of legal systems in each of our cases.

Of the thirty-one democracies under study, only five have common-law systems: Australia, Canada, New Zealand, the United Kingdom, and the United States. Not surprisingly these countries

Table 9.2. Legal system classification and presence of judicial review in thirty-one democracies

Country	Legal System	Judicial review of legislation?
Australia[a]	Common law	Yes
Canada[a]	Common law	Yes (limited)
New Zealand[a]	Common law	No
United Kingdom*	Common law	No—see note
United States	**Common law**	**Yes**
Argentina	Civil law	Yes
Austria[a]	Civil law	Yes[c]
Belgium[a]	Civil law	Yes[c] (limited)
Brazil	Civil law	Yes
Chile	Civil law	Yes[c] (limited)
Colombia	Civil law	Yes[c]
Czech Republic	Civil law	Yes[c]
Denmark[a]	Civil law	Yes
Finland[a]	Civil law	No
France	Civil law	Yes[c] (limited)
Germany[a]	Civil law	Yes[c]
Greece[a]	Civil law	Yes[c]
Hungary[a]	Civil law	Yes[c]
Italy	Civil law	Yes[c]
Mexico[a]	Civil law	Yes
Netherlands[a]	Civil law	No
Poland[a]	Civil law	Yes[c]
Portugal[a]	Civil law	Yes[c]
Spain[a]	Civil law	Yes[c] (limited)
Sweden[a]	Civil law	Yes (limited)
Switzerland[a]	Civil law	No
Japan[a]	Mixed[b]	Yes
India[a]	Mixed[b]	Yes
Israel	Mixed[b]	Yes
Korea	Mixed[b]	Yes[c]
South Africa	Mixed[b]	Yes[c]

Notes: "Limited" means that review is available only to certain persons or entities or is restricted to certain aspects of a constitution (Maddex 2008: xxiv).

* United Kingdom: Judicial review applies only under terms of Human Rights Act of 1998.

[a] Acceptance of International Court of Justice jurisdiction, with reservations (*source:* ICJ, http://www.icj-cij.org/jurisdiction/index.php?p1=5&p2=1&p3=3).

[b] Composition of mixed systems: common/customary/Muslim (India), civil/common/Jewish/Muslim (Israel), civil/customary (Japan), civil/customary (Korea), civil/common (South Africa). In Canada, one province, Quebec, has a legal system based on French civil law. In the United States, one state, Louisiana, has a legal system with French civil-law traditions. The US territory of Puerto Rico has a mixed civil-/common-law system.

[c] Judicial review by a constitutional court or other body that is separate from a regular appellate-court system.

Sources: JuriGlobe (http://www.juriglobe.ca/eng/index.php); Maddex 2008.

are all part of the Anglosphere. Three others have a mixture of common law in their legal systems: India, Israel, and South Africa—all of which experienced rule from London as well. It is worth noting that in both Canada and the United States, the parts of each federation that experienced significant French colonial influence, Quebec and Louisiana, respectively, have civil-law traditions.

The fact that the United States does have a common-law system is the foundation for the strength of its judiciary as a political actor.

2. Strong judicial review. The power to overturn legislation on constitutional grounds is a specifically American innovation, deriving from the landmark *Marbury v. Madison* decision by the US Supreme Court in 1803. The US Constitution nowhere specifically grants the Supreme Court the power to overturn legislation, but the Court asserted that such authority is implied in the text of the Constitution, in Article VI, where it states that the Constitution is the supreme law. If that is the case, reasoned the Court, then acts of Congress or other institutions established by the Constitution that conflict with the supreme law must be invalid. Numerous constitutions drafted in the nearly two centuries since *Marbury v. Madison* have explicitly incorporated judicial review, by establishing that a supreme court or other institution is responsible for ensuring that legislation be in conformity to the constitution.

The United States is hardly alone in terms of judicial review. If we consult table 9.2, we will see that twenty-six of thirty-one countries have some form of judicial review of legislation. Some countries have limited review, as there are constitutional or legal limits on what can be reviewed and by whom. The strongest strictures against judicial review can be found in the Netherlands, where it is expressly forbidden in Article 120 of their constitution, which directly states, "The constitutionality of Acts of Parliament and treaties shall not be reviewed by the courts."

The United States does have the longest tradition of any of the cases under study, and the fact that it is a common-law system that allows for constitutional questions to figure into judicial reasoning in lower-court considerations makes the concept far more central to American politics than is possible in civil-law countries.

3. Concrete judicial review. Constitutional review in the United States is of the concrete variety only, with no abstract review being possible. This places the United States in a minority of our democracies, albeit a large one. Of the twenty-six cases that have judicial review, ten have concrete only, while fifteen have both abstract and concrete review. France is the most unique case, as it has only abstract review. This information is summarized in table 9.3.

4. *A unified supreme court.* In the United States, the Supreme Court functions as both the pinnacle of the appeals process and as the arbiter over constitutionality. In many other democracies, there is a body called the constitutional court, or other similar name, that is institutionally separate from the regular judiciary, as well as a supreme court. In these countries, the supreme court is the court of last resort on legal cases, except those that engage the question of constitutionality of the acts of some part of the government. The latter are decided finally by the constitutional court, which also may often hear cases that have not even arisen from within the judicial system.

The United States is hardly unique in having a unified Supreme Court, as this is the case in almost half of the countries under study. As noted earlier, civil-law systems can only engage in constitutional review via a separate court, so we see that institutional feature in those countries only.

5. *A separate subunit court system.* In the US federal system, each state has its own distinct state judicial system, with its own trial courts, appellate courts, and a court of last resort under state law, usually called the supreme court of the state. Controversies arising within a state are fully dealt with by the state's own courts, unless they also engage issues of federal law or the Constitution, in which case they may ultimately be resolved in the federal judiciary. As such, the only overlap between the state courts and the federal courts is at the Supreme Court of the United States level.

Other federal systems typically have subunit level court systems as well. However, not all have the deeply distinct division between the legal systems that is found in the United States. Austria, for example, constitutionally reserves criminal justice to the national government (while in the United States there are separate and distinct federal and state criminal codes). Also, in the federal case of Canada, provincial and territorial courts may hear cases involving either federal or provincial/territorial laws and hence do not have the same clear-cut divisions that we see in the US case.

Table 9.3. Types of judicial review (abstract and/or concrete) in twenty-six democracies

	Abstract	Concrete
Argentina		x
Australia		x
Austria	x	x
Belgium	x	x
Brazil	x	x
Canada		x
Chile	x	x
Colombia	x	x
Czech Republic	x	x
Denmark		x
France	x	
Germany	x	x
Greece	x	x
Hungary	x	x
India		x
Israel		x
Italy	x	x
Japan		x
Korea		x
Mexico	x	x
Poland	x	x
Portugal	x	x
South Africa	x	x
Spain	x	x
Sweden		x
United States		x

Sources: Ginsburg 2003; Lijphart 2012; Lollini 2011: 65–66; Navia and Ríos-Figueroa 2005: 203; Stone Sweet 2000: 47; Vanberg 1998: 302; Vink, Claes, and Arnold 2009: 31. Also Stephen Gardbaum, personal communication.

6. Political selection of judges. To use the earlier terminology dis-cussion, the United States has a recognition system for the appoint-ment of all federal judges, from the trial-court level to the Supreme Court. In this system, American jurists do not train to be judges but train first, normally at least, to be attorneys and then later may find a second career on the bench.

The American system provides for an explicitly political process of selection for all judges, whereas many other democratic states have career judiciaries with some insulation from the political realm (as discussed in box 9.1 and illustrated by table 9.1—both earlier). However, as table 9.4 illustrates, all of our cases have direct political involvement in terms of the highest courts—either supreme courts in common-law situations, or constitutional courts in civil-law cases. The US system is arguably the most political of them all, as the nomination and confirmation processes (as well as removal) are all in the hands of electorally selected actors.

Typically, political selection means appointment by the executive or legislature or the consent of both branches together. For instance, all US federal judges, from trial courts all the way up to justices of the Supreme Court, are nominated by the president and appointed if confirmed by a majority of the US Senate (and it is a process, as noted in chapter 7, subject to a potential supermajority requirement). In the US states, the process of political selection actually means election of judges in most cases. No other federal system among our democracies that are both federal and have separate state courts has any electoral process for these courts. Additionally, nowhere in our thirty-one democracies are there elections for the selection of judges at the national level.[13]

In addition to formal career judiciaries as noted earlier (such as France and Italy), other examples of how systems may differ from that of the United States include Brazil and Korea. Brazil, a federal, presidential case like the United States but one that mixes career and recognition elements, places appointment power in the hands of the executive, but the president must choose from lists of candidates

---

13. The members of the Japanese Supreme Court are subject to retention elections after ten years. (None has ever lost such an election.)

Table 9.4. Appointment and terms of office of high-court justices and constitutional-tribunal magistrates

Country	Supreme court			Constitutional tribunal		
	No.	How selected	Term	No.	How selected	Term
Argentina	7	Nominated by president, confirmed by senate (2/3)	Life	—	—	—
Australia	7	Appointed by governor general on advice of cabinet	To age 70	—	—	—
Austria	58	By president on advice of government	To age 65	14 + 6 substitutes	Appointed by federal president on recommendation of government and two chambers of legislature	To age 70
Belgium	N/A	Court of Cassation		12	Appointed by monarch from lists from both chambers of legislature; 6 from French-language group and 6 from Dutch	To age 70
Brazil	11	Nominated by president, confirmed by senate	To age 70	—	—	—
Canada	9	Appointed by governor general on advice of cabinet	To age 75	—	—	—
Chile	21	Supreme Court submits list of candidates from which president selects, confirmed by senate	To age 75	10	3 appointed by president, 4 by congress, and 4 by supreme court	9 years (1/3rd replaced every 3 years)
Colombia	23	Appointed from list submitted by Supreme Council of Judicature	8 years to age 75	9	Senate selects from nominations list made by president, supreme court, and Council of State	8 years

(continued)

Table 9.4. (continued)

Country	Supreme court			Constitutional tribunal		
	No.	How selected	Term	No.	How selected	Term
Czech Republic	64[a]	Appointed by president on advice of cabinet	To age 70	15	Appointed by president with consent of senate	10 years
Denmark	15	Appointed by monarch on advice of cabinet	Life	—	—	—
Finland	At least 16	Appointed by president		—	—	—
France	155[a]	Court of Cassation, by president acting on a proposal from Higher Judicial Council		9**	3 by president, 3 by president of National Assembly, 3 by president of senate	9 years
Germany	127[a]	Elected by Judges Election Committee and appointed by president	To age 65	16	8 by Bundestag, 8 by Bundesrat	12 years
Greece	N/A	Court of Cassation	To age 67	14	By presidents of supreme administrative court, supreme court, and court of auditors, and following chosen by lot: 4 councilors of supreme administrative court, 4 members of supreme court, and 2 law professors	2 years
Hungary	83[a]	Court of Cassation; president appoints based on recommendations of president of court	To age 70	11 (15 after 9/1/11)	parliament (2/3 majority)	9 year term (up to 2 terms) to age 70

India	26	Appointed by president on advice of judiciary	To age 65	—	—	—
Israel	14	By president after nomination of Judicial Selection Committee	To age 70	—	—	—
Italy	N/A	Court of Cassation	N/A	15	5 by president, 5 by parliament, 5 by ordinary and administrative courts	9 years
Japan	15	Appointed by cabinet	To age 70	—	—	—
Korea	14	Chief justice by president with legislative consent; others by president with legislative consent as recommended by chief justice	6 years	9	By president: 3 must be from legislative recommendations, and 3 must be from chief justice nominations	6 years
Mexico	11	Nominated by president, confirmed by senate (2/3)	15 years, to age 75	—	—	—
Netherlands	36	Court of Cassation; appointed from list of 3 drawn up by first chamber	N/A	—	—	—
New Zealand	5	Appointed by attorney general from seniormost members of appeals court	To age 75	—	—	—

(continued)

Table 9.4. (*continued*)

Country	Supreme court			Constitutional tribunal		
	No.	How selected	Term	No.	How selected	Term
Poland	81[a]	By president on motion of National Council of Judiciary	To age 65	15	By first chamber	9 years
Portugal	60	Competitive application	N/A	13	10 by legislature, 3 by judiciary	9 years
South Africa	22	By president on advice of Judicial Service Commission	To age 70	11	By president from list compiled by Judicial Service Commission	12 years or until age 70
Spain	74	By monarch on recommendation of General Council of Judiciary	To age 70	12	By monarch	
Sweden	16	Appointed by government	To age 67			
Switzerland	30	Elected by joint session of parliament	6 years	—	—	—
United Kingdom		Selection commission makes recommendation to lord chancellor, who then reports to prime minister and then monarch, who makes formal appointment	To age 70 if appointed after 3/31/95, or else to age 75	—	—	—
United States	9	Nominated by president, confirmed by Senate	Life	—	—	—

Notes: N/A indicates that reliable numbers could not be determined.

[a] Full membership; divided into panels for specialized types of cases.

Sources: Maddex 2008, national constitutions, and official court Web sites.

linked to specific legal career paths.[14] Further, candidates must pass an examination to qualify for the lists. In Korea, the chief justice makes appointments with the consent of the Council of Supreme Court Justices.

7. A mix of appointed and elected judges. At the national level, all judges are appointed by the president and confirmed by the Senate to serve for life on conditions of good behavior. However, at the state level, the process of selecting judges is more varied.[15] Some states have straightforward partisan elections in which candidates for the bench run both in nominating primaries and in the general election under party labels. Others have elections but sans party labels, while others have a process of executive appointment followed by retention elections (where voters are asked whether the given judge should remain in office or be replaced by another appointee).

Of our thirty-one cases, the United States is unique in having any elected judges of any kind.[16] Indeed, the United States is nearly unique globally in this regard, with only Bolivia being another case of elected judges (and that is a recent phenomenon; see Volcansek 2006).

8. Judges with true life terms. Referring back to table 9.4, we can see that life appointment to the bench without mandatory retirement is unusual. Of the thirty-one cases, only the United States and two other countries (Argentina, and Denmark) have life appointments without an age limit. Further, it should be noted that for the United States, life tenure exists for all federal judges, from the district-court level to the Supreme Court. The importance of life appointments (on condition of good behavior) is accentuated by the political nature

14. See Oliveira and Garoupa 2011,

15. For a comprehensive and detailed rundown of these processes in US states, see the American Judicature Society's "Methods of Judicial Selection," available online at http://www.judicialselection.us/judicial_selection/methods/selection_of_judges.cfm?state.

16. Varsho 2007 mentions "some locally elected lay judges" (503) in Finland, a phrase repeated on the Finnish Ministry of Justice's Web site (see http://www.om.fi/en/Etusivu/Ministerio/Oikeuslaitosesite). However, this "election" is by courts (meaning that these are appointed, not elected).

of these appointments (as noted earlier) and the fact that the confirmation process is linked to the Senate, which has, as noted in the chapter on legislative power, a de facto supermajority requirement for action. As this supermajority requirement has become increasingly the norm in the Senate, it has become harder for judges to be confirmed to the bench. It can be argued that the political stakes are increased by the fact that once appointed and confirmed, judges can serve for many, many decades.

In comparative terms it is noteworthy that judges in civil-law systems almost universally have mandatory retirement ages. When it comes to constitutional tribunals, most have delimited terms (ranging from two to twelve years) and even for the two that do not (Austria and Belgium), retirement is mandatory at age seventy. The average tenure for US Supreme Court justices is sixteen years, which surpasses all of the established term lengths noted in table 9.3 save Germany's, which it matches, and Hungary's (where a theoretical eighteen years of service is possible on the constitutional court via two nine-year terms). The longest serving US justice was William O. Douglas, who served just more than thirty-six years.[17]

CONCLUSIONS

The United States has one of the more significant court systems among our cases because it is a constitutionally separate branch of the federal government, and it is one that wields strong judicial review in the context of a deep common-law tradition. Further, the states also have strong court systems that also exist in separation-of-powers circumstances and with judicial review powers over state laws. Indeed, the US court system has special significance because of other institutional features of the US constitutional system, namely separation of powers and federalism. In this regard, it is similar only to the Latin American cases of Argentina, Brazil, and Mexico. It should be noted that, especially since the 1940s, there has been a

17. Term length information via the Supreme Court of the United States: http://www.supremecourt.gov/faq_justices.aspx#faqjustice2.

BOX 9.2. OTHER AMERICAN EXCEPTIONS IN THE JUDICIAL AND CRIMINAL-JUSTICE SYSTEMS

Adam Liptak wrote a series of articles for the *New York Times* called, collectively, "American Exception," which ran from October 2007 to September 2008 and which examined some of the idiosyncrasies of the American court system.[a] We introduce a few of them here.

Bail bondsmen. If one is arrested and wishes to be free in anticipation of a trial, bail must be posted as a means of ensuring that one will show up for trial. This is typically accomplished via the purchase of a bond for the amount of the bail. In the United States, this is a for-profit business. However, Liptak notes (2008a): "In England, Canada and other countries, agreeing to pay a defendant's bond in exchange for money is a crime akin to witness tampering or bribing a juror—a form of obstruction of justice."

Expert witnesses. As part of its common-law (and therefore adversarial) system, the US uses a system of partisan expert witnesses. These witnesses are acquired by the two sides in a court case to testify about facts in evidence in the trial. Liptak notes in his piece that while the notion of expert witnesses exists in other cases, the form that the process takes in the United States is unique: "Partisan experts do appear in court in other common-law nations, including Canada, Singapore and New Zealand. But the United States amplifies their power by using juries in civil cases, a practice most of the common-law world has rejected" (Liptak 2008d).

This creates potential problems, as one study notes, "given that experts are called by one party and paid by that party, there is an inevitable danger of bias in favor of that party" (Mnookin 2008: 1010). To address this problem, other countries employ other methods, such as having experts selected by the courts rather than by the attorneys representing the various parties. Another approach, which is used in Australia, is called "hot tubbing," in which all the experts testify at once and are all subject to questioning at the same time. Yarnall (2009: 323) explains: "Hot tubbing, more formally known as concurrent evidence, involves experts from each side engaging, under oath, in a conversation with each other, the judge, and counsel from both sides of the case." Under such a system, experts from all sides can be heard, but the method of fact-finding is quite different than in the US system.

Exclusionary rule. A key feature of the US criminal justice system is that evidence gathered through problematic means (for example, via police misconduct or without an appropriate warrant) is subject to exclusion at the trial. For example, if a police officer found physical evidence linking a suspect to a crime but obtained that evidence illegally, the evidence would likely be unusable in court. Liptak (2008c) notes:

"'Foreign countries have flatly rejected our approach,' said Craig M. Bradley, an expert in comparative criminal law at Indiana University. 'In every other country, it's up to the trial judge to decide whether police misconduct has risen to the level of requiring the exclusion of evidence.'"

He also states: "The European Court of Human Rights, a notably liberal institution, refused in 2000 to require the suppression of illegally obtained evidence. Using such evidence to convict a man charged with importing heroin into England, the court said, did not make his trial unfair."

The only other study concerning any type of exclusionary rule concerns Germany (Bradley 1983).

Punitive damages. Like expert witnesses, the notion of punitive damages is primarily a common-law phenomenon (which thus limits the number of countries where such damages are awarded). However, the United States is uniquely high in the awards it provides.

NOTE

a. The series can be found online at http://topics.nytimes.com/top/news/us/series/american_exception/index.html?offset=0&s=newes.

global trend to provide for powers of judicial review and to house them in special constitutional tribunals. In general, it also should be noted that as democratic governance has deepened, both globally but also within individual countries, courts have a clear role in protecting the constitutional order of given countries as well as the individual rights and privileges of citizens.

CHAPTER 10

COMPARATIVE CONCLUSIONS

H aving explored the various institutional differences between the United States and the other thirty cases, we now come to a point of asking two questions. The first is, Exactly how different is the democracy in the United States from the others? The second is, How does this matter? The first question is answered by looking at the basic institutional configuration of the United States in terms of various component elements of its institutional framework. This issue is explored in the first section of this final chapter. The second question focuses on public policy and is addressed in the second section of the chapter, which looks not only at a specific case study but at a series of twelve specific comparisons between the United States and the other democratic states under examination.

COMPARING THE INSTITUTIONAL MIX

As was noted in the first chapter of this book, the mix of institutions found in the United States is nearly unique within the universe of democracies that exist around the world. Indeed, if we look closely enough, we can see that US democracy is, in fact, different from all the others in a comparative institutional sense. We have seen in each of the chapters that the United States has features, some small and some large, that are different from any number of other cases within our set. However, now is the time to bring the salient variations together and discuss how much difference they may make in terms of governance. This first section of the chapter looks at this question from two perspectives. The first focuses more on identifying the variations in the institutional recipe of the United States of

America that gives it its own unique flavors. The second is more systematic and focuses on the idea of veto gates within the institutional structure of the United States and how that shapes the question of policy making and governance.

What's in the US Blueprint?

What, then, is the institutional legacy of the political engineers of the Philadelphia Convention, and how after two-plus centuries does it compare to other constitutional orders? Two tables orient the discussion in this section. The first, table 10.1, details noteworthy characteristics of US governmental institutions, whether they are ones that the United States holds uniquely or ones that it shares with only a handful of other cases. The second, table 10.2, provides a comprehensive comparison of all thirty-one cases on several major variables related to the basics of governance. These tables simply summarize significant portions of the discussion laid out in this book. Some general comments about the institutional design that makes up the United States provide a good place to start. Then this section of the chapter discusses two specific factors that are unique to the United States and that warrant special attention: longevity and primary elections.

If we distill the most fundamental variables of governance as a means of narrowing the institutional configuration of the United States, we can start with presidentialism as a filter, which quickly takes us from thirty-one cases to only seven: the United States, Korea, and the Latin American cases: Argentina, Brazil, Chile, Colombia, and Mexico (which is not surprising, given that the postindependence model for the Latin American cases was the US Constitution). The filter of bicameralism eliminates Korea, while federalism removes Chile and Colombia from the mix. So, in terms of the basic ways that power is allocated, considering both executive-legislative relations and the relationship of national and subnational governments, the United States is in a small subset of states (four out of thirty-one).

Another area that the United States shares with only four other, albeit different, states is a common-law legal system—something it

Table 10.1. Basic rundown of US differences/similarities to other democracies

Constitution	—The oldest, continually functioning constitution —One of the shortest (approximately 8,000 words) —An early democratizing state (early first wave) —Achieved full universal suffrage late (1965) —A difficult-to-amend Constitution (one of the most difficult)
Division of power	—A federal state: not unusual (twelve other federal cases in the study)
Electoral system	—Majoritarian electoral system (single-seat plurality) for Congress (only 5 other majoritarian cases in the study, and only 3 of those use plurality rules) —Electoral College to elect the president (unique)
Party system	—An unusually strict 2-party system —Systemwide, long-term usage of primaries to nominate candidates
Interest groups	—Pluralistic interest-group system (not unusual)
Legislative	—Bicameral with strong legislative symmetry (only 7 other cases) —Some asymmetry favoring the second chamber (i.e., Senate's advice-and-consent powers) —Rules of second chamber highly favor the minority party —Fixed size for the first chamber —Short term (2 years) for first chamber (unique)
Executive	—Only 5 other pure presidential systems in the study
Judicial	—Strong judicial review (although judicial review is common across cases) —Only 4 other common-law systems in the study

shares with Australia, Canada, New Zealand, and the United Kingdom. The significance of this is further narrowed when we note that neither New Zealand nor the United Kingdom has strong judicial review, leaving only three total cases in our study that have a common-law tradition and strong review over constitutional questions by the courts. So the United States fits into two different, very small subsets, and it is alone in each set, making the general institutional parameters in question (presidentialism and federalism plus a

Table 10.2. Comparing thirty-one democracies on basic governance

	Unitary or federal	Electoral system	Parties	Uni- or Bicameral	Executive/ legislative	Legal system	Judicial review
Argentina	Federal	PR-Low M	3.31	*Bi*	Pres	Civil	Yes
Australia	Federal	AV	2.28	*Bi*	Parl	Common	Yes
Austria	Federal	PR	3.45	Bi	Semi	Civil	Yes
Belgium	Federal	PR	8.14	Bi	Parl	Civil	Yes
Brazil	Federal	PR	8.74	*Bi*	Pres	Civil	Yes
Canada	Federal	Plurality	2.88	*Bi*	Parl	Common	Yes
Chile	Unitary	PR-low M (M=2)	5.97	*Bi*	Pres	Civil	Yes
Colombia	Unitary	PR	6.30	*Bi*	Pres	Civil	Yes
Czech Republic	Unitary	PR-high threshold	3.87	Bi	Parl	Civil	Yes
Denmark	Unitary	PR	4.72	Uni	Parl	Civil	Yes
Finland	Unitary	PR	5.06	Uni	Semi	Civil	No
France	Unitary	Majority-plurality	2.78	Bi	Semi	Civil	Yes
Germany	Federal	MMP	3.70	*Bi*	Parl	Civil	Yes
Greece	Unitary	PR-bonus	2.35	Uni	Parl	Civil	Yes
Hungary	Unitary	MMM	2.78	Uni	Parl	Civil	Yes
India	Federal	Plurality	5.42	*Bi*	Parl	Mixed	Yes

Country		Electoral system	Parties	Bicameralism	Gov	Legal	Symmetry
Israel	Unitary	PR	6.58	*Uni*	Parl	Mixed	Yes
Italy	Unitary	PR-bonus	4.07	*Bi*	Parl	Civil	Yes
Japan	Unitary	MMM	2.61	*Bi*	Parl	Mixed	Yes
Korea	Unitary	MMM	2.72	*Uni*	Pres	Mixed	Yes
Mexico	Federal	MMM	3.13	*Bi*	Pres	Civil	Yes
Netherlands	Unitary	PR	5.51	*Bi*	Parl	Civil	No
New Zealand	Unitary	MMP	3.35	*Uni*	Parl	Common	No
Poland	Unitary	PR-high threshold	4.73	*Bi*	Semi	Civil	Yes
Portugal	Unitary	PR	2.64	*Uni*	Semi	Civil	Yes
South Africa	Federal	PR	2.11	*Bi*	Parl	Mixed	Yes
Spain	Federal	PR-low M	2.54	*Bi*	Parl	Civil	Yes
Sweden	Unitary	PR	4.15	*Uni*	Parl	Civil	Yes
Switzerland	Federal	PR	5.48	***Bi***	Pres*	Civil	Yes
United Kingdom	Unitary	Plurality	2.32	*Bi*	Parl	Common	No
United States	Federal	Plurality	1.98	***Bi***	Pres	Common	Yes

Notes: Italics for bicameralism indicates medium legislative symmetry; ***bold italics*** indicates high legislative symmetry. Parties = effective number if legislative parties. Pres = presidential system, Parl = parliamentary, Semi = semi-presidential. Switzerland is marked as Pres* because they have formal separation of powers with a head of government called "president," but the arrangement is unique and defies simple classification.

common-law tradition with judicial review) a unique combination found only in the United States.

Beyond the general institutional mix of the United States versus the other states, there are two other factors that deserve some thought: longevity (as it relates to design and long-term function, and really the basic sequence of institutional choices made) along with a specific institutional innovation that is truly unique to the United States: widespread usage of the party primary to nominate candidates.

In table 10.1 (and in previous chapters) we have noted that the United States is old relative to other states both in terms of its adoption of democracy (with all the caveats that accompany such a discussion—such as the evolution of voting rights) and in terms of its initiation of constitutionalism. In terms of our discussion of political engineering and constitution construction, longevity matters because going first in making institutional choices means a lack of practical information about variations and their impacts (at least from the point of view of the political engineer). It also means that the path chosen by a given institutional choice can have follow-up consequences. For example, as noted in chapter 2: a choice was made to have the executive chosen by a body outside of the legislature (even though all initial discussions had had the legislature directly choosing the executive). This choice set the United States on a specific developmental path that created a fully separate executive from the legislature. Had the framers stuck with their original plans, then the US system could have easily more resembled a parliamentary system, because not only would one institution be choosing the other, but such a decision would have required a legislative majority to work together to select the executive. So, not only would legislative-executive relations been different, party development in the legislature would likely have been different as well.

Consider: The way the US system has evolved, candidates mostly run their own campaigns (due to single-seat districts) and party is mostly important as a signaling device in those elections and then in terms of legislative majorities focused on passing bills. However, if the legislature selected the executive, then the candidates would campaign differently, since the issue for voters is different if a member of congress legislates *and* helps select the executive. Hence, the choices made in Philadelphia had long-term consequence for political development well beyond the specific design that was agreed upon. And again, going first meant that there was no way to truly predict how these institutions would actually function.

Two specific issues that illustrate the importance of sequencing in designing institutions in the US case were political parties and elections. First, as we noted in chapter 6, political parties and their role in representative democracy were misunderstood by the political thinkers of the day and therefore played no role in the design of the institutional structure of the United States. And, as noted in the earlier paragraphs, choices about executive-legislative relations had long-term implications for the significance of parties (for example, parties in a parliamentary system play a role that parties in presidential systems do not: they choose the executive). Further, there were no practical guides for electing officials aside from plurality elections at the time. As such, no consideration or discussion was afforded to the implications of electoral rules. This fact has long-term effects on issues like party development and representation.

Additionally, the framers of the US Constitution were starting largely in a vacuum with only a handful of guidelines from which to choose. They had to invent, for all practical purposes, both federalism and presidentialism out of thin air. As such, the actual functioning of these institutional structures took time to sort out (indeed, the fight over some related issues, such as the proper relationship between the states and the national government, persist to this day).

Going first and remaining under the same constitutional order for a long period of time also means a likely conservative bias in terms of governance (and here by "conservative" we mean maintenance of the status quo, or at least slow change, as opposed to adherence to a specific ideology or contemporary partisan affiliation). To paraphrase the first law of thermodynamics so as to adapt it to politics: A political system in motion tends to stay in motion (because the political actors who would have to make moves to change the system are in power because of the existing system). The longer a system operates under a given set of rules, the longer those rules are likely to remain in force. Again, once on the path, it is difficult to deviate from it, and the specifics of the path in question end up dictating where one ends up going.

Beyond broad systemic issues, one institutional feature that evolved in the United States and remains unique in its application is the primary election as the method of nominating candidates for office. While some political parties in some countries have used primaries to nominate some candidates for some offices, no party system in the world comes anywhere near to the usage of primaries found in the United States. Primaries have been systematically used since the early twentieth century and are currently used at all levels for any partisan political office.[1]

Why might this matter? There are several factors worth considering. One is that it leads to the candidate-centric and nonhierarchical parties we noted in chapter 6. Primaries mean that the ability of party leadership to shape a party in a particular direction in terms of philosophy or party choice is quite limited. Rather, the process is one of self-selection by candidates, who choose to adopt a party label and run in the primary, which is then validated or rejected by voters on primary day. Candidates are therefore far more free agents than in systems with more hierarchically structured parties. A second key factor is that the widespread usage of primaries leads to less incentive for groups to form third parties. Consider: If a group of political activists are unhappy with either of the two main parties, they have two options—try to form a third party or try to win nomination within an established party. As we noted in chapters 5 and 6, third parties have had abysmal success rates in US politics (even when we compare the United States to other systems with plurality in single-

---

1. Many local offices are nonpartisan (see ch. 6) and therefore have no need for a nomination process. It is also worth noting, as a caveat to the assertions, that "any partisan office" uses primaries, that some systems that are called primaries in popular discourse really are not actually true primaries. Examples include the "Top Two" system adopted in 2010 in California, or the so-called jungle primary formerly used in Louisiana. They are not partisan primaries because they make it possible sometimes for both candidates in the general election to come from the same party. Both of these systems are variations on a two-round system that narrows the field of candidates rather than nomination mechanisms.

seat districts, such as Canada and the United Kingdom); however, since anyone, in theory, can run within the Democratic or Republican primaries, there is an incentive for insurgent movements to run candidates within one of the main party structures.

Veto Gates

A more systematic way to address the issue of an institutional recipe is to look at the number of veto gates and veto players that exist within a given institutional mix.[2] As we noted in chapter 1 and elsewhere, various institutional actors have the powers to either allow the policy-making process to move forward or not; that is to say, institutions that act like a gate can either stay closed, meaning policy making is halted, or opened, to allow a proposed policy to flow to the next stage. Further, within a given institution, there are actors who either have the unified power to open the gate (as with a president or a single, hierarchically organized party) or there may be multiple actors who have to agree before the gate can be unlocked (as with two or more parties in a legislative coalition).

Any institution that can block the flow of policy can be regarded, therefore, as a veto gate. Legislatures, as we have noted, fulfill this function because if they choose not to act on a given policy, then that policy will not happen. So, as we have seen, for every chamber in a legislature that has power over the legislative process, there is an additional veto gate in the system. If we further add an executive with veto power, then we have added another gate to the process of policy making.

A key comparative question that needs to be asked is, How many veto gates are there in a given system? Each chamber of a legislature through which bills must pass is a veto gate. Hence, a unicameral legislature is a single gate, and a bicameral legislature with either medium or strong symmetrical legislative powers produces two veto

2. The idea of veto players as theoretical concepts can be found in Tsebelis 1995 and 2002, Tsebelis and Money 1997, Stepan 2004b, and Stepan and Linz 2011. Here we are focusing on a narrow aspect of veto players, i.e., policy making.

gates. Executive actors who can veto legislation (that is, many presidents) are also veto gates. Following this logic, all laws in the United States have to pass through three veto gates: the House, the Senate, and the president. Further, as noted in chapter 7, internal fragmentation of parties within the chambers, or more specifically, the power of the minority in the Senate, means that the two chambers of Congress contain numerous veto players who may not be willing to work together to open the veto gates in question.

Table 10.3 classifies our thirty-one democracies in terms of the number of veto gates in each system, combining information from previous chapters, including the strength of bicameralism (table 7.1) and executive veto powers (table 8.9). We can see that the bicameral, presidential systems of the Western Hemisphere (the United States and our Latin American cases) are the only countries with three veto gates. The remaining twenty-five cases have a mix of either two (symmetrical bicameralism or one chamber plus an executive) or only one veto gate (unicameral or asymmetrical bicameral systems with no executive veto). The number of veto players will depend on the party system in each country and whether or not coalitions must

Table 10.3. Veto gates in thirty-one democracies

Number	Veto gates present	Countries
Three (N=6)	First chamber, second chamber, executive	*Argentina, Brazil,* Chile, Colombia, *Mexico, United States*
Two (N=12)	First chamber, second chamber (including second chambers that have medium symmetry)	*Australia, Canada, Germany, India,* Italy, Japan, **Netherlands,** *South Africa,* ***Switzerland,*** **United Kingdom**
	First chamber, executive	Poland
	Unicameral, executive	Korea
One (N=13)	First chamber (bicameral, no second-chamber veto)	*Austria, Belgium,* Czech Republic, France, *Spain*
	Unicameral	Denmark, **Finland,** Greece, Hungary, Israel, **New Zealand,** Portugal, Sweden

Notes: Italics indicates federal system; **bold** indicates no judicial review of legislation.

be formed within the legislature to pass legislation and, if the system is parliamentary, to form and maintain the government.

The earlier discussion is focused on the question of policy making as opposed to policy implementation. The process of implementation may run into two further political actors that may be able to partially, or fully, veto a policy: subunits in federal systems and courts in countries with strong judicial review. As such, the table notes federal cases as well as indicating those cases that lack judicial review of legislation.

Federalism can play a very strong role in policy implementation. As Stepan (2004b: 331) notes, the Argentine and Brazilian state governments have fiscal policy (that is, budgetary) powers over implementing central government policy. Likewise, US states can (as noted in chapter 4 and reiterated later in our discussion of implementing health-care reform) dictate, to some degree, how funds are spent when implementing policy.

As such, the main dimensions in terms of determining veto gates concerning policy design are parliamentary or presidential (that is, is there a separately elected executive with a veto pen?), and unicameral or bicameral (is there a second chamber with equal, or close to equal, legislative powers to the first chamber?). Further factors that require attention and bear on implementation are: Is the system unitary or federal (and do the states have special influence over policy making)? and does the system have courts that have strong judicial review (that is, can they strike down legislation as unconstitutional)? The more veto gates and players in a system, the more complex policy making and governance become.

PUBLIC POLICY

If, as we have shown, the United States is different from other democracies in terms of the makeup and functionality of its institutions, it is fair to ask to what degree it matters for policy outputs. This section of the chapter examines this issue from two approaches. The first is to look at a case study of the process by which major policy is made. Specifically, we do so by examining, in the context of veto gates (as well as other institutional elements of the system) in regards to the passage and implementation of the Patient Protection and Affordable Care Act of 2010 (PPACA). The second is to examine a set of twelve public policy areas to see to what degree the United States conforms to or deviates from the norms within our cases.

Case Study: The PPACA

The Patient Protection and Affordable Care Act, colloquially known as "Obamacare," provides an excellent case to illustrate the institutional parameters of public policy making in the United States, specifically in terms of the various veto points (gates and players) that exist in the process. This illustration is made outside of questions of the normative value of the legislation (which is, we would readily note, a matter of public controversy, as is often the case with major legislative actions). Regardless of one's view on this legislation, it provides an excellent glimpse into how the institutional parameters of the constitutional system of the United States affect policy making in ways that make the United States very different from almost all the other cases under examination. We can see in this case study illustrations of veto gates in action, the idiosyncratic functioning of the US Senate, as well as the role of the courts and primaries.

Table 10.3 shows us that the United States has three veto gates, plus it has judicial review of legislation and is federal.

We can see all of this in action in the recent health-care-reform debate. Specifically we start with the House, Senate, and the president. In 2008 Barack Obama, a Democrat, was elected to the presidency along with large majorities (especially in terms of the recent US context) in both chambers of the legislature. The party mix in the House was 257 Democrats (59.1 percent) to 178 Republicans (40.9 percent). In the Senate the Democrats would eventually (albeit briefly) hold a 60–40 advantage (more on that later). One of President Obama's campaign promises focused on health-care reform, which had been a long-standing Democratic policy goal.[3] Hence, going into

3. It is worth noting that we are here speaking of a general campaign issue. The actual legislation as passed does not fully conform to Obama's stated preferences in the campaign.

the 111th Congress (2009–2011), all three veto gates were poised to be open and allow the passage of some form of health-care reform. And eventually, the bill in question was passed in a 60–39–1 vote in the Senate on December 24, 2009, and then in the house by a 219–212 vote on March 21, 2010, and was signed by the president two days later. So, at that point in the timeline, we see that with all the veto gates unlocked and opened, that policy was made; then the question of implementation arose, which brought in the states and the courts.

Before a full discussion of the role of the states and the courts, let us first note that the passage of the bill was not as simple as the numbers reported in the previous paragraph may suggest. Without getting into specific policy debates about the contents of the bill, its passage in the veto gate of the Senate is worth further scrutiny. As noted in the summary in table 10.1 and as discussed in chapter 7, the US Senate operates under rules that make it an especially difficult veto gate to open, because of the filibuster rule (that is, the supermajority requirement). In simple terms, any coalition of 41 senators can stop the Senate from acting on most legislation by refusing to allow cloture (that is, the formal end of debate). Without 60 percent of the duly elected and sworn-in senators voting to end debate, a measure such as the PPACA cannot be brought to a vote. These numbers are significant because a 60-vote majority is difficult to achieve.

Earlier we noted that in the 111th Congress the Democratic Party had, in fact, achieved a 60–40 margin in the chamber. However, we also noted that this was a temporary situation. The distribution of seats of the Senate by party was a somewhat tricky matter during this period of time. As a result of the November 2008 elections, the seat distribution was 56 Democrats, 41 Republicans, 2 independents (who would caucus with the Democrats), and one seat not yet settled, for a working legislative total of 58–41 which gave the Democrats 58.6 percent of the duly elected and sworn-in members of the chamber. The remaining seat was from the state of Minnesota and would not be fully settled (in the favor of Democrat Al Franken) until July 7, 2009. To make matters more complicated, a number of senators at the beginning of the 111th Congress left to serve in the executive branch, including President Barack Obama, Vice President Joe Biden, and Secretary of State Hillary

Clinton. While each of these persons was replaced by Democratic appointees, it did create some initial upheaval in the composition of the chamber.

The equation became even more complicated when Senator Arlen Specter of Pennsylvania switched parties from Republican to Democrat on April 30, 2009, which took the seat distribution from 58–41 to 59–40. At that point the Democratic caucuses controlled 59.6 percent of the 99 seats. The full 60-vote majority did not occur until the aforementioned seating of Senator Franken in July. Complexity was further increased when Senator Edward Kennedy of Massachusetts died on August 25, 2009. He was replaced first by a Democratic appointee a month later. However, his eventual replacement by special election was a Republican (Senator Scott Brown), and so the Democrats lost their 60-vote status as of February 4, 2010.

To summarize, the Democrats controlled 60 votes in the Senate only from July 7, 2009, to August 25, 2009, and then from September 25, 2009, to February 4, 2010. In legislative terms, especially for major legislation, these were fairly small windows. For the purpose of the theoretical discussion, the main point is that the nature of the Senate as a veto gate changed several times during a roughly one-year period. With a 60-vote majority, the Democrats were in a position to forward legislation. With 41 votes in the hands of the opposition party, the Senate became a closed gate, as the unified Republican opposition was a veto player unwilling to negotiate with the Democratic majority to open the gate. Indeed, the form of the PPACA as it currently exists was passed by the House only because (apart from some budget reconciliation issues[4]) the Senate could no longer pass any changes to the bill without facing a filibuster. The House was faced with the choice of an up-or-down vote on the Senate version that passed during the window in which the 60-vote margin existed or no bill.[5] This entire scenario illustrates why and how the rules of governing can matter greatly.

4. Health Care and Education Reconciliation Act of 2010 (Public Law 111–152).

5. Indeed, it has been assumed that some sort of back-and-forth would take place between the House and Senate, but Senator Kennedy's death and his re-

COMPARATIVE CONCLUSIONS   323

Of course, passage of a law is not the end of the story. The states come into play in two ways. First, a number of state governments objected to the bill and started to engage in the tactic of foot-dragging in terms of implementation. Some states, in fact, asserted that they would not implement aspects of the policy, specifically the expansion of Medicaid (health insurance for the poor) or the insurance exchanges (a policy mechanism intended to facilitate the selling of insurance to the uninsured). Since a significant amount of social policy is implemented at the state level, the federal government must rely on it to put the laws into practice. Second, and more significantly, a number of attorneys general at the state level moved to sue the federal government and challenge the constitutionality of the PPACA. One of the cases, for example, was *Florida v. the Department of Health and Human Services,* which was filed in federal district court, initiated by the government of the state of Florida, which was joined by twenty-six other states.[6] In this case, the district court ruled that part of the law was, in fact, unconstitutional—a ruling that was upheld on appeal and eventually came to be heard before the Supreme Court. The Supreme Court upheld the basics of the law in *National Federation of Independent Business v. Sebelius* (2012), but it also affirmed the states' ability to reject the expansion of Medicaid, if the states saw fit to do so (hence confirming that the states could be veto gates to some portions of implementation of the policy).

Here we get the introduction of the courts as potential veto gates in the process of implementation of policy, because the legal process has dictated that the Supreme Court of the United States exercise its powers of judicial review regarding the law. This also brings in the notion of the Constitution as the final measuring stick of laws and policies, with the high court being the arbiter of the matter. A final point: It is interesting to note that a large number of the primary challenges made by the Tea Party faction of the Republican Party

---

placement with a Republican scuttled that option. The close vote in the House for final passage underscores that many Democrats were not fully happy with the bill.

6. Another example: *Virginia ex rel. Cuccinelli v. Sebelius.*

were made in response to the PPACA. Opposition to the bill has been a key motivator for the Tea Party's candidates.

In conclusion to this section, what this particular situation well illustrates is that the more veto gates involved in policy making, the more difficult it is to make the policy in the first place, as well as it is to implement it. It especially highlights the degree to which minorities in the Senate, acting as veto players, can substantially control the policy-making process in the United States in a way that is wholly unique when compared to other democracies.

US Public Policy in Comparative Perspective

Just as the main chapters of this book detailed a number of ways in which US institutional structures conformed or differed from those in the other thirty democracies in this study, we end the last major section of this final chapter by placing the United States in comparison to our democracies in twelve areas of public policy. Note that the goal here is not to provide a normative assessment, but to note where the United States differs (or not) in comparison to the other cases.

1. Tax policy. Given that all public policy requires funding, a foundation of all such policy is tax collection. The United States is unique to this study in that it has no general consumption tax at the national level, that is, no national sales tax or value added tax (VAT). Indeed, in this regard the United States is part of a very small number of countries on a global scale. The Organisation for Economic Co-operation and Development (OECD) notes that more than 150 countries globally use the VAT, which places the United States in a distinct global minority.[7] The United States does have a handful of targeted consumption taxes, also known as excise taxes, on such items as gasoline and tobacco products. For example, the federal government of the United States collects 18.4 cents in taxes per gallon of gasoline purchased in the United States, and like most consumption taxes, the tax is included in the cost of the item, instead of being added to the bill at purchase, as is the case with general sales

7. See the OECD Web page: http://www.oecd.org/ctp/tax-policy/.

Table 10.4. Total tax collected as a percentage of GDP, twenty-nine democracies, 1990–2009

Denmark	48.89
Sweden	48.40
Finland	44.94
Belgium	44.21
France	43.58
Austria	43.09
Italy	41.96
Netherlands	39.68
Hungary	39.19
Czech Republic	36.75
Germany	36.28
Israel	35.71
United Kingdom	34.91
Poland	34.70
Canada	34.50
New Zealand	34.31
Spain	33.79
Portugal	32.53
Greece	31.58
Australia	28.88
Brazil	29.30
Switzerland	28.73
United States	**27.39**
Japan	26.95
Argentina	23.00
Korea	22.64
Chile	20.14
Mexico	16.87
Colombia	14.70
Median	*34.50*

Note: Data missing for India and South Africa.
Sources: OECD Tax Database, available at http://www.oecd.org/
document/60/0,3746,en_2649_34533_1942460_1_1_1_1,00.html,
and Revenue Statistics in Latin America, available at http://
www.oecd.org/document/54/0,3746,en_2649_37427_49402742_1
_1_1_37427,00.html.

taxes at the state level. Typically, consumption taxes like the VAT are included in the purchase price. In the absence of a VAT or similar broad consumption tax, the US central government funds itself primarily through income and payroll taxes. At the state level, it is a mix of income, sales, and property taxes.

In terms of the share of the national economy collected in taxes, at all levels of government, 27.39 percent of the gross domestic product (GDP) was collected in taxes on average between 1990 and 2009. While this is not the lowest amount of taxes collected within our cases, among long-standing developed economies only Japan collected less over the 1990–2009 period. The US average is well below the median of 34.50 percent.

2. Debt. Another key way that states fund policy is through the acquisition of debt. While no country can exist solely by borrowing (at least not for long), all countries do engage in a mix of borrowing and taxation as a means of funding public policies in a given fiscal year. The United States is not unusual in this regard, as table 10.5 illustrates. While the United States does have debt above the median for our thirty-one cases, it is by no means the most indebted when measured as a percentage of GDP.

One interesting side note on debt in terms of recent US politics: The United States is only one of two countries in the study (indeed, perhaps overall) that requires a specific vote by the legislature to authorize the treasury to borrow funds to cover legislatively budgeted obligations. The other case is Denmark, although the Danish legislature tends to set the ceiling so high that it is not an issue. Some other countries, including Canada and the United Kingdom vote on debt limits, but they are made as part of budget votes, not as separate legislative actions.[8]

3. Health care. The United States spends more on health care by a variety of measures than does any of the other countries in our study, as table 10.6 shows. In terms of the percentage of the economy spent on health care, the United States leads the way with 16.2 percent of GDP. This figure includes both public and private

8. See Christen Simeral, "Debt Ceiling 101," *American Prospect,* 2011, available online athttp://prospect.org/article/debt-ceiling-101.

Table 10.5. Public debt as a percentage of GDP in thirty-one democracies (2011 estimates)

Japan	208.2
Greece	165.4
Italy	120.1
Portugal	103.3
Belgium	99.7
France	85.5
Canada	83.5
Hungary	82.6
Germany	81.5
United Kingdom	79.5
Israel	74.0
Austria	72.1
United States	**69.4**
Spain	68.2
Netherlands	64.4
Poland	56.7
Brazil	54.4
Switzerland	52.4
India	51.6
Finland	49.0
Denmark	46.5
Colombia	45.6
China	43.5
Argentina	42.9
Czech Republic	40.7
Mexico	37.5
South Africa	35.6
New Zealand	33.7
Korea	33.3
Australia	30.3
Chile	9.4
Median	*56.7*

Source: CIA *World Factbook*, https://www.cia.gov/library/publications/the-world-factbook/rankorder/2186rank.html.

Table 10.6. Health care expenditures in thirty-one democracies

	% of GDP 2009	Per capita spending (all)			Per capita spending (public)		
		1990–2010 average	Most recent single year		1990–2010 average	Most recent single year	
United States	**16.2**	**$5,087**	**$7,960**	**2009**	**$2,252**	**$3,795**	**2009**
Mexico	13.8	$569	$934	2010	$258	$442	2010
Belgium	11.8	$2,398	$3,946	2009	$2,016	$2,964	2009
Finland	11.7	$2,084	$3,282	2010	$1,553	$2,463	2010
Portugal	11.3	$1,481	$2,508	2008	$975	$1,633	2008
Switzerland	11.3	$3,418	$5,344	2010	$1,948	$3,154	2010
Austria	11.0	$2,820	$4,128	2008	$2,136	$3,331	2009
Canada	10.9	$2,801	$4,478	2010	$1,983	$3,157	2010
Netherlands	10.8	$2,600	$4,914	2009	$1,306	$1,770	2002
Sweden	9.9	$2,397	$3,722	2009	$2,004	$3,033	2009
Spain	9.7	$1,713	$3,067	2009	$1,242	$2,259	2009
New Zealand	9.7	$1,755	$3,022	2010	$1,400	$2,515	2010
Argentina	9.5						
Israel	9.5	$1,770	$2,165	2009	$1,115	$1,266	2009
Japan	9.3	$1,917	$2,878	2008	$1,543	$2,325	2008
United Kingdom	9.3	$1,979	$3,487	2009	$1,618	$2,935	2009
Brazil	9.0						
Australia	8.5	$2,193	$3,445	2008	$1,461	$2,343	2008
South Africa	8.5						
Chile	8.2	$733	$1,186	2009	$335	$562	2009
Hungary	8.2	$997	$1,511	2009	$746	$1,053	2009
Germany	8.1	$2,815	$4,218	2009	$2,214	$3,242	2009
Czech Republic	7.6	$1,123	$2,108	2009	$999	$1,770	2009
Greece	7.4	$1,596	$2,724	2007	$912	$1,644	2007
Poland	7.1	$665	$1,394	2009	$476	$1,006	2009
Denmark	7.0	$2,597	$4,348	2009	$2,178	$3,698	2009
Korea	6.5	$935	$1,980	2010	$484	$1,154	2010
Colombia	6.4						
Italy	5.1	$2,123	$3,236	2010	$1,596	$2,512	2010
France	3.5	$2,600	$3,978	2009	$2,041	$3,100	2009
India	2.4						
Median	*9.15*	*2,084.286*	*3,282*		*1,542.611*	*2,342.5*	

Note: Some data are missing.

Sources: CIA World Factbook (https://www.cia.gov/library/publications/the-world-factbook/rankorder/2225rank.html), and OECD Heath Data (http://www.oecd-ilibrary.org/social-issues-migration-health/health-key-tables-from-oecd_20758480).

expenditures. The table also notes per capita health-care spending as well as isolating public expenditures only (also on a per capita basis). In all cases, the United States is on top of our set of countries. To find examples of countries that spend more per capita in public monies on health care, we have to move outside our comparison set to Norway and Luxembourg. However, while those countries spend more in public funds, they still spend substantially less overall on a per capita basis when private funds are included. Specifically, Luxembourg spent 4.1 percent of its GDP on health care in 2009, $4,808 per capita overall, and $4,040 per capita in terms of public expenditures alone. Norway's numbers were 9.7 percent, $5,352, and $4,501 respectively. This compares to the United States at 16.2 percent, $7,960, and $3,795.

Despite high levels of expenditure, however, the United States does not rank at the top of several key indicators, including life expectancy, infant mortality, and maternal mortality (as tables 10.7, 10.8, and 10.9 demonstrate). Not only is the United States below the median in life expectancy and above the median in infant mortality rate and maternal mortality, it clusters with states that were classifiable as developing within the last two decades (or in some cases that still are): Brazil, Colombia, and Mexico are all in the second tier of the Human Development Index (that is, "High Human Development"), and India and South Africa are in the third tier ("Medium Human Development"). The United States and the other cases are all in the first tier ("Very High Human Development"). Refer back to table 1.1 for all the HDI numbers for our thirty-one cases.

One last health indicator included here is the obesity rate. Table 10.10 details these numbers for twenty-seven of our thirty-one democracies, which the United States leads.

As noted earlier in the case study discussion regarding the PPACA, health-care reform has been a contentious and long-term policy debate in the United States. On a comparative note, the United States has long been unique in the developed world as a case without systematic universal health care.

4. *Criminal justice.* In comparison to our other cases, the United States has an especially punitive criminal-justice system. Here we provide three metrics: population in prison, presence and application of the death penalty, and life imprisonment for minors.

Table 10.7. Life expectancy at birth for thirty-one democracies (2011 estimates)

Japan	83.91
Australia	81.90
Italy	81.86
Canada	81.48
France	81.46
Spain	81.27
Sweden	81.18
Switzerland	81.17
Israel	81.07
Netherlands	80.91
New Zealand	80.71
Germany	80.19
United Kingdom	80.17
Greece	80.05
Austria	79.91
Belgium	79.65
Finland	79.41
Korea	79.30
Denmark	78.78
Portugal	78.70
United States	**78.49**
Chile	78.10
Czech Republic	77.38
Argentina	77.14
Mexico	76.66
Poland	76.25
Hungary	75.02
Colombia	74.79
Brazil	72.79
India	67.14
South Africa	49.41
Median	*79.78*

Source: CIA *World Factbook*, https://www.cia.gov/library/publications/the-world-factbook/rankorder/2102rank.html.

Table 10.8. Infant mortality rates for thirty-one democracies (2011 estimates)

Japan	2.21
Sweden	2.74
Italy	3.36
France	3.37
Spain	3.37
Finland	3.40
Germany	3.51
Czech Republic	3.70
Netherlands	3.73
Switzerland	4.03
Israel	4.07
Korea	4.08
Denmark	4.19
Austria	4.26
Belgium	4.28
Australia	4.55
United Kingdom	4.56
Portugal	4.60
New Zealand	4.72
Canada	4.85
Greece	4.92
Hungary	5.24
United States	**5.98**
Poland	6.42
Chile	7.36
Argentina	10.52
Colombia	15.92
Mexico	16.77
Brazil	20.50
South Africa	42.67
India	46.07
Median	*4.56*

Source: CIA *World Factbook*, https://www.cia.gov/library/publications/the-world-factbook/rankorder/2091rank.html.

Table 10.9. Maternal mortality rate for thirty-one democracies (deaths per 100,000 linked to pregnancy)

Greece	2
Austria	5
Belgium	5
Denmark	5
Italy	5
Sweden	5
Japan	6
Poland	6
Spain	6
Germany	7
Israel	7
Portugal	7
Australia	8
Czech Republic	8
Finland	8
France	8
Netherlands	9
Switzerland	10
Canada	12
United Kingdom	12
Hungary	13
New Zealand	14
Korea	18
United States	**24**
Chile	26
Brazil	58
Argentina	70
Colombia	85
Mexico	85
India	230
South Africa	410
Median	*8*

Source: CIA *World Factbook,* https://www.cia.gov/library/publications/the-world-factbook/rankorder/2223rank.html.

Table 10.10. Percentage of population classified as obese (based on Body Mass Index) in twenty-seven democracies

Japan	3.1
Korea	3.2
Switzerland	8.2
Italy	9.8
Belgium	10.8
Austria	11.0
Brazil	11.1
Denmark	11.4
Sweden	12.0
Germany	12.9
Colombia	13.7
Portugal	14.2
Czech Republic	15.1
Spain	15.6
Finland	15.7
Australia	16.4
France	16.9
Hungary	17.7
Poland	18.0
Chile	21.9
Greece	22.5
United Kingdom	22.7
Israel	22.9
Canada	23.1
Mexico	23.6
New Zealand	26.5
United States	**33.9**
Median	*15.6*

Note: Data not available for Argentina, India, the Netherlands, and South Africa.

Definitions: "Obesity is defined as an adult having a Body Mass Index (BMI) greater than or equal to 30.0. BMI is calculated by taking a person's weight in kilograms and dividing it by the person's squared height in meters" (CIA *World Factbook*).

Source: CIA *World Factbook*, https://www.cia.gov/library/publications/the-world-factbook/rankorder/2228rank.html.

Table 10.11 contains the imprisonment rates of the population in our thirty-one cases. These numbers include imprisonment regardless of level of government (that is, regardless of whether individuals were imprisoned at the national or subunit level). The United States is strikingly high in this, outpacing South Africa and Israel by a factor of 2.3. Clearly this is a function of policy and culture rather than other factors, as several countries that have marked violence problems (for example, Colombia and Mexico) have far lower incarceration rates, and, interestingly, India, which is large in both territory and population, is at the opposite end of the table. The number of citizens in prison is also of significance to the discussion of representative democracy, as those in prison are usually denied the right to vote. Further, as we noted in chapter 5, felons in the United States often remain unable to vote even after their incarceration ends.

As table 10.12 shows, the United States is in the distinct minority among our democracies in continuing to have the death penalty on the books. Indeed, the United States is one of only three countries in which the death penalty can be applied to ordinary crimes (that is, other than treason), and, indeed, remains in the distinct minority even if we included all countries that have not abolished the death penalty altogether. Additionally, as table 10.13 demonstrates, the United States is far more likely to use this means of punishment than the other five countries that retain a death penalty mechanism. In sum: the United States is both more likely to issue the death penalty as well as more likely to carry it out. This comports with the imprisonment numbers. For whatever reason, the United States is generally more punitive than the general democratic community.

Another area in which the United States is set apart is the sentencing of minors to life sentences. As Liptak notes, "The United States stands alone in the world in convicting young adolescents as adults and sentencing them to live out their lives in prison" (Liptak 2007). An Amnesty International / Human Rights Watch study noted that at least 2,225 minors had been sentenced to life in US prisons, most since 1980 (Human Rights Watch 2005: 1–2).

5. *Defense expenditures.* In terms of military spending as a function of a percentage of the value of the overall economy (table 10.14), the United States spends the second most out of our set of democracies.

Table 10.11. Imprisonment rates (per 100,000 of the national population) in thirty-one democracies, 2009

United States	**760**
South Africa	326
Israel	325
Chile	309
Brazil	242
Poland	224
Mexico	209
Czech Republic	206
New Zealand	190
Colombia	167
Spain	162
United Kingdom	153
Hungary	152
Australia	134
Argentina	132
Canada	116
Greece	109
Portugal	104
Netherlands	100
Austria	99
Italy	97
Korea	97
France	96
Belgium	94
Germany	90
Switzerland	76
Sweden	74
Finland	67
Denmark	66
Japan	63
India	32
Median	*116*

Note: Data as gathered in January 2010. Exact dates per country range from mid-2008 to late 2009.
Source: Based on data collected by the International Centre for Prison Studies (www.prisonstudies.org).

Table 10.12. Status of death penalty in thirty-one democracies

Abolished for all crimes N=24	Argentina, Australia, Austria, Belgium, Canada, Colombia, Czech Republic, Denmark, Finland, France, Germany, Greece, Hungary, Italy, Mexico, Netherlands, New Zealand, Poland, Portugal, South Africa, Spain, Sweden, Switzerland, United Kingdom
Abolished for ordinary crimes N=3	Brazil, Chile, Israel
Abolished in practice N=1	Korea
Retained for ordinary crimes N=3	India, Japan, **United States**

Source: Amnesty International.

Table 10.13. Death sentences issued and executions carried out in seven democracies (2008–2010)

	2008	*2009*	*2010*
Brazil	0 (0)	0 (0)	0 (0)
Chile	0 (0)	0 (0)	0 (0)
India	0 (0)	50 (0)	105+ (0)
Israel	0 (0)	0 (0)	0 (0)
Japan	27 (15)	34 (7)	14 (2)
Korea	2+ (0)	5+ (0)	4 (0)
United States	**111+ (37)**	**105+ (52)**	**110+ (46)**

Notes: Executions in (parentheses). Number with "+" signs reported as "at least" the number given.
Source: Amnesty International.

Only Israel, which has specific and ongoing military threats, spends more. The average amount of GDP spent by the United States for a roughly two-decade period (almost all post–Cold War, but including the War on Terror era) was 3.9 percent of GDP, while Israel spent 9.0 percent. US spending is substantially higher than the median of 1.9 percent.

Table 10.14. Military expenditures as a percentage of GDP for thirty-one democracies

	1990–2009 average	*2009*
Israel	9.0	6.3
United States	**3.9**	**4.7**
Chile	3.6	3.5
Greece	3.3	3.2
Colombia	3.1	3.7
Korea	2.9	2.9
France	2.8	2.5
India	2.8	2.8
United Kingdom	2.8	2.7
Portugal	2.2	2.1
Poland	2.0	1.8
Australia	1.9	1.9
Czech Rep.	1.9	1.4
Italy	1.9	1.8
South Africa	1.9	1.3
Sweden	1.9	1.2
Netherlands	1.8	1.5
Hungary	1.7	1.1
Brazil	1.6	1.6
Denmark	1.6	1.4
Germany	1.6	1.4
Belgium	1.5	1.2
Finland	1.5	1.5
Canada	1.4	1.5
New Zealand	1.3	1.2
Spain	1.3	1.1
Switzerland	1.2	0.8
Argentina	1.1	1.0
Austria	1.0	0.9
Japan	1.0	1.0
Mexico	0.5	0.5
Median	*1.9*	*1.5*

Source: Stockholm International Peace Research Institute at http://www.sipri.org/research/armaments/milex.

In terms of absolute dollars, the United States is the largest spender on its military in the world, and by a substantial margin. The Stockholm International Peace Research Institute noted that the United States spent $711 billion in 2011 in comparison to second-place China, which spent an estimated $143 billion (a difference of a factor of just shy of 5). Sticking to raw dollars, the closest competitor in our set of democracies was the United Kingdom at $62.5 billion, or 11.4 times smaller than the United States.[9]

6. Gun rights. In terms of constitutional rights, only the constitutions of the United States and that of Mexico explicitly state the right of citizens to possess firearms, although the Mexican case builds in more provisos allowing regulation than does the US case. Otherwise, the remaining twenty-seven written constitutions are either silent on the subject or, such as the Chilean and Colombian, they note the right of the central government to regulate the private ownership of firearms. The Austrian constitution cedes the power to regulate firearms to the Länder (states). The most common constitutional reference in our set of countries to arms is the right of citizenry to peacefully assemble "without arms."

The lack of a constitutional right does not preclude gun ownership in our cases, it just sets the general legal context. The United States is unique in recognizing individual gun ownership as a protected constitutional right (which was made clear in the 2010 Supreme Court case McDonald v. Chicago). However, as table 10.15 illustrates, private ownership of firearms exists across all thirty-one cases. The table also underscores the substantially higher level of gun ownership in the United States versus the other thirty cases. The civilian (that is, not militia-related) gun ownership rate in the United States (88.8 per 100 persons) is almost twice that of the second-highest case, Switzerland (45.7 per 100).

In terms of gun ownership policy, GunPolicy.org (a site that compiles data on gun laws globally and is run by Sydney School of Public Health at the University of Sydney) classifies twenty-four of our cases as having firearm regulation regimes at "restrictive," meaning

9. See http://www.sipri.org/research/armaments/milex/resultoutput/trendgraphs.

Table 10.15. Civilian-owned firearms per 100 people in thirty-one democracies (2007)

United States	**88.8**
Switzerland	45.7
Finland	45.3
Sweden	31.6
France	31.2
Canada	30.8
Austria	30.4
Germany	30.3
New Zealand	22.6
Greece	22.5
Israel	17.3
Czech Republic	16.3
Australia	15.0
Mexico	15.0
South Africa	12.7
Denmark	12.0
Italy	11.9
Chile	10.7
Spain	10.4
Argentina	10.2
Portugal	8.5
Brazil	8.0
Belgium	7.2
United Kingdom	6.7
Colombia	5.9
Hungary	5.5
India	4.2
Netherlands	3.9
Poland	1.3
Korea	1.1
Japan	0.6
Median	*12.0*

Source: Small Arms Survey, http://www.smallarmssurvey.org/publications/by-type/yearbook/small-arms-survey-2007.html.

a system in which citizens seeking to purchase a firearm must provide proactive evidence they have reasonable grounds for acquiring the weapon (for example, self-protection, sport, collecting, and so on). Only three countries, including the United States (along with Austria and Belgium), were classified as having "permissive" firearm regulation regimes, meaning systems in which certain classes of persons were prohibited from ownership but otherwise all citizens were eligible. Three additional cases (Israel, Italy, and Portugal) were not classified, although they would appear, based on other criteria, to fall in the "restrictive" category.

Ultimately, the United States stands alone in terms of a clear constitutional right to own arms as well as in terms of the permissiveness of gun regulations. And, certainly, more guns are owned per hundred persons than in any of our other cases.

7. Employee protection. In chapter 6 we noted the low level of unionization in the United States. One area that can be linked to this in terms of public policy is the laws that provide employment protections. These policies focus on the question of the balance of rights between workers and employers and deal with issues such as how difficult it is to fire employees and the degree to which those employees have recourse to legal protection vis-à-vis the actions of employers. Other factors deal with contract rules and collective bargaining rights.

In her study of these types of laws, Venn notes that "the employment protection indicator is (on average) lower in countries with an English legal tradition (1.5) than in those with a French legal tradition (2.7). Countries based on the German (2.3) and Scandinavian systems (2.2) are in between" (Venn 2009: 17). Along those lines we can see on table 10.16 that the United States clusters with other Anglosphere countries—the United Kingdom, Australia, Canada, and New Zealand and the United Kingdom–influenced case of South Africa.

8. Near absolutism in free speech. All of the constitutions under study provide protection for speech. Indeed, freedom of speech is a fundamental democratic right, which must exist for democracy to exist. However, in the US context, the right comes nearer to an absolute one than in our other cases. Specifically we can identify

Table 10.16. Employment protection index in twenty-nine democracies

Mexico	3.23
Spain	3.11
France	3.00
Greece	2.97
Portugal	2.84
Germany	2.63
India	2.63
Belgium	2.61
Italy	2.58
Austria	2.41
Poland	2.41
Czech Republic	2.32
Finland	2.29
Brazil	2.27
Netherlands	2.23
Korea	2.13
Hungary	2.11
Sweden	2.06
Chile	1.93
Denmark	1.91
Israel	1.88
Switzerland	1.77
Japan	1.73
Australia	1.38
South Africa	1.35
New Zealand	1.16
United Kingdom	1.09
Canada	1.02
United States	**0.85**
Median	*2.23*

Source: OECD. To find out more about the methodology used to calculate the OECD employment protection indicators, see www .oecd.org/employment/protection.

differences on hate speech, slander, and campaigning/campaign finance rules.

Hate speech has political significance, as it pertains to certain kinds of extremist political parties and their activities, especially in public. The interpretation of the First Amendment by the Supreme Court has been such that it allows groups like the Ku Klux Klan or the National Socialist Party of America to engage in public activities, even when the community has a high probability of being offended by said activity. This is not the case in all of our democracies. For example, as Schauer notes:

> Germany, Israel, and France are among the nations that prohibit the sale and distribution of various Nazi items, including swastikas, Nazi flags, and, on occasion, images of Adolph Hitler and copies of *Mein Kampf.* Canada, Germany, and France, along with others, permit sanctions against those who would deny the existence of the Holocaust. France imposes fines with some frequency on public utterances espousing the racial or religious inferiority of various groups, or advocating the exclusion of people from France on the basis of their race, their religion, their ethnicity, or their national origin. The Netherlands outlaws public insults based on race, religion, or sexual preference. (2005: 708)

He further notes: "South Africa, New Zealand, Australia, Canada, the United Kingdom, and all of the Scandinavian countries, among many others . . . mak[e] it a crime to engage in the incitement to racial, religious, or ethnic hatred or hostility" (708). All of those mentioned are permissible under the prevailing interpretations of the First Amendment of the US Constitution.

Not only is politically extreme speech more protected in the US case, defamatory speech is likewise more protected, especially in terms of application to public figures, including politicians. Another comparative study noted:

> Under the rule of *New York Times v. Sullivan* and its subsequent extensions, laws imposing liability on those who defame government officials or other public figures are constitutionally permissible only when such speech is made with "actual malice"—that is, knowledge that the statement is false or reckless disregard of its truth or falsity. This rule has expressly been considered and

rejected under both the Canadian and Australian Constitution as insufficiently protecting the conflicting values of reputation and dignity, a position mirrored in most other countries, including Germany. (Gardbaum 2008: 402–3)

Another key area worth considering, especially as it pertains to electoral politics, is that of campaign speech and its linkages to campaign finance. In regards to campaign speech, the US system is one that allows for very few restrictions on campaign advertising. For example, there are controls on paid advertisement and broadcasting in the United Kingdom that could never withstand court scrutiny in the United States. As Gardbaum notes: "The exceptional understanding of the right to free speech as permitting at most only very limited regulation of broadcasting companies means that the common ban elsewhere on paid political advertisements in favor of free, mandated airtime for electoral candidates would be unconstitutional in the United States" (2008: 403). Not only are controls over broadcast commercials not possible, but the general situation is such that campaign-finance controls are limited because they have been seen by the Supreme Court as First Amendment issues. Specifically, the Supreme Court of the United States recently expanded the application of political free-speech rights to group actors, including corporations in the *Citizens United* case in 2010. The case also made explicit a notion in American campaign-finance policy that money is speech in the sense that the main way by which political speech is made public is via the spending of money. This, therefore, produced a legal regime that made the curtailing of campaign spending difficult.

9. Citizenship. The Fourteenth Amendment to the Constitution explicitly states, "All persons born or naturalized in the United States, and subject to the jurisdiction thereof, are citizens of the United States." The original purpose of this clause was to find a comprehensive method for ensuring that all freed slaves were recognized as citizens in the post–Civil War period (as well as to explicitly overturn aspect of the infamous *Dred Scott* case that has declared that freed slaves were not citizens). Subsequent to its original purpose, this clause also has been recognized to grant citizenship to any person born in the United States, regardless of the citizenship status of the parents. As such, the United States has what is known as birthright citizenship, also referred to by the Latin term *jus soli*, which means "right of soil." This is to be contrasted with citizenship policies that require that one inherit one's citizenship from one's parents, which is called *jus sanguinis* ("right of blood").

Of our thirty-one cases, only the United States and six other cases have automatic birthright citizenship. These are Canada (since 1977) and the Latin American cases (Argentina, Brazil, Chile, Colombia, and Mexico). Indeed, according to the Center for Immigration Studies, pure birthright citizenship regardless of one's parent's status is a Western Hemispheric phenomenon.[10]

10. Environmental policy. The best indicator of how well countries do with regard to protecting the environment is the Environmental Performance Index, produced by a team of environmental experts at Yale University and Columbia University. It is a broad and comprehensive index that rates the performance of most of the countries in the world on twenty-five indicators in ten policy areas, including environmental health, air quality, water resource management, biodiversity and habitat, forestry, fisheries, agriculture, and climate change (Yale Center for Environmental Law and Policy 2010). A pilot project was published in 2006, and full reports were released in 2008 and 2010. Table 10.17 uses the average ratings for the latter two years received by our thirty-one countries. Countries are rated on a scale from 100, indicating the best performance, to 0, indicating the poorest performance, although in practice no country is rated even close to 0. The more economically developed countries tend to have the better environmental performance, but there are clear exceptions. For instance, Colombia and Chile are in the top half of the table with ratings above the median, and Australia, the Netherlands, and Belgium are well below the median. The United States is also in the bottom half—ranked number twenty-third out of thirty-one countries.

11. Distribution of wealth. A policy dimension to consider that is focused less on a policy as much as on outcomes is the distribution

10. See John Feere, "Birthright Citizenship in the United States: A Global Comparison," online at http://cis.org/birthright-citizenship.

Table 10.17. Environmental performance in thirty-one democracies, 2008–2010

Switzerland	92.3
Sweden	89.6
Austria	83.8
Finland	83.0
France	83.0
Colombia	82.6
New Zealand	81.2
United Kingdom	80.2
Germany	79.8
Portugal	79.4
Italy	78.6
Japan	78.5
Chile	78.4
Spain	76.8
Hungary	76.6
Denmark	76.6
Canada	76.5
Czech Republic	74.2
Mexico	73.6
Brazil	73.0
Australia	72.8
Netherlands	72.6
United States	**72.2**
Poland	71.8
Argentina	71.4
Israel	71.0
Greece	70.6
Belgium	68.2
Korea	68.2
South Africa	59.9
India	54.3
Median	*76.6*

Source: Based on data in Yale Center for Environmental Law and Policy, 2010; http://epi.yale.edu.

of income within our cases and how the United States fits into the discussion. All of our cases include tax provisions, for example, that cause wealthier citizens to pay more in taxes both in relative and absolute terms. As such, all of these systems can be said to have some sort of redistributionist elements. However, redistribution for redistribution's sake is likely not the goal, but policies such as public education have redistributionist elements. To wit: Property taxes collected in a US municipality to help pay for K–12 education will help poor children receive an education that can help them move out of poverty because of the enhanced employment prospects afforded to the education, even though their families paid proportionally fewer taxes into the system than did wealthier residents.

The notion of redistribution as a general principle is not especially popular in many sectors of US society, although the question of wealth distribution became a more prominent political topic of discussion as a result of the financial crisis and recession of the late 2000s. In regard to public sentiment, a 2011 Gallup poll asked about policies to fix the economy, and only 13 percent of national adults chose, "Take steps to distribute wealth more evenly among Americans," whereas 84 percent preferred, "Take steps to improve overall economic conditions and the jobs situation."[11] A separate 2011 poll on the more specific policy question, "Do you think our government should or should not redistribute wealth by heavy taxes on the rich?" the result was 47 percent yes, 49 percent no, and 4 percent no opinion.[12] The notion is, depending on how the question is asked, either unpopular or polarizing.

Of course, much of this relates, in a practical political fashion, to the note earlier on tax policy, insofar as noted in table 10.4, the United States is well below the median in taxes collected as a percentage of GDP. In terms of actually measuring distribution, table 10.18 details

11. See "Americans Oppose Income Redistribution to Fix Economy" online at http://www.gallup.com/poll/108445/americans-oppose-income-redistribution-fix-economy.aspx.

12. See "Democrats, Republicans Differ Widely on Taxing the Rich" online at http://www.gallup.com/poll/147104/s-republicans-differ-widely-faxing-rich.aspx.

Table 10.18. Gini index for household income in thirty-one democracies

Denmark	24.7
Japan	24.9
Sweden	25.0
Czech Republic	25.8
Finland	26.9
Germany	28.3
Austria	29.1
Hungary	30.0
Netherlands	30.9
Korea	31.6
Australia	32.5
Canada	32.6
France	32.7
Belgium	33.0
Switzerland	33.7
Greece	34.3
Spain	34.7
Poland	34.9
Italy	36.0
United Kingdom	36.0
New Zealand	36.2
India	36.8
Portugal	38.5
Israel	39.2
United States	**40.8**
Mexico	48.1
Argentina	50.0
Chile	52.0
Brazil	55.0
South Africa	57.8
Colombia	58.5
Median	*34.3*

Source: Human Development Report 2009, http://hdr.undp.org/en/global-reports.

the Gini Index rankings for our thirty-one democracies on the issue of household income.

The Gini Index is a mathematical formula used to measure distribution of items and is a standard metric for measuring wealth/income distribution. The Gini Index runs on a theoretical scale from 0 to 100 with a measure of 0 meaning that everyone has an equal share of whatever is being distributed, and a measure of 100 meaning that one person has everything.[13] Reality in any given distribution, especially in terms of income, is somewhere between 0 and 100. In table 10.18 we see that of our thirty-one democracies, Denmark has the most even distribution, with a Gini Index of 24.7, and Colombia is the most maldistributed, with a Gini Index of 58.5. The United States has an index of 40.8, which is significantly above the median of 34.3. Hence, in terms of actual distribution of incomes by household, the United States is one of the more unequal examples in our comparison set and, as with a number of other policy examples noted earlier, clusters with cases that were recently (or still) classified as developing.

This topic is linked to a broad belief in the United States of social/economic mobility as manifested in the "American Dream," that is, that the United States has a purely meritocratic system wherein hard work will be rewarded with upper mobility in the social structure. Such a notion also assumes that existing distributions are the result of that meritocratic system. However, recent studies have noted that this is not the case, but rather that "in tests of intergenerational mobility, the higher the correlation between one's generation's family income and education and the next generation's, the lower the mobility" (Stepan and Linz 2011: 852). In other words, in comparing the United States to other advanced industrial democracies, the macro-level finding is that one's chances of upward mobility are predicated substantially on one's family position than on one's own hard work. Stepan and Linz go on: "In all of the studies, the United States emerges as having the lowest levels of intergenerational upward mobility, with the exception of the UK" (852). One study, by

13. It can also, and often is, expressed as being between 0 and 1, with measures given in decimals, e.g., .45 rather than 45.

Corak, summarized the situation as follows in a statement that includes several of our other democracies: "The United States, the United Kingdom, and to a slightly lesser extent France, stand out as being the least mobile societies, with 40–50% of fathers' earnings advantage being passed on to sons. At the other extreme are Denmark, Norway, Finland, and Canada with about 15–20% of earnings advantage passed across generations, and in an intermediate position Germany and Sweden with about 30%" (2006: 11).

If the main predictor of how one will fare economically generation to generation is the status of one's parents and not personal factors, then the notion of substantial economic mobility has to be questioned, if not rejected, in terms of the perception of how US society functions.

12. Governmental effectiveness. Finally, we can go beyond specific policies and look to two data sets for the measurement of the overall effectiveness of government and policy making as well as the overall quality of democracy in our thirty-one countries: the Worldwide Governance Indicators (WGI)—based on expert assessments of several dimensions of good governance in most of the countries of the world—and the data of the Democracy Index project of the Economist Intelligence Unit (EIU). Table 10.19 shows five of the WGI measures, averaged over nine years, from 2002 to 2010. The first column contains the averages of the five scores for each country. All of the scores are on a scale ranging from −2.5 to +2.5. The first performance variable, political stability and the absence of violence, measures the likelihood that the government will be destabilized by unconstitutional or violent means, including terrorism. Government effectiveness is a composite measure of the quality of public services, the quality of the civil service and its independence from political pressures, the quality of policy formulation and implementation, and the credibility of the government's commitment to such policies. Regulatory quality measures the government's ability to formulate and implement sound policies and regulations that promote private sector development. Rule of law is a self-explanatory term; it specifically includes the quality of property rights, the police, and the courts, as well as the risk of crime. Control of corruption comprises not only the degree to which public power is used for private

Table 10.19. Effective government and policy making in thirty-one democracies, 2002–2010

	Effective government and policymaking	Political stability and absence of violence	Government effectiveness	Regulatory quality	Rule of law	Control of corruption
Finland	1.96	1.52	2.17	1.74	1.94	2.42
Denmark	1.90	1.10	2.22	1.82	1.93	2.45
Sweden	1.80	1.25	1.99	1.63	1.89	2.22
New Zealand	1.79	1.21	1.79	1.73	1.85	2.37
Switzerland	1.76	1.24	2.00	1.62	1.84	2.10
Netherlands	1.69	0.97	1.87	1.76	1.76	2.11
Austria	1.68	1.14	1.84	1.60	1.87	1.97
Canada	1.65	1.01	1.88	1.61	1.74	1.99
Australia	1.63	0.91	1.81	1.66	1.77	1.99
Germany	1.49	0.86	1.59	1.54	1.65	1.82
United Kingdom	1.46	0.36	1.70	1.73	1.67	1.81
Belgium	1.31	0.82	1.72	1.33	1.31	1.37
United States	**1.26**	**0.16**	**1.58**	**1.54**	**1.55**	**1.50**
France	1.23	0.51	1.60	1.24	1.41	1.39
Chile	1.20	0.65	1.19	1.47	1.26	1.41

Japan	1.18	0.97	1.38	1.04	1.27	1.24
Portugal	1.06	0.95	1.03	1.13	1.12	1.06
Spain	0.97	0.02	1.25	1.25	1.15	1.17
Hungary	0.85	0.85	0.85	1.16	0.85	0.52
Czech Republic	0.85	0.92	0.97	1.15	0.86	0.34
Korea	0.70	0.26	1.06	0.80	0.90	0.45
Greece	0.59	0.37	0.69	0.87	0.76	0.26
Poland	0.55	0.61	0.52	0.80	0.50	0.29
Italy	0.54	0.49	0.58	0.94	0.45	0.26
Israel	0.51	−1.47	1.21	1.03	0.87	0.90
South Africa	0.30	−0.08	0.59	0.57	0.11	0.31
Brazil	−0.08	−0.12	0.01	0.12	−0.36	−0.04
Mexico	−0.14	−0.49	0.17	0.35	−0.50	−0.26
India	−0.38	−1.21	−0.04	−0.31	0.06	−0.41
Argentina	−0.43	−0.18	−0.11	−0.72	−0.69	−0.46
Colombia	−0.53	−1.92	−0.07	0.12	−0.60	−0.20
Median	*1.18*	*0.65*	*1.25*	*1.24*	*1.26*	*1.24*

Source: Based on data in Kaufmann, Kraay, and Mastruzzi, "Worldwide Governance Indicators," http://govindicators.org.

gain, including both petty and grand forms of corruption, but also the "capture" of the state by elites and private interests (Kaufmann, Kraay, and Mastruzzi 2010). The table lists the thirty-one countries in decreasing order of the mean scores (in the first column) on these five dimensions. Generally, we find the older democracies above the median score of 1.18 and the newer democracies below the median. The United States is also above the median, but only in thirteenth place. On the individual indicators, the United States ranks between eleventh and fourteenth, except with regard to political stability and the absence of violence, where it is in twenty-third place, well below the median.

The sixth dimension measured by the World Governance Indicators is called "voice and accountability," defined as the extent to which citizens are able to participate in selecting their government, as well as freedom of expression, freedom of association, and a free press. It is a good comprehensive measure of the quality of democracy.[14] Table 10.20 shows the average scores of our thirty-one countries in the years 2002–2010 in decreasing order. The older democracies generally rank higher than the newer ones, but the United States is only in fifteenth place, only one place above the median.

More detailed and inclusive measures of the quality of democracy have been devised by the Economist Intelligence Unit. The average scores (on a 10-point scale) in its three reports for 2006, 2008, and 2010 are shown in table 10.21. The EIU's overall index of democracy is an average of the scores in five categories. Each category is composed of an average of twelve subcategories. To give a few examples of the questions that the EIU asks about each country, the first category, electoral process and pluralism, includes the following: "Are elections for the national legislature and head of government free [and fair]?"; "Are municipal elections both free and fair?"; "Do laws provide for broadly equal campaigning opportunities?"; and "Do opposition parties have a realistic prospect of achieving government?" Questions in the second category, the functioning of government,

14. Note that *voice* here means more than just freedom of speech, but whether popular preferences are effectively translated into government policies.

Table 10.20. Quality of democracy (voice and accountability) in thirty-one democracies, 2002–2010

Denmark	1.62
Finland	1.58
Netherlands	1.56
Sweden	1.56
Switzerland	1.56
New Zealand	1.55
Canada	1.46
Australia	1.42
Germany	1.41
Belgium	1.41
Austria	1.38
United Kingdom	1.36
Portugal	1.29
France	1.26
United States	**1.20**
Spain	1.17
Hungary	1.07
Chile	1.04
Italy	1.01
Czech Republic	1.01
Japan	1.00
Greece	0.98
Poland	0.95
Korea	0.69
Israel	0.64
South Africa	0.61
Brazil	0.45
India	0.42
Argentina	0.28
Mexico	0.16
Colombia	−0.29
Median	*1.17*

Source: Based on data in Kaufmann, Kraay, and Mastruzzi 2011, http://govindicators.org.

Table 10.21. The Economist Intelligence Unit's Democracy Index, 2006, 2008, and 2010

	Overall index	Electoral process and pluralism	Functioning of government	Political participation	Political culture	Civil liberties
Sweden	9.75	9.86	9.88	9.63	9.38	10.00
Denmark	9.52	10.00	9.64	8.89	9.38	9.71
Netherlands	9.39	9.58	9.05	9.26	9.38	9.71
Finland	9.23	10.00	9.88	7.59	8.96	9.71
New Zealand	9.15	10.00	8.93	8.70	8.13	10.00
Australia	9.13	10.00	8.93	7.78	8.96	10.00
Switzerland	9.09	9.58	9.29	7.78	9.17	9.61
Canada	9.07	9.31	9.52	7.78	8.75	10.00
Germany	8.67	9.58	8.33	7.59	8.54	9.31
Austria	8.56	9.58	7.98	7.78	8.34	9.12
Spain	8.32	9.58	7.98	6.30	8.33	9.41
United States	**8.21**	**8.89**	**7.86**	**7.22**	**8.54**	**8.53**
Czech Republic	8.18	9.58	7.02	6.85	8.13	9.31
Japan	8.16	9.03	8.09	5.93	8.33	9.41
United Kingdom	8.13	9.58	8.33	5.37	8.34	9.02
Belgium	8.12	9.58	8.21	6.11	7.29	9.41

Portugal	8.08	9.58	7.97	5.93	7.50	9.41
Greece	8.06	9.58	7.14	6.67	7.50	9.41
Korea	8.00	9.44	7.50	7.22	7.50	8.33
France	7.97	9.58	7.38	6.48	7.50	8.92
South Africa	7.87	8.75	7.98	7.22	6.67	8.72
Italy	7.85	9.44	6.55	6.30	8.13	8.82
Chile	7.82	9.58	8.81	4.63	6.46	9.61
India	7.59	9.58	8.33	5.19	5.42	9.41
Israel	7.41	8.89	7.21	8.15	7.50	5.29
Hungary	7.39	9.58	6.31	5.19	6.88	9.02
Brazil	7.29	9.58	7.74	4.63	5.21	9.31
Poland	7.22	9.58	6.07	6.11	5.21	9.12
Mexico	6.79	8.47	6.78	5.37	5.00	8.33
Argentina	6.70	8.75	5.24	5.56	5.84	8.14
Colombia	6.50	9.17	5.62	4.63	4.17	8.92
Median	*8.12*	*9.58*	*7.98*	*6.67*	*8.13*	*9.31*

Source: Based on data in Economist Intelligence Unit 2006, 3–5; 2008, 4–8; 2010, 3–8. London: The Economist.

are: "Do freely elected representatives determine government policy?"; "[Do] special economic, religious or other powerful domestic groups . . . exercise significant political power, parallel to democratic institutions?"; "Are sufficient mechanisms and institutions in place for assuring government accountability to the electorate in between elections?"; and "Is the functioning of government open and transparent, with sufficient public access to information?" The third category, political participation, has questions about interest and participation in elections, political parties, other organizations, lawful demonstrations, and women's legislative representation. The fourth category, political culture, focuses on the degree to which citizens express faith in and support for democracy. The fifth category, civil liberties, looks at the traditional freedoms of expression, association, and religion, a free and robust press and other media of communication, equal treatment under the law, and an independent judiciary (Economist Intelligence Unit 2010: 33–42).

Our thirty-one countries are ranked in decreasing order of their scores on the EIU's overall index of democracy. On this index, too, the older democracies tend to rank above the median and the newer ones below the median, but Spain and the Czech Republic, relatively young democracies, are above the mean. The United States is in twelfth place between these two countries. It is also above the median with regard to political participation (a shared twelfth to fourteenth place with Korea and South Africa) and well above the median on political culture (a shared eighth and ninth place with Germany). However, the United States scores much lower on electoral process and pluralism (a shared twenty-seventh and twenty-eighth place with Israel), functioning of government (nineteenth place), and civil liberties (twenty-seventh place).

FINAL CONCLUSIONS

There are, of course, any number of other areas of public policy that could be discussed, but this chapter has provided an overview of a variety of policy areas, measures, and ideas that demonstrate the ways in which US policy is different from (as well as similar to) other cases in our study. The fundamental issues beyond the description of these outcomes is to point back to the institutional structures of the US government and how they differ from the vast majority of our cases and how that, along with other factors, like culture and historical circumstances, produce some of the differences we see. Certainly there are additional areas of policy that could be included, and each of them could be a chapter, if not a book, by itself.

It should be noted that despite the differences being discussed, all thirty-one of these cases are representative democracies in which the reins of government are placed in the hands of elected officials for a specific amount of time to govern under the constraints of an institutional order created by a constitution. In all of these cases there are substantial political rights in place to allow citizens to pursue their interests and attempt to influence said government. In short, the argument here is not the United States has a different regime type than the other thirty. Rather, just that its democracy does differ on a number of institutional and policy-related parameters. Ultimately, the issue is how a given institutional order creates the circumstances for governance and, hence, policy outcomes. We can return to the notions introduced in chapter 1 and consider the principal-agent model introduced in figure 1.1. The question becomes, in terms of delegation of power and the seeking of accountability, how does this function in the US context? What we have demonstrated is that there are numerous ways to do what Madison described in *Federalist 10*: "delegate[ed] . . . the government . . . to a small number of citizens elected by the rest" (Madison, Hamilton, and Jay 1987: 126). The question of how power is delegated and to whom has been a central theme of this study, especially as it pertains to the creation of veto gates and players. Because of the large number of veto gates in the US system, the authority delegated by the citizens as principals, to the US government as agents is highly diffused. It is diffused between national and state governments, where it is then further diffused to various institutional actors. If we focus just on the national government, power is then divided between two chambers of the legislature and between the legislature and the executive. Consonant with the design of the political engineers of the Philadelphia Convention, this structure decreases the ability for consolidated power to act. On the one hand, diffusion of power means that policy decisions, especially dramatic ones, require consensus building. On the other hand, diffusion of power also makes accountability more difficult. If policies fail, or if inaction creates new difficulties, who is to blame? Should the voters, as principals, punish members of the House, the Senate, and/or the president?

Further, as noted earlier, the diffusion of power in the United States is such that policy formulation and passage is quite difficult, given the number of veto gates and the special veto power inherent in the Senate, especially in the past decade or so as the filibuster has become the norm. Ultimately, the institutional circumstances of the United States are fundamentally conservative, meaning that they lend themselves to maintaining the status quo.

By contrast, our survey of the United States in comparative perspective has shown that most other democracies have institutional configurations that diminish the number of veto gates, and therefore are less complex in their operation. Specifically we found that most of the democracies in our comparison group have a parliamentary executive, proportional representation with multiparty systems, and are more likely to be unitary and unicameral (or at least to have a weaker second chamber). An institutional configuration that approximates the one just sketched implies either one veto gate or one that dominates over the others. With one veto gate primarily shaping government policy, the process of responding to policy challenges may be far less complex, and also more rapid, if a cohesive majority exists in the first or sole chamber of the legislature. Of course, less complex and rapid processes are not always better, but the point is that the policy involves fewer actors who can block a change, which makes policy change more likely.[15] In countries with a single veto gate but a coalition government, the one gate is able to be opened only when two or more transacting parties consent to change.[16] This

15. Examples would be New Zealand before its electoral reform in 1996 (as discussed in ch. 5 and other chapters) or the United Kingdom before the coalition that was formed in 2010. In the United Kingdom, there is a second chamber, the House of Lords, but as noted in ch. 7, it is not nearly as powerful in practice as is the US Senate.

16. Prominent examples among our comparative cases would be New Zealand after its change to a Mixed-Member Proportional electoral system in 1996, or the United Kingdom Coalition Government formed in 2010.

adds complexity to the policy-making process beyond the case of a single cohesive majority party, because each of the parties in coalition is a veto player. However, very few coalition-based parliamentary systems have a policy-making process as complex as that of the United States, even if they also happen to be federal.[17] The reason is that multiple veto players in such systems are transacting to open the veto gate created by a single dominant institution, the legislature, whereas in the United States, the policy-making process involves separate institutions acting as veto gates.

Of course, evaluations of the situation need to be divided into empirical and normative considerations. Our goal here has been to provide an empirical description of the institutions of democratic governance in the US case and then to detail some of the outputs of that system. Normative preferences on these outcomes range from positive evaluations of a system that must move slowly, to negative in terms of how difficult policy making can be in this context.

Certainly the institutional parameters under which politicians compete for power, and under which they operate when making policy once in power, matter greatly. Regardless of anything else, this analysis should underscore that there is a great deal of institutional variation among functioning democratic states around the world, and that in many ways, the United States of America is different on several key counts from its democratic siblings. We hope that we have inspired more thought and study on this topic.

17. For example, Germany, where governments are always coalitions, and they must transact with states and a powerful second chamber. However, the second chamber has neither equal representation for different-size states (see ch. 4) nor fully symmetrical legislative authority (see ch. 7).

REFERENCES

Ansolabehere, Stephen, and Shanto Iyengar. 1995. *Going Negative: How Attack Ads Shrink and Polarize the Electorate.* New York: Free Press.

Benedict, Michael Les. 2006. *The Blessings of Liberty: A Concise History of the Constitution of the United States.* 2nd ed. Boston: Wadsworth.

Beth, Richard S., and Stanley Bach. 2003. *Filibuster and Cloture in the Senate.* Washington, DC: Congressional Research Service.

Blackwell, Christopher W. 2003. "Athenian Democracy: A Brief Overview." In "Athenian Law in Its Democratic Context," ed. Adriaan Lanni. *Center for Hellenic Studies On-line Discussion Series.* Republished in C. W. Blackwell, ed., *Dēmos: Classical Athenian Democracy* (A. Mahoney and R. Scaife, eds., *The Stoa: A Consortium for Electronic Publication in the Humanities* [www.stoa.org]), edition of February 28, 2003.

Brooks, Stephen. 2009. *Understanding American Politics.* Toronto: University of Toronto Press.

Buchanan, Bruce. 1988. "The Six-Year One Term Presidency: A New Look at an Old Proposal." *Presidential Studies Quarterly* 18, no. 1 (Winter): 129–42.

Burnham, Walter Dean. 1987. "The Turnout Problem." In A. James Reichley, ed., *Elections American Style,* 97–133. Washington, DC: Brookings Institution.

Butler, David, and Bruce Cain. 1992. *Congressional Redistricting: Comparative and Theoretical Perspectives.* New York: Macmillan.

Butler, David, and Austin Ranney. 1994. *Referendums Around the World: The Growing Use of Direct Democracy.* Washington, DC: AEI Press.

Carey, Henry F., and Robert M. Howard. 2004. "Is an Independent Judiciary Necessary for Democracy?" *Judicature* 87, no. 6 (May/June): 284–90.

Carey, John. 2000. "Parchment, Equilibria, and Institutions." *Comparative Political Studies* 33, no. 6/7 (August/September): 735–61.

———. 2009. *Legislative Voting and Accountability.* Cambridge: Cambridge University Press.

Carroll, Royce, and Matthew Søberg Shugart. 2007. "Neo-Madisonian Theories of Latin American Institutions." In *Regimes and Democracy in Latin America.* Vol. 1: *Theories and Agendas,* ed. Gerardo Munck. New York: Oxford University Press.

Casper, Gerhard. 1989. "Changing Concepts of Constitutionalism: 18th to 20th Century." *Supreme Court Review:* 311–32.

Casto, William R. 2002. "The Early Supreme Court Justices' Most Significant Opinion." *Ohio Northern University Law Review* 29: 173–207.

Cheibub, José Antonio. 2007. *Presidentialism, Parliamentarism, and Democracy.* Cambridge: Cambridge University Press.

Chen, Jowei, and Jonathan Rodden. 2013. "Unintentional Gerrymandering: Political Geography and Electoral Bias in Legislatures." *Quarterly Journal of Political Science* 8: 1–31.

Central Intelligence Agency. *The World Factbook.* Washington, DC. https://www.cia.gov/library/publications/the-world-factbook/index.html.

Corak, Michael. 2006. *Do Poor Children Become Poor Adults? Lessons from a Cross Country Comparison of Generational Earnings Mobility.* IZA Discussion Paper no. 1993. Bonn, Germany. Available online at http://ftp.iza.org/dp1993.pdf.

Council of State Governments. 2003. *The Book of the States.* Lexington, KY.

Cox, Gary, and Scott Morgenstern. 2001. "Latin America's Reactive Assemblies and Proactive Presidents." *Comparative Politics* 33, no. 2: 171–90.

Cutler, Lloyd N. 1980. "To Form a Government." *Foreign Affairs* 59, no. 1 (Fall): 126–43.

Dahl, Robert A. 1998. *On Democracy.* New Haven: Yale University Press.

———. 2001. *How Democratic Is the American Constitution?* New Haven: Yale University Press.

Denmark, David. 2001. "Choosing MMP in New Zealand: Explaining the 1993 Electoral Reform." In *Mixed-Member Electoral Systems: The Best of Both Worlds?* ed. Matthew Søberg Shugart and Martin P. Wattenberg. Oxford: Oxford University Press.

Department of Justice (Canada). 2005. *Canada's Court System.* Ottawa, Ontario: Communications Branch, Department of Justice, Canada.

Diamond, Larry. 1999. *Developing Democracy: Toward Consolidation.* Baltimore: Johns Hopkins University Press.

Diamond, Larry, and Marc F. Plattner, eds. 2006. *Electoral Systems and Democracy.* Baltimore: Johns Hopkins University Press.

Dippel, Horst. 1996. "The Changing Idea of Popular Sovereignty in Early American Constitutionalism: Breaking Away from European Patterns." *Journal of the Early Republic* 16, no. 1 (Spring): 21–45.

Du Bois, François. 2006. "Judicial Selection in Post-Apartheid South Africa." In *Appointing Judges in an Age of Judicial Power: Critical Perspectives from Around the World,* ed. Kate Malleson and Peter H. Russell. Toronto: University of Toronto Press.

Duverger, Maurice. 1986. "Duverger's Law: Forty Years Later." In *Political Laws and Their Political Consequences,* ed. Bernard Grofman and Arend Lijphart, 69–84. New York: Agathon.

Dworkin, Ronald. 1990. "Equality, Democracy, and Constitution: We the People in Court." *Alberta Law Review* 28, no. 2: 324–45.

Economist Intelligence Unit. 2006. *Index of Democracy.* London: The Economist.

———. 2008. *Index of Democracy, 2008.* London: The Economist.

———. 2010. *Index of Democracy, 2010.* London: The Economist.

Elgie, Robert. 2011. *Semi-Presidentialism: Sub-Types and Democratic Performance.* Oxford: Oxford University Press.

Elkins, Zachary, Tom Ginsburg, and James Melton. 2009. *The Endurance of National Constitutions.* Cambridge: Cambridge University Press.

———. 2010. *Chronology of Constitutional Events, Version 1.1.* Comparative Constitutions Project. Last modified: May 12, 2010. Available online at http://www.comparativeconstitutionsproject.org/index.htm.

Elliot, Jonathan, ed. 1888. *Debates of the Adoption of the Federal Constitution.* Vol. 1. New York: Burt Franklin.

Farrell, David. 2011. *Electoral Systems: A Comparative Introduction.* 2nd ed. New York: Palgrave Macmillan.

Federal Court of Justice. 2010. *The Federal Court of Justice.* Karlsruhe, Germany. Available online at http://www1.worldbank.org/prem/PREMNotes/premnote54.pdf.

Fellner, Jamie, and Marc Mauer. 1998. *Losing the Vote: The Impact of Felony Disenfranchisement Laws in the United States.*

Washington, DC: Human Rights Watch and the Sentencing Project. Available online at http://www.sentencingproject.org/doc/File/ FVR/fd_losingthevote.pdf.

Frankenberg, Erica, Chungmei Lee, and Gary Orfield. 2003. "A Multiracial Society with Segregated Schools: Are We Losing the Dream?" Cambridge, MA: Civil Rights Project at Harvard University. Available online at http://civilrightsproject.ucla.edu/ research/k-12 education/integration-and-diversity/a-multiracial -society-with-segregated-schools-are-we-losing the-dream.

Franklin, Mark N. 2004. *Voter Turnout and the Dynamics of Electoral Competition in Established Democracies Since 1945.* Cambridge: Cambridge University Press.

Freeman, Richard B. 2004. "Fighting Turnout Burnout: Why Europeans Turn Out at Higher Rates and How to Improve American Participation." *American Spectator* 15, no. 6 (June): A16.

Frohnen, Bruce, ed. 2002. *The American Republic: Primary Sources.* Indianapolis, IN: Liberty Fund.

Gallagher, Michael. 1991. "Proportionality, Disproportionality and Electoral Systems." *Electoral Studies* 10, no. 1 (March): 33–51.

Gallagher, Michael, and Paul Mitchell, eds. 2005. *The Politics of Electoral Systems.* Oxford: Oxford University Press.

Gardbaum, Stephen. 2008. "The Myth and Reality of American Constitutional Exceptionalism." *Michigan Law Review* 107 (December): 391–466.

Garoupa, Nuno, and Tom Ginsburg. 2008. "Guarding the Guardians: Judicial Councils and Judicial Independence." University of Chicago Law School, University of Chicago, Olin Law and Economics Program, Research Paper Series. University of Chicago Law and Economics, Olin Working Paper no. 444. Available online at http://ssrn.com/abstract=1303847.

———. 2011. "The Comparative Law and Economics of Judicial Councils." *Berkeley Journal of International Law* 27, no. 1: 52–82.

Georgakopoulos, Nicholas. 2000. "Discretion in the Career and Recognition Judiciary." *University of Chicago Law School Roundtable* 7: 205–25.

Ginsburg, Tom. 2003. *Judicial Review in New Democracies: Constitutional Courts in Asian Cases.* Cambridge: Cambridge University Press.

Grofman, Bernard. 1999. "SNTV: An Inventory of Theoretically Derived Propositions and Brief Review of the Evidence from Japan, Korea, Taiwan, and Alabama." In *Japan, Korea, and Taiwan under the Single Non-Transferable Vote*, ed. Bernard Grofman, Sung-Chull Lee, Edwin A. Winckler, and Brian Woodall. Ann Arbor: University of Michigan Press.

Grofman, Bernard, and Scott L. Feld. 2004. "If You Like the Alternative Vote (a.k.a. the Instant Runoff) Then You Ought to Know about the Coombs Rule." *Electoral Studies* 23: 641–59.

Grossman, Joel, and Charles Epp. 1995. "Judicial Systems." In *Encyclopedia of Democracy,* ed. Seymour Martin Lipset. Washington, DC: CQ Press.

Hajnal, Zoltan L., and Paul G. Lewis. 2003. "Municipal Institutions and Voter Turnout in Local Elections." *Urban Affairs Review* 38, no. 5 (May): 645–68.

Harvard Law Review. 2011. "Advisory Opinions and the Influence of the Supreme Court over American Policymaking." *Harvard Law Review* 124 (June): 2064–82. Available online at http://www.harvardlawreview.org/issues/124/june11/Note_8268.php.

Hayter, Susan, and Valentina Stoevska. 2010. *Social Dialog Indicators: Trade Union Density and Collective Bargaining Coverage, International Statistical Inquiry 2008–2009.* Geneva: International Labour Office. Available online at http://www.ilo.org/public/english/dialogue/ifpdial/downloads/papers/tbm-2010-dialogue.pdf.

Heath, Anthony, Siana Glouharova, and Oliver Heath. 2005. "India: Two-Party Contests in a Multi-Party System." In *The Politics of Electoral Systems, ed.* Michael Gallagher and Pail Mitchell. New York: Oxford University Press.

Howard, Marc Morjé. 2005. "Variation in Dual Citizenship Policies in the Countries of the EU." *International Migration Review* 39, no. 3: 697–720. Available online at http://www.u.arizona.edu/~jag/POL596A/IMRDualcitz.pdf.

Human Rights Watch. 2005. *The Rest of Their Lives: Life Without Parole for Child Offenders in the United States.* New York: Human Rights Watch.

Huntington, Samuel P. 1991. *The Third Wave: Democratization in the Late Twentieth Century.* Norman: University of Oklahoma Press.

Inter-Parliamentary Union. 1995. *Women in Parliaments, 1945–1995: A World Statistical Survey.* Geneva.

International City/County Management Association. 2004. *The Municipal Year Book.* Chicago.

Jackman, Robert W. 1993. *Power Without Force: The Political Capacity of Nation-States.* Ann Arbor: University of Michigan Press.

Karatnycky, Adrian, Aili Piano, and Arch Puddington. 2003. *Freedom in the World: Political Rights and Civil Liberties, 2003.* New York: Freedom House.

Katz, Richard S. 1997. *Democracy and Elections.* New York: Oxford University Press.

———. 2006. "Electoral Reform in Italy: Expectations and Results." *Acta Politica* 41: 285–99.

Katzenstein, Peter J. 1985. *Small States in World Markets: Industrial Policy in Europe.* Ithaca, NY: Cornell University Press.

Kaufman, Herbert. 1963. *Politics and Policies in State and Local Governments.* Englewood Cliffs, NJ: Prentice-Hall.

Kernell, Samuel, ed. 2003. *James Madison: The Theory and Practice of Republican Government.* Stanford, CA: Stanford University Press.

Koger, Gregory. 2010. *Filibustering: A Political History of Obstruction in the House and Senate.* Chicago: University of Chicago Press.

Laakso, Markku, and Rein Taagepera. 1979. "'Effective' Number of Parties: A Measure with Application to West Europe." *Comparative Political Studies* 12, no. 1 (April): 3–27.

Law Library of Congress. 2004. *Nations of the World.* Washington, DC: Library of Congress (www.loc.gov/law/guide/nations.html).

Lijphart, Arend. 1994. *Electoral Systems and Party Systems: A Study of Twenty-Seven Democracies, 1945–1990.* Oxford: Oxford University Press.

———. 1999. *Patterns of Democracy: Government Forms and Performance in Thirty-Six Countries.* New Haven: Yale University Press.

———. 2004. "Constitutional Design for Divided Societies." *Journal of Democracy* 15, no. 2 (April): 96–109.

———. 2012. *Patterns of Democracy: Government Forms and Performance in Thirty-Six Countries.* 2nd ed. New Haven: Yale University Press.

Linder, Wolf. 1994. *Swiss Democracy: Possible Solutions to Conflict in Multicultural Societies.* New York: St. Martin's Press.

Lipset, Seymour Martin. 1996. *American Exceptionalism: A Double-Edged Sword.* New York: W. W. Norton.

———. 2003. *The First New Nation: The United States in Historical and Comparative Perspective.* Piscataway, NJ: Transaction.

Liptak, Adam. 2007. "Lifers as Teenagers, Now Seeking Second Chance." *New York Times,* October 17. Available online at http://

travel.nytimes.com/2007/10/17/us/17teenage.html?ref=american exception.

————. 2008a. "Illegal Globally, Bail for Profit Remains in U.S." *New York Times,* January 29. Available online at http://www.nytimes .com/2008/01/29/us/29bail.html?ref=americanexception.

————. 2008b. "Foreign Courts Wary of U.S. Punitive Damages." *New York Times,* March 26. Available online at http://www.nytimes .com/2008/03/26/us/26punitive.html?_r=1&ref=americanexceptio n&gwh=A48E6177B83F98F7D5E87AC884CE0EC.

————. 2008c. "U.S. Is Alone in Rejecting All Evidence If Police Err." *New York Times,* July 19. Available online at http://www.nytimes .com/2008/07/19/us/19exclude.html?ref=americanexception.

————. 2008d. "In U.S., Expert Witnesses Are Partisan." *New York Times,* August 12. Available online at http://www.nytimes.com/ 2008/08/12/us/12experts.html?ref=americanexception.

Lollini, Andrea. 2011. *Constitutionalism and Transitional Justice in South Africa.* Bologna, Italy: Segretariato Eureopo per le Pubblicazioni Scientifiche.

Lutz, Donald S. 1994. "Toward a Theory of Constitutional Amendment." *American Political Science Review* 88, no. 2 (June): 355–70.

Mackie, Thomas T., and Richard Rose. 1991. *The International Almanac of Electoral History.* 3rd ed. London: Macmillan.

Maddex, Robert L. 2008. *Constitutions of the World.* 3rd ed. Washington, DC: CQ Press.

Madison, James. 1966. *Notes on the Debates in the Federal Convention of 1787 Reported by James Madison.* Athens: Ohio University Press.

Madison, James, Alexander Hamilton, and John Jay. 1987. *The Federalist Papers.* New York: Penguin Books.

Malleson, Kate. 2006. "The New Judicial Appointments Commission in England and Wales: New Wine in New Bottles?" In *Appointing Judges in an Age of Judicial Power: Critical Perspectives from Around the World,* ed. Kate Malleson and Peter H. Russell. Toronto: University of Toronto Press.

Massicotte, Louis, André Blais, and Antoine Yoshinaka. 2004. *Establishing the Rules of the Game: Election Laws in Democracies.* Toronto: University of Toronto Press.

Matland, Richard E., and Donley T. Studlar. 2004. "Determinants of Legislative Turnover: A Cross-National Analysis." *British Journal of Political Science* 34, no. 1 (January): 87–108.

Mauer, Marc. 2003. *Comparative International Rates of Incarceration: An Examination of Causes and Trends.* Washington, DC: The Sentencing Project. www.sentencingproject.org.

McDonald, Michael P., and Samuel L. Popkin. 2001. "The Myth of the Vanishing Voter." *American Political Science Review* 95, no. 4 (December): 963–74.

Meyers, Marvin. 1981. *The Mind of the Founder: Sources of the Political Thought of James Madison.* Rev. ed. Hanover, NH: University Press of New England.

Migration Policy Institute. 2004. *Global Data Center.* Washington, DC: Migration Policy Institute/www.migrationinformation.org.

Mnookin, Jennifer L. 2008. "Expert Evidence, Partisanship, and Epistemic Competence." *Brooklyn Law Review* 73, no. 3 (Spring): 1009–34.

Müller, Wolfgang C. 1999. "Austria." In *Semi-Presidentialism in Europe,* ed. Robert Elgie. Oxford: Oxford University Press.

Navia, Patricio, and Julio Ríos-Figueroa. 2005. "The Constitutional Adjudication Mosaic of Latin America." *Comparative Political Studies* 38, no. 2 (March): 189–217.

Neale, Thomas H. 2009. *Presidential Terms and Tenure: Perspectives and Proposals for Change.* Washington, DC: Congressional Research Service. Available online at http://www.fas.org/sgp/crs/misc/R40864.pdf.

Norris, Pippa. 1995. "The Politics of Electoral Reform in Britain." *International Political Science Review* 16, no. 1 (January): 65–78.

———. 1997. "Choosing Electoral Systems: Proportional, Majoritarian and Mixed Systems." *International Political Science Review* 18, no. 3 (July): 297–312.

Oliveira, Angela Jardim de Santa Cruz and Nuno Garoupa. 2011. "Choosing Judges in Brazil: Reassessing Legal Transplants from the United States." *American Journal of Comparative Law* 59: 529–560.

Palmer, Matthew S. 1995. "Toward an Economics of Comparative Political Organization: Examining Ministerial Responsibility." *Journal of Law, Economics and Organization* 11, no. 1: 164–88.

Paterson, Alan. 2006. "The Scottish Judicial Appointments Board: New Win in Old Bottles?" In *Appointing Judges in an Age of Judicial Power: Critical Perspectives from Around the World, ed.* Kate Malleson and Peter H. Russell. Toronto: University of Toronto Press.

Poole, Keith, and Howard Rosenthal. 1997. *A Political-Economic History of Roll Call Voting.* New York: Oxford University Press.

———. 2007. *Ideology and Congress.* Piscataway, NJ: Transaction.

Ranney, Austin. 1981. "Candidate Selection." In *Democracy at the Polls: A Comparative Study of National Elections,* ed. David Butler, Howard R. Penniman, and Austin Ranney. Washington, DC: American Enterprise Institute.

Rottinghaus, Brendon. 2003. *Incarceration and Enfranchisement: International Practices, Impact and Recommendations for Reform.* Washington, DC: International Foundation for Election Systems. Available online at http://felonvoting.procon.org/sourcefiles/RottinghausDisenfranchisement.pdf.

Samuels, David J., and Matthew S. Shugart. 2010. *Presidents, Parties, and Prime Ministers: How the Separation of Powers Affects Party Organization and Behavior.* Cambridge: Cambridge University Press.

Samuels, David, and Richard Snyder. 2001. "The Value of a Vote: Malapportionment in Comparative Perspective." *British Journal of Political Science* 31, no. 3: 651–71.

Sartori, Giovanni. 1962. "Constitutionalism: A Preliminary Discussion." *American Political Science Review* 56, no. 4 (December): 853–64.

———. 1968. "Political Development and Political Engineering," *Public Policy* 17: 261–98.

Schattschneider, E. E. 1942. *Party Government.* New York: Rinehart.

Schauer, Frederick. 2005. *The Exceptional First Amendment.* Faculty Research Working Paper Series. Harvard University, John F. Kennedy School of Government. Available online at https://research.hks.harvard.edu/publications/workingpapers/citation.aspx?PubId=2554&type=WPN.

Schuck, Peter H., and James Q. Wilson, eds. 2008. *Understanding America: The Anatomy of an Exceptional Nation.* New York: PublicAffairs.

Scruggs, Lyle, and Peter Lange. 2002. "Where Have All the Members Gone? Globalization, Institutions, and Union Density." *Journal of Politics* 64, no. 1 (February): 126–53.

Sentencing Project. 2007. *Barriers to Democracy: A Petition to the Inter-American Commission on Human Rights for a Thematic Hearing on Felony Disenfranchisement Practices in the United States and the Americas.* Washington, DC: Sentencing Project. Available

online at http://www.sentencingproject.org/doc/publications/
fd_PETITION%20TO%20IACHR_final_formatted.pdf.

———. 2012. *Felony Disenfranchisement Laws in the United States.*
Washington, DC: Sentencing Project. Available online at http://
www.sentencingproject.org/doc/publications/fd_bs_fdlawsinus
_Jun2012.pdf.

Shugart, Matthew Søberg. 2005. "Semi-Presidentialism: Dual Executives and Mixed Authority Patterns." *French Politics* 3, no. 3:
323–51.

Shugart, Matthew Søberg, and John M. Carey. 1992. *Presidents and
Assemblies: Constitutional Design and Electoral Dynamics.* Cambridge: Cambridge University Press.

Siavelis, Peter M., and Scott Morgenstern, eds. 2008. *Pathways to
Power: Political Recruitment and Candidate Selection in Latin
America.* University Park: Pennsylvania State University Press.

Stepan, Alfred. 2004a. "Toward a New Comparative Politics of
Federalism, Multinationalism, and Democracy: Beyond Rikerian
Federalism." In *Federalism and Democracy in Latin America,* ed.
Edward L. Gibson. Baltimore: Johns Hopkins University Press.

———. 2004b. "Veto Players in Unitary and Federal Systems." In
Federalism and Democracy in Latin America, ed. Edward L. Gibson. Baltimore: Johns Hopkins University Press.

Stepan, Alfred, and Juan J. Linz. 2011. "Comparative Perspectives
on Inequality and the Quality of Democracy in the United States."
Perspectives on Politics 9, no. 4 (December): 841–56.

Stone Sweet, Alec. 2000. *Governing with Judges: Constitutional Politics in Europe.* Oxford: Oxford University Press.

Strøm, Kaare. 2000. "Delegation and Accountability in Parliamentary
Democracies." *European Journal of Political Research* 37, no. 3
(May): 261–89.

Taagepera, Rein. 1972. "The Size of National Assemblies." *Social
Science Research* 1: 385–401.

———. 2007. *Predicting Party Sizes: The Logic of Simple Electoral
Systems.* Oxford: Oxford University Press.

Taagepera, Rein, and Matthew Søberg Shugart. 1989. *Seats and
Votes: The Effects and Determinants of Electoral Systems.* New
Haven: Yale University Press.

Taylor, Steven L. 2009. *Voting Amid Violence: Electoral Democracy
in Colombia.* Boston: University of New England Press.

Teixeira, Ruy. 1992. *The Disappearing American Voter.* Washington,
DC: Brookings Institution.

Tokaji, Daniel P. 2006. "The Story of *Shaw v. Reno:* Representation and Raceblindness." Public Law and Legal Theory Working Paper Series. The Ohio State University Moritz College of Law.

Tschentscher, Axel. 2010. *International Constitutional Law.* Berne: Institut für Öffentliches Recht, Universität Bern (http://www.servat.unibe.ch/icl/info.html).

Tsebelis, George. 1995. "Decision Making in Political Systems: Veto Players in Presidentialism, Parliamentarism, Multicameralism and Multipartyism." *British Journal of Political Science* 25, no. 3 (July): 289–325.

———. 2002. *Veto Players: How Political Institutions Work.* Princeton, NJ: Princeton University Press.

Tsebelis, George, and Eduardo Alemán. 2005. "Presidential Conditional Agenda Setting in Latin America." *World Politics* 57, no. 3 (April): 396–420.

Tsebelis, George, and Jeannette Money. 1997. *Bicameralism.* Cambridge: Cambridge University Press.

Ungar, Mark. 2001. *Elusive Reform: Democracy and the Rule of Law in Latin America.* Boulder, CO: Lynne Rienner.

United Nations Development Programme. 2009. *Human Development Report 2009.* New York: United Nations Publications. Available online at http://hdr.undp.org/en/reports/global/hdr2009/.

United States Census Bureau. 2010. *International Database.* Washington, DC: US Census Bureau. Available online at http://www.census.gov/ipc/www/idb/.

Van der Kolk, Henk. 2008. "Supplementary Vote: Analysis, Applications, and Alternatives." *Electoral Studies* 27: 417–23.

Vanberg, Georg. 1998. "Abstract Judicial Review, Legislative Bargaining, and Policy Compromise." *Journal of Theoretical Politics* 10, no. 3: 299–326.

Varghese, John. 2011. "Judicial Appointments—The Domain Game." Available online at http://ssrn.com/abstract=1604487 or http://dx.doi.org/10.2139/ssrn.1604487.

Varsho, Kelly J. 2007. "In the Global Market for Justice: Who Is Paying the Highest Price for Judicial Independence?" *Northern Illinois University Law Review* 27, no. 3 (Summer): 445–518.

Venn, Danielle. 2009. *Legislation, Collective Bargaining and Enforcement: Updating the OECD Employment Protection Indicators.* OECD. Available online at http://www.oecd.org/dataoecd/36/9/43116624.pdf.

Vink, Maarten, Monica Claes, and Christine Arnold. 2009. "Explaining the Use of Preliminary References by Domestic Courts in EU Member States: A Mixed-Method Comparative Analysis." Presented at the 11th Biennial Conference of the European Union Studies Association (April 24). Available online at http://aei.pitt.edu/33155/1/vink._maarten.pdf.

Volcansek, Mary L. 2006. "Judicial Selection in Italy: A Civil Service Model with Partisan Results." In *Appointing Judges in an Age of Judicial Power: Critical Perspectives from Around the World,* ed. Kate Malleson and Peter H. Russell. Toronto: University of Toronto Press.

Vowles, Jack. 1995. "The Politics of Electoral Reform in New Zealand." *International Political Science Review* 16, no. 1 (January): 95–115.

Watt, Nicholas. 2009. "Labour Plans to Guarantee Referendum on Electoral System Reform." *Guardian,* December 1. Available online at http://www.guardian.co.uk/politics/2009/dec/01/electoral-system-reform-referendum-plan.

Wilson, Graham K. 1998. *Only in America? The Politics of the United States in Comparative Perspective.* Chatham, NJ: Chatham House.

Wiseley, D. Eric. 2004. *Constitution Finder.* Richmond, VA: School of Law, University of Richmond (confinder.richmond.edu).

Wolfinger, Raymond E. 1994. "The Rational Citizen Faces Election Day or What Rational Choice Theorists Don't Tell You About American Elections." In *Elections at Home and Abroad: Essays in Honor of Warren E. Miller,* ed. M. Kent Jennings and Thomas E. Mann. Ann Arbor: University of Michigan Press.

World Bank. 2001. "Governing the Justice System: Spain's Judicial Council." *PREMnotes* 54, no. 2 (June). Available online at http://www1.worldbank.org/prem/PREMNotes/premnote54.pdf.

Yarnall, Megan A. 2009. "Dueling Scientific Experts: Is Australia's Hot Tub Method a Viable Solution for the American Judiciary?" *Oregon Law Review* 88: 311–40.

Yale Center for Environmental Law and Policy. 2010. *Environmental Performance Index, 2010.* New Haven. http://epi.yale.edu.

Index